THE MANYOSHU

A NEW AND COMPLETE TRANSLATION

THE
MANYOSHU

A NEW AND COMPLETE TRANSLATION

By

H. H. HONDA

1967

THE HOKUSEIDO PRESS

To the Memory of

my Beloved Wife,

Honda Tsuruko

PREFACE

Poetry is a theme which always interests me, and as a young student of English poetry I once thought how nice it would be if I could render Japanese verse into English, using the English rhythm.

Scores of years have passed by since then, and I am already an old man.

And here is a realization, if I may call this work so, of the cherished dream of my young days.

October, 1966

H.H.H.

THE MANYOSHU
A NEW AND COMPLETE TRANSLATION

CONTENTS

How to Translate the Tanka

Many scholars both native and foreign have translated Tanka into English. They are, to name a few, Basil H. Chamberlaine, Clay MacCauley, F. V. Dickens, William N. Porter, F. A. Lombard, Dr. Nitobe, Kenneth Yasuda, and S. Nishimura. The quintet was the metrical form in which the Tanka was rendered by some of these, while others used the quatrain.

Those who preferred the quintet divided the 31 syllables of the Tanka into five lines, namely: 5-7-5 7-7 the upper hemistich, and the lower hemistich, respectively. To cite an example (which is the only Tanka found in Dr. Nitobe's *Bushido* and translated by the same author):

> Isles of blest Japan!
>   Should your Yamato spirit
> Strangers seek to scan,
>   Say—scenting morn's sun-lit air,
>   Blows the cherry wild and fair!

This translation is to Dr. Nitobe's credit, though Dr. Wadagaki, his colleague, pointed out one blemish in the fourth line. 'Scenting' should be some other word suggestive of the effect on the eye rather than on the nose.

Now, to scan this verse, the first four lines have three feet, while the last alone four. This irregularity of beat always accompanies this form of translation unless the rendering is done throughout in trochaic measure (which is the metre employed by William Porter in his translation of the *Tosa Diary*).

The trochaic measure, however, as everybody who has studied something of prosody is aware, is a sprightly measure, not to say, warlike. It is like heady wine lacking in mellowness, especially when it is uniformly used. A good instance of it is Longfellow's "Hiawatha".

Now, one of the Tanka's peculiarities is elegance. It is, generally speaking, like cherry-blossoms seen through vernal mist. Its nature is feminine, static, and as calm and sweet as an idle dream. That is why many ancient poets preferred composing Kanshi (Chinese verses) to writing Tanka.

To quote another example. This is from Sanetomo, the third Shogun of the Minamoto Clan; it is one of his masterpieces and against what I have just mentioned, rather masculine: a rare example testifying that the usually graceful feminine Japanese language can be transformed in the hands of a master craftsman to fit in with a most dashing and powerful verse. The translator is Mr. Kenneth Yasuda.

> Ocean-waves that rush
>   and hurl like pounding thunder
>   against the rock-shore,
> Break and scatter, whirl and crash
>   with their wild tumultuous roar!

The first line and the fourth are in trochaic measure, the number of feet in the five lines being 3, 3, 2, 4 and 3 respectively. In other words, the upper hemistich has 8 feet, and the lower 7; whereas in the above-quoted Dr. Nitobe's translation 9 feet are for the upper hemistich and 7 for the lower.

I have cited the above two example, because I think they are excellent translations done in the quintet.

For long years I myself kept rendering Tanka in this metrical pattern. A voice in me, however, kept whispering there was something inappropriate if not wrong in this use of the quintet. For whenever I read my translation aloud, or had somebody read them for me, I would notice some hitches in them, caused by irregularities of beat.

The reader enjoys a translation of Tanka, if it is good, whether it be a quatrain or a quintet. And this is what it should be. However, the translator is not so free, because he knows that the Tanka like the sonnet is a poem of fixed form. And once he works out his method which he thinks the best vehicle for Tanka's translation, he feels obliged to stick to it. This I think is the psychology and practice of not only a translator of verses but of all craftsmen. The translations of Omar Khayyam by Edward Fitzgerald are a good example of this.

On the other hand there are scholars who advocated the quatrain. Dr. Taketomo was one of them. In his "Tanka in English Translation", he dwelled at large on the merits of the quatrain as a vehicle for the translation. After dealing with the nature of both Japanese and English poetry, he comes to the conclusion that the metrical form for Tanka's translation should be the quatrain. As regards the rhyme scheme, the alternate rhyme is in his opinion the most graceful and the couplet and enclosed rhyme should be avoided. To endorse his argument he translated fifty poems from the Manyoshu, including them at the end of his essay. This is one of them:

> Nor silver, nor gold, nor the gem
>   Has any charm in life's career,
> What treasure could there be found in them,
>   More precious than my children dear?

As for me, I prefer the quatrain as a pattern for Tanka's translation to the quintet. And if I have to give reasons, the chiefest is the latter's irregularities of beat which appear almost of themselves. In my opinion poetry must first appeal to the ear. In the quatrain the flow of rhythm, if the verse is well written, is not disturbed, whereas in the quintet, as I have already mentioned, hitches in the rhythm are unavoidable unless the measure be trochaic.

The following is reprinted from part of my article which appeared some time ago in the English Mainichi, and with the reader's permission, I will avail myself of it to illustrate my views on this subject:—

Japanese Tanka, as students of Japanese know, are not necessarily written in five lines, but may be written in any lines less than five. They are also aware that Japanese verses, with a very few exceptions, lack rhymes. In poetry what is essential is rhythm, and rhyme is only of secondary importance; wherein lies the raison d'être of blank verse.

Now the worst drawback in the 5-7-5 7-7 verse form lies in its too great artificiality, its too much attention to the number of syllables at the expense of rhythm. I have come to this conviction after hundreds of my own translations of Tanka. Far be it from me to detract from others' merits. All I want to say is that I have reached such a conclusion.

The Tanka, however, is a verse of fixed form. And I am of the opinion that it should preferably be translated as such. By investing it with some definite form, it will be recognized at a glance as a Tanka. But without any such form, the reader will be at a loss to know what it is. Suppose he is shown an anthology wherein some translated Chinese and Japanese verses are put together. Perhaps in most cases he will find it difficult to tell Japanese pieces from Chinese. But once the Tanka is dressed in a definite English garb, he will readily take it for such.

Now, there are lots of English verses composed of four lines with 31 or 32 syllables. Robert Louis Stevenson's "Requiem" is an example:

> Under the wide and starry sky
> Dig the grave and let me lie;
> Glad did I live and gladly die,
> And I laid me down with a will.
>
> This be the verse you grave for me:
> *Here he lies where he longed to be;*
> *Home is the sailor, home from sea,*
> *And the hunter home from the hill.*

The first stanza has 31 syllables, while the second 32. The following stanzas composed by A. E. Housman are all in 31 syllables:

> Loveliest of trees, the cherry now
> Is hung with bloom along the bough,
> And stands about the woodland ride
> Wearing white for Eastertide.
>
> Now, of my threescore years and ten,
> Twenty will not come again,
> And take from seventy springs a score,
> It only leaves my fifty more.
>
> And since to look at things in bloom
> Fifty springs are little room,
> About the woodland I will go
> To see the cherry hung with snow.

Each stanza is made up of iambic tetrameter, excepting one line which is trochaic with the same feet. After efforts extending over long years, I have come to believe that this is an ideal mould for recasting Tanka. The following is a piece of Tanka translated in four lines with 32 syllables by Hidesaburo Saito:

> I look out o'er a tangled mass
> Of cherry's bloom and willow's green;
> The metropolis is in spring
> A rich brocade of brilliant sheen.

If you replace the word metropolis in the third line with 'capital', and insert 'the' between 'in' and 'spring' of the same line, the verse will be in perfect four feet. Saito was a great scholar of English. But to err is human. And he must have mispronounced the word metropolis. Save for this blemish this is a fine translation worthy of his parts and scholarship.

To translate either prose or verse is not easy. And we must admit the translator's lot is hard without his being snubbed. All translators may be said to be in the same boat. They, therefore, might do well to sympathize with one another. On the contrary, some of them are more against their poor fellow-workers than otherwise. Another noted Japanese scholar, himself a translator, criticizing Arthur Waley's translation of the "Genji Monogatari", said it was full of mistakes without so much as taking into consideration its literary merits. It was as if mistakes were this man's sole concern. No one could be perfect. If he is so interested in finding fault with others' mistakes, the wisest thing for him to do is not to make mistakes himself lest he should incur the same fate. To be frank, I, for one, much prefer a good translation with mistakes to a bad one without mistakes. A good translation with mistakes does less harm to the original than a bad translation with few mistakes. For the reader can recognize and enjoy something of the beauty of the original work through the former, whilst the latter only leads him to consider that the original is not worth while to read.

GLOSSARY

of English equivalents for terms retained in Japanese

ajisai, hydrangea.
ashibi, staggerbush. It grows into a tall tree in Japan.
ayu, sweetfish.
chisa, a wild tree bearing clusters of white flowers.
Dazaifu, the local government of Kyushu.
fuji, wistaria.
hagi, lespedeza, bush clover.
hanifu, ochre.
hanka, résumé of a longer song.
Hohrai, the island of eternal youth.
kajika, singing frog living by a limpid stream.
katsura, Judas tree believed to be standing in the moon.
koto, Japanese harp.
kuzu, arrowroot.
miru, a kind of seaweed.
mon, old coin: one tenth of a sen.
musasabi, flying squirrel.
obana, also called susuki, eulalia, plume grass.
ominaeshi, patrinia.
oshidori, mandarin duck.
saké, Japanese wine.
shigi, snipe.
shikimi, aniseed tree.
shishi, wild boar.
shinsen, an archaic term for a kind of fairy or witch.
sumo, Japanese wrestler.
tamamo, seaweed; duckweed.
Tanabata, seventh day of the seventh month.
tsuki, a kind of zelkova tree.
uguisu, a bush warbler.
utsugi, called also unohana, deutzia.

THE MANYOSHU

BOOK I

FOREWORD

Book I as well as Book II differs greatly from the rest of the anthology.

"All the verses are ancient, and sung in the manner of the court; and their age and authors are well known," says one of the greatest Manyo scholars, Kamono Mabuchi. The songs were written at the time when Imperial courts were held at the following places, each situated in the present-day Kinki District (the figures denote the year in which capitals were transferred):

Asakura Palace, 479?　(Emperor Yuryaku, 418–479)

Okamoto Palace, 639　(Emperor Jomei, 593–641)

Asuka Kawara, 658　(Empress Saimei, 655–661)

Late Okamoto Palace　(Ditto)

Otsu Palace, 667　(Emperor Tenji, 626–671)

Asuka Kiyomihara Palace, 675　(Emperor Temmu, 631–686)

Fujiwara Palace, 694–710　(Empress Jito, 645–702 and Emperor
　　　Mombu, 683–707)

Nara Palace, c. 712 (Empress Genmyo, 661–721)

Book I contains 84 verses, including 16 so-called longer songs, and 68 verselets.

As to the poets, besides Emperors Yuryaku, Jomei, Tenji, Temmu, and Empress Genmyo, Empress Jito, Princes Shiki, Naga, and Princess Minabe, Lady Nukada stand prominent together with Kakinomotono Hitomaro, Takechino Kurohito, Yamanoeno Okura, Kasugano Oyu, etc.

MISCELLANEOUS SONGS

Emperor Yuryaku
No. 1

A basket in hand, a good basket,
and a trowel in hand, a little trowel,
O Maiden, you pick herbs upon this hill.
Tell me your house,
and your name.
Over this land, Yamato, I reign;
over this land I rule.
Call me your Lord.
Know you not my house and name?

> This unsophisticated song tells us the way
> people got married in ancient times. Theirs
> was a free marriage. On suing for the hand of
> a girl, first a man asked her family pedigree
> and her name; and when she gave an answer,
> that meant her consent. As an act of etiquette
> the man had to tell his lineage and name also
> at the same time.

*Written by Emperor Jomei on the occasion
when he stood upon Mt. Kagu
contemplating the country lying below*
No. 2

Among hills soaring in Yamato
there Mt. Kagu perfect stands,
from where we see our fertile fields,
with wreaths of smoke from houses rising,
and plovers o'er the vast lake flying.
How fair a country is Yamato!

No. 3

I hear the sound
of the Emperor's catalpa bow
which he ever takes when to the morning
and evening hunt he deigns to go.
HASHIBITONO OYU

Hanka*
No. 4

The Emperor goes hunting,
and horses tread the meadow.

* The Hanka (or kaeshiuta) resembles the envoy in the
ballade. It comes after a so-called longer lay, serving as
résumé.

No. 5

I yearn for home, and weep
upon this vernal day.
How the wind, sweeping down the mountain
where the Sovereign stays,
blows and saddens me,
though a warrior brave,
and like the salt they make upon the shore
my heart burns too.
PRINCE IKUSA

Hanka
No. 6

I hear the night wind sweep
down the mountain drear,
and it keeps me from sleep,
yearning for my wife so dear.

No. 7

Never shall I forget
that cottage thatched with the obana
the men had reaped from autumn fields
when the Imperial progress stopped at Uji!
LADY NUKADA

No. 8

At Nigitatsu
waiting for flood tide are we.
Now the moon appearing,
we can put out to sea.
DITTO

*On the occasion of the Imperial visit to
Kii hot springs by Lady Nukada*
No. 9

Across the beautiful Yoshino mountains
I go to the Sacred Oak
under which my gentle lover stands.

> (Usually considered the most textually difficult
> song in the Manyoshu. This translation follows
> Tsuzuki Shogo's interpretation.)

No. 10

I wish that we could know
    how long our life would be.
Here let us tie the grass roots,
    praying for longevity.

No. 11

Should you, my husband, resting on your journey,
find naught to thatch your temporary dwelling,
pray search beneath the little pine trees,
and line your shelter with the hidden grasses.

No. 12

I saw Nujima island,
    view of my desire,
but found no pretty pebbles
    to take home and admire.

Written at the time when Empress Saimei
was reigning, by Prince Nakano Ohye,
later Emperor Tenji

No. 13

THE CONFLICT OF MOUNTAINS

Yearning to marry fair Unebi Hill,
Kagu with Miminashi fell in strife.
Thus even in the Age of Gods, alas,
these mountains had to fight to get a wife;
shall mortals then avoid it in our life?

Hanka

No. 14

Abo, the god, came to Inami field to see the quarrel
between Mt. Kagu and Mt. Miminashi.

No. 15

Behold, the setting sun lights up
    the clouds resembling banners bright
over the watery plain. Meseems
    the moon will be serene tonight.

EMPEROR TENJI

No. 16

Though winter passes into springtime,
and birds that have kept silent sing;
though flowers that have long slept blow.
(the vernal woods, so dense with growth,
offering no means for a maid to cull them,)
it is the autumn which delights our hearts:
the golden maple leaves are fair to see.

LADY NUKADA

No. 17

Longing for the view of Miwa,
I looked back at each turning of the highway,
but oft the peaks of Nara
concealed it with the clouds together.

DITTO

Hanka

No. 18

O Clouds, why are you hiding Miwa still?
You would pity me,
if but you knew how eagerly
I wish to see the lovely hill.

No. 19

The hagi flowers attract my eyes.
So does my husband dear.

    A note in the anthology says this does not seem
    to be a song.

No. 20

Riding through the purpling field
roped off for your Imperial family,
you beckon me, but oh my love,
what will the watchman think?

LADY NUKADA

No. 21

Oh if I had no love for you
    beautiful as a violet bright,
would I, alas, sue for your heart,
    aware thereto I have no right?

EMPEROR TEMMU

No. 22

As in the rapids rocks remain
    bright and unmossed, so may
your Highness be as young and fair
    for ever as today.

FUKINO TOJI

Feeling pity for Prince Omi banished
on the Isle of Irago

No. 23

The prince become a fisherman
    searches on Irago's shore
for herbs of meagre sustenance—
    a courtier no more.

No. 24

Though life ephemeral, I live it still;
though drenched by brine, I seek my herbs
upon Irago Isle.

PRINCE OMI

No. 25

Upon Mimiga's peak of fair Yoshino
snow falls incessantly,
or rain falls endlessly.
Now like the snow that ever snows,
or like the rain that ever rains,
each bend of the mountain path,
as I came tracing it,
has found me thinking of you.

EMPEROR TEMMU

No. 26

The same as above

No. 27

How beautiful Mt. Yoshino
where men of old were wont to go!
Look, therefore, on the mountain well
of which the ancients loved to tell.

DITTO

No. 28

Spring is already gone, and now
it seems the summer's come, for lo,
all white is yonder Kagu's brow
with garments airing row on row.

EMPRESS JITO

Passing the old Ohmi Palace
by Kakinomotono Hitomaro

No. 29

When Emperor Jimmu reigned in Kashiwara
Court,
the capital was in Yamato.
Later it was moved to Nara.
Again the Emperor Tenji changed it by Lake Biwa,
living in the Ohmi Palace,
I hear this is the site,
but I see only vernal grasses,
and the old Court stands
deserted in the mist.

No. 30

The scenery of Karasaki
remains as beautiful as ever,
but now, alas, no courtiers come
to sail upon the waters.

KAKINOMOTONO HITOMARO

No. 31

Deserted is the capital
and though Lake Biwa calm may lie,
no courtiers now will ever come
as they did in the days gone by.

DITTO

No. 32

Alas, I, like an aged man,
stand and behold in sorrow here
the capital destroyed, deserted,
lying in ruins drear.

TAKECHINO FURUHITO

(Probably a misreading for Kurohito)

No. 33

Here deserted lies the ancient capital.
Oh, how the dreary spectacle gnaws at my soul!

No. 34

How many years have passed, I wonder,
since men of bygone days
here hung the offerings on the pines
upon the beach by white waves washed?

PRINCE KAWASHIMA

No. 35

This is Mt. Se* in Kii Province
I have been yearning so to view.

* meaning, "husband".

At the Yoshino Imperial Villa
by Kakinomotono Hitomaro

No. 36

Vast is the land ruled by our Emperor,
and from it he has chosen for his villa Akitsu.
Here every morning and evening courtiers come
and go by boat.
How beautiful the hills and streams—
this town of cataracts!

Hanka

No. 37

Often would I come again
to see this limpid stream, Yoshino!

No. 38

Our Sovereign is a deity,
living in a palace girdled by the clear Yoshino.
As she looks around her from the tower,
she sees in spring their mountain majesties with
    flowers,
in autumn crimson tree leaves in their hair,
the river nymphs present their fishes for her table,
Thus all are glad to serve the Empress.

KAKINOMOTONO HITOMARO

No. 39

Lo, like the goddess waited on
by mountain sprites, and river nymphs,
Our Sovereign takes ship now to shoot
The rapids at Kauchi pool!

DITTO

No. 40

Do the court ladies take delight
    in boating now on Ago Bay,
on the rising tide with scarlet skirts
    sparkling amid the azure spray?

DITTO

No. 41

Are the courtiers
hunting for seaweed
now on the promontory
Of Tohshi?

DITTO

No. 42

Are our court ladies in the boat
bound for Irago isle
amid the heavy sea roar now?
I only see the promontory.

DITTO

No. 43

Where is my husband,
    traveling today?
Over Nabari's mountain range
    does he wend his weary way?

Wife of TAGIMANO MAHITOMARO

No. 44

Is it because the peaks are lofty
that I can not behold Yamato?

No. 45

The Prince my master is a deity.
He goes out of his spacious palace in the morning
along the paths on Mt. Hatsuse where thrive
    cypress trees,
and in the evening roams in snowy Aki Meadow
where obana flowers sway to the wind.

KAKINOMOTONO HITOMARO

No. 46

The travelers lying side by side
on yonder Aki Field perhaps
can not sleep for the memories
they have of days gone by.

DITTO

No. 47

Though Aki now is wilderness,
yet here our late prince used to come
ahunting: on that graceful lord
I muse in this abandoned field.

No. 48

Eastward upon the plain I see
    the dawning. I turn round and now
behold the setting moon
    above yon western mountain brow.

DITTO

No. 49

At this time last year
    the Crown Prince people did adore
went hunting, horses speeding
    up and down the field, but ah! he is no more.

DITTO

No. 50

The Emperor we serve is pleased
to build a palace new in Fujiwara Town,
and orders cypress trees to be brought
from Mt. Tanagami down the Uji River.
All men are glad to work for him,
forgetting both home and themselves.
They labor in the water, making rafts,
and carry them adown the stream.

No. 51

The court's no longer in Asuka.
The wind that used to set aflutter
the gay sleeves of the ladies
is vainly blowing now.

PRINCE SHIKI

On the well in the Fujiwara Palace grounds

No. 52

When the Emperor moved to the palace new
in Fujiwara Town,
and looked around him,
standing on the shore of Lake Haniyasu,
he saw Mt. Kagu in the east
all clad with vernal green,
fair Mt. Unebi in the west,
and Miminashi soaring in the north,
and crystal water welling in the palace grounds.

ANON.

Hanka

No. 53

May our Emperor enjoy longevity!
I envy maidens who will serve him after me.

No. 54

O that in spring I might
see Kose's sight:
camellia trees that grow
upon the hillsides all ablow!

SAKATONO HITOTARI

No. 55

How blest are Kii people
who daily see Mt. Matsuchi!

TSUGINO OBITO OHMI

No. 56

Never shall I tire of wandering
Kose's field in spring
where the camellias blow
along the river row on row.

KASUGANO OYU

No. 57

Men of the retinue, resting in Hikumanu Field
where hagi shrub is flowering,
dye your garments with the bloom
in memory of this journey!

NAGANO OKIMARO

No. 58

Oh where will yonder little ship
head past Are tip?

TAKECHINO KUROHITO

No. 59

Upon this night, a cold wind blowing,
lonely and wayworn must my husband sleeping be.

PRINCESS YOSA

No. 60

Oh, how long since my love
left for her journey!
Has she fashioned for herself
a shelter in Nabari Village?

PRINCE NAGA

No. 61

Noble as is the warrior who
stands upright with a bow in hand,
ready to let an arrow fly,
so fair is Mato* and its sand!

Daughter of a gentleman-in-waiting

* Mato Bay. The word means target.

No. 62

As you sail across Tsushima Straits,
give offerings to the deity of the sea,
and after duty done abroad,
return posthaste to me.

KASUGANO OYU

Written in China yearning for home

No. 63

O, Comrades, could we but go home
to see our good friends in Japan
and those old pine trees that must yearn
on Mitsu Beach for our return!

YAMANOENO OKURA

No. 64

Upon a chilly twilight when
    even on the wild ducks frost comes down
as they swim about among the reeds,
    my thoughts return to Nara town.

PRINCE SHIKI

No. 65

How beautiful the view
of the pine grove in Suminoe
I see with you,
Otohi, my dear singing girl!

PRINCE NAGA

No. 66

Though here upon Takashi Beach
    under pretty pines I lie,
I only yearn for home:
    my thought is not of scenery.

OKISOMENO AZUMATO

No. 67

If on my solitary way
I should not hear the plaintive lay
from the love-whispering shigi, I,
pining alone, shall die.

TAKAYASUNO OHSHIMA

No. 68

Oh how can I forget my darling wife,
though years are wasted in this traveling life?

No. 69

Had I but known so soon you would be going,
I would have dyed your clothes with bright hanifu.

No. 70

A cuckoo bird goes flying
over Mt. Kisa.
Does it wing its lonely way
toward Yamato today?

TAKECHINO KUROHITO

No. 71

Oh, Cranes! Why do you cry
above the shoal so heartlessly,
when yearning after home I sigh,
and sleepless in my bed I lie?

OSAKABENO OTOMARO

No. 72

I shall not row my boat out where
they gather herbs of ocean
that will remind me of the hair
of my sweet love I yearn for.

FUJIWARANO UMAKAI

No. 73

O sweet Breeze, go inland across this cove,
and breathe upon the dwarf pines and camellias
    of my love!

PRINCE NAGA

No. 74

The chilly wind is sweeping down
    the mountain high,
and I throughout this night
    alone must lie.

ANON.

No. 75

How chilly blows the morning wind
    over the mountains sweeping down,
and I a traveler, can find
    no kindly maid to lend a gown*.

PRINCE NAGAYA

* In those times there was no difference between the gowns
worn by men and women.
    This is not a love song, since no particular maid is referred
to, and it is classified under Miscellaneous Songs.

No. 76

The wristguards of yon archers ring:
    the upright shields are set in rows,
and led by their captains, all the men
    practise shooting with their bows.

EMPRESS GEMMYO

No. 77

O my dear Liege, be free from care.
Whatever happens I am there.
PRINCESS MINABE, sister of the Empress

*In February of the third year of Wado when the
Fujiwara Palace was moved to Nara, stopping
the palanquin at Nagaya Field on the way,
Empress Gemmyo composed the
following song:*

No. 78

Once I leave Asuka town for Nara,
perhaps again I shall not see your dwelling.

No. 79

Her Majesty has moved the capital,
and so I left my home,
setting a boat afloat in Hatsuse's River.
All day long I took joy in the scenery from the
  stream;
then went into the Saho waters,
and on the morrow saw the moon while half
  asleep.
Like a white sheet the night frost fell;
and like a rock the river froze.
Oh, how eventful was my trip from Fujiwara
  Town
to the new Capital of Nara.
ANON.

Hanka
No. 80

Though you in Nara, I in Fujiwara be,
my friend, you ever dwell in me.

No. 81

I went to Yamanobe
    where gush the crystal waters,
and happened to behold
    a group of Ise daughters.
PRINCE NAGATA

No. 82

Sad am I
beneath the sky
with nothing nigh
but raining, raining.

No. 83

When can I go across Tatsuta's peak to see
my darling wife so long awaiting me?
(Perhaps the above two were old folk songs.)

No. 84

How still the heights! And fair as now
    though lonelier they will be when winds
of autumn come and stags are heard
    belling sadly for their hinds.
PRINCE NAGA

THE MANYOSHU

BOOK II

FOREWORD

Book II is composed of love songs and elegies, whereas, as we have seen, Book I contains only miscellaneous verses. The oldest song in Book I is by Emperor Yuryaku (5 Century), but the oldest in this book are anterior to it; since they were composed in the reign of Emperor Nintoku (4 Century), but these are only a few in number.

No mention is made of the time when these love songs were written.

The number of verses are 149 of which longer songs are 19, the remainder being verselets.

Emperors Tenji, Temmu, and Empress Jito, and Iwanohime, wife to Emperor Nintoku, Princess Kagami, Lady Fujiwara, Princesses Ohku, Tajima, Princes Ohtsu, Arima appear in this book, but the foremost figure is Kakinomotono Hitomaro, who stands head and shoulders above the other authors. His masterpieces are found here.

Indeed Book II may be said to be the greatest in the anthology. We can also see Fujiwarano Kamatari, Emperor Tenji's righthand man, Mikata Sami, Yamanoeno Okura, Nagano Okimaro, Lady Ishikawa, Lady Kose, etc. therein.

The greater part of the songs are related to the Imperial Household, and among passionate love songs and pathetic elegies are found verses uncovering conflicts of princes and tragedies arising from them.

LOVE SONGS

4 songs by Empress Iwano Hime,
wife of Emperor Nintoku

No. 85

How many days and months have passed
    since you, my Lord, left me to roam!
Now to the mountains should I go,
    or wait and wait for you at home?

No. 86

Better to die upon a rock
    amid high mountains than to yearn,
sitting at home, after my Lord,
    and wait in vain for his return!
       (Ascribed to the Empress, but not certain)

No. 87

Oh, must I wait, and always wait
    until the last hour of my time,
until my waving raven hair
    is black no longer, white as rime?

No. 88

The morning fog will disappear
    from autumn fields with harvest blest,
but oh when will the trouble clear
    from off this miserable breast?

No. 89

Though my black hair with frost be white,
I wait for you throughout the night.

No. 90

Same as No. 85

No. 91

O that I dwelled upon the peak
of Yamato's Ohshima, then should I
day in day out,
still gaze on your dear house.
              EMPEROR TENJI

In reply by Lady Kagami

No. 92

I love you, though you love not me,
like water flowing silently
where fallen leaves in gold and red
conceal the faithful rivulet's bed.

No. 93

If 'tis after dawn you leave me,
shall I not be talked about?
              LADY KAGAMI

No. 94

Pray, first let me lie with you,
then, circumspect, I take my leave.
              FUJIWARANO KAMATARI

No. 95

Oh I have won the maiden fair:
    Yasumi whom the world did court
is mine! And what words do I know
    to tell about this wonder wrought?
              DITTO

Songs when Kume Zenshi took Lady Ishikawa
to wife

No. 96

If I draw a bow of love,
can I hit your heart, my dove?
              KUME ZENSHI

No. 97

How do you know
whither arrows go
before they leave the bow?
              LADY ISHIKAWA

No. 98

If you make love to me, I will be yours,
but still I wonder if you speak the truth.
              DITTO

No. 99

When a warrior draws a bow, does he
not draw it with sincerity?

KUME ZENSHI

No. 100

As the box with the first rice ears within,
a present for the Court,
is tied fast to the horse,
so is my darling to this heart.

DITTO

No. 101

The tree that flowers and bears no fruit
the jealous gods claim for their own.
I counsel you: become my love
lest you belong to them alone.

OHTOMONO SUKUNE to LADY KOSE

No. 102

Whose love is it that but comes into bloom,
and bears no fruit? Such is not mine!

LADY KOSE

Sent to Lady Fujiwara by Emperor Temmu
No. 103

Oh such a heavy snowfall here!
You have not had the snow, I fear—
and only of its news must hear
in far Ohara Village.

Reply to the above by Lady Fujiwara
No. 104

Why boast, my Sire, so of your snow?
'Tis what I prayed for, you must know,
besought the mountain to bestow
at least some portion of our snow!

No. 105

To see my darling brother go
Yamato-ward, outside in rue
I stood at midnight to be drenched
with early morning dew.

PRINCESS OHKU

No. 106

'Tis difficult for even two
to cross the autumn mountain drear;
and now to see you leaving all alone
fills me with fear.

DITTO

No. 107

Bent on my tryst, I wait
and wait upon the hill till late,
but you do not come, and for you
my robe is wet with chilly dew.

PRINCE OHTSU

No. 108

You tell me you were wet and chill,
waiting alone upon the hill.
O that I could have been the dew
so lucky as to be with you.

LADY ISHIKAWA

No. 109

Fair haven, no haven!
If fortune reveal it—
"You two were together"—
Why need we conceal it?

PRINCE OHTSU to LADY ISHIKAWA

No. 110

Shall I forget you even awhile?
Do you not dwell within my heart?

PRINCE KUSAKABE to LADY ISHIKAWA

No. 111

Oh, Past! does he too yearn—
the bird that flies
about the well?

(PRINCE YUGE to LADY NUKADA, reminded of his father, Emperor Temmu on the occasion of his visit to the Yoshino Palace)

No. 112

Is it a cuckoo bird, I wonder,
that yearns, as I do, for your father?

LADY NUKADA

No. 113

Behold, together with a pine sprig of Yoshino
now I bring to you this letter.

DITTO

To Prince Hozumi by Princess Tajima

No. 114

Like ears of rice plants in the fall
    my heart leans heavy to one side,
and ill though folk may speak of me,
    steadfast in love will I abide !

To Prince Hozumi again by Princess Tajima

No. 115

You left me. Yearning now in vain,
    should I but waste my time away?
I too will go, so as a sign
    tie ropes on trees along the way.

No. 116

I leave the palace for no one knows where.
Across the morning river rumor drives me.

PRINCESS TAJIMA to PRINCE HOZUMI

No 117

Never in unrequited love
shall I fall, thought I, alas.
Now poor fool, I find myself
head over ears in love.

PRINCE TONERI

In reply

No. 118

The string that ties my hair is wet.
Is it because you love me so?

Daughter of a gentleman-in-waiting

*4 Songs to Princess Kii
by Prince Yuge*

No. 119

Ever flows Yoshino's river.
Ever wish I to be with you.

No. 120

I'd rather be a hagi flower
than live like this.
O that instead of yearning endlessly
I bloomed with grace, and then fell scattered.

No. 121

Ere evening's rising tide at Suminoe
from the cove of Asaka will cut me off,
I'll gather now tamamo.

No. 122

Like a ship that rocks from side to side
troubled am I, thinking of another's bride.

*3 songs when Mikatano Sami was taken ill
soon after he wedded the daughter of
Sononoomi Ikuha*

No. 123

How I desire to see
the tresses of my bride
too short to dress,
too long to hang !

No. 124

They say my hair is long enough to dress,
my lord, but I am waiting for your leave.

No. 125

I am ill abed,
and can not go to where my wife is,
only yearning after her.

No. 126

What kind of gentleman are you,
refusing me admittance to your house?

LADY ISHIKAWA

In reply

No. 127

Noblesse oblige: a gentleman indeed
at times a lady's visit must forgo.

OHTOMONO TANUSHI

No. 128

What I hear is true: your foot ails you.
Oh pray, my lord, take good care of yourself.
                              LADY ISHIKAWA

No. 129

I am old enough to know how to behave
but now in love, cry like an innocent.
              LADY ISHIKAWA to OHTOMONO NAMARO

No. 130

Wading Nifu's rapids, I would come to thee,
but can not; do thou, my dear Brother, come to me.
                      PRINCE NAGA to his brother

Written by Kakinomotono Hitomaro
No. 131

People may say that Tsuno
in Iwami has no harbor fine.
Good port or no,
the wind at morn and eve
comes from the sea
where fishermen catch whales
to the seashore over wavering sea-tangle.
Now I leave behind
my wife as yielding as those herbs,
and at every turning of the road
I look back, and see
our town receding in the distance.
Mountains after mountains I have traversed.
Would that these mountains
could be leveled to the ground
for me to see her bower.

Hanka
No. 132

Can my love see
from behind the tree
on Takatsuno's peak the sleeve
I now on parting wave?

No. 133

Noisily the bamboo grass
    is rustling in the wind,
but all my thought is of my love
    I left behind.

No. 134

Same as No. 132

No. 135

In the sea of Iwami
off the cape of Kara
miru grows,
and by the strand
other herbs of the brine.
They cling to rocks
as my wife clung to me.
I love her deeply as the sea,
but alas,
how few those nights I spent with her.
We part now like the creeping ivy.
How my heart aches!
I look back and see her standing on Watari hill,
waving her sleeve half hidden
by the falling crimson leaves.
None but miss the moon when hidden in the
    clouds.
She fades away, and in the evening light
I who thought myself a manly courtier
now wet my sleeves with tears.

Hanka
No. 136

Too swift ran my white horse,
and the abode where dwelt my darling
soon was left behind among the clouds.

No. 137

Oh, Maple trees upon the hill,
    stop shedding leaves upon the road
that I, though even for awhile,
    may get a glimpse of her abode.
                      KAKINOMOTONO HITOMARO

No. 138

Same as No. 131

No. 139

Same as No. 132

No. 140

Though soon you say you will return,
yet all the same I long and yearn.
                      HITOMARO'S wife, YOSAMI

ELEGIES

2 Elegies by Prince Arima
No. 141

I will tie guide-knots on these pines
    here upon Iwashiro beach,
and hope to see them once again
    when proved not guilty of that breach.

No. 142

Where I at home, then I would have
    a bowl for my rice, but oh grief,
as I am traveling, I must eat
    my food off of an oaken leaf.

*2 songs composed by Nagano Okimaro in tears
on seeing the guide-knots on the pines*
No. 143

Alas, no more did he behold the beach,
he who tied the guide-knots on the pines!

No. 144

When I behold the pines of Iwashiro,
I am reminded of the tragic prince.

No. 145

No one knows his spirit might come back
like the wingèd bird
to see the beach again
except the pines.

              YAMANOENO OKURA

No. 146

Could he see the pines again
whereon he left the fated knots?
          KAKINOMOTONO HITOMARO

*When Emperor Tenji was ill
by Empress Yamato*
No. 147

The sky is clear and bright:
a lucky sign,
although the Emperor is ill.
May he live long!

No. 148

I see upon the mausoleum funeral banners flutter-
    ing,
and in fancy picture the Emperor's spirit on the
    wing.

              EMPRESS YAMATO

No. 149

Others may forget the Emperor,
but ever shall I keep him in my memory.
              DITTO

No. 150

Alas, the Emperor is gone.
Now we are in a different world.
Every minute of the day do I miss him.
Were he a jewel, I would ever keep him on my
    hand.
Were he a garment, I would never take him off.
Yesternight I saw him in my dream:
the only means for me to meet him now.
              ANON.

2 songs mourning Emperor Tenji's Death
No. 151

Alas, no human power could
detain him in this world.

No. 152

Are the pines at Karasaki waiting
for the Imperial vessel that will never come?

No. 153

O yonder boats now coming
shoreward o'er the lake,
do not splash
with oars to scare the fowl
my husband loved so deep,
and make them start.
          The Empress Dowager

No. 154

O Forest Ranger, the Emperor is no more.
What do you rope the hill off for?
            LADY ISHIKAWA

No. 155

By Mt. Kagami where the Imperial Mausoleum
  stands
I weep both day and night.
A year has passed by since the burial day,
and all the courtiers now will leave the tomb
  behind them.

                                    LADY NUKADA

3 Songs by Prince Takechi on
Princess Tohchi's death
No. 156

O that the dead princess would come into my
  dream,
but I can have no slumber. How could she appear?

No. 157

The life of the princess was brief,
whom now I call to mind in grief.

No. 158

I would draw water from the place
where yellow roses ever flower,
but I, alas, know not the path
to that tenebrious spring.

No. 159

Would my Lord could speak about
the golden leaves of Kamioka
at daybreak and again at twilight!
I see the mountain now alone,
and never my wet sleeves have time to dry.
                                    EMPRESS JITO

2 Songs by Empress Jito
No. 160

A fire could safely be put in a bag, 'tis said;
then why, oh why could I not meet my lord now
  dead?

No. 161

Though months have gone by since my lord's
  demise,
for ever sorrow in my bosom lies.

Sung in a dream
No. 162

The Emperor who held a court
at the Kiyomihara Palace
liked to go to Ise
where sea breeze scented blows.

                                    EMPRESS JITO

2 Songs by Princess Ohku after the burial of
Prince Otsu's remains in the tomb of
Futakami Hill
No. 163

Far better had I stayed in Ise
  at the Grand Shrine; for now I know
my darling brother has been killed,
  leaving me in this grief and woe.

No. 164

My brother whom I came to see
  is now no more. In vain, indeed
have I returned then all the way
  only alas, to tire the steed.

2 songs by Princess Ohku
No. 165

Now you are dead, and still I live;
forevermore will I regard
Futakami's mountain as a brother,
for there you are entombed.

No. 166

The flowering ashibi branches
  on yonder rock I wish to have;
but now to whom can I give them,
  for he alas, is in the grave?

On the Demise of Crown Prince Kusakabe
by Kakinomotono Hitomaro
No. 167
At the beginning of the world
all the deities gathered by the Heavenly River
and decided, after consultation, Hirumeno Mikoto
    should
rule Heaven together with the country of Yamato.
Thus the first ancestor, Ninigino Mikoto descended
    to our clime.
One of his descendants, the good Emperor Temmu,
built a stately palace at Asuka.
All people hoped with glad anticipation
that his son, young Kusakabe, would succeed
to the throne, and bless the land,
but alas, he, dying suddenly,
now sleeps upon Mayumi Hill,
leaving all his servants masterless, dismayed.

2 Hanka
No. 168
The palace of the young prince
which I looked on as I do the sky,
will now be desolate,
since he is gone.

No. 169
The sun shines in the sky,
but now alas,
the moon has disappeared
behind the clouds.

No. 170
Even the fowl in yon pond are forlorn,
because our young crown prince is gone.

23 songs by the gentlemen-in-waiting
mourning the Prince's death
No. 171
Alas, the prince is gone,
and the palace stands forlorn.

No. 172
O Birds that live upon the pond,
stay there, although our prince is gone.

No. 173
If but the prince were here,
how could the palace be so drear?

No. 174
By the Mayumi Mausoleum I abide
to keep watch day and night upon the mountain-
    side.

No. 175
How sad! I never dreamed of keeping
watch thus by the mausoleum.

No. 176
Alas, the prince I hoped to serve for e'er
is gone, and life's become all drab and bare.

No. 177
Weeping we sit all night beside the tomb;
and though the sun come out, we are in gloom.

No. 178
I see the park where oft our prince went wander-
    ing,
and again tears gush forth like the garden spring.

No. 179
I served the prince in Shima's Palace with great
    pride,
and now keep watch beside his tomb upon the
    mountainside.

No. 180
O Birds, fly not away this year,
but stay yet in his garden here.

No. 181
I view the garden pond
the late prince used to contemplate,
and find rank grasses covering
the ground beside the spring.

No. 182

Wild Geese the prince loved, when you leave your
     nest,
fly to Mayumi's hillside where he lies at rest.

No. 183

Alas, our crown prince is no more,
and how I his demise deplore.

No. 184

Vainly I went to the court today and yesterday
to serve the prince well knowing he had passed
     away.

No. 185

Today I leave this palace, and no more shall I
     behold
the azaleas blowing by the rocks here in the garden
     old.

No. 186

Many a time did I pass through the gateway in
     one day,
but now the prince is gone, I have no will to go
     that way.

No. 187

If I return now to the mausoleum,
who will remain to guard the palace?

No. 188

When the morning sun conceals itself behind the
     clouds,
I am reminded of the prince's death, and weeping
     stand beside his pond.

No. 189

Within the house I hear no sound,
only solitude profound.

No. 190

I feared no grief or pain,
but now to sorrow I give rein.

No. 191

I cherish memories of Uda meadow
where oftentimes our late crown prince went
     hunting.

No. 192

Like birds beside the Sada Mausoleum
I hear the keepers nightly crying.

No. 193

We go now to the grave along the way
where palanquins wend night and day.

*To Princess Hatsusebe
by Kakinomotono Hitomaro*
No. 194

The tamamo growing in the upper reaches of
     Asuka
flows pliantly downstream.
Like the tender herb you used to lie beside your
     lord,
but he is gone, and lonely is your bower.
Daily alas, you wander in Ochi field,
your garments wet with dew
to meet him who can never come.

Hanka
No. 195

Though you roam about the field,
no hope have you to meet your love.

*On the death of Princess Asuka
by Kakinomotono Hitomaro*
No. 196

The wavering tamamo in the upper rapids
where stepping stones are laid,
and also in the lower rapids
spanned with a wooden bridge
grows afresh, although it withers.
And oh why have you, graceful as the herb,
left the palace, never to return.
You used to deck your hair with flowers in spring,
and with golden maple leaves in autumn.
You loved Prince Osakabe,
took delight in walking side by side with him,
but sleep now, your mouth and eyes tight closed.
Forlorn, the prince roams all disconsolate.
Alas, how sad! All I can do
is remember you as long
as the stream, your namesake, runs.

No. 197

Even the river swift as the Asuka
can be stemmed,
but alas, how can we hold her back
in life?

No. 198

As swift Asuka's stream the same—
I never shall forget her name.

On the death of Prince Takechi
by Kakinomotono Hitomaro

No. 199

With the profoundest reverence I speak
of Emperor Temmu who sleeps
in Magami field, and of the gallant prince
who went across Mt. Fuwa,
summoned soldiers from the East,
and girding on a sword and bow in hand,
led the brave army.
On the field drums sounded loud as peals of
    thunder;
the horns like roars of tigers;
banners fluttered in the wind
red as the wild fire in the spring,
and bowstrings rang, reminding one of blizzards
raging over winter forests,
with arrows flying thick as snowflakes.
The enemy fought bravely too,
but amidst the fight
suddenly black clouds veiled the sky,
darkening the sun: dread gusts arose,
the beaten foe escaping with bare life.
Thus the Imperial army won the day.
The Emperor ruled in peace
with Prince Takechi as his righthand man.
But now, alas, our prince is dead.
His palace is all veiled in black.
Though the sun go down after dyeing Haniyasu
    field,
the servants in white hempen clothes
still stay with heads down
to guard the palace all night through.
Now the funeral goes through Kudara field,
though yet grief has not subsided in their breasts,
to Kinoe Mausoleum decided as the everlasting
    resting place,
leaving behind the palace on Mt. Kagu masterless,
    forlorn.

No. 200

How I yearn for the prince,
who now rules in heaven!

No. 201

Alas, alas, the prince is gone,
and masterless retainers wander.

No. 202

Though I went to the shrine
    for him to pray,
offering wine,
    yet he has passed away.

LADY HINOKUMA

After the death of Princess Tajima
by Prince Hozumi

No. 203

Fall not copiously, O Snow,
to keep me from Igai hillside where she sleeps.

Upon the death of Prince Yuge
by an Eastlander

No. 204

Alas, Prince Yuge
has gone to heaven,
and all day long,
and all night through
I only sigh in sorrow.

No. 205

Very much the same as No. 235

No. 206

I thought you would enjoy long life,
but now alas, you on a sudden die.

On the death of his mistress
by Kakinomotono Hitomaro

No. 207

My love lived on the Karu.
I ever longed to see her,
but fearing others,
who would spread rumors, I desisted.
Secret as a pool among the mountains
she remained.
But she is gone,
gone as the sun goes down at dusk,
gone as the shining moon hides in the cloud.
The sad news came,
and thinking mere sight of her village
might soothe me, I roamed about the mart of
  Karu,
but nowhere could I hear her voice,
not a maid passed who resembled her.
I vainly cried her name, and waved my sleeve.

No. 208

Ah in the mountains where is she
    mid golden foliage wandering?
O that I had the means to see
    where she now could be loitering!

No. 209

The maple leaves are falling fast;
    and now, this grievous news I hear,
and call to mind those past days when
    under golden foliage I met her.

Elegy by Kakinomotono Hitomaro

No. 210

Beautiful was the tsuki tree upon the bank
my dear wife and I used to view
which in springtime was bedecked
with fresh green leaves,
and as beautiful was she.
I loved her with all my heart.
But none can flee the inevitable.
The funeral procession started in the morning
with white flags fluttering,
and through the wild field

where the heat wave shimmered
it reached the hill.
Our boy kept crying for his milk since then,
but with no food to give,
I only tried to soothe him,
carrying him in my bosom.
Now calling for his mother,
I've come along the rocky path on Hagai Hill
where is her grave.

No. 211

The moon is shining clear tonight—
    the selfsame moon I viewed last year,
but how the days have passed
    my cherished memory to blur!

No. 212

Leaving her tomb upon the hill
    as I alone retrace the way,
deep sorrow overwhelms my heart,
    and I am lorn as on that day.

No. 213

Same as No. 210

No. 214

Same as No. 211

No. 215

Same as No. 212

No. 216

Returning to the lonely bower,
to my distress and grief I see
the cherished pillow of the dead,
as if discarded, thrown aside.

(Good care was taken of the pillow in those
days, and, even after the death of the owner,
was placed on the bed as before.)

ELEGIES

On the death of the beautiful girl
by Kakinomotono Hitomaro

No. 217

O Woman, beautiful as an autumn leaf,
and supple as a young bamboo,
why did you die so young,
when life was long before you?
Dew falls at morn,
and disappears at eve,
as men are wont to say,
and mist, it comes at eve,
vanishing at morn.
I have heard the sad word,
and calling you to mind,
deplore your death.
How much more will your husband grieve
who slept upon your arm,
and miss and yearn for you!
Alas, you dying ere your time
like morning dew,
like evening mist!

No. 218

Whenever I behold the road
her funeral passed along
with sorrow I call her to mind.

No. 219

Only a glimpse upon that day
had I—and ever since have longed for more.

On the dead man upon Samine Island
by Kakinomotono Hitomaro

No. 220

Sanuki is a province good blessed by the gods.
My ship now leaves the port of Naka,
and goes amid the roaring billows
in the raving wind.
The rowers pull the oars with all their strength,
and we reach the island of Samine.
I land, and build a shed to stay in for the night,
then wander out, and am surprised
to find a dead man on the beach.
Alas, where is his wife, all unaware,
waiting for his return?

No. 221

If his love lived beside the hill,
she would have culled the starwort fresh.

No. 222

You sleep upon the shore
where wild waves roar.

On the eve of his death
by Kakinomotono Hitomaro

No. 223

My wife will still be waiting
     to see me come home after I
have died, and pillowing my head
     on rocks of Kamo Mountain lie.

2 songs on the death of Kakinomotono Hitomaro
by his wife

No. 224

You I awaited day and night are now adream,
lying with the shells of Ishikawa's stream.

No. 225

O Vapor, hang above the Ishikawa river, for
you will remind me of my husband sleeping on
     its shore.

On behalf of Kakinomotono Hitomaro
by Tahino Mahito

No. 226

Who will tell my wife that I
wet with the river spray now lie?

No. 227

My lord is buried in a distant province,
and dreary lies my life before me.

2 songs written by Kawabeno Miyahito in the
fourth year of Wado on seeing a drowned
maiden in the pine grove of the
Isle of Hime

No. 228

Oh let your name remembered be
     until these pine trees young and small
on Hime Island grow to see
     hoar moss bedeck them all.

No. 229

Oh Tide, pray, do not ebb to leave
    Naniwa Bay adry,
for at its bottom would I grieve
    to see the maiden drownèd lie!

On the death of Prince Shiki

No. 230

I asked, "What fire is that upon Mt. Takamado?—
Burning off the grass are they?"
The man stopped, shedding tears like rain and
    said,
"Prince Shiki died, and yonder go the torches
carried by mourners in the funeral procession."

   (this verse appears in the collection of poems
   by Kasano Kanamura.)

No. 231

Now the prince is gone, the hagi
on the mountain will be vainly blowing.

No. 232

Our good prince has not been long gone,
but grassy now the palace road and lorn!

No. 233

O Hagi flowers in the field, pray do not fall,
since looking on you, I the late prince can recall.

No. 234

Same as No. 232

THE MANYOSHU

BOOK III

FOREWORD

Book III is divided into 3 parts, i.e. miscellaneous verses, songs in metaphor, and elegies. The longer songs are 13, and verselets 140. Most of the songs in metaphor, numbering 25, are love songs.

Such a distinguished writer as Prince Shohtoku appears in this book. Other authors are Princes Ohtsu, Yuge, Shiki, Kasuga, Nagata, Nagaya and Kakinomotono Hitomaro, Yamabeno Akahito, Takechino Kurohito, etc.

Unlike Books I & II, many poems by authors related to Ohtomo Family appear; Ohtomono Tabito, and his son Yakamochi stand prominent among them. Especially Tabito's "13 Songs in Praise of Wine" may be called unique in the whole of the Manyoshu because of their buoyant hedonism.

MISCELLANEOUS VERSES

Written by Kakinomotono Hitomaro on the occasion when Empress Jito went up Ikazuchino Oka, the Hill of Thunder

No. 235

A goddess is Her Majesty,
    and upon the Hill of Thunder
she sojourns with a sea
    of Heaven's clouds extending under.

From Empress Jito to Duenna Shii

No. 236

The tales you always would be telling,
    I felt myself compelled to hear.
But somehow, now I hear them not,
    a haunted silence strikes my ear.

From the Duenna to the Empress

No. 237

For whose ears were the tales intended?
    Not mine: you asked for stories still,
or so I thought. The tales now ended.
    It seems I told them 'gainst your will.

No. 238

Still and serene the Villa stands,
    but here the fishermen's voices reach,
calling for helping hands
    to pull the laden nets onto the beach.
NAGANO OKIMARO

On Prince Naga
by Kakinomotono Hitomaro

No. 239

Even wild deer and boars, and quail bow to our
    prince
when he goes, followed by his suite,
stalwart riders in hunting garbs.
We, his servants too, adore him like the beasts
    and birds.

No. 240

Lo, catching in his net the moon
    that sails on high, our prince has made
it like a canopy of silk
    to rest beneath its silvery shade.

No. 241

I look upon Prince Naga as divine:
by his command we have a lake amidst the hills.

No. 242

Ever as clouds veil Mt. Mifune
that overlooks the waterfall,
so could I wish my presence
perdured forever on this earth.
PRINCE YUGE

Prince Kasuga in Response

No. 243

You will live ever as the clouds
that never vanish from the sight.

No. 244

Almost the same as the above.

2 songs by Lord Nagata

No. 245

How noble Mizu Isle and fair!
Oh pray, what island can compare
in fame with its reputation fine,
in beauty to this isle divine?

No. 246

O Sea, be calm, for I set sail
now from this cove to go to Mizu Isle.

No. 247

Even though the billows roar
elsewhere along and off the shore,
around your ship may no waves rise
wherever she at anchor lies!
LORD ISHIKAWA

No. 248

Away on the horizon I beheld
Satsuma Straits today.
LORD NAGATA

8 songs by Kakinomotono Hitomaro

No. 249

The men were taking shelter in the cove,
but now the sea is calm, and they row out.

No. 250

Behold, our ship, passing Minume seaboard,
has approached, the promontory of Nujima!

No. 251

Here on Nujima Promontory in Awaji Isle
the sash my love tied flutters in the briny air.

No. 252

A traveler I, but in such mean attire
as sea-bass fishers' in Fujie Cove.

No. 253

As we sailed off the plain of Inabi,
I sighted Kako Point for which I had been yearning.

No. 254

When the ship enters the Akashi Strait,
the houses on the shore will disappear.

No. 255

After a long trip as I come,
   yearning to see my darling love,
yonder I view Yamato's land
   from this Akashi's lovely cove.

No. 256

The Sea of Muko must be calm today,
for I see fishing boats out in the bay.

On Mt. Kagu by Kamono Kimitarihito
No. 257

When Mt. Kagu is veiled in vernal mist,
Lake Haniyasu ripples in the sylvan breeze,
and cherry trees bloom all at once.
On the shores gulls and plovers cry;
but alas, no more come courtiers here,
with pleasure-boats abandoned oarless,
since Prince Takechi is gone.

No. 258

No courtiers come to row the boats,
and duck and drake upon them rest.

No. 259

The prince's death—it seems but yesterday.
How can already be this overlay
of slow-grown moss on his beloved cedars?

No. 260

Same as No. 257

To Prince Niitabe
by Kakinomotono Hitomaro
No. 261

It is my greatest joy
to serve Prince Niitabe.
Would that I could
attend on him for ever!

No. 262

How fast descends upon Yatsuri Hill the snow,
even the lofty trees concealing now!

No. 263

O Man, ride not posthaste for my sake:
so beautiful the view along the lake!
                    OSAKABENO TARIMARO

No. 264

Onward—how far onward?—go the waves
though pikes are set against them
wickerwork-fashion in the Uji river.
                    KAKINOMOTONO HITOMARO

No. 265

How heavy falls the rain,
   nor yet a house can I behold
about the ferry
   upon the cape of Miwa cold!
                    NAGANO OKIMARO

No. 266

O evening Plovers, how your cries
   over the billows on the lake
bring back old memories to me,
   causing my heavy heart to break!
                    KAKINOMOTONO HITOMARO

No. 267

A flying squirrel rashly sought
   higher to soar, and higher still;
risking too much, was seen and caught
   by the shrewd old huntsman of the hill.
                    PRINCE SHIKI

No. 268

Do you not hear the plovers cry?
    They wait for you, my friend, and they
will welcome you back to the town.
    Like us, they yearn to greet that day.
                              PRINCE NAGAYA

No. 269

Alas, the pretty hill is scorched and bare.
Would I could dress it with my own bright clothes!
                              LADY ABE

8 songs by Takechino Kurohito

No. 270

As after home I yearn, I see
    a vessel painted with red clay
that lay at anchor 'neath the hill
    go sailing far away.

No. 271

The cranes go crying toward Sakura,
following the tide now ebbing,
and Ayuchi Lagoon
will lie bare soon.

No. 272

Crossing Mt. Shihatsu overlooking the sea,
I view many a little boat behind the isles.

No. 273

As off the rugged shore we go, I hear
cranes crying on the waters far and near.

No. 274

The night is far advanced,
so we will stay in Hira Port.

No. 275

Where shall I lodge this evening,
if I'm benighted on Kashino field?

No. 276

We are one in mind and body now, my darling,
and can not part one from the other at this cross-
    roads.

No. 277

Alas, why did I not come earlier here
to see the leaves of gold zelkova trees?

No. 278

Busy gathering seaweed, boiling salt,
Shika maidens have no time to comb their hair.
                              LORD ISHIKAWA

2 songs by Takechino Kurohito

No. 279

Now have I shown my love Inano Field,
but when will she see Mt. Nasugi, and the pines
    at Tsuno?

No. 280

Friends, let us go back to Yamato,
gathering white sedge for our families.

Kurohito's wife in reply

No. 281

On your way out and back
you savoured the view of Hari Field.
Now through your gift,
the white field shines for me.

No. 282

Far spent the night, and still Iware is ahead.
Alas, when can I traverse Mt. Hatsuse?
                              KASUGANO OYU

No. 283

From Enatsu here in Suminoe
I see ships leaving Muko Harbor.
                              TAKECHINO KUROHITO

No. 284

I never shall forget the maiden
I chanced on in Suruga.
                              KASUGANO OYU

*On crossing Mt. Seno in Kii
by Nihino Kasamaro*

No. 285

Mt. Seno means Mt. Husband.
Were it Mt. Wife, I'd be reminded of home.

In response by Kasugano Oyu

No. 286

Mt. Wife? No, never:
Husband is fitter.

No. 287

Afar off is my house:
the hills I crossed are veiled in clouds.

LORD ISONOKAMI

No. 288

Should I survive my exile,
then once again will I behold
these white waves lave the shore.

LORD HOZUMI

*2 songs on the moon
by Hashihitono Oura*
No. 289

How pleasant on the road of night
to see the moon, a bow of white
amidst the heavenly field!

No. 290

Same as No. 1763

No. 291

Yearning for home, as I traverse Mt. Se,
the drooping cypress branches know my grief.

LORD ODA

4 songs by Rokuno Maro
No. 292

Where long ago the stone ship, sent from heaven
with Amano Sagume at Takatsu,
was sheltered, time has silted up the harbor.

No. 293

Let us go see the Mitsu maiden divers
gathering sea-given herbs.

No. 294

The fishing boats came back to shore.
Too high the wind and waves at sea.

No. 295

The fair pine grove at Suminoe
recalls the Emperor who once stood there.

2 songs by Lord Taguchi
No. 296

The view of Miho seabeach is so fair
that it has cleared me of all care.

No. 297

The scenery of Tago Beach
is truly everyone's delight,
but swift on errands of my lord
I pass it in the sightless night.

No. 298

This eve I will cross Mt. Matsuchi,
and sleep alone upon the riverside.

PRIEST BENKI

No. 299

Weak rain, hold off, for beautiful the snow
that lies upon the mountain sedge.

OHTOMONO TABITO

*2 songs composed, stopping the horse
on Mt. Nara by Prince Nagaya*
No. 300

At Nara pass with its secluded shrine,
my prayer is for the welfare of my love.

No. 301

Despairing of crossing the mountain,
my grief I voice aloud
with no one by to hear me.

No. 302

The moon sails fast tonight. Ah! would that I,
before it sinks, could reach my dear love's house.

ABENO HIRONIWA

2 songs by Kakinomotono Hitomaro
No. 303

Rolling in serried ranks, Inami's waves
mask from my rearward glance my lost Yamato.

No. 304

How far I have to go!
Between the Court at Nara
and far provincial Kyushu lie
many and many a strait.

No. 305

Where once the capital stood my heart misgave
me going.
Now sadly I behold it—Oh, truth-presaging heart!

TAKECHINO KUROHITO

No. 306

I wish the waves upon the Ise Sea were flowers
that I might give some to my love at home.
                                    PRINCE AKI

3 songs on the hermit's cave at Miho in Kii
Province by Priest Hakutsu

No. 307

Here in this cave once lived a youthful hermit.
Who would tire of dwelling in such grandeur?

No. 308

The cave remains for ever,
but the hermit, where is he?

No. 309

O Pine tree, growing by the cave,
you must have seen the hermit once.

No. 310

The young tree I bought at the fair has grown
    tall now;
for so long have I not seen you, sweet.
                                    LORD KADOBE

No. 311

From Buzen now I take my leave,
and I shall long for sight of Mt. Kagami.
                        KURATSUKURINO MASUHITO

No. 312

Naniwa so long a little town
is now a capital grand to see.
        FUJIWARANO UMAKAI, who was ordered
            to build a new capital at Naniwa

No. 313

I never knew the old days of Yoshino,
but stories handed down awake my heart.
                                    TORINO SEMURYO

No. 314

How clear the voices of the running river,
far and near foaming in the rapids.
                                    HATANO OTARI

When Emperor Shomu visited the detached
palace of Yoshino in late spring,
composed by Ohtomono Tabito

No. 315

Behold, the Palace at Yoshino
is noble, set among its mountains,

and in quiet streams serene.
This Villa of Yoshino shall not change,
but, even as heaven and earth, shall stand eternal.

No. 316

The River Kisa I see now again,
and find it no less clear than as of yore.

On Mt. Fuji
by Yamabeno Akahito

No. 317

Since heaven parted from the earth
there has been standing high
Mt. Fuji in Suruga's skies.
When I look up, I see the sun
itself quite hidden by the mount;
even the moon rides all obscured;
the white clouds dare not pass its front.
Our songs of praise shall never end:
Oh Fuji peerless, Oh divine!

Hanka

No. 318

From Tago Beach I see the sight
    of Fuji's lofty brow serene
now covered over with the white
    of snow descending all unseen.

No. 319

MT. FUJI

Behold Mt. Fuji yonder in the sky
lording it o'er both provinces of Kai,
and of Suruga. Even the clouds hang low
on high afraid to pass its lofty brow;
the birds upon their pinions dare not seek
from awe to wander near its sacred peak.
The snowflakes struggle to subdue the fire
that rises from the rugged craters dire;
the flaring flames fight back and melt the snow.
Lake Seno Umi vast as is the brine
lies at the bottom of this mount divine.
The river by which people come and go
originates there from its virgin snow
and foaming courses over rocks and sand.
Art thou a spirit, pray, that guards this land,
Yamato, or didst thou from earth rise there
to bless us as a treasure mountain fair?
O noble Fuji, never shall our eyes
cease to enjoy thy sight with ecstasies!
                    Ascribed to TAKAHASHINO MUSHIMARO

2 Hanka

No. 320

The winter snows on Fuji by mid-June
have melted; at mid-June the first snow falls.

No. 321

Holding in awe Mt. Fuji high,
even the clouds of heaven lie
hanging before it streamer-wise,
afraid to pass across the skies.

Composed on the occasion of his visit to Iyo
Springs by Yamabeno Akahito

No. 322

Many hot springs spout out of this sacred land,
but the spring welling up here at the foot
of the lofty peak is peerless.
Once Prince Shotoku stood
composing verses on this Isaniwa Hill
where I see old firs around,
and birds are singing still just as of yore.

Hanka

No. 323

Many centuries have passed by since that day
when the courtiers took ship at Nigitatsu.

On Mt. Kannabi by Yamabeno Akahito

No. 324

I go up Mt. Kannabi, and look down at Asuka,
    the ancient capital
surrounded by high hills and run through by long
    streams.
On vernal days one sees the mountains green;
on autumn nights clear sounds of rills are heard.
Here in the morning clouds cranes fly;
and in the evening vapor stream frogs sing.
Everything seen in the town from Mt. Kannabi
brings to mind fond memories of yore.

No. 325

In Asuka here
I hold so dear
I look around
with love profound.

No. 326

Fishing torches now shine clear
    in Akashi Cove,
and in my face, my sweet,
    you can see burning love.

                              PRINCE KADOBE

To a girl who teased him to resuscitate a dried
abalone, by Priest Tsukan

No. 327

My incantation is of no avail:
the sea itself could not refill this shell.

No. 328

Like flowering plums ablaze
    exhaling fragrance soft and sweet,
Nara, the Capital, displays
    her vernal splendour full complete.

                              ONUNO OYU

2 songs by Ohtomono Yotsuna

No. 329

Of all the land benignly ruled by the Emperor
I hold the capital most dear.

No. 330

Do you not from this distant province
with everywhere wistarias in bloom
yearn after Nara town
where they are now in all their glory?

5 songs by Ohtomono Tabito

No. 331

How can an aged man e'er hope
    his prime of manhood to regain?
I live away from Nara, and
    never shall see my home again!

No. 332

O that now I could see
    Kisa's stream once more,
the view of which I oft enjoyed
    in days of yore!

No. 333

In meditation I spend the time,
and yearn for Nara rich as bright brocade.

No. 334

Now the day lily do I fasten to my girdle,
trying to forget the village by Mt. Kagu.

No. 335

I shall not be gone long,
     Oh crystal Pool of Dream.
Be as you are,
     letting water slowly go downstream.

No. 336

This cotton of the Western shore
     most comfortable looks, and rare.
It makes me warm indeed before
     a garment lined with it I wear.
                                    SAMI MANSEI

*Bidding farewell to his friends at the feast,
by Yamanoeno Okura*

No. 337

Goodby, friends, for my children dear
perhaps are crying now, I fear,
and their fond mother giving ear
to hear my footsteps drawing near.

*13 songs in praise of wine
by Ohtomono Tabito*

No. 338

Pray, take no thought you cannot prize,
but drink stout wine up to the eyes
from vessel of a goodly size.
No more than this can I advise.

No. 339

How I admire those ancients wise
who could for wine a name devise
and called it sage that, in this guise,
they might to the occasion rise!

(The allusion is to the drinkers of ancient
China. Once a Chinese emperor forbade his subjects to drink wine. So the folk could neither
drink nor speak openly of wine. But they had
the wit to call it 'sage'. And whenever they
wanted to take wine, they probably said, "Now,
let us go and see our sage.")

No. 340

Even the seven men of yore
loved drinking, and did wine adore.
Nothing could please those wise men more
than having of wine a goodly store.

(The Seven Wise Chinese of the Bamboo Grove
are well known here in Japan too, and have
often been the theme of poetry and painting.)

No. 341

'Tis better cups of wine to drain
and maudlin cry than wisdom feign;
for greater joys I rack my brain
and find the effort all in vain.

No. 342

Well do I know that none can try
wine and its worth to praise too high;
its virtues wine will ne'er belie,
nor any gem its powers defy.

No. 343

If I were not a man, then ask
I would to be of wine a cask;
how sweet indeed would be my task
to drink of it in such a mask!

No. 344

Ugly indeed are they who feign
wisdom, and from wine abstain!
Look at their faces. Are they sane?
They but resemble monkeys vain.

No. 345

Better to taste the cup divine
than to have gems however fine!
The greatest pleasure 'tis of mine
to drink cup after cup of wine.

No. 346

Better to drink and take delight
in this our life and choose aright
than to be rich in jewels bright
that sparkle in the dark of night!

No. 347

The best of pleasures here below
is that of drinking, one must know;
drunken, released, with joy I crow
or sudden sad, tears freely flow.

No. 348

If in this world well I can fare,
for after life I little care.
What matter were I bird of air,
or worm? Oh, what should I not dare?

No. 349

We mortals who are made of clay
must willy-nilly go the way
of all, and so fate I obey
and dare enjoy life while I may.

No. 350

Pray, then your vanity o'ercome,
and, if you choose, to wine succumb,
or drinking, weep; but ne'er be glum,
nor trying to look wise be dumb.

No. 351

To what this life shall I compare?
    'Tis like a vessel which at break of day
starting, leaves no traces where
    upon the waves she made her way.
                              SAMI MANSEI

No. 352

Cranes cry upon the shore among the reeds.
Is a cold wind blowing over Tsuwo Promontory?
                              PRINCE WAKAYUE

No. 353

Clouds fear to pass Takaki's Peak,
and hang before it streamer-wise.
                              PRIEST TSUKAN

No. 354

At eve the smoke from boiling salt
can not go past the mountain, but stays there.
                              HEKINO OYU

No. 355

Ohnamiji, Sukunahiko,—
those gods of yore—this was their dwelling,
but oh! how long since gods walked here!
                              OFUSHINO MAHITO

No. 356

How I yearn for the Asuka River where
kajika sing at evening!
                              KAMINO FURUMARO

6 songs by Yamabeno Akahito
No. 357

From Nawa Cove we see the distant isle,
and rowing in the foreground is a ship.
Whose ship? Perhaps some fisherman's.

No. 358

How picturesque the boats
seen far and near about the Cove of Muko!

No. 359

On Abe Island, thronged with cormorants,
incessantly as the overlapping waves,
I yearn for Yamato.

No. 360

I'll cull the salt tamamo at ebb tide
to take home to my darling wife.

No. 361

How cold the autumn wind on Sano Hill,
which you are crossing.
Would I could wrap you in my own gown.

No. 362

Where the ospreys hover
and the rock-mosses grow,
tell, tell me your name.
I would be your lover,
though your parents might know.

No. 363

Same as No. 362

2 songs by Kasano Kanamura

No. 364

Pulling at my bow with strength, I shoot.
Let afteryears still tell how strong I was.

No. 365

My old horse stumbles, as I'm crossing Mt. Shiotsu
to tell how much they yearn for me at home.

Composed by Kasano Kanamura

No. 366

Launching their many-oared ship at Tsuruga,
they rowed panting, and I saw upon the beach
smoke of salt being made by women divers.
Alone I could not take joy in the view,
my thought flying to Yamato and my wife.

Hanka

No. 367

This beautiful Tayuhi Cove
reminds me of Yamato and my love.

No. 368

Down to the sea
in a many-oared ship
at our lord's command go we.

No. 369

A loyal warrior should obey
the Emperor without complaint.

KASANO KANAMURA

No. 370

Though not raining, yet no light
comes down from the sky tonight,
and as I wait outside for you
the air is moist with dew.

ABENO HIRONIWA

No. 371

O Plovers that cry on Ou's shore,
you remind me of your Saho River.

LORD KADOBE

Composed by Yamabeno Akahito

No. 372

On Mt. Mikasa clouds hang every morn;
where cuckoos love to sing.
Like the clouds afloat,
and like the cuckoos I've no rest,
being in unrequited love,
and day and night I yearn
after the heartless maid.

Hanka

No. 373

Like a cuckoo I
may cease to cry,
but again I grieve anew,
sighing for you.

No. 374

O sweet Mt. Kasa,*
shelter me,
not some one else
when the raining starts.

* Kasa means umbrella.

No. 375

In the pool of the Natsumi River in Yoshino,
overshadowed by mountains, mallards are crying.

PRINCE YUHARA

*2 songs at a banquet
by Prince Yuhara*

No. 376

Look at the girl who dances there,
waving her sleeves of gauze
like wings of dragonflies
what do you think of her?

No. 377

I never tire of seeing
the clouds above yon mountains,
nor do I of you,
although I meet you every day.

Looking at the garden of the late Prime Minister,
Fujiwarano Fubito, by Yamabeno Akahito

No. 378

Although time has worn down this ancient bank
by the neglected pond,
untended thrive the water plants.

No. 379

O Guardian God of the Ohtomo,
to you I offer sacred branches from the mountain,
and dig the ground to bury jars to hoard good
  wine.
Upon my bended knees I pray to you.
Let me see my lover I adore.

Hanka

No. 380

O God, accept these rolls of cotton cloth,
and grant that I may see my lover.

                    OHTOMONO SAKANOENO IRATSUME

No. 381

Be not too eager, Traveler, to go home.
Beware, because the seas are high.

                              A Girl of Tsukushi

Climbing Mt. Tsukuba
by Nihino Mabito

No. 382

Many a mountain is there in Azuma,
but none that can compare with Mt. Tsukuba.
I long wished to go up this peak to overlook the
  plains,
and on I plod although the path is slushy.

No. 383

I only saw Tsukuba from afar,
but now I climb upon the mountain's path.

No. 384

I sowed the seeds of cockscomb in my garden.
They grew and withered, but undaunted now I
  sow again.

                              YAMABENO AKAHITO

No. 385

Kishimi's peak is steep, and no grass growing,
I helped my wife together to ascend.

No. 386

Though mulberry twigs come floating down the
  stream,
having no weir, pray, how can we get one tonight?

No. 387

People of old took with a weir
all the mulberry branches that came floating.

On travel, recited by Wakamiyano Ayumaro

No. 388

Praises be to the sea god who,
setting Awaji Isle between the mainland and
  Shikoku,
orders the ocean to encircle all,
making tide come at eve, and go at dawn
athwart Akashi Strait.
I have been waiting on the island
for the wild waves to subside,
and do not know when day will break,
but now I hear a pheasant cry near by,
and the ocean has grown calm.
So, 'tis time for the sailors to set sail.

Hanka

No. 389

We go from isle to isle,
and crying cranes remind us of Yamato.

LOVE SONGS IN METAPHOR

No. 390

Even wild ducks that swim about the pond of Karu
do not sleep upon the water plants alone.

                              PRINCESS KI

No. 391

I went to Mt. Ashigara to cut trees to build a ship,
but who forstalled me, and got them in his pos-
  session?

                              SAMI MANSEI

No. 392

Why did I leave unplucked that eve
the fair plum spray I chanced to see
to have my heart now keenly smart,
calling to mind the flowers?

OHTOMONO MOMOYO

No. 393

Oh who will not long for the moon
that hides herself behind the peak?

SAMI MANSEI

No. 394

The little pine at Suminoe
I rope off, hoping 'twill be mine for ever.

KOMUNO MYOGUN

3 songs to Ohtomono Yakamochi
by Lady Kasa
No. 395

I dyed my robe in purple at Tsukuma field,
but people came to know before I wore it.

No. 396

The grassy field of Manu is
far, far away up in the north.
You seem to be now as remote;
still you live within my heart.

No. 397

I pledged my love to you. The vow
is deeply rooted in my heart,
as is the sedge beside the rock
of the remotest mountain range.

2 songs on plum blossoms
by Fujiwarano Yatsuka
No. 398

The plum tree at your bower will bear fruit,
when we shall greet our wedding day.

No. 399

We shall be wed, my love,
when your flowering plums bear fruit.

No. 400

Fallen already most flowers gay,
so I hear people say;
but I hope my plum
is still fair in bloom.

OHTOMONO SURUGAMARO

At a feast
No. 401

Not knowing that there was a ranger,
I roped the wood off, and was shamed.

OHTOMONO SAKANOENO IRATSUME

In reply
No. 402

True I have a ranger,
but no one shall take off your sign.

OHTOMONO SURUGAMARO

No. 403

How can I keep the gem
I wish to see each day and night?

OHTOMONO YAKAMOCHI

3 songs
No. 404

Were not Kasuga field
devoted to the shrine,
therein would I sow millet
and reap the crop for mine.

A girl

In reply
No. 405

If you sowed millet in the field
would I not come for it like deer?
But oh! the shrine stands near.

SAEKI AKAMARO

No. 406

'Tis not my god that is enshrined,
but yours. So worship well.

The same girl

To Ohtomono Ohkiiratsume
No. 407
The small plant in Kasuga field
must be full grown by now.

OHTOMONO SURUGAMARO

No. 408
I wish you were a flowering pink
for me to see with pleasure every morning.

OHTOMONO YAKAMOCHI

No. 409
After the gem I yearn
a thousand times a day,
but can not have it as my own.

OHTOMONO SURUGAMARO

No. 410
I will think twice——remorse would be too late—
before I plant this orange at my door.

OHTOMONOE SAKANOENO IRATSUME

In reply
No. 411
Your sweet orange tree grows well beside my
house.
I wait the day it bears me golden fruit.

No. 412
Peerless the string of gems you wear upon your
head;
as fair are you, my love, and I adore you.

LORD ICHIWARA

No. 413
I am not used to garments rough
fishermen wear on making salt.

PRINCE OAMI

No. 414
How hard 'tis to uproot the grass beside a crag!
So I shall be contented with the thought that she
is mine.

OHTOMONO YAKAMOCHI

ELEGIES

No. 415
Had he but stayed at home,
his head would now be laid
upon his wife's arm,
but he lies dead on the grass.

PRINCE SHOTOKU

No. 416
No more shall I behold the mallards fly
over Iware's pond and hear them cry.

PRINCE OHTSU

*3 songs on the burial of Prince Kauchi
at Mt. Kagami by Princess Tamochi*
No. 417
On Mt. Kagami where he longed to be
Prince Kauchi sleeps eternally.

No. 418
Beneath Kagami's Peak he closed the rocky door,
and though I wait and wait, he'll come no more.

No. 419
O that I had the strength
to break the door of stone!
but I'm a woman weak
and can not open it alone.

*On the death of Prince Iwata
by Princess Nifu*
No. 420
The handsome prince is dead,
and buried on bleak Mt. Hatsuse,
so goes the news;
whereat I scarcely can believe my ear.
But 'tis the truth: endless is his sleep
upon the dreary mountain rocks.

No. 421
O that the news were false, but he is dead,
and lies upon the dreary mountain's bed.

No. 422

Never shall I forget
our prince whom I regret.

*On the death of Prince Iwata
by Prince Yamakuma*

No. 423

When Prince Iwata went each morning to his love
along Iware road, he thought,
"In May when cuckoos sing,
I'll weave a wreath with irises and orange flowers,
and, in September when it showers, a garland of
    red maple leaves."
But now, ah he can visit her no more.

Hanka

No. 424

Shattered is the gem the woman
of Hatsuse cherished!

No. 425

In the cold wind blowing from the river
the broken-hearted woman wanders.

*On the dead man at the foot of Mt. Kagu
by Kakinomotono Hitomaro*

No. 426

Whose husband he that lies
upon the road, forgetting all?

No. 427

Alas, my friend is gone,
If I prayed at every temple in the land,
could I see him once more?

OSAKABENO TARIMARO

*When the remains of the maiden, Hijikata, were
cremated on Mt. Hatsuse, composed
by Kakinomotono Hitomaro*

No. 428

The vapor hanging over Mt. Hatsuse
is she, is she?

*2 songs, when the drowned maiden of Izumo
was cremated at Yoshino, by
Kakinomotono Hitomaro*

No. 429

Alas, is she the fog
now hanging over Mt. Yoshino?

No. 430

The raven tresses of the maiden of Izumo
flow upon the waves of the Yoshino River!

*On lovely Tekona's tomb
by Yamabeno Akahito*

No. 431

Long, long ago here lived a handsome youth
who had a cottage built, 'tis said, and who
with hempen sash both twilled and striped begirt
went to Tekona good and fair to woo.
Now, here her grassy grave is said to lie,
but is it for the cypress foliage dense,
or is it for the pine roots overspread,
(because so many years have passed by thence),
that nowhere can I find the maiden's tomb?
All save her legend is in forest gloom.

Hanka

No. 432

Lo, I beheld the tomb I tell you of,
the grassy tomb of the maiden, Tekona
of Mama in the shire of Katsushika!

No. 433

I am reminded of Tekona
who gathered herbs of ocean
in the cove of Mama.

4 songs

No. 434

I feel sad to behold the white azaleas on the beach,
for they remind me of the graceful youth who
    once lived here.

No. 435

Once the graceful youth of Kume
may have touched these shoreward grasses
I see them now, but all is withered.

No. 436

Let rumor spread!
O that you were a jewel
I could carry with me.

No. 437

The limpid river brims between its banks:
so clear should be your trust,
for so deep is my love.

3 songs by Ohtomono Tabito

No. 438

Never shall I lend to other women
my arm whereon my dead wife laid her head!

No. 439

The time comes for me to return,
    but since my dear wife is no more,
no one have I to comfort me
    at Nara as of yore.

No. 440

To think of dwelling all alone at home—
the thought is lonelier than alone to roam.

After Prince Nagaya's death
by Princess Kurahashibe

No. 441

Faithful to his lord's command,
from dying he stayed not his hand.
No mourning marks his obsequy,
but hid behind the clouds is he.

On the death of Prince Kashiwadebe

No. 442

As if to prove that life is but in vain,
the shining moon itself is bound to wax and wane.

ANON.

Composed by Ohtomono Minaka on the death of
his subordinate Hasetsukabeno Tatsumaro

No. 443

My warrior known as courageous in the distant
    East
has served the Court with great devotion.
He always told his family
that men at arms should not disgrace the good
    name of their clan.
Ever since he left his mother has been praying
the gods with all her heart to see his safe return,
but he, alas, is dead before his time.

Hanka

No. 444

Yesterday he was with us,
but today is with the clouds above the pines.

No. 445

Your safe return your wife on tiptoe waited,
but alas, you are no more.

5 songs on his way home
by Ohtomono Tabito

No. 446

The juniper of Tomo Beach
    that she beheld remains for aye.
But now where is my darling?
    Oh, never will she come my way.

No. 447

Juniper tree on Tomo Beach!
    How you remind me of my wife,
for I beheld you once with her
    who has departed from this life.

No. 448

If of the juniper I ask
    where my beloved now may be
perhaps the tree
    will tell the place to me.

No. 449

Minume Promontory now alone
I pass, which on my outward journey
I saw together with my wife,
and tears gush from my eyes.

No. 450

Upon the outward trip together
with my wife I saw this cape,
but now, behold it all alone.
And oh! how heavy is my heart!

3 songs on returning home
by Ohtomono Tabito

No. 451

How lonely is the hearth
where no longer is my wife!
I feel more miserable now
than voyaging upon the way.

No. 452

Leafy and tall have grown the trees
    she and I planted with delight,
making the garden fair to view,
    but dawnless now remains my night!

No. 453

Whenever I behold the trees,
  I weep, and think with grief of life,
remembering the happy days
  when they were planted by my wife.

*Lord Ohtomono Tabito died in 731, at the age of 67,
within a few years of his wife's decease; and
deploring his death, his friend Konno Myohgun
(life unknown) writes:*

No. 454

No more for me, day after day,
can send my lord, now passed away.

No. 455

So oft he fondly asked me,
"Your hagi—has it blown?"
Now he is gone.

No. 456

Deeply deploring your demise,
  like lonely cranes amid the reeds,
I cry and cry both morn and eve.
  Ah woe is me with heart that bleeds!

No. 457

My lord, since you I would have served
  for aye now lie within the tomb,
I've lost the heart to keep alive,
  myself left weary in deep gloom.

No. 458

Since you are gone, I all alone
  both day and night your death deplore,
and like a child naive and wild
  I moan and crawl about the floor.

*Lamenting the death of Ohtomono Tabito
by Inukaino Hitokami*

No. 459

His presence never ceased to be
the greatest of delights to me,
but since my lord is gone,
oh how should I live on?

*On the death of the nun Rigen
by Ohtomono Sakanoeno Iratsume*

No. 460

Our nun came from Korea to this country
far from kinsmen, far from home;
and not caring for a prosperous town,
chose the hill of Saho for her dwelling place,
and for many years lived there.
But "every one is doomed to perish,"
and during the absence of her journeying friends
she went the way of all.
She sleeps now on a hill
beyond Kasuga field across the Saho.
And I roam about with tears I wish would change
into rain to pour upon her grave.

Hanka

No. 461

She departs this life
now—this world of strife.

*On the death of his love
by Ohtomono Yakamochi*

No. 462

Coldly the autumn wind will blow
  and from now on
how can I spend the lonely night,
  since my love is gone?

*Sympathizing with his brother,
by Ohtomono Fumimochi*

No. 463

Weary must be the night
  you sleep alone.
With sorrow I think
  of your love now gone.

No. 464

The pinks my love set in the garden
for me to see with joy in autumn
are now in bloom, but where is she
who left the gift to me?

OHTOMONO YAKAMOCHI

No. 465

I know life is ephemeral,
  but as the dreary autumn wind
comes coldly blowing over all,
  my faithful love I call to mind.

DITTO

Written by Ohtomono Yakamochi
No. 466

Although our pinks have blown,
I have no consolation.
Were my love with me,
we could take joy in them together,
but she is gone, alas, like dew—
gone like evening's setting sun.

Hanka
No. 467

Alas, she passed away,
leaving a child to me!

No. 468

Oh! if I only knew the road
leading to the other world,
would I not set a barrier
to let her stay with me?

No. 469

My tears have not yet dried,
but now the flowers are gone.

5 more songs by Ohtomono Yakamochi
No. 470

I prayed for the welfare of my wife
in vain: so brief indeed her life!

No. 471

I could not make her stay with me,
and now she sleeps among the hills.

No. 472

Though 'tis the common fate, I know,
of man to die, still I can not
be reconciled to this sad lot,
and mourn my love, and cry in woe!

No. 473

Whenever I behold mist hanging o'er Mt. Saho,
in tears I call to mind the smoke she vanished in.

No. 474

Once I thought Mt. Saho strange,
but time goes by and all things change.
Now I hold the mountain dear:
my love laid in its sepulcher.

6 songs on the death of Prince Asaka
by Ohtomono Yakamochi
No. 475

This is a thing I fear to think of;
this is a thing I fear to utter:
the prince I served has passed away.
Alas, in springtime when the mountain
is bedecked with flowers,
and in the river sweetfish leap,
by white-robed men his bier was shouldered up
   the hill.
Now I know not how to beguile my days;
the tears obscure my weeping eyes.

Hanka
No. 476

Wazukasoma, once like any other mountain,
is now ennobled by the prince's tomb.

No. 477

As cherry blossoms fall, in which
   all the surrounding mountains shone,
so our beloved prince, alas,
   now at the height of youth is gone.

No. 478

Prince Asaka summoned chiefs of warriors
serving the Court to go ahunting.
He roused deer and wild boars in the morning,
and quail and pheasants in the evening.
He brought his stallion to a halt
and contemplated all the land around;
but now the flowers on leafy Ikuji have all faded,
and he I wished to serve for ever,
catalpa bow in hand,
armed with a sword and quiver,
sleeps in the tomb.
Smiles no longer light the faces of his men,
and nothing seems the same since he is gone.

No. 479

Silent now is Mt. Ikuji
where our prince once loved to hunt.

No. 480

Bearing the quiver of the famed Ohtomo,
eternally I would have served
that peerless Prince, Asaka.

Mourning his dead wife
by Takahashino Ason

No. 481

We vowed that we would live together
till our locks all white became,
but alas, my wife is gone,
leaving a piteous child with me,
buried now in drear Mt. Sagara.
I go out in the morning, thinking
of the days I spent with her,
and nightly in the lonely cottage mourn her death.
Whenever the child begins to cry,
I take him in my arms or on my back,
crying myself, and yearning after the deceased.

Hanka

No. 482

Mt. Sagara drear
I now hold dear.
All true the change,
although so strange.

No. 483

As morning birds will sing away,
    so do I cry in vain;
for now no opportunity
    have I to see my love again.

THE MANYOSHU

BOOK IV

FOREWORD

Book IV contains only love songs. The number of the longer poems is 7, sedohka one, and verselets 301—309 in all. The oldest song, written by one of the sisters to Emperor Nintoku to be sent to her brother in Yamato, appears at the beginning of the book (No. 484).

There are songs also by Emperor Jomei. These are the only verses written anterior to those of Emperor Tenji, and most were written after the capital was removed to Nara.

Some songs were composed in the era of Jinki (724–728), but mostly no mention is made as to the years in which they were written. It may be said that Book IV contains poems written in the same period as most of those that are found in Books III and VIII.

SEDOHKA

Unlike the tanka which is made up of 5, 7, 5, 7, 7 syllables, the sedohka is composed of 5, 7, 7, 5, 7, 7 syllables. It numbers 63 in the whole Manyo anthology. In Book VII, 25 songs by Kakinomotono Hitomaro are in this form. In Book XI, where verses of anonymous writers are mostly collected, this form often appears. It seems that this is a verse form rather prevalent in olden times.

Sedohka was sung then, perhaps, in a chorus. And it has declined abruptly since the Manyo Period, as poetry lost its chanting quality and developed into pure literature.

In No. 529 (Book IV) we find the first example:

> Along Saho's stream/ on the high parts of the bank/ do not gather the brushwood.
> For if it remains/ when springtime comes we shall go/ and meet there, hiding ourselves.

LOVE SONGS

*To Emperor Nintoku
by his sister*

No. 484

Only a single day
one would fain wait,
but oh how can I bear
so long an absence!

3 songs by Emperor Jomei

No. 485

Many people have lived in this land
ever since the blest days of the gods.
Now I see passers come and go,
but they are utter strangers.
And all day long I only yearn for you;
all night through I sleepless pine.

Hanka

No. 486

Many people come and go
over the mountain, making noises
like so many mallards, but
I sit forlorn without my love.

No. 487

I do not know your mind,
and wonder if you long for me.

*To Emperor Tenji
by Lady Nukada*

No. 488

As I sit longing for my lord,
    there comes, instead, the autumn wind,
making a visit to my bower,
    tap-tapping at the bamboo-blind.

No. 489

I envy you, my sister, whom
    at least the wind calls on; if I
could but wait for a man to come,
    I should be glad, and never sigh!

LADY KAGAMI

2 songs by Lady Fuki

No. 490

I ever think of you,
and see you in my dreams.

No. 491

Do come to me
at any hour,
for I keep open my door
to welcome you.

(Same as No. 1931)

4 songs by Tanobeno Ichiiko

No. 492

Like a child clinging to the sleeve
not to let its mother go
I wish to get you to remain.
Still have you the heart to leave?

No. 493

If I depart from you,
    will you lie the livelong night in bed
yearning for me,
    with your raven tresses spread?

No. 494

How I long for my love!
and now
I have a grudge against the man
who first sent her to me.

No. 495

How sad to leave my love behind
in a far town beyond the mountains!

No. 496

A hundred times I yearn for her,
but even once we can not meet.

No. 497

Did they also suffer
in olden times,
pining in love?

No. 498

It is not only we, but folk of yore
also wept and moaned in love.

No. 499

However oft I hear from thee,
it never wearies me.

No. 500

Is my husband lying on the reeds
far away on windy Ise's beach?

Wife of GONO DANOCHI

3 songs to his wife
by Kakinomotono Hitomaro
No. 501

Long is the fence around the shrine on Furu Hill,
and long have I been yearning after you, my dear.

No. 502

Never shall I forget you,
my sweetest love, oh never!

No. 503

Leaving my love disturbed and sad,
I started on my way.

Written by his wife
No. 504

I never shall forget, my lord,
that once I went to your abode.

2 songs by Abeno Iratsume
No. 505

Why shall I worry now?
    I but rely on you. My soul
is yours, and I
    consign to you my all.

No. 506

My dear lord, set thy heart at ease!
    Am I not here to go for thee,
no matter what the circumstance,
    into the fire, into the sea?

No. 507

My love for you is deep
but sad, and I, tears running down the pillow,
lie afloat as on the billow,
crying even in my sleep.

SURUGANO UNEME

No. 508

Since we are parted,
each will never see again the other,
and we shall go on yearning,
alas, for evermore.

On the Way to Tsukushi
by Tajihino Kasamaro
No. 509

I lay on Mitsu beach my scarlet sash untied,
yearning for my wife,
and crying like a crane in morning fog.
To soothe myself I stood up,
and looked toward home,
only to see Mt. Katsuragi hidden in the clouds.
But now I embark and westward go
past Awaji Isle and Awa,
hearing the sailors singing in the morning sun,
and oars' sweet music in the evening calm;
the ship sails off Inami,
and comes to Iyejima* held dear by all travelers.

* The name means 'Home Island'.

Hanka
No. 510

Liefer would I midst all that busyness
have sat with my dear wife
and reckoned up the days till my return!

No. 511

Same as No. 43.

No. 512

Even so innocent an act
as our sweet love-tryst will attract
the folk's eye, and to vex us sore
their poisoned tongues wag evermore.

A country maid

No. 513

How long have I been waiting for this chance?
Now at last I have her at my side.
PRINCE SHIKI

No. 514

My love for you is so profound
that in each stitch I gave with care
it went into your robe, and there
like thread with thread is closely bound.
LADY ABENO IRATSUME

To Lady Abeno Iratsume
by Nakatomino Azumabito
No. 515

I went to bed (alone, alas),
and woke to find myself ungirt.
How shall I bind a raveled sash?
Chagrined, I cried as though from hurt.

In reply to the above
No. 516

Your sash that came apart—how sad!
Were I but there where you're sojourning,
to mend it strongly were I glad,
with three-ply thread—mere one-ply spurning.
LADY ABENO IRATSUME

No. 517

He lives secure though he has touched
the consecrated tree,
must I then fear to touch my dear,
though she another's be?
OHTOMONO YASUMARO

No. 518

You often came across the mountain path;
and why not now, my dear?
ISHIKAWANO IRATSUME

No. 519

Always the rain
makes you indoors remain,
and yesternight
you came not again.
OHTOMONO IRATSUME

No. 520

While it rains, while it pours,
with you by my side
I'll snugly stay indoors.
ANON. in response to
the preceding verse.

No. 521

Standing mowing in the fields,
spreading hemp for sun to dry,
thinking of you,
your maid of the east country—
do not forget me.

3 songs to Ohtomono Iratsume
by Fujiwarano Tayu
No. 522

As girls hide combs within their boxes,
my love lived secretly,
and years have passed without a tryst.
Alas, how old today is she?

No. 523

Some men can pass a twelvemonth unconcernedly
without sight of their wives, but I
only awhile have been away from mine,
and yet already now I pine.

No. 524

Though I am lying now in bed
wrapped in a warm, warm counterpane,
I am forlorn and cold,
since you, my dear, are not with me.

4 songs by Ohtomono Iratsume
No. 525

Pray, come, though it be once a year,
astride your steed, the jet-black horse,
crossing the Saho River,
scattering pebbles in your course.

No. 526

As rippling waves are ever seen
and heard on Saho rapids where
plovers fly crying, so day and night
love harries me with ceaseless care.

No. 527

Many a time you broke your word
    and did not come. Now I reply
though you think you've a tryst assured
    I shall not wait. Oh! why should I?

No. 528

The mouth of Saho's stream is wide,
    where only plovers' cries we hear,
but I will bridge the roaring tide
    that you may cross and have no fear.

No. 529

I would they left unreaped the grass
that grows so thick on Saho's banks,
for in the gentle spring we'll hide
within it, shunning people's eyes.

          OHTOMONO SAKANOENO IRATSUME

To Princess Unakami
by Emperor Shohmu
No. 530

Horses are kept within a fence
    to make them safely stay.
Your heart is likewise in my care.
    From me it shall not get away.

In response to the above
by the Princess
No. 531

Like arrows ringing from catalpa bows
your words arrive at my delighted ear.

2 songs by Ohtomono Sukune
No. 532

The palace lures her like a shining dream,
and I dream of the girl who wants to go.
Oh shall I keep her here and spoil her dream,
or shall I let her go and spoil my own.

No. 533

I envy courtiers who can see
that maid as often as they like.
while I, alas, am all alone,
and have no girl to care for me.

Composed by Lord Aki
No. 534

My wife is far away,
and I feel ill at ease.
I wish I were a cloud that sails,
or a bird that soars on high
to go back and talk,
sitting side by side with her!

Hanka
No. 535

Alas, a twelvemonth has passed over me,
my head not resting on her dainty arm.

No. 536

I know not if you still remember me,
but I will go a long way to see you.

          LORD KADOBE

6 songs to Lord Imajo
by Lady Takada
No. 537

You lightly talk of breaking with me,
but if I did not see you
even for a day, then I should suffer.

No. 538

I fear the rumors that they spread;
so I did not see you,
but do not understand me wrong,
thinking ill of me.

No. 539

My lover, if you truly wished
to see me, then no matter how
they might have talked about me, I'd
have ventured to meet you.

No. 540

Did I have a premonition
of not seeing you again?
For sad and lorn I felt this morning
when you left me.

No. 541

People like spreading rumour.
Therefore, let us await, my love,
the opportunity to see
each other in the world to come.

No. 542

How happy I was in those days
when you used to come!
Alas, no messenger
now do you send to me.

"Ghostwritten" for a woman
by Kasano Kanamura
No. 543

My husband who went with others
in the retinue of the Emperor
along the road of Karu,
passing fair Unebi Hill, to Kii,
you may have seen red maple leaves
on Mt. Matsuchi falling in the wind,
and fascinated by their beauty,
lost the thought of me.
A thousand times I think of following you,
but not knowing how to answer
the barrier-keepers on the road,
I pine for you in vain.

Hanka
No. 544

Better 'twould be
to go to Kii
than thus but yearn
for his return!

No. 545

I can not go and follow him, alas,
no barrier guardsman suffering me to pass.

On meeting a girl on the journey
by Kasano Kanamura
No. 546

Accompanying the Emperor, I lodge at Mikanohara.
I, meeting you upon the way, made love,
and now by the mercy of the gods of heaven and
  earth
you are my mistress for the night—
the happy night I wish to last for evermore.

Hanka
No. 547

Since I saw you on the way
You have become my all-in-all.

No. 548

Happily met are we.
May this night last eternally.

3 songs by Ishikawano Tarihito
No. 549

May the gods of heaven and earth
help and protect you who start now
upon your journey that you may
return to live again with us.

No. 550

Steadfast as a mighty ship
you are my strength. When you are gone,
my days are filled with longing
until you come again.

No. 551

As wave on wave rolls in to dash
ceaselessly against the island shores,
so I yearn for you
both day and night.

No. 552

Oh, does my love wish me to die?
She thinks not of me enough,
and grudges time to spend with me,
and many a night I lie alone.

OHTOMONO MIYORI

2 songs to Ohtomono Tabito in far Tsukushi
by Lady Nifu
No. 553

You live far from me as the cloud of heaven,
but our love brings us together.

No. 554

Kindly you gave me millet wine;
but if I be intoxicated, then what should I do?
Pray, send to me a mat, too, of bamboo.

To Tajihino Agatamori
by Ohtomono Tabito
No. 555

Alas, the saké that I brewed,
desiring to enjoy with you
upon Yasuno field, I drink
companionless now, all alone.

To Ohtomono Miyori
by Lady Kamo
No. 556

No vessel from Tsukushi has come yet
to carry you away from home,
but I'm sad to see you
already querulous, so cold!

2 songs by Hanishino Mizuchi
No. 557

Eager to see my love at home, I start
even though the vessel dash against the rocks and
 sink.

No. 558

Give me back the offerings, O god;
you can not still the waves for me
who return to see my love.

4 songs by Ohtomono Momoyo
No. 559

Living a peaceful life so far,
I am an aged man, but now,
falling in passionate love,
I am tormented night and day.

No. 560

What care I for the other world
 after I die lovelorn?
I wish but here below to live
 with you, not thus alone.

No. 561

If I should tell you that I love you
 when I do not, it is the god, enshrined
in yonder forest of Mikasa,
 that will punish me, and you need never mind.

No. 562

In vain I scratch my eyebrow,
for you refuse to meet me.

> (It was believed that when someone loves
> you, it makes your eyebrows itch.)

2 songs by Ohtomono Sakanoeno Iratsume
No. 563

Have I fallen in love so deep? Oh ne'er
even when young, when raven was my hair.

No. 564

Laying all blame on me, alas,
where now are you, and with what lass?

No. 565

Never will I let others know, I vow to you,
that on a moonlit night we had a rendezvous.

LADY KAMO

2 songs on seeing off friends
No. 566

As you depart for grassy-pillowed travel,
yearning we ride abreast on Shika beach.

OHTOMONO MOMOYO

No. 567

When you cross Iwakuni, oh my friends,
pause to pray there at the mountain shrine.

YAMAGUCHINO WAKAMARO

4 songs by officials in the local government,
sending off Ohtomono Tabito
No. 568

Like a thousand waves drawn to the shore
are we to you, our lord whom we adore.

KADOBENO ISOTARI

No. 569

Like purple of Korean dye
 that ever stays unfadingly
our hearts are steeped in sorrow deep
 since now we have to part from thee.

ASADANO YASU

No. 570

The day you go back to Yamato
    is drawing near,
and plaintive cries of stags
    upon the field I hear.

DITTO

No. 571

Look, how senene the moon!
And hark, how sweet the river's tune!
Let us all who stay, or leave
for home, enjoy this memorable eve!

OHTOMONO YOTSUNA

2 songs to Lord Ohtomono Tabito
by Sami Mansei

No. 572

Left behind now by my lord,
a lonely life I have to live
of weary morning,
of dreary night.

No. 573

My black hair has turned all white,
yet I experience at this age
how hard it is to part
from you, friend of my heart!

2 songs in reply by Ohtomono Tabito

No. 574

Though I am here in Nara,
I can not help but wonder
in what direction lies Tsukushi?
Oh white Cloud, hanging on the mountain,
I think you point the way.

No. 575

Oh like a lonely crane that feeds
among the seaside reeds
I am without a good friend here,
and daily life to me is drear.

After Lord Ohtomo left for home
by Fujino Ohnari

No. 576

Lonely will be the mountain road
leading to Dazaifu Castle,
and weary from now on,
since homeward you are gone.

To Lord Takayasu by Ohtomono Tabito

No. 577

Never give others, pray, this gown, my gift to you,
although you show it to the Naniwa fishermen.

No. 578

Here I wish to be
    like heaven and earth for aye,
but leaving my dear garden,
    I must go away.

OHTOMONO MIYORI

2 songs to Komuno Myogun
by Ohtomono Yakamochi

No. 579

Since you departed is but little time,
yet long it seems to me, and I am lorn.

No. 580

How I wish that thou couldst come to me,
my friend, that I might be again with thee!

4 songs to Ohtomono Yakamochi
by Ohtomono Sakanoeno Ohkiiratsume

No. 581

Alive, opportunities we have to meet.
    Why did you say
then in my dream
    you soon would pass away?

No. 582

That my lord pines in love I know,
but it is naught beside a woman's woe.

No. 583

Your love is like a dayflower,
and will change as quickly.
For days have passed, and oh
you send me not a word.

No. 584

You are lovely as Kasuga Hill all veiled in mist
which I wish to look on morning after morning.

No. 585

Of all times, why do you leave me now
when you say you yearn so after me?

OHTOMONO SAKANOENO IRATSUME

To Tamurano Ohkiiratsume by Ohtomono Inagimi
No. 586
Oh why did I have sight of you
only to languish day and night?

24 songs to Ohtomono Yakamochi
by Kasano Otome
No. 587
Look at this gift of mine as often as you may
to bring to mind one who remembers you for aye.

No. 588
O Pines upon the hill,
like you, I pine
for him to come.

> In the original also there is a pun on matsu
> (pine), and matsu (wait).

No. 589
Oh why do you not come?
You know I live in Tamu.

No. 590
How sweet our months of secret bliss!
O my beloved, never tell my name!

No. 591
I dreamed my precious comb-box was unlocked.
I fear you have divulged our secret love.

No. 592
As people hear the crane cry in the murky night,
I only hear of you, and have no sight.

No. 593
Yearning and longing after you,
I feel my love grow deeper still,
and stand and grieve beneath a pine
upon the side of Nara Hill.

No. 594
Ah short-lived as the evening dew
that lies upon our garden bed,
languishing in my love for you,
soon, very soon shall I be dead.

No. 595
Never shall I forget my dove,
while yet upon this earth I move.
And daily will my love grow too,
ever to you remaining true!

No. 596
Think you not, Keeper of the Isle,
the beach, to cross which takes above
eight hundred days, a promenade,
compared with my hard task of love?

No. 597
Alas, e'er shunning others' eyes,
I spend my days in heaving sighs.

No. 598
Do we not sigh in love and die?
And every month by day and night
unknown I peak, and growing weak,
I shall soon perish in my plight.

No. 599
How can it be
that I am yearning unto death
for her whom only dimly
I glimpsed in morning mist?

No. 600
Alas, I love a courtier
too high in social standing.

No. 601
Although no hill or river be
between us—you and me,
yet for your sight I care
as if there were.

No. 602
I met you first at evening,
and yearn especially at twilight.

No. 603
If yearning were to die,
a thousand deaths had I.

No. 604
Yesternight I dreamed I wore a sword.
It is an omen I shall see my lord.

No. 605

If deities grant not my prayers,
I'll perish from my love for you.

No. 606

Ceaselessly across the cove of Ohnawa*
the breezes blow.
Ceaselessly I yearn for you.
Forget me not!

> * Following Keichu's interpretation of Ohnawa as a place
> name.

No. 607

I hear the night bells telling us
    to go to bed, but when I deep
in love now lie and yearn for you,
    to my eyes comes no sleep.

No. 608

No better to love a courtier who is cold
than idolize the temple devil famished, old.

2 songs by Kasano Otome

No. 609

Happy was I in thy vicinity;
but alas, I have no hope now to meet thee.

No. 610

So happy in your neighborhood,
was I, but now I only brood.

> (The above 2 songs were sent to Ohtomono
> Yakamochi after she separated from him.)

2 songs in reply by Ohtomono Yakamochi

No. 611

I'm weary and forlorn,
alas, since you are gone.

No. 612

Why did I not let you alone?
Now, alas, I am lovelorn.

> (Almost the same as No. 2899)

*5 songs to Ohtomono Yakamochi
by Lady Yamaguchi*

No. 613

I am forlorn,
and brood alone.

No. 614

Alas, I weep, and wet my sleeves with brine,
harassed by unrequited love of mine.

No. 615

If I can't dream of you, my darling,
let me at least dream of your pillow.

No. 616

Years have passed o'er me
without a tryst with thee.

No. 617

I love you more and more
as tides yearn for the shore.

To Ohtomono Yakamochi by Ohmiwano Otome

No. 618

Now in the night I long for you,
and mewing plovers make me lonelier.

Written by Ohtomono Sakanoeno Iratsume

No. 619

You vowed you would be true,
and won my heart that I had tried
to keep clear as a mirror.
Since then I have relied on you
as one relies upon a lofty ship.
But oh! what is amiss?
By the divine will are we separated
or by mortal men?
Anyway you come not to me,
nor does your messenger,
and all day long, the livelong night,
not knowing what to do,
Like 'a weak woman' they call me I only weep,
vainly waiting word from you.

Hanka

No. 620

Had you made to me no vow,
my love, I should not suffer now.

No. 621

Journeying still you love me dear,
for in my night's dream you appear.
Wife of SAEKI AZUMAHITO

In reply
No. 622

I have been traveling long o'er hill and stream—
so long that now I have become but dream.

SAEKI AZUMAHITO

Recited at a feast by Lord Ikebe
No. 623

I see the moon now setting over yon pine tree,
and know tonight in vain we have awaited thee.

To Princess Sakabito by Emperor Shomu
No. 624

When we two met, thou smiledst on me,
and ever since I've longed for thee.

On sending a carp to a lady
by Lord Takayasu
No. 625

This is the carp I sought
throughout the pond,
and, as it hiding lay beyond
the duckweed dense, I caught.

No. 626

I feel as if my ears were sullied with such rumors;
I go to purify them in Asuka River.

To Saeki Akamaro by a woman
No. 627

Can still you want to lie with me in bed
when gray from tears of sorrow is my head?

In reply by Saeki Akamaro
No. 628

You say your head is gray—but that's no harm,
and as for tears—they are an added charm.

At a feast
No. 629

Thou only sendst a messenger to me,
while I await no one but thee.

OHTOMONO YOTSUNA

No. 630

Gone will be the bloom I love,
but I,
backward and shy,
only look, and make no move.

To a girl by Prince Yuhara
No. 631

You shut your door to me. How cold you are
to me who came to see you from afar!

No. 632

How could I reach to you?
You I can see,
but can not touch
like the famous lunar tree.

(The tree five thousand feet high in the moon
of the Chinese legend.)

2 songs by a woman
No. 633

In my dream did you appear,
and now I know you hold me dear.

No. 634

How happy now I am, my lord,
that thus I go with you upon the road.

2 songs by Prince Yuhara
No. 635

I've brought my love
with whom together do I roam,
and still I hold her like the pearl
hidden within the case at home.

No. 636

My love, I leave my gown with you to wear:
when wrapped in it, remember my embrace!

No. 637

The robe my lover left me,
all silently tells me
of him it once enfolded:
may we be never parted.

The woman

No. 638

Only a night passed by
without your company;
and yet, it seems, I own,
as if a month had gone.

PRINCE YUHARA

No. 639

You love me deep,
and will not let me sleep,
for every night I see
in dreams you come to me.

The woman

No. 640

Not so far distant is your town,
and yet as if it were the land of clouds
I yearn. I yearn though but a month away.

PRINCE YUHARA

No. 641

You want to break with me, but hesitate:
how can I live a happy life in such a state?

The woman

No. 642

Loving you, I wish now I were dead.
Alas, at first I fondly thought
you might take me as easily
as the reel will roll up thread.

PRINCE YUHARA

3 songs to Lord Aki by Kino Otome

No. 643

I, a woman, find
me lingering here,
afraid to wade Anase's stream
to overtake my husband.

No. 644

Ah me! dismayed,
since you whom I hold dear
as life itself
I now see go.

No. 645

The day approaches—
the day of parting, of waving the white sleeves.
Already I grieve in my heart,
already I weep.

No. 646

You make me grieve for you,
and this day you will surely rue.

OHTOMONO SURUGAMARO

No. 647

Since custom keeps my love away,
I languish for him every day.

OHTOMONO SAKANOENO IRATSUME

No. 648

Days have passed we do not meet.
How fares it now with you, my sweet?

OHTOMONO SURUGAMARO

No. 649

What ails you now, I wonder,
that you send me no message?

OHTOMONO SAKANOENO IRATSUME

No. 650

In what enchanted land have you been dwelling,
that, parting long and now beholding you,
I find you ever young and fair?

OHTOMONO MIYORI

2 songs by Ohtomono Sakanoeno Iratsume

No. 651

'Tis autumn, and now frost is falling,
and they at home await my coming back.

No. 652

To the happy bridegroom's care
will I commit my daughter fair,
and carrying the pillow all alone,
resigned, shall to my room repair.

3 songs by Ohtomono Surugamaro

No. 653

I yearn for you again and yet again,
but ah! alas, a month has passed in vain.

No. 654

The month in which we met is not yet out.
If I say I yearn,
you will say I lie.

No. 655

The gods of heaven and earth may punish me,
if on pretence I say that I love thee.

6 songs by Ohtomono Sakanoeno Iratsume
No. 656

I love you true,
and wonder if you do.

No. 657

Though to free myself from love I oft desire,
my heart will never let me quench the fire.

No. 658

I know in vain for you I yearn,
but ah still I can naught but burn.

No. 659

Though I met you but awhile, my lord,
the buzz of gossip is abroad.

No. 660

Never believe what people say:
bent on splitting us are they.

No. 661

I long and yearn for you,
so when we meet be kind to me.

No. 662

In Ago inlet girt with hills
a maid was fishing, and of her I dream.
LORD ICHIWARA

No. 663

My lovely wife is of my choice,
and sweet as songbirds' is her voice.
ABENO TOSHITARI

No. 664

What matter if it rains? I'll come to you,
keeping the promise for our rendezvous.
OHTOMONO KATAMI

No. 665

I can not find it in my heart
from you, my darling love, to part.
ABENO MUSHIMARO

2 songs by Ohtomono Sakanoeno Iratsume
No. 666

I have not seen you for awhile,
and find it hard time to beguile.

No. 667

My love, the moon is still on high.
We have time yet ere you bid me goodby.

No. 668

Oh how can I forget you
fair as the mountain cloud in autumn?
LORD ATSUMI

No. 669

The golden-fruited orange trees upon the broad-
    based mountain
hide not their color: why should you and I?
Let us then freely meet and talk.
PRINCE KASUGA

No. 670

Come on a moonlit night serene:
    the way is short and even too,
and there no mountain lies between
    to make the pathway hard to you.
PRINCE YUHARA

In reply
No. 671

Even though the moon shines clear,
my night within is dark and drear,
and how can I your dwelling find
in this condition of my mind?

ANON.

No. 672

I, obscure, ah me !
languish so for thee.
ABENO MUSHIMARO

2 songs by Ohtomono Sakanoeno Iratsume
No. 673

Innocent, if I accept this offer,
I may go on repenting.

No. 674

You say you will be ever true.
Your words, folk tell me, I shall rue.

5 songs to Ohtomono Yakamochi
by Nakatomino Otome
No. 675

Consumed in love so fervent,
day and night I suffer.

No. 676

The day will come,
though years may pass,
whereon I shall meet you
whom I love true.

No. 677

Half-glimpsed like Mt. Kasuga
in the morning cloud,
I yearn for him
I scarcely know.

No. 678

The only way, if there be one, to see
my mind at rest is to come face to face with thee.

No. 679

I will say once again to you,
if you do not love me, I do.

3 songs to a friend by Ohtomono Yakamochi
No. 680

Oh, why do you not come, my friend? I wonder
if you take seriously remarks malicious.

No. 681

If you will break with me,
I shall cease to love you.

No. 682

I know I love you true,
and go on yearning after you.

7 songs by Ohtomono Sakanoeno Iratsume
No. 683

Slanderous are people in this place.
Therefore, though fatal may prove care.
never, never, in your face
betray the secret thoughts of love.

No. 684

What care I if I die,
     for though I live on in this life,
never you will agree
     to take me willingly to wife.

No. 685

Alas, because of custom,
we both live separated.

No. 686

A moment passed without the sight of you
does seem a thousand years indeed to me.

No. 687

Your smiles impel me toward you:
no weir can stem the river utterly.

No. 688

Let not your smile upon me be
conspicuous as white clouds o'er green mountains,
lest people come to know
and talk of our relation.

No. 689

No sea or mountain separates us,
and yet, alas, we rarely meet.

No. 690

The shining day obscuring,
my weeping tears
bedew my garments
with none to dry them.

OHTOMONO MIYORI

2 songs to a lady by Ohtomono Yakamochi
No. 691

Though many ladies serve at court, my sweet,
you are the only one I wish to meet.

No. 692

How cold you are!
whom yet I love so much.

No. 693

White clouds are ever hanging o'er Akitsu field.
Would you could be the clouds and I Akitsu field.

OHTOMONO CHIMURO

2 songs by Lady Hirokawa

No. 694

I labor under love,
and have none to reprove.

No. 695

Of love I thought I had been dispossessed,
but still I find it tenanting my breast.

No. 696

Those at home,
oh how can I forget them,
now with kajika trilling
in this village of Izumi
where I have lived so long?

ISHIKAWANO HIRONARI

No. 697

When word from you I hear,
I newly pine, my dear.

No. 698

Translated, almost the same as No. 693

No. 699

A thousand ways within the rapids
each drop of water goes,
and yet goes onward, reunites,
and so shall I with you.

At the gate of a house
by Ohtomono Yakamochi

No. 700

Alas, I've come a long, long way,
and you tell me to go away.

2 songs to Ohtomono Yakamochi
by Kochino Momoyo

No. 701

When will you come again to me,
you who left me so hurriedly?

No. 702

Since that moonlit night
even till today, ah! unforgettable,
because I love you!

2 songs by a maid

No. 703

I have been yearning for you since that day
when we parted, and you went away.

No. 704

I pray to live long: why?
Only for the chance of meeting you.

To a maid by Ohtomono Yakamochi

No. 705

With a garland in my dream did you appear,
and since then I yearn after you, my dear.

In reply by the maid

No. 706

I never wear a garland,
and whom you love I wonder.

2 songs to Ohtomono Yakamochi by a maid

No. 707

Freedom from care not knowing,
my love for you
brings me to extremity.

No. 708

If you should chance again to come,
I will not let you leave for home.

No. 709

The paths you tread are rough, my dear;
wait for the moon, pray, to appear.

A maid

No. 710

I only met him in the dim moonbeam,
and now love and see him in my dream.

DITTO

3 songs by Taniwano Ohme
No. 711

That I am true you are aware.
So, never liken me to leaves
wafting upon the waters where
mallards are swimming free from care.

No. 712

Oh ! is it for that sin of mine
to touch the sacred cedar tree
beside the Miwa shrine
that you, my love, I can not see?

No. 713

Oh, does he mind the rumors spread
that separate us like a fence,
or is he going to avoid me,
using them as mere pretence?

7 songs to a maid by Ohtomono Yakamochi
No. 714

I ever hold you dear,
but with no opportunities
to meet you, do I live alone,
yearning, and only heaving sighs.

No. 715

Over the sparkling rapids where
the ferry plies, and plovers cry,
astride my charger when can I
go to meet my lady fair?

No. 716

Dost thou not pity me
who yearn both day and night for thee?
Pray, now let me hear:
in thy dream did I appear?

No. 717

Cursed is he who loves
an unresponsive lass,
suffering alone
in unrequited love, alas.

No. 718

I yearn more, having seen you smile,
my darling, in my dream.

No. 719

Alas, I thought myself a warrior brave,
who now am naught but tender passion's slave.

No. 720

Alas, perhaps you do not know
from love of you I suffer so.

Presented to the Court
No. 721

I ask your pardon on my knees
for this my songlet; I abide
upon the lonely mountainside
a stranger to urbanities.

ANON.

No. 722

O that I were of stone or wood
which no afflictions ever move !
For day and night I only brood;
I suffer for my thoughts of love.

OHTOMONO YAKAMOCHI

To Ohtomono Sakanoeno Ohkiiratsume
from her mother
No. 723

My daughter saw me off when I left home,
standing beside the iron-studded gate,
sunken in thought with face disconsolate,
as if in foreign lands I were to roam.
Only of her I think now day and night,
and haggard and all gaunt have I become,
wetting my sleeves with tears in sorrow deep.
Alas, if I go on like this, how can I sleep
or live a single month out of her sight?

Hanka
No. 724

Oh, does my daughter pass the night,
her mind confused as hair at morn?
For in my dream I saw her sight,
which even now makes me forlorn.

2 songs presented to the Court
No. 725

O Waterfowl there swimming about the lake,
go take our Liege my love now for his servant's
sake.

No. 726

I'd liefer be a mallard in the Imperial pond
than thus afar adore our Sovereign.

2 songs to Sakanoeno Ohkiiratsume
by Ohtomono Yakamochi

No. 727

Alas, love racks me even now with care,
though for my amulet
day lilies on my sash I wear.

No. 728

Oh if there were a country where
no people dwell, there would I now repair
with my sweet love to live alone,
well satisfied, and free from care.

3 songs to Ohtomono Yakamochi
by Ohtomono Sakanoeno Ohkiiratsume

No. 729

Were you a gem, my dear, I would be dight
therewith to be together day and night.

No. 730

My darling, I met thee,
and now they talk of me.
Oh why did I set sight
on thee that very night?

No. 731

I take no care of gossip,
unless it give you trouble.

3 songs again by Ohtomono Yakamochi
No. 732

All for your sake, my lady fair,
a thousand rumors will I bear;
and should it fall upon my chance,
I'll lend myself to your romance.

No. 733

I, a mortal, could not live again,
and life without you would be all in vain.

No. 734

O that a priceless gem I were!
Then I should not be thus forlorn,
but on your tender arm could be,
with you abiding night and morn.

To Ohtomono Yakamochi
by Sakanoeno Ohkiiratsume
No. 735

The moon is shining o'er the hill, and on
this lovely night how could I sleep alone?

Again to Sakanoeno Ohkiiratsume
by Ohtomono Yakamochi
No. 736

I went into the moonlight, yearning after thee,
revolving in my mind if thou wouldst welcome me.

2 songs to Ohtomono Yakamochi
by Sakanoeno Ohkiiratsume
No. 737
People spread the rumors,
but we shall disregard them.

No. 738

Alas, alas, above
all things one grieves in love.

2 songs to Sakanoeno Ohkiiratsume
by Ohtomono Yakamochi
No. 739

The slightest hope of seeing
my love gives heart to go on being.

No. 740
You give me hopes for trysts.
Be sure they are not vain.

15 more songs to Sakanoeno Ohkiiratsume
by Ohtomono Yakamochi
No. 741

Empty was the dream, ah me.
I woke and vainly felt for thee.

No. 742

I've pined away in love for you,
and now my sash goes thrice round me.

No. 743

No thousand men could move
this rock of love
which round my hapless neck
hangs sevenfold.

No. 744

With my doors unshut I wait
that you may come into my dream.

No. 745

I did yearn even when I saw you every day.
Pity me who live from you now far away.

No. 746

You have sent me a gift elaborate, fair.
Never have I seen a purse so rare!

No. 747

I wear your gift, the gown, next to my skin,
and shall not part with it until we meet again.

No. 748

Though I die,
though I be pierced by people's tongues,
what care I?
My only thought is you.

No. 749

Why in my dream do you no more appear?
Do you want me to die from love, my dear?

No. 750

I lived apart from you in grief,
and meet you now to suffer more.

No. 751

Only a few days have passed since our tryst,
and for the next I madly long and yearn.

No. 752

How can I live out of your sight,
dreaming like this day and night?

No. 753

Thy sight, instead of soothing me,
makes me yearn more, alas, for thee.

No. 754

I still behold you, looking as sad and forlorn
as you looked when I left you at dawn.

No. 755

Whenever I take leave of you at dawning,
I feel as if my heart were cut or burning.

4 songs to Sakanoeno Ohkiiratsume
by Tamurano Ohkiiratsume

No. 756

Sister, eager am I to behold you;
and plan for our reunion.

No. 757

Sister, we live nearby,
but can not meet, oh why?

No. 758

Sister dear, I love you,
and think but of you.

No. 759

When will you come
to see me, dear, at home?

2 songs to Ohkiiratsume from her mother,
Ohtomono Sakanoeno Iratsume

No. 760

Translated, same as No. 3088

No. 761

My child, now I must part,
though it grieves my heart.

2 songs to Ohtomono Yakamochi by Kino Otome

No. 762

Though I am old, my joy is to be with my dear;
but the morning's solitude he leaves me in I fear.

No. 763

We are like jewels set upon a string,
and fate some day will bring us both together.

In reply by Ohtomono Yakamochi
No. 764

Why talk of age, my darling?
In love that never matters.

*Thinking of his wife, Sakanoeno Ohkiiratsume
by Ohtomono Yakamochi*
No. 765

Although a mountain stands us both to separate,
this moonlit night she may await me at her gate.

In sympathy by Fujiwarano Iratsume
No. 766

The way is long, and though you do not come, still
she
must now be waiting for you eagerly.

2 more songs to his wife by Ohtomono Yakamochi
No. 767

We live afar, and even in my dream, my dear,
although I pray, now you do not appear.

No. 768

My yearning in this capital of Kuni
is only to return to you, my darling.

To Kino Iratsume by Ohtomono Yakamochi
No. 769

When on a day of rain
    I sit alone, my dear,
upon the mountainside,
    all is forlorn and drear.

5 songs to his wife by Ohtomono Yakamochi
No. 770

Although I do not come to thee,
my dear, thou dwellest e'er in me.

No. 771

Do you not know when folk deceive you,
    they will pretend to tell the truth?
How try to get me to believe you,
    then, when you say you love in sooth?

No. 772

Even in dreams to see your sight
ungirt in bed I lie at night;
but never do I see you come,
and to my ardor you are dumb.

No. 773

Even innocent ajisai flowers change hue.
I trust you, but know that I am betrayed by you.

No. 774

You love me a thousand times you say,
but prove me that it is true, I pray.

*To Kino Otome
by Ohtomono Yakamochi*
No. 775

We seldom met in Nara,
and now I yearn in Kuni.

In reply
No. 776

My dear, 'tis you who said you love me,
and now, oh why do you reprove me?

*5 more songs to Kino Otome
by Ohtomono Yakamochi*
No. 777

If I approach your hedge,
will you dismiss me from your gate?

No. 778

To tell the truth, it is for you I care,
and not the hedge however fair.

No. 779

I have enough material to thatch your roof.
Tomorrow I will bring it from the nearby woods.

No. 780

If I bring wood and reeds to thee,
my darling, wilt thou smile on me?

No. 781

I'll go again along the darkling way;
so this time do not refuse me, pray.

On sending a gift to a friend
by Kino Otome
No. 782
The wind was blowing high today, dear friend of
  mine,
when I picked this herb of ocean wet with brine.

3 songs to a maid by Ohtomono Yakamochi
No. 783
I've loved you these two years, my sweet,
and wonder why we can not meet.

No. 784
We are not allowed to see each other.
Therefore let me dream of you, my darling.

No. 785
What though my life be brief as morning dew?
I am content if I can live with you.

3 songs to Lord Fujiwarano Kusumaro
by Ohtomono Yakamochi
No. 786
Though vernal rain fall ceaselessly,
is it because so young the tree
that your fair plum,
does not come into bloom?

No. 787
I felt as if I were adream
when I beheld your messenger,
for what delight it is to hear
I am allowed to come to you!

No. 788
I set a young plum tree not yet in flower,
and people talk of me.

2 more songs to Fujiwarano Kusumaro
by Ohtomono Yakamochi
No. 789
You wrote to me upon a misty vernal day,
and your words cast me into dismay.

No. 790
I but entreat your promise, and will wait
for you to make it good, however late.

2 songs in reply by Fujiwarano Kusumaro
No. 791
Deep rooted as the mountain-rock-bound sedge
is my undying gratitude to you.

No. 792
Waiting for the vernal rain to flower,
my young plum tree is budding.

THE MANYOSHU

BOOK V

FOREWORD

Book V consists of miscellaneous poems, some of which are verses that in other volumes are classed in the group of elegies. Conspicuous in this book are verses written by Ohtomono Tabito, which remind one of something fey (a), and long poems treating of social miseries by Yamanoeno Okura (b).

Examples: (a) 2 songs by Tabito on sending a Japanese koto made of paulownia to Lord Fujiwarano Fusasaki (Nos. 810, 811).

There is a note affixed to the first song, which reads, "This koto turned to a maiden in my dream and said, 'I took root on the rugged peak of a remote isle, and had my trunk exposed to the sun's brilliant light. For a long time I was also veiled in the mist, and enjoyed my stay amidst the natural scenery. Looking afar at the billows, I feared that I might prove useless, and lie rotting in the vale in a hundred years' time. Happily, however, I met a good artisan, and became a little koto. Though I know that I am modest in quality and tune, I yearn to be laid at the left side of a man of noble character,' and it sings, What day and what time/ shall I be able to find/ one who can enjoy/ my voice and lay myself then/ on his knees for a pillow?

And I (who present the koto to you) reply:

Though you are speechless/ being made of simple wood/ you shall presently/ become the pet instrument/ of an honorable man."

(b) A Poor Man's Sympathy for the Poorer (No. 892).

This book shines brilliant not only among the rest of the Manyoshu, but in the whole history of Japanese poetry. The number of longer poems is 10, that of verselets 104.

MISCELLANEOUS POEMS

No. 793

The more I know
that life is mutable,
the more forlorn
does it grow.

OHTOMONO TABITO

*An Elegy (written by Yamanoeno Okura either
in sympathy with his friend, Ohtomono Tabito,
who had lost his wife, or when he himself
met the death of his spouse)*

No. 794

You came, yearning for me
all the way to Tsukushi,
only a short time ago;
but, yielding to an illness, died.
How can I voice my sorrow?
Your body still remains with me,
but it can not stay long.
Oh why have you to go so soon,
leaving me all alone?

Hanka

No. 795

Must I return now to my house
so desolate without my spouse?

No. 796

Alas, my wife is gone,
leaving me forlorn.

No. 797

How I mourn the death
of my wife so dear
who never went around
to see the scenery here!

No. 798

The flowers will fall too which she eyed
before my woeful tears are dried.

No. 799

Ohno Hill is veiled in vapor.
It might be caused by my deep sighing.

*An admonition to those who wish to become
hermits by Yamanoeno Okura*

No. 800

How noble are our parents,
and how lovable our wives and children!
Our ties with them are close, inseparable.
A man who leaves them like shoes broken
is no better than a rock or stock.
If there be any such, woe be to them.
You may do what you like in the next world;
but while here below
you have the Emperor above,
who suffers none to act
as freely as his fancy moves him.

Hanka

No. 801

To go back home, and work aright
is better than to play the eremite.

On the children by Yamanoeno Okura

No. 802

When I eat a melon,
I recall my children.
When I eat chestnuts,
I wish that they were here.
In my dream oft they appear,
and take my sleep away,
for they demand to stay
in any wise
before my eyes.

Hanka

No. 803

What do I care for silver, gold,
or jewels sparkling fair?
My offspring dearer do I hold
than any gems however rare!

"The World is Hard to Live in"
by Yamanoeno Okura

No. 804

Time goes on like the flow of water
burdened with trials and privations.
Today's maiden—gray-haired crone tomorrow,
wrinkles filling her once-rosy cheeks.
Where is the warrior wearing swords,
astride a bay horse, bow in hand?
Alas, there only goes a crippled dotard.
Even the love of my young days
now looks on me with cold indifference.

Hanka

No. 805

'Tis the way of all: to age
though one determines to stay young.

2 songs to a friend by Ohtomono Tabito

No. 806

O for a wingèd horse
for me to go to Nara and return.

No. 807

I have no means to be with you.
So come into the dream I nightly dream.

2 songs in reply

No. 808

I'll seek a wingèd horse for you
who wish thereon to go to Nara.

No. 809

You have stayed long away.
So let me dream of you.

2 songs on sending a koto to Lord Fujiwara
by Ohtomono Tabito

No. 810

(*Koto appearing as a maiden in the dream*)
What day, what time can I meet
one who appreciates my music?

No. 811

(*Dreamer*)
Koto, you are a speechless piece of wood;
I will find such a person now for you.

In reply by Lord Fujiwara

No. 812

"A speechless piece of wood," you say, but I will
   treasure
your beautiful gift, my friend, with gratitude and
   pleasure.

The following legend is handed down
by Tatebeno Ushimaro

No. 813

When the Empress Jingu went
to conquer three states of Korea,
she was with child,
but by the virtue of the magic stones she cherished
the child stayed in her for a long, long time.

Hanka

No. 814

The stones are here to tell
of their mysterious powers to posterity.

32 songs on plum flowers written at a feast held
on January 13 in the second year of Tempyo (730)
in the Kyushu residence of Lord Ohtomono Tabito

No. 815

Come January, let us take delight
in viewing plums with flowers all bedight.
                              LORD KI

No. 816

Stay as you are, O Plums in flower.
Keep redolent and sweet my bower.
                              ONUNO OYU

No. 817

My friends, let us weave garlands
with fresh green willow branches from the garden
together with these red and white plum flowers.
                              LORD AWATA

No. 818

No joy were it to view alone
the plums beside my cottage
the first to flower in spring.
                              YAMANOENO OKURA

No. 819

In such a world of love,
who would not a plum flower be?

OHTOMONO MIYORI

No. 820

We are in spring,
and plums are blossoming.
Let us now wear
their flowers in our hair.

LORD FUJII

No. 821

Fall now if you like, Plum flowers,
since we have dined with garlands
woven with you and willows.

PRIEST SAMI

No. 822

How beautiful the flowering plum
    shedding its bloom before my eye!
Like snowflakes they soft drifting come
    out of the azure of the sky.

OHTOMONO TABITO

No. 823

Where do I see plum blossoms falling?
Only the snow descends now from the mountain.

OHTOMONO MOMOYO

No. 824

Amid our bamboo grove I hear the uguisu
lament the falling of his dear plum blossom.

No. 825

Let us enjoy the banquet,
wearing garlands woven
with plum flowers from the garden
and strands of verdant willows.

No. 826

The waving vernal willows
and flowering plums are vying
for beauty in my garden.

No. 827

When happy springtime comes
sweet uguisu sing on plums.

No. 828

Behold plum flowers fair
in every person's hair!

No. 829

Sing of spring,
happy spring:
after plum
cherries come.

No. 830

A thousand years may come and go,
still plum flowers shall as ever blow.

LORD SAEKI

No. 831

Spring has brought the flowering plum.
I longed and waited for its coming.

ITAMOCHINO YASUMARO

No. 832

We are enjoying this spring day so fair,
wearing plum flowers in our raven hair.

KAMUTSUKASANO INAFU

No. 833

Thus let us feast each spring that comes,
wearing flowering plums like combs.

NOSHI SUKUNAMARO

No. 834

Behold, the plum trees now are blossoming.
Soon with a thousand birds will come the spring.

TASHI HIBITO

No. 835

To grace this banquet, plums have burst in flower;
the longed-for bloom is here for springtime.

TAKANO YOSHIMITSU

No. 836

Now we know no satiety of pleasure,
as wearing plum flowers we enjoy our leisure.

ISOSHI NORIMARO

No. 837

The plum trees by my bower are blossoming,
inviting uguisu now to come and sing.

SHISHI OHMICHI

No. 838

The spring is come and on the hill
in ecstasies the uguisu trill.

ENOKISHI HACHIMARO

No. 839

Upon a misty spring day, lo,
plum blossoms fall as thick as snow.

TASHI MAHITO

No. 840

The plum flowers I was using for my garland—
who has put them in my wine?

MURASHI OCHIKATA

No. 841

To the sweet music of the uguisu
the petals of the plum fall in my garden.

TAKANO OYU

No. 842

Grieving the falling plum flowers in the garden
I hear the uguisu sadly crying.

TAKANO AMA

No. 843

Fair the plum flowers in the locks
of the guests, reminding me of courtiers.

HANISHI MIMICHI

No. 844

The plum flowers fall as thick as snow
outside my dear wife's bower now.

ONUNO KUNITATA

No. 845

The plum flowers long awaited by bushwarblers
blow.
Let them not fall awhile: my love admires the
sight.

KADOBE ISOTARI

No. 846

With beautiful plum flowers my locks bedight
I in this misty spring day take delight.

ONUNO AWAMARO

2 songs, yearning for home by Ohtomono Tabito

No. 847

The magic draught that lets you climb the sky
brings not your youth again—and old am I.

No. 848

It needs no tonic: I were no more old,
if but the capital I could behold.

4 songs on plum blossoms by Ohtomono Tabito

No. 849

Plum flowers, survive the snow
that lies upon your bough.

No. 850

Plum flowers vie for beauty with the snow,
I wish you could behold them with me here.

No. 851

In this brief moment while the plums appear
at their flowering best I would my friend were
here.

No. 852

The spirit of the plum spoke in my dream,
    "Am I not fair?
Take now your cup of wine,
    and put me there."

2 songs by Ohtomono Tabito

No. 853

No mere child of fisherman art thou.
I know thou art a noble maiden now.

No. 854

I live far up the Tamashima River;
shy I didn't tell it you, however.

3 songs by a traveler

No. 855

The maiden's skirts are wet, as she stands fishing
beside the clear Matsura for swift sweetfish.

No. 856

Where are the houses of the maidens
who fish for ayu by the waters?

No. 857

Will I not woo and win her
who fishes by the stream for sweetfish?

3 songs in reply

No. 858

Men fish for ayu
in Matsura River eddies.
So eddying ever in thoughts of you,
do I not hope to catch you?

No. 859

My friend, now that 'tis spring,
sweetfish wait for you,
leaping in our village stream.

No. 860

Matsura loiters in its seven pools,
but never can I rest from seeking you.

3 songs by Ohtomono Tabito

No. 861

With scarlet skirts splashed by the current
are the maidens angling still for sweetfish?

No. 862

All travelers praise Matsura Tamashima;
when comes the day for me to go and see it?

No. 863

How I envy those who watch the maidens
angling for young ayu by the river!

No. 864

Left behind,
not longing thus for you,
ah! would I were a plum flower in your garden.

No. 865

I wonder if the maids be mermaids
who wait for you at Tama harbor?

2 songs, thinking of a friend

No. 866

Cloud on cloud divides us:
you in Tsukushi, I in Nara.

No. 867

Many a year has passed since you left for Tsukushi:
your trees at home grow tall and hoary.

*3 songs to Ohtomono Tabito
by Yamanoeno Okura*

No. 868

How I wish to see the hill
whence Lady Sayo waved her scarf
at parting from her husband bound for Chosen.

No. 869

The stone that long ago
divine Princess Tarashi stood to fish by,
what has become of it, I wonder?

No. 870

It needs no hundred days,
the highway to Matsura—
one goes today,
comes back tomorrow.
Then, what keeps me here?

No. 871

Once Lady Sayo of Matsura, yearning for her
love,
stood here, and waved her scarf—and, lo,
henceforth the mountain took its name from this.

OHTOMONO IRATSUKO

No. 872

Did Lady Sayo dream her simple deed
would in the people's mouths rename the mountain?

OHTOMONO TABITO

No. 873

She waved her scarf upon the hill,
and is remembered by it still.

DITTO

2 more songs by Ohtomono Tabito

No. 874

Perhaps she waved her scarf
as if she could recall the parting ship.

No. 875

How sad she was to see her lover's ship
bound for Korea fade into the distance!

4 songs at a feast sending off Ohtomono Tabito by Yamanoeno Okura

No. 876

I would a bird I now could be
so that to Nara I might carry thee.

No. 877

We are all sad to see you go. Never forget us
even when your horse draws near to Mt. Tatsuta.

No. 878

So I say, and you will understand,

. . . .

will it not be sad with you not here?

> Note: The middle line is unintelligible in
> the original.

No. 879

Help his Majesty to rule the land.
I only pray you may live long.

3 songs by Yamanoeno Okura

No. 880

So far from Nara have I lived these five years
 gone,
oh what a bumpkin figure must I cut by now!

No. 881

Every day I sigh for Nara,
living in this dreary province.

No. 882

If my lord should help, then could I see the spring
I long for, once again in Nara.

No. 883

I have not seen Matsura yet,
though I know it by repute,
where Lady Sayo waved her scarf.

2 songs in sympathy for Ohtomono Kumagori (see below) by Asadano Yasu

No. 884

Alas, I die now on the way,
yearning for my parents far away.

No. 885

I know that life is like the morning dew,
but oh! why must I die
here far away from my dear parents?

6 songs by Yamanoeno Okura in sympathy for Ohtomono Kumagori who died at the young age of eighteen on his way to the capital

No. 886

Sent to the Court,
I took leave of my parents;
and crossing many a mountain
I went with other travelers,
when sudden I fell ill.
I lay down in the grass,
thinking that I should be tended by
my parents if I were at home;
but now, alas, I perish like a dog astray.

No. 887

O Mother dear, away from home,
now I must depart this life.

No. 888

Alas, how shall I go on my next journey—
a long, long road and unfamiliar plodding?

No. 889

Were I at home,
then I could die,
tended by my mother.

No. 890

How my parents must be waiting,
expecting so soon my return,
counting the days upon their fingers!

No. 891

No more again here in this world
shall I behold my dear old parents!

"A Poor Man's Sympathy for the Poorer"
by Yamanoeno Okura
No. 892

Upon a rainy night and windy,
and a snowy night again with sleet
cold makes me bite and taste crude salt,
and sip the broth of saké lees
softened in a pan of boiling water.
I snuffle and I clear my throat,
then stroke caressingly my beard,
proud of myself and now content.
Still pinched, however, by the cold,
I jump beneath the hempen counterpane
with all my cotton garments piled thereon.
Then I think of the poorer folk,
and of their starving, shivering parents,
and children begging food with cries.
Alas, how do they get along?

Although our world is wide,
it seems to be a narrow place;
and though the sun and moon shine bright,
they do not give us light enough.
I wonder what may others think of this?
How lucky to be born a man!
He can work hard, and till the land,
and yet to what end?
For no wadded clothes he wears.
His hang in rags and tatters,
reminding one of tangled seaweed.
Now spreading straws upon the ground
of their low, dingy hut,
in one corner lie the parents,
the wife and children in another,
huddled and sighing anxiously.
No smoke comes up out of the chimney;
spiders weave webs in the rice chest,
because no rice is ever brought in.
And, to make matters worse, here comes
the village headman, whip in hand,
crying loudly for the tax.
Alas, is such the way of life?

No. 893

I wish for wings to let me flee
this narrow world so drear!

To Tajihino Hironari, the Envoy to China,
by Yamanoeno Okura
No. 894

The country of Yamato is loved by the gods,
blessed with a beautiful language.
Since the days of yore it has been said,
and we people of today believe 'tis true.
Now from among the numerous courtiers you are
    chosen,
as a descendant of a noble family,
for an envoy to Cathay.
The gods who guard both land and sea
will keep you safe,
piloting your vessel at the prow.
And when you return,
they will guide you all the way again
straight past Cape Chika to Ohtomo Beach.

Hanka
No. 895

Return as swiftly as you can.
I shall be waiting your return, my lord,
making festive pine-clad Mitsu Beach.

No. 896

When I hear your ship arriving at Naniwa,
I'll hurry to put on my best and meet you.

7 songs on falling ill by Yamanoeno Okura
No. 897

All of us wish to live at peace,
but such is life, and sometimes woe
comes after woe as salt is put
on the abraded skin
or a heavier load upon a weary horse.
I have grown old;
and, illness enervating me, year after year
all day long and all night through
I suffer pain.
I wish to die; but when I think
of my dear children
noisy as flies of May,
I only weep and moan.

No. 898

Nothing I have to soothe my breast.
I cry but like a bird, and know no rest.

No. 899

To be freed from the pain of the world is my
  prayer,
but my children—can I leave them there?

No. 900

The children of the rich
    have more clothes than they need:
many and many a silk
    and cotton robe so warm indeed.

No. 901

But few rough clothes can I afford my children.
I weep to see them, urchins, scantily dressed.

No. 902

Though life be unsubstantial
like foam atop the wave,
I pray that mine may plumb
a thousand fathoms.

No. 903

Only for my children's sake would I
live on, who wish to die.

*3 songs on the death of his son Furuhi
by Yamanoeno Okura*

No. 904

What care I for the seven treasures people prize?
I loved my child Furuhi better than them all.
He would insist upon my playing with him as I
  woke in bed,
nor let me slumber when I went to my repose,
and begged to let him sleep between my wife
  and me.
With great anticipation I looked forward to his
  future,
but smitten with an ague, ill he lay.
I prayed the gods for his recovery,
yet every day he languished, fell unconscious,
dying at last.
With desperation I appeal to heaven and earth
for the departed jewel,
but only echoes come back for my cries.

Hanka

No. 905

Pray, let me ask you with a gift,
O Guardsman of the Nether World;
carry my young son on your back
along the way he does not know.

No. 906

Oh merciful Buddha, I have prayed
    and offerings given.
Now I implore of you to lead
    my little son to Heaven.

THE MANYOSHU

BOOK VI

FOREWORD

This book contains only miscellaneous verses, just as Books I & V: many songs on travels (especially royal progresses), the capital, and banquets are found in this volume, covering 21 years from the year of Yohro (723) till approximately Tempyo 16 (744).

The prominent writers are Emperor Shohmu, Princes Ichihara, Yuhara, Yamabeno Akahito, Kasano Kanamura, Takahashino Mushimaro, Tachibanano Moroe, Lady Sakanoeno Iratsume, Ohtomono Yakamochi, and others. The styles of the poems are long, Sedohka, and short, 27, 1 and 132 respectively.

MISCELLANEOUS VERSES

*On the Yoshino Detached Palace
by Kasano Kanamura*
No. 907

How the Akitsu Palace looms in grandeur!
Is it because the guardian spirit of the province
  makes it so,
or that the scene itself is beautiful?
Serene it stands here since the days of old.

Hanka
No. 908

Yearly I wish to come here to Yoshino
to behold its limpid, foaming river.

No. 909

Where lofty mountains soar,
Kohchi's rapids foaming roar.

No. 910

Beloved of the gods must be Yoshino;
forever would I view its foaming river.

No. 911

As the river flows on for eternity,
so e'er would I behold it.

No. 912

The foam of the rapids here
resembles the fields of cotton
tended by the women of Hatsuse.

At Yoshino by Kuramochino Chitose
No. 913

As I look down from the wooded mountain at
  Yoshino,
at morn I see mist o'er the rapids of the river,
and at nightfall hear kajika trill.
I am a traveler lone,
and only wish my people could behold this view.

No. 914

The lofty mountain strikes my heart with awe,
yet in my breast the thought of home remains.

No. 915

Ceaseless, Yoshino's stream runs, plovers crying
  above,
and so I ever yearn for my dear love.

No. 916

I haven't been long away from home, but now
  already I,
standing by the foggy river of Yoshino, sigh.

In Kii Province by Yamabeno Akihito
No. 917

Behold, far in the distance from the Saiga Villa
you see upon a windy day
along the shores of yonder islands white waves
  roll,
and when the tide is out, folk gathering seaweed.
How beautiful the landscape which remains
the same as in the ancient days.

No. 918

If the pearly sea grass hide beneath the wave,
tide flowing in, I'll yearn to see the grass again.

No. 919

Tide flowing into Waka Cove,
   no ground is left bare in the bay;
so for the shore where rushes grow
   the crying cranes now wing their way.

*On the Detached Palace of Yoshino
by Kasano Kanamura*
No. 920

With thunderous sounds reverberating in the
  mountains high,
the rapids of Yoshino runs.
Plovers cry in the upper reaches,
and in the lower, calling for their mates, kajika
  trill.
Many a courtier comes and goes along the banks.
I hope the Villa here may flourish ever.

No. 921

The Villa stands beside the foaming river,
which none shall ever tire of viewing.

No. 922

How I wish our life to be
peaceful and changeless as this scenery!

Songs on Yoshino by Yamabeno Akahito
No. 923

The Imperial Villa at Yoshino stands
encircled by the mountains green,
and girded by the rivers clear.
In spring wild flowers,
and in autumn mists bedeck the scene;
and along the paths the courtiers come and go.

No. 924

Many birds I hear now singing
among the trees upon Mt. Kisa.

No. 925

Deep at midnight plovers cry
the clear Yoshino River nigh.

More songs by Yamabeno Akahito
No. 926

Behold, in yon Akitsu field
there rides our Majesty.
Spread are trackers far and near,
and archers set upon the hills.
They start wild deer and boars at morn,
and countless sylvan birds at eve.
Astride, the hunting men are seen
upon the vernal grasses green.

No. 927

Over the hills and fields men hie,
disturbing the quiet of the scenery.
Arrows in their hands they have—
our Sovereign's huntsmen brave.

*On the occasion of the Emperor's visit in winter
of the second year of Shinki to the Naniwa
Palace, composed by Kasano Kanamura*
No. 928

Every one thought Naniwa was a poor old town,
but now it is a capital magnificent,
for by the Imperial order
a gorgeous palace is erected,
and many a residence stands in Ajifu Field.

Hanka
No. 929

Lo, the august Liege coming,
the wilderness becomes a thriving city.

No. 930

Sojourning at Naniwa, I hear
the sound of sculls by maidens worked.

Written by Kuramochino Chitose
No. 931

Fair is the beach,
and over the seaweed wavering
a myriad of ripples come
at the morning calm,
and at the evening calm.
Like the gentle wave
however oft I come
to view this Suminoe shore,
I never tire of it.

Hanka
No. 932

I will dye my clothes here with the earth
of the beach laved by the waves.

Written by Yamabeno Akahito
No. 933

Eternal as heaven and earth,
and endless as the flow of time,
the Imperial family shall last.
We pay homage to the Emperor
who now reigns at Naniwa.
Fishermen at Nujima Isle
dive to the sea floor and present
the Court with priceless pearls.

Hanka
No. 934

I hear the sound of working sculls
now at the morning calm.
Are they bringing presents to the Court?

Written by Kasano Kanamura
No. 935

On Matsuho seabeach of Awaji
seen afar from Nakizumi
I hear maids gather seaweed
at the morning calm;
and at the evening calm
they boil sea salt,
but I can not go there without a boat and oars,
and only yearn to see them work.

No. 936

Oh how I yearn to go and view
the maiden divers gathering pearly grass of sea,
and how I wish to have a boat and oars,
although the waves are high.

No. 937

How beautiful Funase Beach!
I come and go but to behold
the white waves laving the shore.

Written by Yamabeno Akahito
No. 938

How beautiful Inami field with a detachèd villa
where our Emperor often comes to stay!
Out on Fujii Cove now I see boats with fishermen
clamoring to catch tuna fish,
and people on the seashore boiling salt.
Well for our Sovereign that he comes
here to view this beach so fair.

No. 939

I see the fishermen all busily engaged
upon Fujii Cove, because the sea is calm.

No. 940

Many a night I spent upon Inami plain,
and long now for my folk at home.

No. 941

Tomorrow I shall take my homeward way
along Akashi bay.

On passing Karani Island
by Yamabeno Akahito
No. 942

As my ship nears Karani Island
after passing Kojima Isle
I look back toward where my wife is,
but see only mountains and blue skies.
Thinking of my home at every cove
and every point, I go upon my voyage.

No. 943

Alas, I yearn for home, and find it hard time to
beguile.
O that I were a cormorant upon Karani Isle.

No. 944

Passing Karani Island,
afar off I behold a vessel
sailing toward dear Yamato.

No. 945

As it is windy, and the seas are high,
in Tsuta Cove at anchor now we lie.

Passing Minume Cove by Yamabeno Akahito
No. 946

Off the shore of Minume
facing Awaji Island
they gather deep-sea miru,
and nearer the beach
other good herbs of the brine.
But no one cares for me,
no messenger comes to me
with word of my love.

Hanka
No. 947

A lonely traveler, I trudge or rest
only holding you, my darling, in my breast.

*Written when by the Imperial order all the court
was confined in the dormitory*

No. 948

This is the spring the courtiers long awaited.
The mist hangs over Mt. Kasuga,
and on Mt. Takamado uguisu sing.
They see the wild geese,
and dream of vernal fields,
of going there together with their friends,
but alas, they are in custody.
If this calamity had been foreseen,
they could have purified themselves
in Saho's stream where plovers cry
with the holy sedge root growing there
to be rid of the pleasure-seeking lust.

Hanka

No. 949

Without permission having seen
    plum flowers and willow trees one day,
now under this confinement
    kept are they.

4 songs ascribed to Kuramochino Chitose

No. 950

Will I not go up even to the mountain
the Emperor forbids all men to climb?

No. 951

I will possess the pearl
hidden among the rocks.

No. 952

How I wish some one would
hang jewels on the pine at Nara!

No. 953

Stags cry upon the mountain as I leave;
and even now would you not see me, love?

No. 954

How I envy the wild geese
    that feed among the reeds at morn,
at evening fly back to Yamato:
    my home for which I yearn.

PRINCE KASHIWADEBE

No. 955

Do you yearn still
after Saho Hill
where you know well
many courtiers dwell?

ISHIKAWANO TARIHITO

No. 956

I enjoy my life here as at home,
since this place too is ruled by the Emperor.

OHTOMONO TABITO

No. 957

At low tide though our sleeves may get wet, let
    us hunt
after sea herbs for breakfast in Kashii Bay.

DITTO

No. 958

I know wind rises as tide comes in;
so now I'll gather sea herbs in the bay.

ONUNO OYU

No. 959

I love the fine view of Kashii Bay,
but to return home I must go away.

UNUNO OHITO

No. 960

I love the scenery of this West Country deep,
but more that of Yoshino's stream where ayu leap.

OHTOMONO TABITO

No. 961

Out among the reeds I hear cranes crying.
Are they, like me, for their mates yearning?

DITTO

No. 962

You ask me now to write a lay,
and I'm bewildered what to say.

FUJIINO HIRONARI

Written by Ohtomono Sakanoeno Iratsume

No. 963

ON MT. NAGO (MT. CONSOLATION)

This mountain was created by two gods,
and named Mt. Consolation;
but it does not console me,
suffering so from love.

No. 964

I suffer, longing for my lover.
Even awhile I wish I could forget him.

2 songs by the singing girl, Kojima

No. 965

Were you not a nobleman, now as you leave,
with all my heart would I not wave my sleeve?

No. 966

Afar off in the clouds your home, Yamato, is.
Despise me not for waving sleeves on parting.

2 songs in response by Ohtomono Tabito

No. 967

If I pass Kojima Isle in Kibi Province on my
  homeward way,
shall I not call to mind its namesake?

No. 968

I think I am a gallant heart,
but weep, so sad from you to part.

2 songs at Nara by Ohtomono Tabito

No. 969

I will go see the Kamunabi River
where pools turn overnight to churning rapids.

No. 970

I wish to go now to Kurusu field,
and bring my offering of hagi to the gods.

*To Lord Fujiwarano Umakai who is Departing for
Tsukushi, by Takahashino Mushimaro*

No. 971

When white-clouded Mt. Tatsuta stands
dressed in crimson with the autumn dews,
over this peak and many others
you go your long, long way
to Tsukushi where your men you delegate
to the farthest corners of the land,
and defend against intruding foes our state.
You guard its safety, and see how affairs are,
even as far as where the echoes only could attain,
or patient toads go crawling.
When after winter springtime comes again,
prithee, quick as a bird to us return.
I will wait on Tatsuta highway then
amid the fair azalea blooms that burn
all red, and mountain cherries in full flower
to welcome you with all within my power.

Hanka

No. 972

I look upon you as a man
who makes no idle speech, but goes
forward to beat the enemy—
though numerous as clouds up in the sky.

To the governors by Emperor Shohmu

No. 973

You go to the distant provinces
to rule on my behalf.
Thanks to your good service,
I can rest here in the capital.
Believe me I, your Sovereign, love you deep,
and will keep this wine
for all of us to drink on your return.

Hanka

No. 974

Start on your journeys,
proud of your missions.

No. 975

The life that we enjoy here thanks to thee—
may it go onward to longevity.

ABENO HIRONIWA

2 songs by Kamikosono Imiki Oimaro

No. 976

I'll look well at the scene
of Naniwa Bay now at low tide,
to tell my wife about it
when I return home.

No. 977

The sea here at Naniwa is called 'sparkling',
perhaps because 'tis radiant when seen from this
mountain.

Falling ill by Yamanoeno Okura

No. 978

How grievous for a man to die
without a name to leave posterity!

No. 979

Pray, let not the wind blow coldly on my nephew
till he returns home, for he now is in thin
garments.

OHTOMONO SAKANOENO IRATSUME

No. 980

Is it because the mountain is so high
no moon comes out though midnight is now nigh?

ABENO MUSHIMARO

*3 songs on the moon
by Ohtomono Sakanoeno Iratsume*

No. 981

With great impatience I await the moon to rise
now from behind Mt. Takamado in the skies.

No. 982

How forlorn I feel to see the moon
shining dimly through the mist of midnight!

No. 983

I love to see the moon above the mountain rise,
and go on sailing bright across the skies.

No. 984

I wonder if you also wish, my love,
to see the moon concealed behind the clouds
above?

A woman of Buzen Province

2 songs on the moon by Prince Yuhara

No. 985

I will present you with a gift,
O Moon serene and bright,
so make five hundredfold long
this beautiful night.

No. 986

Behold, the moon is shining bright
the paths you come along to light.

No. 987

The moon which I await is still
hidden behind Mikasa Hill.

FUJIWARANO YATSUKA

To his Father

No. 988

Spring flowers soon fall, my father;
be thou as changeless as a rock that stays for ever.

PRINCE ICHIWARA

No. 989

Taking off my well-tempered blade
in honoring this mellow saké,
lo, I, a happy courtier, drink and drink,
and now I am all drunken!

No. 990

This old pine standing on the mountain
has survived a thousand winters.

KINO KABITO

No. 991

How fair the river of Hatsuse
that, foaming, courses over pebbles!

DITTO

No. 992

Reverend though be the old Asuka temple,
more dear to my heart is the new one
amid the greens and reds of Nara.

OHTOMONO SAKANOENO IRATSUME

No. 993

My eyebrows itched, whereby I knew
you loved me. Here am I with you.

DITTO

No. 994

I look up at the crescent,
which reminds me
of the blackened eyebrow
of that lovely maiden.

OHTOMONO YAKAMOCHI

No. 995

Now let us drink, enjoy our fill while young.
Look at tree leaves. They thrive in springtime
but fall, when autumn comes,
and by the wind are scattered.

OHTOMONO SAKANOENO IRATSUME

No. 996

The joy of your subject does not wane,
    for is it not the height
of bliss now in this reign
    to live and to enjoy the sight
    of all things prosperous and bright?

AMANOINUKAINO OKAMARO

6 songs
No. 997

Like the shellfish at low tide
love within my breast I hide.

ANON.

No. 998

Where will lie tonight yon vessel
headng for Awa with high mountains
resembling women's eyebrows?

LORD FUNE

No. 999

O Fishermen, protect the drying net.
Rain is coming from the sea.

LORD MORIBE

No. 1000

Now at morning if my wife were here,
the cranes' cries on the seashore she would also
    hear.

DITTO

No. 1001

The men go hunting with the Emperor;
the women trailing red skirts play upon the beach.

YAMABENO AKAHITO

No. 1002

Our horses here at Suminoe we will stay
to dye our garments with the famed red clay.

ABENO TOYOTSUGU

No. 1003

Are the women divers seeking pearls,
for they go out despite the roaring waves?

FUJIINO OHNARI

No. 1004

Alas, you did not stay to hear the music
of sweet-voiced frogs consorting by our river.

KURATSUKURINO MASUHITO

*On the Detached Palace of Yoshino
by Yamabeno Akahito*
No. 1005

See the Yoshino Palace hidden in the clouds,
because it towers upon the peak;
the limpid river here makes music all the time.
The mountains soar above the river,
and the magnificent palace stands for ever.

Hanka
No. 1006

From olden times here stands the palace
to cap the landscape picturesque.

No. 1007

Even the speechless plants have kindred of their
    own,
while I, alas, all brotherless, sisterless live alone.

PRINCE ICHIWARA

No. 1008

As one awaits the moon that rises
from behind the mountain,
I've been expecting you to come, but
only night advances.

IMBENO KUROMARO

*Composed and given to Prince Katsuragi by
Emperor Shohmu together with the name
'Tachibana' (Orange Tree) when the
latter descended to a subject*

No. 1009

The orange tree remains green till the wintertime
when on its branches comes descending hoary
rime.

Tachibanano Naramaro in response

No. 1010

However thick and fast descends the snow,
the orange leaf shall stay upon the bough.

2 songs by Fujiino Hironari

No. 1011

If you've invited friends to come
   and see the plums in white array,
after that the vernal wind may come
   to blow the bloom away.

No. 1012

Never forget, my friend, to call on me in springtime
when uguisu come to warble on our plum boughs
flowering.

2 songs at a feast

No. 1013

If I had known your visit to my dwelling,
I'd have spread pebbles everywhere around it.
               PRINCE KADOBE

No. 1014

I have been fortunate to see you last three days
   on end;
yet again tomorrow do I wish to see you, friend.
          TACHIBANANO FUMINARI

Prince Enokii in response

No. 1015

Good to see stones spread everywhere,
but this surprise call I prefer.

At a feast by Lord Kose

No. 1016

I, a fairy, came across the ocean
to see the courtiers here in life take pleasure.

No. 1017

I came across Osaka Hill, and wonder
in what field tonight I shall be sheltering.
     OHTOMONO SAKANOENO IRATSUME

*Composed by a monk of the Genkoji Temple,
complaining that no one knows his worth*

No. 1018

Satisfied the pearl is with itself, though none
appreciate it, aware it is a precious stone.

Taking pity on Isonokami Otomaro

No. 1019

Intriguing with a worthless girl,
the courtier Otomaro
hands bound, by bowmen guarded,
rides off to distant banishment.

No. 1020
No. 1021

O God of Suminoe,
guard the ship aboard which Otomaro sits,
protect it, pray, from wind and wave,
and let him come home soon in safety.

No. 1022

I am a darling of my parents.
I pray, give offerings at the shrine
upon our slope,
and then take ship across the sea for Tosa.

No. 1023

Banished, here I pass, and can't enjoy at leisure
the lovely landscape of the seabeach of Obama.

4 songs at a feast

No. 1024

As yonder island lies for ever,
so may you live a thousand years!
            LORD KOSOBE

In response by the Minister of the Right, Tachibanano Moroe

No. 1025

Kind Lord I too wish you
a thousand years of life.

No. 1026

Some courtiers seem too busy
to come here to this banquet.

A court lady

No. 1027

Hiding love deep in my breast,
I sit at a banquet as a guest.

DITTO

On presenting the Court with a flying squirrel

No. 1028

This is a flying squirrel that came down to Nara,
fleeing the hunt upon Mt. Takamado.

OHTOMONO SAKANOENO IRATSUME

No. 1029

Here in this temporary hut
I have spent many a night,
and now yearn for my love,
now crave her sight.

OHTOMONO YAKAMOCHI

No. 1030

Many crying cranes I see
o'er the now-bare lagoon beyond the pines.

EMPEROR SHOHMU

No. 1031

I pray, making offerings to the gods at Shide Point
for the safety of my darling wife at home.

TAJIHINO MAHITO

2 songs by Ohtomono Yakamochi

No. 1032

Now I am in the retinue of the Emperor,
and for a month my wife I have not seen.

No. 1033

I see out on the sea a ship with fishermen,
catching perhaps fish for the Emperor.

At the Tagi Villa in Mino Province

No. 1034

Ever since of old it has been told
this foaming water makes one young.

OHTOMONO AZUMABITO

No. 1035

The water of the Tado River is so clear.
Perhaps that's why here was the Villa built.

OHTOMONO YAKAMOCHI

No. 1036

If there were no barrier here,
I'd hasten home to see my wife so dear.

DITTO

No. 1037

Well may the palace be erected
here at Kuni for its lovely landscape!

DITTO

2 songs by Takaokano Kochi

No. 1038

Beyond that mountain high is Nara—
the former capital I yearn for.

No. 1039

The mountain hides the moon, my friend,
but what of that, were you with me?

No. 1040

The rain is raining, so my friend,
I will stay with you tonight.

OHTOMONO YAKAMOCHI

No. 1041

I will stay at home,
and wait for you to come.

ANON.

2 songs, drinking in January under a pine tree

No. 1042

How many winters has this pine tree left behind
amid the soft or boisterous music of the wind?

PRINCE ICHIWARA

No. 1043

I know not to what age I live.
I wish I could live as this pine.

OHTOMONO YAKAMOCHI

3 songs on the deserted capital of Nara

No. 1044

Loving the capital deserted,
I have no heart to leave it.

No. 1045

The glorious capital of Nara is no more,
and the vicissitude of life do I deplore.

No. 1046

I wish I could be young again
to see once more the capital of yore.

On the deserted Capital

No. 1047

The province of Yamato was a seat of government
since the reign of Emperor Jimmu.
In Nara cherries bloomed in spring,
songbirds twittering ceaselessly.
In the fall among the hagi flowers
on Mt. Ikoma stags were heard to cry for hinds.
Every mountain in the neighborhood was fair to
    view;
every village pleasant to live in.
But now, alas, the city is deserted,
and not a man or horse is to be seen upon its
    streets.

Hanka

No. 1048

Deserted now the capital so sweet,
rank grasses growing on the street.

No. 1049

Deserted, Nara looks so drear,
as alone I wander here.

In praise of the new Kuni Palace

No. 1050

Beautiful all the provinces ruled by the Emperor,
but more so the landscape where the Kuni Palace
    stands.
The murmur of the river stills,
the songs of birds enliven, the heart.
In autumn wild stags cry for hinds;
In springtime flowers prank the hills.
Well the Sovereign built his palace here.

Hanka

No. 1051

A palace so magnificent is built upon this site,
perhaps because so fair the landscape of Futagi
    field.

No. 1052

The mountains soar, and streams run clear.
May this Kuni Court thrive here!

No. 1053

The Kuni Court stands by the wooded mountain,
and foaming river. In spring when uguisu come,
brocades of flowers beautify the place;
In autumn mid the cries of stags for hinds
cold rain spreads golden leaves upon the ground.
Oh may the Imperial family reign here for all
    eternity.

5 Hanka

No. 1054

Here Izumi's stream runs on for ever,
and the palace ever shall remain.

No. 1055

Lo, Mt. Futagi soars as if to bless
the Imperial Palace underneath.

No. 1056

Behold, a capital is set up
here at the bottom of Mt. Kase.

No. 1057

Upon Mt. Kase trees are prospering,
where every morning uguisu sing.

No. 1058

The Izumi is too wide, I fear,
for cuckoos singing on Mt. Koma to come here.

*Sorrowing for the deserted capital of Kuni
in Mikanohara*
No. 1059

The beautiful town now lies forlorn:
the houses stand all empty;
none goes in the deserted streets.
Although flowers smile still in the field,
birds twitter in the woods,
alas, here no folk live.

2 Hanka
No. 1060

The capital is no more at Kuni,
and the place looks all deserted.

No. 1061

Even now flowers remain,
but not a courtier stays.

On the Naniwa Palace
No. 1062

The palace at Naniwa where the Emperor oft
comes
stands on the seashore where folk gather pebbles.
Here one can hear waves rolling, sound of sculls,
plovers calling for their mates above the bar,
and crying cranes among the rushes on the beach.
How fair the scenery which none will tire of
viewing!

2 Hanka
No. 1063

The palace overlooks the sea
where fishing women's boats they see.

No. 1064

The palace stands near where one hears the
cranes
calling their mates among the rushes at ebb tide.

Passing Munume Cove
No. 1065

Since the days of old
this has been a haven good
where hundreds of ships ever lie at anchor.
The waves rise with the morning wind;
seaweed drifts in with the evening tide,
and people stroll upon the sands.
Well they speak of this cove with love.

2 Hanka
No. 1066

No ship can pass Unume Cove
without admiring its fine view.

No. 1067

Numberless ships have lain at anchor by Ohwada
Beach
since ancient times to view its lovely scenery.

**(The above 21 songs are from Tanabe
Fukumaro's Anthology.)**

THE MANYOSHU

BOOK VII

FOREWORD

This book contains 350 songs, which are divided into miscellaneous songs and songs in metaphor, besides elegies; and but for 25 Sedohka, all are verselets.

The absence of longer lays is conspicuous in this book. Kamono Mabuchi says that the verses in this volume, like those in Book X seem to belong to the beginning of the Nara Period. The compiler is unknown, but gathering from the classifications of this book which are similar to those of Book III, it appears that the chief editor was Ohtomono Yakamochi.

MISCELLANEOUS VERSES

Song of Heaven
No. 1068

Behold, the waves of cloud are seen
upon the sea of heaven, and
the moon, a ship, goes sailing
amid innumerable stars.

KAKINOMOTONO HITOMARO

18 songs on the moon
No. 1069

How I regret to see the moon so bright
vanish behind the clouds tonight!

No. 1070

Fair and serene
the field of Karitaka,
and clear and bright
this moonlit night.

No. 1071

I waited for the moon to come out
from behind the mountain brow,
but alas, the night is far spent now.

No. 1072

Tomorrow I'd fain spare myself your sight,
O Moon, so doubly shine tonight!

No. 1073

I take no pleasure in the moon which looks forlorn,
viewing it alone through bamboo blinds.

No. 1074

The moon shines bright upon Kasuga Hill,
and as brightly on my sweet love's bower.

No. 1075

It seems the moon tonight shines brightly on the
sea,
but here upon the beach it sheds dim light on me.

No. 1076

How brightly shines the moon tonight
at their feast the courtiers to delight!

No. 1077

Oh for a barrier in the heavens
to keep the shining moon from setting!

No. 1078

The moon is in the middle of the sky.
My love now must be waiting at her gate.

No. 1079

The harvest moon is shining dim,
perhaps concealed by clouds or mist tonight.

No. 1080

Behold, the moon still shines
as clear as in the age of gods.

No. 1081

While I enjoyed the moon,
night dew fell on my clothes.

No. 1082

Even the bottom of the stream
we see. So brightly shines the moon.

No. 1083

Clouded the sky; the moon unseen—
is frost descending now so thick?

No. 1084

Same as No. 1071

No. 1085

O Clouds, do not hide the moon
that rises from beyond the woods,
for to my wife I'll wave my sleeve.

No. 1086

Behold, the bright moon shines on us,
warriors of Ohtomo Clan,
who fight with quivers on our backs.

2 songs on clouds by Kakinomotono Hitomaro
No. 1087

The waves are roaring in Anashi's stream.
It seems rain clouds are coming over us.

No. 1088

The boisterous water roars here in the river,
and clouds are gathering over Mt. Yuzuki.

No. 1089

As far as the eye can reach
not an isle is to be seen.
Only white clouds are afloat
above the undulating seas.

ANON.

No. 1090

This gentle drizzle
that moulds her red skirts to my wife—
I shall stay out in it myself.

No. 1091

Let not the rain descend so hard
as to wet me through,
for I wear a precious garment,
my wife's gift, underneath my gown.

3 songs on mountains by Kakinomotono Hitomaro

No. 1092

Today I am so glad and happy
to see this famous wooded mountain.

No. 1093

Mt. Makimuku stands majestic
above the rest of the Mimuro mountains.

No. 1094

The maple leaves on Mt. Mimuro now have
    colored.
O that I could dye red my clothes with them!

No. 1095

Mt. Miwa held so sacred
resembles Mt. Hibara.

No. 1096

Mt. Kagu is a noble peak
with many a legend handed down.

No. 1097

Mt. Kose* stands here by my bower,
but, my dear love, you do not come.

> * There is a pun on Kose, the name of the mountain, and *kose*, "Let him come".

No. 1098

Mt. Man and Wife are said to stand in Kii.
Our Futagami is a husband with a spouse.

No. 1099

If I plant acorns on this mountain,
can I one day enjoy the shade in summer?

No. 1100

I'll always come Anashi's stream to see,
as it flows on ceaselessly.

No. 1101

Tonight the river's raving.
Where is the storm now raging?

No. 1102

Clear is the murmur
    coming from the rill
that flows around the bottom
    of Mikasa Hill.

No. 1103

How blessed I, who never thought of seeing
again this river and its pool.

No. 1104

To see Yoshino's river
we came riding side by side,
across the mountains
to its waterfalls.

No. 1105

I knew the river of Yoshino
only by repute.
So what delight to see
its Mutsuda Pool today.

No. 1106

I stand by this clear stream today
    where river frogs are heard to sing,
but when can I come here again
    across the mountains wandering?

No. 1107

I came a long, long way
to see Hatsuse's river,
and its limpid rapids
foaming like the cotton flower.

No. 1108

Fast are the rapids
of this Hatsuse River; and
clear the murmur of the waves
that run across the weir.

No. 1109

We cross the rapids of the River
    Hinokuma side by side;
and if I reach, my arm to give her
    shall we be by gossip tied?

No. 1110

To sow the sacred seeds
I sought a new rice field,
wandering gaitered,
and wading in the rapids.

No. 1111

I wonder if the ancients too
loved to visit here to listen
to the sweet music of this river
and its rapids.

No. 1112

Like maidens wearing
feathers in their tresses
this Iza River looks so sweet
with its rapids clear.

No. 1113

When the god and goddess made an oath a mist
    arose, 'tis said;
and lo, such vapor veils this little river now.

No. 1114

Translated, almost the same as No. 1100

No. 1115

Many a man of old enjoyed
the view of this meandering river.

No. 1116

The dew that falls upon my jet-black hair
vanishes at a touch.

No. 1117

So sweet upon the island shore
    the flowers that I chanced to see,
spite raging wind and rolling wave
    to cull them there again I'll be.

No. 1118

Did folk of yore too break
    the twig of cypress standing there
upon Hibara Hill
    to wear it in their hair?

No. 1119

No one else now comes to break the sprig
of cypress tree as did the ancients,
and lonesome in its greenness
stands Hibara Hill.

No. 1120

I marvel at the mossy carpet
overspread upon Aone Peak,
wondering who wove it all
without or warp or woof.

No. 1121

You Scrub Bamboos, and you Obana
growing on the path I take
to see my darling love, bend, pray,
bend as I, passing, make my way.

No. 1122

Behold, there go a flight of ducks
    over the mountains; and I pray
no waves may in the river rise
    where they alight upon the way

No. 1123

Oh how can I forget the plovers
crying over Saho's limpid rapids
and the sweet-throated frogs
piping beside the stream?

No. 1124

When in the night I hear
the plovers' cries so drear
over Saho's stream
I can not dream a peaceful dream.

No. 1125

In my home village of Kamnabi
do plovers still cry for their mates
over the rapids;
and veiled in vapor stands the hill?

No. 1126

It seems so short a time ago
the court was moved—and yet
to cross Asuka stream
there are no longer any stones.

No. 1127

I see the fountain welling forth its limpid waters,
and am detained here by the sight.

No. 1128

In your munificence
you have given us this well
with ever freshening water
flowing over its coping.

No. 1129

Whenever I try to play the koto,
I'm seized with sorrow.
Is my wife's memory
imbued within the very instrument?

No. 1130

How fascinating is the view
    of yon Divide
where rugged rocks we see
    side by side!

At Yoshino

No. 1131

People admire Yoshino's scenery,
and well they may.
I marvel at its mountains high,
and rivers crystalline.

No. 1132

It was my one desire to view
    the famed Yoshino's Pool of Dream.
Now the long-cherished wish comes true,
    and I behold it, standing by the stream.

No. 1133

Like men of yore who served their prince I also
will take me to the palace at Yoshino.

At Yoshino

No. 1134

How beautiful the scene
of this Yoshino River!
I would come here as changeless
as the old rocks on the banks.

No. 1135

The River Uji never rests
in pools where one can ford it:
Even the tenders of the wicker fish-traps
must shout to cross by ferry.

No. 1136

I would gather water-moss
here growing in the river to take home
as a souvenir,
but too fast runs the stream.

No. 1137

Things are oft compared to wickerwork
here in Uji, and if I were one
set in the river, I might catch
your heart instead of wood adrift.

No. 1138

Although I shout to get a boat,
    the river is too wide, I fear,
for ferrymen to hear me,
    and no sound of oars comes near.

No. 1139

Serene and crystalline
 the Uji waters flow,
and fascinated travelers
 are loath to go.

No. 1140

As I cross Inano field,
 the evening fog conceals the sight
of Mt. Arima, and I have no shelter
 now for the night.

No. 1141

The current of the River Muko
was so swift that I was wet
with splashes made by my bay horse
in crossing it astride.

No. 1142

Wishing for long life,
 I scooped the water from Tarumi's rill—
the water crystalline—
 in both my hands and drank my fill.

No. 1143

The night is far advanced, and there
 in the canal a boat now goes.
Its sound of oars is loud to hear:
 perhaps the current swiftly flows.

No. 1144

Alas, the tide is flowing in,
 for I hoped the scenery
to view of Suminoe Beach,
 strolling at leisure by the sea.

No. 1145

For your dear sake
I gathered shells
in Chinu's Sea
and wet my sleeves,
and still they drip!

No. 1146

How I would love
 to see the famous clay
upon the shore
 of Suminoe Bay!

At Suminoe Cove
No. 1147

If I have time to spare,
 I will go to the cove
to gather shells which bring
 forgetfulness of love.

No. 1148

Today I rode together
with friends to see the famed red clay
on Suminoe shore, and there
oft I would repair.

No. 1149

Yesterday I saw the shells
said to make the beholder
forget his love,
but all the same I suffer still.

No. 1150

Oh how I wish to have a house
upon the shore of Suminoe
that I might enjoy the sight of billows
rolling and roaring out upon the sea!

At Mitsu Beach of Ohtomo
No. 1151

The white waves come
 to lave the sands, but where
they go
 none are aware.

No. 1152

Far away the sound of oars is faint.
Is it the women divers
setting out to gather seaweed?

No. 1153

Never shall I forget
the pleasure of the ride
we took to Suminoe beach
to gather shiny shells!

No. 1154

Heigh-ho, how it rains!
And I must thatch my cottage in it.
How can I have time to gather shells
at low tide in Ago Cove?

No. 1155

How I wish to go to see
seaweed left scattered on the beach
at the ebb tide of the morn
today as it was yesterday!

At Oriono of Suminoe

No. 1156

Alas, the color of the dress
I dyed with hagi flowers gay
gathered in this vicinity
has faded all away.

At Ago Bay

No. 1157

The coming tide may bring a wind.
So, while the inlet is still dry,
I'll gather ocean herbs
left upon the shore.

At Suminoe

No. 1158

I take joy in the sight
of silvery breakers throwing spray
and in hearing billows roar
far, far away.

At Suminoe

No. 1159

Sweet is the sound
of rolling waves, as they
lap the bared roots of old pine trees
standing beside the bay!

At Naniwa Lagoon

No. 1160

As I look at ebb tide
over the bared ground,
I see a flight of cranes
for Awaji Island bound.

No. 1161

The autumn wind blows cold on me
now on a journey,
and yon flight of wild geese honking
makes me feel still colder.

No. 1162

Perhaps the waves are rising now;
for, hark, the birds upon the shoal
are crying loudly for their mates
to fly together to the shore.

No. 1163

Does yon lagoon lie bare?
It must; for in the harbor we
behold no boats this morning:
all are way out at sea.

No. 1164

When the tide goes out, together
to the lagoon the cranes repair.
Now their cries come from afar.
Are they feeding at the cape?

No. 1165

When the wind drops in the evening
we see cranes hunt for food,
but at flood tide, when billows rise,
they clamor for their mates.

At Manu's Harihara

No. 1166

Now I stand upon this field
where the ancients came
to dye their clothes with hagi flowers.
O that I too could do the same.

No. 1167

I went to hunt for fish
left by the waves, and there
saw seaweed. Now I wonder who
will gather it, what islander.

No. 1168

I wonder if the seaweed
under billow on white billow
is now wavering in profusion.

At Lake Biwa

No. 1169

Innumerable bays are found
along the lake; in one of which
I know your boat is moored,
and you are praying for safe journey now,
tying grass together.

No. 1170

When o'er Mt. Namikura clouds appear,
we've rain in this vicinity,
'tis said. So pray, my husband dear,
before it rains, come home to me.

No. 1171

I picture in my mind
the Imperial vessels lying
beside the shore, awaiting
calm weather and fair wind.

No. 1172

Whence did those sailors come—
at what harbor anchor weigh—
who now put out to sea
from Katori Bay?

No. 1173

How fast the River Nifu!
Woodcutters float their timber on it;
people call easily across it,
but no boat dares traverse it.

At Kashima Promontory
No. 1174

The billows are so high
here off the promontory,
that only from afar I glimpse
the celebrated scene.

No. 1175

Yamato, my home province
comes to mind, now that I see
o'er the Hakone mountains
cranes winging their way westward.

At Unagami Lagoon
No. 1176

In the lagoon, above the bar,
I see a flight of seabirds,
and hear them crying loudly,
but alas, no word from you, my love.

No. 1177

How fair Mikata's lake!
I come and go along the beach,
for the lovely scene
never ceases to charm me.

No. 1178

I've passed Inami field already,
and behold now
high waves roaring in Higasa cove
yonder, in front of me.

No. 1179

I shall remember,
long after I get home, the sight
of Inami meadow
of this moonlit night.

No. 1180

Afraid to cross the roaring waves
dashing against the strand,
we will not land upon Awaji,
though it lies near at hand.

No. 1181

Upon the morn of spring
when I set sail,
I must part from the sight
of Mt. Tatsuta and its hazy veil.

No. 1182

I thought at first the boats had spread
their white sails out in Tomo cove,
but second glance assures me that
they are but sparkling waves.

No. 1183

Upon my homeward trip
I will come here again and see
on the shore of Tomo cove
the soul-enchanting scenery.

No. 1184

I feel so lonely
when I hear roaring waves
at sea aboard a ship
floating like a bird.

No. 1185

At the morning calm I left
Mitsu beach where stand pine trees
and now I but perceive them
distantly across the waves.

No. 1186

So hard to dry the clothes
of the fishing maid
drenched with the brine.

No. 1187

People may look on me
who came to see the view
of Aku Beach as fisherman
that lives by drawing nets ashore.

No. 1188

Azaleas growing on the rocks
of Totsu Beach, pray, do remain
in bud till on my homeward way
I come to see you once again.

7 songs by Lord Fujiwara
No. 1189

May the gods protect
our ship from harm till we
reach Ina Bay, forbidding
the storm to come across the sea!

No. 1190

How beautiful Nagoe Beach!
I'll build a hut ashore,
and drive in stakes to moor my boat,
and there at ease enjoy the view.

No. 1191

The current in the river
runs so rapidly
the old horse stumbles: maybe
my people yearn for me.

> (There was a belief that, when your horse
> stumbles, the people at home are thinking of
> you.)

No. 1192

As I was riding o'er the river
running under Mt. Matsuchi
my old horse lost its footing:
perchance my people think of me.

No. 1193

The stronger mountain stands
face to face with the fair
whose hand, perhaps, is given him;
for now a bridge connects the pair.

No. 1194

As I go out on Saiga Beach
fishing torchlights I behold
now vanish, now appear
amid the surges of the sea.

No. 1195

Whenas I wear the hempen clothes,
they bring to mind the maiden fair
who upon Imose Hill in Kii
sows the hemp, and tends it there.

No. 1196

I gather shells as souvenirs
for my beloved family.
So wet me not,
O white Waves from the offing.

No. 1197

The oracle of fishermen is false;
I took in hand a shell
said to make one forget all troubles,
but it was to no purpose.

No. 1198

Behold, here is the dawn of day,
bringing in a cold wind from the sea;
and cranes that hunt for food ashore
are crying for their mates.

No. 1199

A boat is coming from the offing,
loaded with ocean herbs.
And yonder, cranes are on the wing
o'er Imo Island and Katami Cove.

No. 1200

I wish my vessel would not go to sea,
   because a boat is in the cove,
wherein, so eager to see me,
   is waiting now my darling love.

No. 1201

How the billows roar
in the angry ocean,
as our boat we oar
to reach the lovely shore!

No. 1202

I love the wild beach here,
but more that solitary isle
far out upon the sea,
and oft I see it in my dream.

No. 1203

This is my souvenir, a pearl
   for which I dived oft to the ocean floor,
warming myself between times by a fire
   of driftwood gathered on the shore.

No. 1204

As I sit upon the beach,
   drinking in the scenery,
although I am not fishing,
   for a fisherman folk will take me.

No. 1205

I am rowing now across the sea,
but my strength fails me.
I fear the town I can not reach,
for still so distant is the beach.

No. 1206

The rolling waves bring seaweed here
   and many a shiny shell with them,
but none whatever can compare
   with you, my dearest sparkling gem.

No. 1207

To go to Awa Island
   the seas have I to brave,
for in Akashi Straits
   the billows roar and rave.

No. 1208

I cross the pass, and go on still,
   recalling my own dearest one;
and see with envy yon Se Hill*
   standing so calm alone.
   * 'Se' meaning 'husband'.

No. 1209

Were those mountains human,
they had been surely reared in love:
look, how content the couple seem,
standing beside the River Kii.

No. 1210

After my dear wife yearning,
I go my way, and see with envy
a pair of mountains standing
in blessed conjugality.

No. 1211

On my way I pass
Mt. Imo* veiled in clouds.
Oh how I wish I were at home,
sitting face to face with my dear wife.
   * 'Imo' meaning 'wife'.

No. 1212

I traversed Ate county
and came to Mt. Itoka
where cherries are abloom. I pass them,
hoping they will stay till I return.

No. 1213

Mt. Nagusa* now I see
good but in name, because I am
neither healed from loving, nor
any better than before.
   * 'Nagusa' meaning 'consolation'.

No. 1214

O Cypress trees on Mt. Osute,
for long I have not seen you;
and now your aged boughs
are decked with hoary moss.

No. 1215

Look at Tama Island well.
People at Nara
may ask about its landscape.

No. 1216

What will the women divers do
    while working off the strand,
if the tide should take them unawares?
    All's hidden in the sea god's hand.

No. 1217

I grudge myself the view
of beautiful Tama Island;
lest I suffer when at home,
desiring to see it again.

No. 1218

The maids of honor take delight
in fishing, and the sea,
is red because their dresses
are reflected in the water.

No. 1219

When white waves rise
    in Waka Cove,
and winds blow coldly from the sea,
    I languish for Yamato and my love.

No. 1220

I spent all day
at Yura Promontory
in gathering shells
as souvenirs for you.

No. 1221

Oh do not row our boat back yet;
    for from Yamato here I came,
yearning to see the view
    of this beach so rich in fame.

No. 1222

Never I tire of seeing
Tama Isle so fair.
Could I not wrap it up,
to take home for a souvenir?

No. 1223

I wish the wind would rise
waveless, and send our ship
toward yonder beach, for I
desire to view the scene.

No. 1224

Mt. Ohba's veiled in mist,
and far advanced the night;
and in what harbor
will our ship drop anchor?

No. 1225

The shouts of boatmen setting out at midnight
made me uneasy: shouts as though of fear.
Have they in safety harborward returned?

No. 1226

The high waves dash against the shore
    about the cape of Miwa now and oh!
whatever passage can I take,
    finding no path whereby to go?

No. 1227

I stand upon the beach and stare
over the wide expanse, and only see
a boat for gathering seaweed there,
and suddenly a flight of ducks.

No. 1228

The fishermen who row
    Miho's seabeach off
are shouting. Why?
    Are the waters getting rough?

No. 1229

We will anchor in Akashi Bay.
So let us make now for the shore,
since far spent is the night.

No. 1230

Since I have safely passed the perils of Kane
    Point,
never shall I forget the god enshrined on Shika
    Isle !

No. 1231

The sky is overcast with clouds;
  the wind comes from the west and south.
I hear the billows roar and rave
  off Oka's river mouth.

No. 1232

Dreadful the ocean waves,
  but no harm will come to me,
if to the gods I pray,
  and then put out to sea.

No. 1233

The view of Taku Isle, how fine
as it is seen out on the brine!

No. 1234

If people see me on this shore,
  for I can not put out to sea,
as the incoming tide is swift,
  they for an angler will take me.

No. 1235

Sailor, the waves are high.
What will you do—at anchor lie,
or set your sails again,
and sleep upon the main?

No. 1236

Heigh-ho, the livelong day
  I think about my home;
again night after night,
  into my dream the darlings come.

No. 1237

The waves are lapping yonder shore,
and their sound comes to my ear,
as in the stillness
of my bower I sit.

No. 1238

My temporary hut is still,
  though foaming runs the stream;
and in this solitude I sit,
  and of my home I dream.

No. 1239

How fair the beach!
  I wish to go ashore,
braving the waves that seem
  to shake the ocean floor.

No. 1240

I went to Mt. Mimuro.
  So lovely was its scenery,
it brought the memories
  of other days to me.

No. 1241

I came this morning
  across Mt. Raven Hair*,
and my own got wet
  with fine mist in the air.

  * Mt. Kurokami.

No. 1242

If I'm benighted traveling,
and seek a lodging,
perhaps a lass will come out of an inn
and let me in.

No. 1243

My village looks near, but the road is roundabout.
This is where my love at parting waved her sleeve.

No. 1244

Let not clouds come
and hide Mt. Yufu,
for I stand looking
toward my home.

No. 1245

The strength of Shika rope
  that fishermen haul boats with is not mine;
I could not bear our parting, and
  in my love for you I pine.

No. 1246

Shika's fishermen are boiling salt,
  but the wind blowing shrill,
the smoke will not ascend,
  streaming before the hill.

No. 1247

I see a pair of mountains,
    soaring in the skies.
'Tis said they were created
    by two divinities*.

    * Ohnamuchi and Sukunamikami.

No. 1248

Thinking it as my dear one dead,
    I'll look into the ocean floor
at pretty blooming seaweed
    when'er they are in flower.

No. 1249

I went and gathered
    waternuts upon the lake,
and wetting my new sleeves,
    I plucked these for your sake.

No. 1250

For you I went into the mountains
to hunt for sedge seeds, and
losing my way,
returned but now, and lost all day.

Colloquy (Nos. 1251 and 1252)

No. 1251

Plovers who cry upon the Saho River,
why do you go thus flying,
scouring the leafy landscape,
for the upper reaches?

No. 1252

Man extols the river but with words,
    yet plovers love it true.
It is for every creature.
    So spare your weightless words, we ask of you.

Colloquy (Nos. 1253 and 1254)

No. 1253

On Shiga's ever-rippling waters
let not the divers without me
conduct their trade, no matter
though the lake be calm.

No. 1254

Had I a stout ship many oared,
to do my fishing from,
without you I'd not ply my trade,
though the lake be calm.

No. 1255

I came into the field to dye
    the garment with dayflowers for you,
and lo, already it is colored
    with the yellow blossoms wet with dew.

No. 1256

There is a short cut through the field;
    I know, but I prefer to meet
and talk with you, and so I came
    by a long, circuitous way, my sweet.

No. 1257

We met, you smiling like a lily
amid the wayside grass; and ever since then
have I looked upon you as my life,
and my beloved future wife.

No. 1258

I can distinguish
between the truth and comforting speech.
So, ne'er endeavor to relieve me
with your jejune refrain, "believe me."

No. 1259

Though the flowers they hold be scattered,
yet would I clasp her hands in mine—
the maid of Mt. Saeki.

No. 1260

The hagi is not flowering yet
    in Shima field, but I wish there
to go and dye my cloth to get
    a parti-colored garment fair.

No. 1261

It seems my ranger of the mountain
    has forgotten to come to me;
and now the paths are wild,
    overgrown with grass and tree.

No. 1262

The hunter lies
　　for deer in wait.
And you seem eager too
　　to see your mate.

No. 1263

Why make haste to leave me,
only to grieve me?
Though crows tell the time is dawn, yet on the
　hill,
the trees as yet stand still.

No. 1264

How gullible I,
who went alone to West mart,
and bought the silk they offered me!

No. 1265

O Guardsman going to Tsukushi,
　　when your hempen garments wear
through their shoulders, who
　　will mend for you the tear?

No. 1266

Rowing, rowing out into the raging sea,
I still retain before me
the lustre of her eyes.

No. 1267

The crawling waves come from afar,
　　undulating o'er the place whereon once stood
the capital of Ohmi
　　long since underneath the flood.

No. 1268

Mt. Makimuku soars now as before,
but we are human, and we change:
no more can I behold my dear
to be together as of yore.

No. 1269

I'm nothing but an earthly creature
short-lived as the foam
floating upon the river
that runs thundering beneath Mt. Makimuku.

No. 1270

The moon that shines above yon hill
　　will never stay the same, but wane
and wax. And so is our life too,
　　as transitory and as vain.

No. 1271

The cottage where my sweet love lives
is in the distant mist, still far away.
So, speed on, run your swiftest,
my black Horse, to get there.
　　　　　KAKINOMOTONO HITOMARO

No. 1272

My darling love is gathering ivies now.
Does she intend to weave my clothes therewith?

No. 1273

The dress the rider wears was woven
by a skilful woman weaver.

No. 1274

Reap not the reeds on Suminoe Beach,
for among them I will hide to see the maidens
go with wave-wet scarlet skirts.

No. 1275

"Oh you who reap the fields of Suminoe,
have you no serving-man to do it for you?"
"A serving-man have I, but by myself
I do the labor for my sweet wife's sake."

No. 1276

Reap not the grass beneath the tall tree by the
　　pond,
since it is there that we once had a rendezvous.

No. 1277

Reap not the grass, my love,
for fear your tresses should be soiled.

No. 1278

My love who cuts a robe for me,
line it, and do not make it tight.

No. 1279

Wait until the gulfweed blows,
for with the flower I'll come to you.

No. 1280

I roamed about the highway to the court to meet
   you,
and had my lovely skirt all frayed with walking.

No. 1281

This is the garment I took pains in weaving.
What color shall I dye it for your vernal wear?

No. 1282

O rising Cloud, why hide Mt. Kurahashi,
when I so desire to see it?

> (Keichu took this song for a verse in
> metaphor, and thought, as rising clouds, though
> beautiful, can not be touched by hand, they
> are compared to a girl, though seen, can not
> be met in rendezvous. Others, however, think
> it is only a descriptive song.)

No. 1283

Oft did I cross the Kurahashi River,
stepping over stones when I was young.

No. 1284

I reaped the sedge beside the River Kurahashi,
but did not make a hat of it.

> Meaning: only a promise, and no marriage.

No. 1285

Upon this balmy vernal day
yet single,
the young man tills the fields alone.

No. 1286

Never pluck up grass about the shrine,
though you find it rank and prosperous.

No. 1287

O that I could meet some one as I roam,
to tell him tales of Ohmi, my dear home.

No. 1288

"Who cut these rushes at the estuary?"
"Better to see my parting husband wave his
   sleeve, I did."

No. 1289

My lord who call your dogs to go ahunting,
rest your horse upon the wooded hill.

No. 1290

Never tell that we
like plants all hidden by the brine
stay here, my love and I.

No. 1291

O Children reaping grass upon the hill,
pray, leave some for my lover's horse.

No. 1292

My husband waits, his sleeves tucked up,
for deer and wild boars to appear.

No. 1293

However oft one cuts the branches
of the willows by the Ado,
new sprigs will come out soon again
upon their sappy, sturdy trunks.

No. 1294

I see the harvest moon rise from behind yon
   mountain.
Let those who left their wives at home be soothed
   now by the view.

No. 1295

The moon has risen over Mt. Kasuga,
and in our wine cups now it is reflected.

SONGS IN METAPHOR

No. 1296

The new-made parti-colored robe
which will become me well,
though I haven't donned it yet,
is e'er before my eye.

No. 1297

I wish to dye my garment red,
but the color would draw folk's attention,
and soon rumors might be spread.

No. 1298

Tongues wag this way, that way.
As for me,
I persevere in weaving
my white linen cloth.

No. 1299

Oh let not others know
that I, the orient pearls to gain,
now row out on the main
where many seafowls go.

No. 1300

How I wish to find the pearl
hidden in a cavern
under the sea,
by others all unnoticed.

No. 1301

For the pearl of the ocean god
I dive into the sea.

No. 1302

Many and many a time the diver said,
"still will I dive, until
with my own eyes I see
the ocean god's white pearl."

No. 1303

The fisher-diver asks to see
    the pearl, but it unable yet
to know the god's mind, is not fain
    to have itself before him set.

No. 1304

My heart is like a tree concealed
in clouds that veil the mountain,
and no one but its leaves know it.

No. 1305

The foliage that bedeck the mountain
    of that remote land do I crave;
their sight will never tire me.
    Oh how I wish those leaves to have!

No. 1306

I glimpsed a pretty flower
under the autumn leaves,
and now for it I yearn.

No. 1307

Navigable is the river,
but alas, at every ferry
there is a man who keeps
a strict watch on the waters.

No. 1308

In the harbor
peopled by lofty ships
should misadventure overtake us,
whither will you succor me?

No. 1309

The tempest roars; the seas run wild.
But if it seem a long time
for you to wait until
tomorrow, fain would I obey your will.

No. 1310

Your parents are as awesome
    as the god enshrined upon the isle.
So I come not to you,
    but deeply love you all the while.

No. 1311

People who are in rags
    look so free from care,
and I long now
    to be in clothes threadbare.

No. 1312

Did I not hold it dear,
would I be putting on for all to see
the robe so long worn secretly?

No. 1313

Will people talk of me,
if I don as outer garment
the red gown I have worn
so long beneath my robe?

No. 1314

Strange to say, tonight I want
   the other clothes to doff
and don the garment
   I have had washed oft enough.

No. 1315

So far from such a river
as dyers bleach their cloth in
am I here in Tachibana
that I must make my underrobe
from cloth unbleached.

No. 1316

Repeatedly I use Kawachi thread;
'tis only single ply,
and yet it will not snap.

No. 1317

The wind may blow; the waves may rage,
   but repeatedly
I'll try to get the pearl that lies
   deep at the bottom of the sea.

No. 1318

I eagerly wish to see the pearl
   down at the bottom of the main,
and a thousand times did ask
   the sea god for his leave in vain.

No. 1319

O Sea god, pray, let me acquire
   the pearl that sparkling lies
upon the ocean floor;
   bid the wind not to rise!

No. 1320

Why do I yearn to get the pearl
   set on the ocean shelf?
Because I eagerly wish to treasure
   it all to myself.

No. 1321

Alas for me, is such the world?
The string of pearls has broken,
and my love's word is vainly spoken!

No. 1322

The diver took the pearl away
   off the ocean floor.
Then long he looked and looked at it,
   loving it the more.

No. 1323

I know not how to get the pearl
   that lies beneath the brine,
yet day and night, alas,
   for it I pine.

No. 1324

Behold the knot is tied
   as tightly as I can,
and it shall never be
   unloosed by any man.

No. 1325

To keep a pearl aye in a box
   will do the jewel harm.
Better to take it often out
   and wear it on the arm.

No. 1326

I wish I could acquire the pearl
the jewel merchant has on him;
then, changing the old string to new,
most fondly would I wear it too.

No. 1327

O Autumn Wind, blow not
until I get the pearl that lies
deep beneath the sea,
and wear the gem on me!

No. 1328

Were there no obstacles, should I
suffer so, and sigh for her?

No. 1329

If I drew her near
as I pull an arrow
on the bow string,
would it make a scandal?

No. 1330

O Spindle tree upon the hill,
   wait and let none know
that you are here until I come again
   to make a strong bow from your bough.

No. 1331

I love you, though
you are as noble
as a lofty rugged mountain,
and I am but a humble woman.

No. 1332

I've wandered far into the mountain
where rock on rock impedes me,
but so fair the view
I can not leave it now.

No. 1333

Saho hill I long regarded
   with little care.
Now I look on it with love.
   O Wind, blow gently there!

No. 1334

How I respect the mountain
strewn here and there with moss,
but love abides with the respect,
and I yearn after it.

No. 1335

How I love Mt. Unebi!
   and now, behold, thereon
have set a mark
   denoting 'tis my own.

No. 1336

O Men who set
   the field of spring afire,
are you not content therewith?
   To burn my bosom too do you desire?

No. 1337

Alas, I should have marked
   that meadow as my own.
It is too late, and now
   its loss I moan.

No. 1338

O fairest Flower
   growing in my dwelling place,
never be used to dye the garment of another
   even as an act of grace.

No. 1339

Dayflower, I wish to dye my cloth
   in your hue, but I know
your color changes easily,
   which causes me to suffer so.

No. 1340

I twist a purple thread
in hopes of stringing
the golden oranges
from the broad-based hill.

No. 1341

How I regret I did not reap
the sedge already;
for some one else are cutting
the grass to keep.

No. 1342

The mountain soars, and oh,
   behind it now has sunk the sun.
'Tis dark; too late am I to mark
   the meadow as my own.

No. 1343

Although it is not mine,
   determined am I to reap
the forest grass
   as my own to keep.

No. 1344

O that I had a love
   I could dress with the cloth I dye
with the sedge growing in the moor
   where we see eagles in the sky.

No. 1345

I dreamed a dream:
   an iris was in flower
out in a pretty field, for which
   I still yearn at this hour.

No. 1346

Strong is the kuzu
 growing beside the lake
of Sakisawa field.
 So from it my garment I will make.

No. 1347

Out in the moor I saw a sedge's flower
 as fair as you, my lass,
and prayed that none might harm
 that marshland grass.

No. 1348

Since I roped off as my own
 the rushes on the moor,
I've come to love them
 even ere reaping them to keep in store.

No. 1349

How like this stunted bamboo, left behind
upon Araki's snowy plain,
am I, as I grow older
all unfulfilled.

No. 1350

Oh how I long to make my arrows
from Yabase bamboo in Ohmi!
How can I shoot without them?

No. 1351

I will dye my clothes
 in brilliant dayflower hue.
What care I if they fade
 when wet with morning dew?

No. 1352

My heart is buoyant,
and like a floating water flower
can not stay still, but goes
now toward, now away from shore.

No. 1353

Though ears are not yet on the rice,
 do stretch a rope around the patch.
Then a guardsman I will be
 to keep for you a careful watch.

No. 1354

The Manu hagi flower
is not my heart's desire,
and yet I dyed my robe its color.

No. 1355

The woodman planting cypresses
 has good use of the wood in view.
He does not raise the trees
 to build a little hut anew.

No. 1356

O Peach tree on the peak,
one whispered in my ear of you,
"Does it bear fruit?"
Beware of him.

No. 1357

My mother raises silkworms at home.
I've seen how from the lowly mulberry
finally gorgeous garments come.

No. 1358

My cherished peach tree
all leafy and in flower,
will it not bear me fruit?

No. 1359

I plucked a twig from yonder red-bud tree,
and yearn to see it flower.

No. 1360

With all my heart I love you, yet
I know that like the flower of mountain chisa
you have changed.

No. 1361

When can I wear the garment new
of the iris color blue?

No. 1362

The coxcombs I intended
to transplant when autumn comes,
now where are they,
and who took them away?

No. 1363

The hagi have begun to flower
in Kasuga meadow now.
I'll wait until
they all are in full bloom.

No. 1364

I loved the hagi,
and yearned to see its bloom.
Now it has broken into flower,
and I muse upon the seed.

No. 1365

I enjoyed the hagi in full flower
outside my bower.
Now it has gone to seed,
which I cherish all the more indeed.

No. 1366

The waterfowl that live
upon the seven-rapids pools
make no noise
and hide themselves.

No. 1367

The musasabi living
    upon the high branch of the tree
is anxious to acquire its prey;
    and so am I my love to see.

No. 1368

Would I could be a cloud
floating above yon field
for the wind to take
me where I wish to go!

No. 1369

O Lightning flashing high
    among the clouds, thou art so dread to see,
but sometimes I do yearn
    for the sight of thee.

No. 1370

I thought it scarcely rained,
but a puddle is made in the garden.
Let it not flow
lest people know.

No. 1371

I do not go out in the rain, and yet,
alas, my sleeves are always wet.

No. 1372

Every night though I
see the moon up in the sky,
yet I can not go near by.

No. 1373

The mountain's high. It is too dark
to find the precious sedge among the stones,
and vainly do I wait
for the moon to ride the sky.

No. 1374

Murky the night;
    I await the moon,
but she tarries.
    O that she would rise soon.

No. 1375

Life is like the morning dew,
and all too soon we die;
but only for your sake
do I pray for long life.

No. 1376

If the red earth
of Uda County stick to you,
people will go on talking of us two.

No. 1377

Never do I pretend
    to be too good to woo you.
I only fear the talk
    others gossip to you.

No. 1378

Since so in love am I,
shall I not trespass on the precincts
of the bark-hung shrine?

No. 1379

If the Asuka River
    cease to flow,
will not folk wonder,
    wishing the why to know?

No. 1380

At every rapids
of the Asuka River
we see duckweed growing,
but weirs keep it from coming and going.

No. 1381

Shallow you are as a rill,
yet I deeply love you still.

No. 1382

If off the surface of Hatsuse's stream
foam disappeared altogether,
only then, would I give you up,
part from you, and make you free.

No. 1383

If I cry aloud,
people will know;
so I suppress my passion,
though it be wild as rushing rapids.

No. 1384

Like the mountain current
    though my passion may run high,
will I not bide the time,
    even if I daily sigh?

No. 1385

Any attempt to hide our secret
    will be in vain.
Lovers resort to it,
    but nothing gain.

No. 1386

I went to sea
aboard a lofty ship with many oars
and there, though it was at low tide,
fathomless was the ocean under me.

No. 1387

Better for me to have gone by
    a roundabout safe way
than, coming thus across the beach,
    be drenched through by the spray.

No. 1388

Behold, the white waves can approach
    the seashore with impunity,
but if I sometimes come to you,
    people will talk of me.

No. 1389

White Waves that lave my beach,
if you love me,
linger here,
stay near the sands.

No. 1390

Should I wait till the lifting of the wind
    and quiet grows the lake,
till myself becoming old,
    no strength is left my oars to take?

No. 1391

Now in the morning calm
    I long the waves to see,
but all windless,
    no wave comes toward me.

No. 1392

On Nataka's golden strand
as we passed along the lane,
our sleeves brushed each other.
Is this the only touch we are to know?

No. 1393

Why should I grieve,
    if he love me, and if that I know?
but, bitten by the fangs of doubt,
    daily I live in woe.

No. 1394

As under water, when the tide is in,
lies the sea moss growing on the rock,
so my love, for whom I yearn,
seldom can I see.

No. 1395

As seaweed drifts ashore,
    borne by rolling billows of the brine,
so driven by wild love,
    I only wish you could be mine.

No. 1396

I wait for you, my dear, to come to me
as one awaits herbs drifting from the sea.

No. 1397

Awesome the breakers beating
    against the rugged shore,
but fair the herbs they bring
    out of the ocean floor.

No. 1398

Can I forget the maid
    I met beside the lake?
Alas for me
    who ever languish for her sake.

No. 1399

I can't forget that voyage,
    oh nay;
nor can I forget the maiden
    I met that day.

No. 1400

Resembling a little boat
am I, waiting out the storm,
and growing superannuated,
no longer fit to go to sea.

No. 1401

Eager am I to land,
    but my small boat nears the shore in vain,
the heavy wind now tossing
    the spray like driving rain.

No. 1402

Oh why did you not send me word
when I was away from you?
Behold, here I am in the harbor.
Why refuse to see me now?

No. 1403

Entering a sacred forest, I cut wood,
and almost had my hand ax confiscated.

No. 1404   *see 1416*

To me familiar as my mirror
were you,
whose ashes now, like orange flowers,
I place within the urn.

No. 1405

Whenever I hear of Akitsu field,
    I am reminded of the morrow
when I sowed her ashes there,
    weeping, overwhelmed with sorrow.

No. 1406

Like a cloud hung o'er Akitsu field
was the smoke left by the burning pyre,
but now, alas, 'tis gone.
Still day after day I moan.

No. 1407

The mist now veils Hatsuse's hill
where sadly I cremated her.
Alas, is it the smoke
left by the funeral pyre still hovering?

No. 1408

Oh is it true
    what people say
that my love lies on Mt. Hatsuse,
    having passed away?

No. 1409

Enjoying golden leaves, my love
    entered the autumn mountain bright,
and her return I wait and wait,
    vainly now day and night.

No. 1410

Alas, she can not live again.
My wish to reunite is vain.

No. 1411

How blessed the man !
    Although his once-black hair has grown all
        white,
yet he can hear
    still the sweet voice of his heart's delight.

No. 1412

Little knowing that my husband would
be early taken from me,
I refused him in our bed,
and now, too late, I grieve.

No. 1413

Alas for me
    who mourn your death
as ceaselessly
    as I take breath.

No. 1414

Alas, now that my wife is dead,
    all the same is my plight
no matter whether long or brief
    be the night.

No. 1415

Was my love of gems?
for as I sow the field
with her ashes now,
they scattered fall like them.

No. 1416

It seems my love was flowers;
for as I sow her ashes,
over the field I see
them fall like blossoms off a tree.

No. 1417

The morning ocean
    did I sail,
and heard the Nago
    sailors hail.

THE MANYOSHU

BOOK VIII

FOREWORD

This book is divided into 8 parts: Spring miscellaneous songs, Spring love songs, Summer miscellaneous songs, Summer love songs, Autumn miscellaneous songs, Autumn love songs, Winter miscellaneous songs, and Winter love songs.

The whole volume is classified into the 4 seasons, and further divided into miscellaneous and love songs. This classification has given an example to later anthologies compiled by Imperial command, which are edited, classifying songs into four seasons.

The number of verses contained in the book is 246. These are divided into 6 longer lays, 4 Sedohka, and 236 verselets.

Among the verselets there is one peculiar song of which the upper hemistich is composed by a nun; and the lower hemistich by Ohtomono Yakamochi (No. 1636). This verse may be regarded as a forerunner of later renga. A large number of the songs are written by young Ohtomono Yakamochi (his verses numbering as many as 53) and his relatives.

SPRING MISCELLANEOUS SONGS

No. 1418

Behold, the spring at last has come
when on Tarumi's hillock where
the waterfalls plunge o'er the crags
brackens put forth their tender shoots.

PRINCE SHIKI

No. 1419

O Cuckoo Bird,
    singing in Iwase Wood, pray, cease
to bill your sylvan song
    to make my love for him increase.

LADY KAGAMI

No. 1420

Are leaves of flowers descending
    from on high,
or tiny flakes of snow
    out of the sky?

SURUGANO UNUME

2 songs by Owarino Muraji
No. 1421

I like to see the sashes white
of maidens gathering young herbs
when the trees of vernal mountains
are radiant, decked with flowers.

No. 1422

It seems that spring is come,
    for the trees seen far away
upon the misty hills
    grow fairer day by day.

No. 1423

Behold, the plum
    outside my bower
which last spring I set,
    has broken into flower.

ABENO HIRONIWA

4 songs by Yamabeno Akahito
No. 1424

I went into the vernal field
    to gather violets there.
and yearning to stay longer,
    slept in the open air.

No. 1425

Were the cherry trees abloom
    day after day,
should I love the flowers so much
    as now? Oh, nay.

No. 1426

Abloom the plum trees of my garden,
to view them I invited you,
but, alas, the snow has fallen,
hiding the flowers with its white.

No. 1427

I marked the field intending
to cull young herbs tomorrow,
but yesterday was snowy, and
today goes on with snow unending.

No. 1428

Passing Naniwa,
I traverse Mt. Kusaka
in the gloaming,
and see ashibi trees in flower
as I hie myself
to your bower.

> (The commentator remarks that the name
> of the author, being of obscurity, not men-
> tioned.)

2 songs recited by Wakamiyano Ayumaro
No. 1429

How beautiful
the cherry flowers
opening everywhere
throughout this land !
Maidens wear them
in their tresses;
courtiers weave them
in their garlands.

ANON.

Hanka
No. 1430

You saw last year
    my cherry's sheen.
The tree is ready
    again now to be seen.

No. 1431

In Kudara field I saw a warbler perched
    on the old hagi bough,
waiting for the spring.
    Is he singing now?

YAMABENO AKAHITO

2 songs on willows
by Ohtomono Sakanoeno Iratsume

No. 1432

You go and see the willows green
    fringing the Saho way,
but I live now remote from it. Oh! would
    that I could even see their cut-off spray.

No. 1433

Saho's stream is fringed
    with willows green.
'Tis springtime, and the trees
    budding must be seen.

No. 1434

Frost and snow
still are falling,
but in our village
plum trees are ablow.

OHTOMONO MIHAYASHI

No. 1435

Are the yellow roses blowing,
reflected in the Kamunabi pool
where the sweet-throated frogs
trill at this time, inviting the coolness?

PRINCE ATSUMI

2 songs on plum trees by Ohtomono Murakami

No. 1436

We had a snow
this morn, and so
has the budding plum
come into bloom?

No. 1437

O Plum flowers opened luxuriantly
    here in Kasuga town,
may you not be scattered in the gale
    sweeping the mountain down.

No. 1438

The plum flowers of Kasuga village
veiled in vapor—
with what a brimming heart
I come to view them!

No. 1439

To show that spring is here
yonder mountain,
although still white with snow,
in softening mist is veiled.

NAKATOMINO MURAJI

No. 1440

This unremitting rain of spring—
what happens to the cherry trees in flower
on Takamado?

KAWABENO AZUMABITO

No. 1441

The snow falls from the sky
overcast with murky clouds,
but in my garden
already uguisu sing.

OHTOMONO YAKAMOCHI

No. 1442

My man has gone to Naniwa,
and all the lonelier I feel
to see a housewife gathering herbs.

TAJIHINO MAHITO

No. 1443

Into the field enveloped
    in mist I go my way
to hear uguisu sing
    his year's first lay.

TAHINO OTOMARO

No. 1444

The violets are in bloom,
vying in grace with flowering yellow roses.
They are all wet with rain of spring
without cease falling.

LADY TAKATA

No. 1445

The wind and snow now mingling come
upon our blossoming plums.
I pray they'll scatter not the flowers
before the trees set fruit.

OHTOMONO SAKANOENO IRATSUME

No. 1446

The pheasant cries ayearning
for his mate, alackaday,
letting his nest be known,
and to a hunter falls a prey.

OHTOMONO YAKAMOCHI

No. 1447

No one enjoys the voice
of cuckoos at another time,
but since 'tis spring, all people
delight to hear their chime.

OHTOMONO SAKANOENO IRATSUME

LOVE SONGS OF SPRING

To Sakanoeno Iyeno Ohkiiratsume

No. 1448

When will the pinks, whose seed I sowed,
come into flower? I wait now
for that time, imagining the bloom,
my darling, to be you.

OHTOMONO YAKAMOCHI

*To Sakanoeno Ohkiiratsume from her sister,
Ohtomono Tamurano Ohkiiratsume*

No. 1449

You seem to me a vernal violet sweet,
Sister dear, whom I now long to meet.

No. 1450

Every maid in love feels melancholy
when spring mist veils the landscape

OHTOMONO SAKANOENO IRATSUME

*To Ohtomono Yakamochi
from Kasano Otome*

No. 1451

When spring bedecks the mountains,
more than any other season
do I yearn for my lover.

No. 1452

I am aware you do not come
upon a murky night,
but why not on a moonlit eve
when plum in flower stands bright?

KINO OTOME

*To the Envoy to China,
by Kasano Kanamura*

No. 1453

By the command of the Emperor, you whom I love
leave Mitsu Point where cranes cry in the twilight,
and go across the billowy deep from isle to isle.
I remain at home, and making votive gifts,
pray gods for your return.

Hanka

No. 1454

Your ship will vanish like an isle
behind the waves, and I shall only sigh.

No. 1455

O that I were the tiller of your ship
rather than be yearning thus for you.

To a young girl

No. 1456

Each petal of these cherry blossoms
    I offer you today
conceals a thousand tender thoughts
    my longing to convey.

FUJIWARANO HIROTSUGU

In reply

No. 1457

Laden is your thought with tender love,
    concealed within the flowers, you say.
This heaviness—was it the cause
    that so bent down and broke the spray?

The young maid

No. 1458

The wind is blowing through the pines.
    I fear the cherry trees in flower
are shedding petals now,
    my dear, outside your bower.

PRINCE ATSUMI

In reply

No. 1459

Nothing remains the same:
    all things change here below.
Our cherry flowers are falling now.
    They too the way of all must go.

KUMENO OTOME

2 songs to Ohtomono Yakamochi
by Kino Otome

No. 1460

All for your sake
in fields of spring

the healthful herbs
a-gathering
that now I bring—
please take,
    and flourish!

No. 1461

The flowers of silk trees blow by day,
yearning for the sun,
and close their leaves by night. I've one
of which I offer you a spray.

2 songs in reply by Ohtomono Yakamochi

No. 1462

Am I then in love with you,
that still I stay so thin
despite your gift of healthful herbs,
which, though I take, I pine?

No. 1463

The silk spray you sent me
is beautiful to view,
but it will bear no fruit,
and pass away.

To Sakanoeno Ohkiiratsume
by Ohtomono Yakamochi

No. 1464

The misty mountain is between us,
    you living far away.
I have spent a lonely month
    without a single happy day.

MISCELLANEOUS SONGS OF SUMMER

No. 1465

Sweet bird that charms the listening ear,
    Cuckoo, not yet your voice expend.
Upon the Summer's thread I'll string your songs
    like pearls. So yet awhile attend.

LADY FUJIWARA

No. 1466

When will cuckoos come
    and sing among
our trees. I daily yearn
    for their sweet song.

PRINCE SHIKI

No. 1467

O for a quiet country where
  no cuckoo sings at any time;
for its heart-rending song gives me
  insufferable pain here in this clime.
                    PRINCE YUGE

No. 1468

I have come to the field
  where cuckoos live, but here,
the autumn wind now blowing, and
  hagi abloom, few songs I hear.
                    PRINCE OHARITANO HIROSE

No. 1469

O Cuckoo, if you cry,
  you will remind me of my dear
I left behind, and I shall feel
  lonely here.
                                SAMI

No. 1470

O Cuckoo in the forest, fill
with your sweet song my ear,
for I am yearning now to hear
you in the shadow of this hill.
                    TORINO SENIRYO

No. 1471

Lo, the wistaria is abloom
but she, alas, sleeps in her tomb.
                    YAMABENO AKAHITO

No. 1472

Together with utsugi flowers
that mark the season of the dead,
did you too come to sing,
  O Cuckoo?
            ISONOKAMINO KATSUWO

  (Cuckoos were believed to be birds of the
  nether world.)

No. 1473

The cuckoo in the village where
  the orange flowers fell cries,
like me, lamenting for the fond
  unforgettable memories.
                    OHTOMONO TABITO

No. 1474

I am back home,
and wonder if the cuckoos yet
have finished with their song
upon that far-off Ohki Hill.
            OHTOMONO SAKANOENO IRATSUME

No. 1475

O Cuckoo crying now above,
your summer song
ever makes me long
after my love.
                                DITTO

No. 1476

I am forlorn this evening
as I sit alone, and hear a cuckoo
singing so sadly.
Is the sweet bird taking pity on me?
                    OWAIDANO HIROMIMI

No. 1477

Utsugi have not yet blown,
  but cuckoo birds are singing here
upon the mountainside
  their first songs of the year.
                    OHTOMONO YAKAMOCHI

No. 1478

When will our kumquat trees now blossoming
bear fruit large enough for you to string?
                                DITTO

No. 1479

Lonely in my cottage
I went out for a ramble,
and heard cicadas singing,
which made me still more lonely.
                                DITTO

2 songs by Ohtomono Fumimochi
No. 1480

O Cuckoo, come and let me hear
  your throat, your happy dower,
for the moon is shining clear,
  brightly lighting up my bower.

No. 1481

My friend is here, so Cuckoo,
  come and test
your throat from out our flowering oranges
  for my guest.

No. 1482

Even though the utsugi flowers pass away,
O Cuckoo
shall I e'er forget your sweet, sweet lay?
                    OHTOMONO KIYONAWA

No. 1483

I have come to your bower
to see the orange trees in flower,
hoping too a cuckoo may
come and sing its summer lay.
                    AMUNOKIMI MOROTATSU

No. 1484

O Cuckoo, cease to sing your melancholy song
  until
it wearies me who live alone, and make me sadder
  still.
              OHTOMONO SAKANOENO IRATSUME

No. 1485

Our late-blossoming plums are now in flower,
and spring soon will be gone.
I fear that coming rain
will fade their lovely color.
                    OHTOMONO YAKAMOCHI

2 songs on cuckoos by Ohtomono Yakamochi
No. 1486

The oranges are abloom
    outside my bower, and if their flowers leave
ere cuckoos sing upon their boughs,
    how I shall grieve.

No. 1487

No cuckoos come,
    and now the orange trees outside my bower
have grown all thick and dark with foliage,
    leaving not a flower.

No. 1488

A cuckoo came here to our town,
    and sang its song today.
I know not how it is elsewhere,
    but I have heard its lay.
                    OHTOMONO YAKAMOCHI

No. 1489

The kumquat flowers are gone,
    and now the fruit are glowing red
for me to string the same as I
    do pearls upon a thread.
                              DITTO

No. 1490

No cuckoo comes
to let me hear him sing.
Oh is the day still far away
when iris flowers we arrange in garlands?
                              DITTO

No. 1491

Do cuckoos love utsugi flowers so?
    For here they come to see
them and sing, although the rain is falling
    ceaselessly.
                              DITTO

No. 1492

The orange blossoms at your bower
    have dropped their petals now, and in their
      place
have set green fruit.
    I grieve I came not during the flowering grace.
                         A singing girl

No. 1493

Alas, the orange flowers are gone.
    They were so beautiful
that cuckoos came to sing among them,
    scattering the petals, one and all.
                    OHTOMONO MURAKAMI

2 songs on cuckoos
by Ohtomono Yakamochi
No. 1494

Hark to the cry, that comes
    from yonder summer mountain now,
of a cuckoo bird
    perched on a leafy bough.

No. 1495

Hark, the cuckoo's song
    coming from far away
from among the trees. I hear it now
    and shall remember aye.

No. 1496

The pink's flowers by our bower
are at their best. I look on them,
and wish I had a maid to whom
I could present a nosegay.

              OHTOMONO YAKAMOCHI

No. 1497

If I go to Mt. Tsukuba,
    can I hear a cuckoo hail
with his echoing voice,
    covering the hill and dale?

              TAKAHASHINO MUSHIMARO

No. 1498

Cuckoo, go flying
    and ask my love for whom
I yearn
    why he does not come.

              OHTOMONO SAKANOENO IRATSUME

At a feast
No. 1499

My friend comes not to me.
He has no time, says he.
But you at least, my cuckoo bird,
are at my gate, and keep your word.

              OHTOMONO YOTSUNA

No. 1500

My love for him is like a little lily
    blowing among the grasses high
of summer's meadow, all concealed
    from people's eye.

              OHTOMONO SAKANOENO IRATSUME

No. 1501

Cuckoo, I miss my friend.
Why does he not come?
Every day I wait.

              OWARIDANO HIROMIMI

No. 1502

How fair this lei
of orange flowers of May!
I've culled and strung them all
for you before they fall.

              OHTOMONO SAKANOENO IRATSUME

No. 1503

You are not willing to see me;
    and so, say, "later." Egoist,
I know, you are. You might as well
    flatly refuse my hoped-for tryst.

              KINO TOYOKAWA

No. 1504

Pressed with affairs,
though it be May,
the flowering oranges of my love
I have to hurry by.

              TAKAYASU

To Ohtomono Yakamochi
by Ohmiwano Iratsume
No. 1505

I sent to you a cuckoo bird,
    telling him to sing for you;
and wish to know, my dear,
    if to your bower he flew.

To Ohtomono Sakanoeno Ohkiiratsume
by her sister, Tamurano Ohkiiratsume
No. 1506

As my messenger I sent
    a cuckoo which perhaps you hear
now on your hill. Did he
    tell you my words, my sister dear?

To Sakanoeno Ohkiiratsume
by Ohtomono Yakamochi

No. 1507

As the month of May was nearing,
the orange branches by my bower were in flower.
I took much care to keep them,
hoping you would come upon a moonlit night
to view them,
but silly cuckoos came this dawn
and scattered nearly all the flowers.
So I cannot invite you now,
and only send a sprig to you.

Hanka

No. 1508

These are the orange flowers
    I wished my heart's delight
would come and see
    upon a moonlit night.

No. 1509

Cuckoos came before you,
scattering all our orange flowers
I had kept only for you.

To Lady Kii by Ohtomono Yakamochi

No. 1510

Withered the pinks, they say,
    as soon as they had blown.
But I hope they were not of the field
    I had marked as my own.

AUTUMN MISCELLANEOUS SONGS

No. 1511

When night falls,
    the cries of deer come from our mountain
        deep;
but no belling do I hear this eve,
    Are they then all gone to sleep?

                                EMPEROR JOMEI

No. 1512

On golden tree leaves like brocade
woven by some angelic hands,
of which the warp and woof are one,
O Autumn frost, pray, do not fall.

                                PRINCE OHTSU

2 songs by Prince Hozumi

No. 1513

This dawn I heard wild geese, reminding
    me of Mt. Kasuga now all bright
with crimson leaves, but still I thought
    autumn was lone though ne'er so bedight.

No. 1514

Gone with summer now the sedge bloom by my
    bower,
and soon the autumn hagi will come into flower.

No. 1515

I wish I were not in this town
    of gossips, by their tongues all torn,
but could escape with those wild geese
    that go crying in the sky this morn.

                                PRINCESS TAJIMA

Deploring the fall of autumn leaves
by Prince Yamabe

No. 1516

How beautiful the hills
    with golden leaves bedight!
And all the more I shall
    sigh for autumn after this fair sight.

No. 1517

How sad I feel to see the fall
  of autumn tree leaves which adorn
Mt. Miwa where the priests
  pray in the old shrine night and morn.
                    PRINCE NAGAYA

*12 songs on the night of
the seventh of July by Yamanoeno Okura*

No. 1518

Parted are we by the Heavenly River,
but this eve comes my long-yearned-for husband,
and I am waiting with my sash unloosened.

No. 1519

My love comes rowing—what delight—
across the Heavenly Stream this night.

No. 1520

Since heaven and earth divided were
the Cowherd has been on one bank
of the Heavenly River, and the Weaver
on the other. The azure waves obstruct
the view; white vapor keeps them separate.
Were there a crimson boat with jeweled oars,
morning calm would see the husband paddling,
and eventide would find him rowing back.
The happy pair could spread a carpet on the shore,
and locking their fair arms could lie
through nights of bliss—not Seventh Month's
  alone.

Hanka
No. 1521

Wind and cloud come over the Celestial River;
but ah! they, being not messengers,
will not bring word from my darling Weaver.

No. 1522

The stream is narrow, and a stone,
if cast, would reach the other bank,
yet apart, we only sigh forlorn.

No. 1523

Here is my love for whom I have been waiting
since the autumn wind began to blow.

No. 1524

Narrow is the Heavenly River
  where no high waves appear,
but my lover can not come
  save only once a year.

No. 1525

Narrow is the stream,
  and if I waved my sleeve, my lover sweet
might see me, but, alas,
  except one autumn night we can not meet.

No. 1526

If after this short rendezvous,
I part from you,
then till again we meet,
yearning ever shall I be, my sweet.

No. 1527

Veiled in spray is the Heavenly River.
Is the Cowherd rowing to his Weaver?

No. 1528

I come and go, awaiting you
by the misty stream,
my skirt all wet with dew.

No. 1529

I hear the waves
  roaring in the river.
Is the boat being rowed
  by my lover?

2 songs at a feast
No. 1530

I see Ashiki field,
for the first time today,
where hagi is abloom
with other autumn flowers.

                                        ANON.

No. 1531

How glad I am to see
Ashiki river gently flow.
I never shall forget
this lovely view!

                                        ANON.

2 songs by Kasano Kanamura
No. 1532
The hagi are in flower.
They will stain
the clothes of travelers
passing by.

No. 1533
On Mt. Ikao I behold
    hagi in flower,
reminding me of the obana
    beside your bower.

No. 1534
Take home these autumn flowers
    and give them to your daughter fair
who will beg for a souvenir,
    when you, my friend, get there.
                    ISHIKAWANO OKINA

No. 1535
I wait for him to come
    across the stream to me. And oh
this is the happy, happy time:
    I hear the fall wind blow.

No. 1536
The hagi has now fallen,
    leaving Nabari field forlorn.
I wait for golden leaves
    the world now to adorn.
                    PRIEST ENUTACHI

2 songs on autumn flowers by Yamanoeno Okura
No. 1537
On my fingers do I count
    the meadow flowers of the fall,
and find their number is
    seven in all.

No. 1538
Bush clover, eulalia, arrowroot,
pinks, patrinia, agueweed,
and bellflower—these they call
the seven flowers of the fall.

2 songs by Emperor Shomu
No. 1539
It is the hour of dawn, but still 'tis dark,
    and yet already I hear wild geese cry
honk-honk in a flock
    up in the tranquil sky.

No. 1540
Coldly cry wild geese this morning,
and the sedge in the field is colored red.

2 songs by Ohtomono Tabito
No. 1541
To our hillock comes a stag
among the hagi flowers which
he loves much as he loves his doe.
Oh, listen to his plaintive cry.

No. 1542
The wind will scatter soon
    the hagi bloom upon our hill.
I wish some friend would come
    while the flowers are there still.

No. 1543
Behold, the hill is of a golden hue.
It seems a dyestuff is the autumn dew.
                    PRINCE MIHARA

2 songs on Tanabata by Prince Yuhara
No. 1544
Sad the Cowherd must feel now
    since the night is spent so far,
and I in sympathy
    look at the departing star.

No. 1545
O Cranes flying over
    the Silver Stream on high,
at daybreak while the Cowherd lad still lies
    with the Weaver do not cry.

No. 1546
On my way to her bower
    lies the river, and as I
cross it avoiding others' eyes
    already dawn is nigh.
                    PRINCE ICHIWARA

No. 1547

The stag left pearls unbrushed-off from the hagi

. . . .

who will so adorn his arm?

FUJIWARANO YATSUKA

Note: The meaning of the central line seems
to be lost beyond recovery.

No. 1548

I love not flowers that open
too early and soon fall away.
I love that which, though tardy, keeps
long, and enjoys each given day.

OHTOMONO SAKANOENO IRATSUME

No. 1549

I'll cull the flowers of pinks on Tomi Hill
and take them to my friend at Nara town.

IKINO KABITO

No. 1550

The hagi scattered falls,
and from afar we hear,
coming on the air,
the plaintive cries of deer.

PRINCE YUHARA

No. 1551

The autumn rain
has fallen many a day,
and soon on the hill we'll see
the leaves all colored gay.

PRINCE ICHIHARA

No. 1552

Upon this moonlit night
when I feel so lonely, I
hear in my dewy garden
short-lived crickets cry.

PRINCE YUHARA

No. 1553

After the ceaseless rain
we now
behold on Mt. Kikasa
golden leaves on every bough.

OHTOMONO INAKIMI

No. 1554

Have the leaves on Mt. Mikasa fallen away
in the heartless rainstorm of today?

OHTOMONO YAKAMOCHI

No. 1555

Time flies! Since fall set in
but a few days are gone,
and yet already coldly
blows the wind of morn.

PRINCE AKI

No. 1556

The shed built for the keeper
of the fields is still standing,
and yet already wild geese cry
so coldly in the frosty sky.

IMIBENO KUROMARO

3 songs at a feast in the nunnery of the deserted capital

No. 1557

Hagi were blowing
on the hillock at the bend
of the Asuka River.
Will they fall with this shower?

TAJIHINO KUNIHITO

No. 1558

With good acquaintances
did I enjoy
the autumn hagi blooming
amid the crying quails of the deserted capital.

A nun

No. 1559

The hagi season is now passing,
and will you leave
without adorning your hair
with their flowering sprigs?

A priest

2 songs by Ohtomono Sakanoeno Iratsume

No. 1560

O autumn Hagi
upon Hatsumi Promontery,
never, never let your flowers fall
this month before I take delight.

No. 1561

Pathetic sound the cries of stags
now coming on the air.
They are belling for their mates
upon Mt. Ikai.

No. 1562

Who heard the wild geese fly,
crying for their mates?
How sweet the sound!
                    Daughter of KAMUKONO MASO

In reply
by Ohtomono Yakamochi
No. 1563

The crying wild geese
of which you ask me
went farther, farther on
among the floating clouds.

No. 1564

On hagi flowers is laid
    the morning dew,
but soon 'twill perish
    like me who waste in love for you.
                    Daughter of HEKINO NAGAE

No. 1565

I'm doubly glad to welcome you,
    for if today you came not to my bower,
our hagi bush must have
    vainly been in flower.
                    OHTOMONO YAKAMOCHI

4 songs by Ohtomono Yakamochi
No. 1566

Despite the dreary rain
    there among
the clouds geese go
    singing their song.

No. 1567

As wild geese fly above,
winging for the fields of autumn which
are bright with golden rice ears rich,
so do I yearn for you, my love.

No. 1568

Long was I kept indoors
    by the rain both day and night.
Now I go out and see
    Mt. Kasuga colored red and bright.

No. 1569

O Clouds, pray, do not come
    to hide the clear moonlight;
now the rain has passed,
    and lovely is the night.

2 songs by Fujiwarano Yatsuka
No. 1570

Alas, the rain
    falling day and night,
I must remain
    indoors, yearning for Kasuga's sight.

No. 1571

The rain is falling on Kasuga field,
    and Mt. Takamado soon will wear,
golden leaves, and we
    too prank therewith our hair.

No. 1572

I wish that I could keep the dew
    on our obana flowers laid,
stringing it on a thread, as we
    do jewels for a maid.
                    OHTOMONO YATSUKA

No. 1573

A traveler now wet
    all through with rain, I feel forlorn,
yearning for the cottage where
    my dear wife lives alone.
                    OHTOMONO MURAKAMI

7 songs at a feast held by Tachibanano Moroe,
Minister of the Right
No. 1574

I live far, far away
    as is the cloudy zone,
but only to see you,
    my friend, I came alone.

No. 1575

Coldly cry the geese
    among the clouds. Now is the time
when hagi leaves on lower sprays
    are colored red by rime.

No. 1576

As hunters try all means
to catch deer on the hill,
so will I do
to please my lord.

                KOSOBENO TSUSHIMA

2 songs by Abeno Mushimaro

No. 1577

Pushing apart obana flowers
of the autumn meadow,
here I came, and to reward my labor
I now see you, my lord, before me.

No. 1578

Coldly crying,
wild geese went this morning,
and the sedge on the autumn field
has begun to color.

2 songs by Fumino Imiki Umakai

No. 1579

I opened sliding doors this autumn morning,
feeling melancholy;
then I saw our hagi
all white with dew drops.

No. 1580

The hagi flowers,
    bitten by the rime,
have fallen on the meadow
    where stags come from time to time.

11 songs at a banquet held
by Tachibanano Naramaro

2 songs by the host

No. 1581

How regretful it would be,
    should the maple leaves fall ere
I pluck some twigs to deck my locks!
    I have been thinking, but here one I wear.

No. 1582

This is a maple spray with golden leaves
    I brought to show my guest,
braving the rain. You see
    the colored leaves are at their best.

No. 1583

I came here in this ceaseless rain
    which wets the maple leaves now red and
        bright;
and with the golden twig you gave
    my hair is dight.

                PRINCESS KUME

No. 1584

This is the truth:
    you are as full
of grace as maple leaves
    adorning the hill of fall.

            Daughter of NAGANO IMAKI

No. 1585

The maple leaves on Nara Hill
fall now at a touch.
So brittle are they made
by autumn rains.

              INUKAINO YOSHIO

No. 1586

Whenever I behold the fall
    of golden leaves, I can't but grieve.
So I brought a maple twig,
    wearing it in my hair this eve.

              INUKAINO MOCHIO

No. 1587

Perhaps red maple leaves
    this evening drifting, jump and leap
down the rapids of the stream
    beneath the mountain deep.

            OHTOMONO FUMIMOCHI

No. 1588

I brought some leaves from Nara Hill,
    to wear this evening in my hair,
and little now about the foliage
    of the forest do I care.

            MITESHIRONO HITONA

No. 1589

I see the leaves so beautified by frost
    the lovely maids wear in their hair.
Now, for the foliage of the woods
    nothing soever do I care.
                        HATANO KOBEMARO

No. 1590

The maple tree leaves of October
    rain-beaten and now frail,
scattered by a gust of wind,
    soon on the air will sail.
                        OHTOMONO IKENUSHI

No. 1591

Lest golden leaves fall soon,
    together we have met, and I
desire this memorable night
    will last long, for eternity.
                        OHTOMONO YAKAMOCHI

2 songs by Ohtomonono Sakanoeno Iratsume
No. 1592

Alas,
now in my cottage by the fields
I sit surrounded by the golden grain,
and think of the capital in vain.

No. 1593

Mt. Hatsuse is all clad in crimson.
Has an autumn shower fallen on the mountain?

Recited accompanied by the koto
before the Buddha's Image by several persons
No. 1594

O Rain, descend not, pray,
both night and day,
for sad 'twould be
the fallen leaves to see.

No. 1595

Even though I perish
like the dew on hagi branches,
I'll keep my love for thee
hidden well in me.
                        OHTOMONO KATAMI

At the gate of a maiden
by Ohtomono Yakamochi
No. 1596

I came to view the paddy fields
    beside the bower of my love
whom, alas, I can not see.
    Only the moon is shining bright above.

3 autumn songs by Ohtomono Yakamochi
No. 1597

The hagi flowering
    now in the field are blown
by the cold wind, sparkling
    with dew upon them sown.

No. 1598

A buck stands in the autumn field
    pranked with flowering hagi, and on them
is laid the morning dew.
    each drop sparkling like a gem.

No. 1599

Behold, the hagi flowers
    scattered lie:
perhaps their time was come,
    or bucks passed by.

2 songs by Ishikawano Hironari
No. 1600

The hagi of the mountain
    whereon the stag oft cries
for his doe are falling now
    to the ground where the cold frost lies.

No. 1601

Alas, the autumn's passing by
    though the obana by the bower
of my love are so beautiful,
    the cold wind swaying their white flower.

2 songs on deer by Ohtomono Yakamochi
No. 1602

I live alone beside a hill
    where bucks bell for their does
until in echo after echo
    the plaintive crying goes.

No. 1603

I hear the crying of a stag
for his mate somewhere far away,
echoing and reechoing
through the morning woods.

On the deserted capital, Nara
by Oharano Imaki

No. 1604

Whenever autumn came, we used to take
    joy in the golden foliage here
on lovely Mt. Kasuga, but alas,
    our Nara town is now deserted, drear.

No. 1605

Does the hagi bush
    upon Mt. Takamado bear
flowers now, prompted by
    the morning dew so fresh and fair?

OHTOMONO YAKAMOCHI

No. 1606

Same as No. 488

No. 1607

Same as No. 489

No. 1608

Alas, I waste in love,
and wish to perish
like dew upon the hagi flowers
that soon will vanish.

Recited by PRINCE YUGE

No. 1609

Even the stag that goes
pushing apart the hagi bush on Uda Field,
could not yearn so much
after his mate as I yearn for my love.

TAJIHINO MAHITO

To Ohtomono Tabito by Princess Nifu

No. 1610

The pinks in bloom on Takamado field
every one was proud of wearing once
are now neglected, since
things are no longer as they used to be.

No. 1611

I love him from my heart:
    a gentleman of few words he,
and husband true of mine,
    whose image dwells in me.

PRINCESS KASANUI

No. 1612

Though not young I could accept
    your offer now, but sad am I,
for I would needs betray myself:
    I took a vow to single die.

ISHIKAWANO KAKENO OMINA

No. 1613

You were gone like a deer
that speeds at morning
across the autumn field,
leaving no trace;
but again to my delight,
I meet you now.

PRINCESS KAMO

To Emperor Shomu
by Lord Sakurai

No. 1614

O Wild geese of September,
why not bring me a royal message?

In reply by Emperor Shomu

No. 1615

I send no word,
but ever think of you
like waves that run,
seeking for the beach.

To Ohtomono Yakamochi by Kasano Otome

No. 1616

Every morning by my bower
    flowering pinks I see.
Oh how I wish that you were here
    to rejoice with me.

To Ohtomono Yakamochi
by Princess Yamaguchi
No. 1617

When the wind blows, as the dew cascades
from off the hagi branches,
so, yearning after you,
my tears are ever falling.

To a maiden by Prince Yuhara
No. 1618

Keep the pearls of dew,
    stringing them as they
are laid upon the leaves
    of autumn hagi spray!

No. 1619

Oh have sympathy
    for me, my dear,
for though the way was long,
    yearning, came I here.
                    OHTOMONO YAKAMOCHI

In reply by Ohtomono Sakanoeno Iratsume
No. 1620

The month has passed. How fleet
but sad, because we could not meet;
and nightly in my dream, my dear,
did I see you appear.

No. 1621

The hagi are in flower
beside my humble bower.
Come to see them, for they
in a few days will pass away.
                    Daughter of KAMUKOBENO MASO

2 songs to Ohtomono Sakanoeno Ohkiiratsume
by Tamurano Ohkiiratsume
No. 1622

The hagi in my garden
    have broken into flower;
and what delight, could I have you
    come at the twilight hour.

No. 1623

Whenever I behold these maple leaves
    all crimson here
in my garden,
    I am reminded of you, Sister dear.

To Ohtomono Yakamochi
by Sakanoeno Ohkiiratsume
No. 1624

This garland is made of the ears
    of rice from fields of mine.
Look at it, and think of me
    ever proud of being thine.

In reply by Ohtomono Yakamochi
No. 1625

With thanks I now receive thy gift—
    the rice-eared garland fine.
I never tire of seeing
    this handicraft of thine.

No. 1626

Now I wear the robe, your gift,
    since the wind blows cold and drear,
thinking of you with love
    and gratitude, my dear.
                    OHTOMONO YAKAMOCHI

2 songs to Ohtomono Sakanoeno Ohkiiratsume
by Ohtomono Yakamochi
No. 1627

Wistarias in my garden are
    blooming out of season, and the grace
thereof reminds me
    of the charming smile upon your face.

No. 1628

This is our hagi
with leaves now golden,
though the autumn wind
is not yet blowing.

To his wife, Lady Sakanoeno Ohkiiratsume
by Ohtomono Yakamochi
No. 1629

We went out hand in hand into the garden
in the morning,
and slept in the selfsame bed
at night,
yet 'twas but a short time.
Even a pheasant flies across the gorge
to meet his mate upon the peak,
but now, alas, I have to sigh in vain.
To soothe my heart I roam about the field,
but sweet flowers only make me languish
more for you.

Hanka

No. 1630

Even the flowers in Takamado field
remind me of my darling wife.

To Abeno Otome
by Ohtomono Yakamochi

No. 1631

Ah me, alone
    in this capital new
I lie the livelong night
    yearning for you.

To his wife, Sakanoeno Ohkiiratsume
by Ohtomono Yakamochi

No. 1632

I live beneath the hill
    of the capital new,
and in the autumn wind
    I yearn for you.

2 songs sent to a nun by a man

No. 1633

A hagi did I plant,
    and for its growth took care.
Now 'tis in flower
    so lovely, and so fair.

> Note says a story of interest must lurk behind.

No. 1634

Over the paddy field for which
    I stained my clothes with soil,
I like a scarecrow watch
    after daytime's toil.

A nun composed the first part of the following
lines, but could not go on, and
Ohtomono Yakamochi completed the verse
for her, being asked to.

No. 1635

The rice set in the fields
    with water drawn from little streams
is reaped by others than the one
    who finally eats the grain, it seems.

WINTER MISCELLANEOUS SONGS

No. 1636

O Snow, descending on Magami Field,
    do not fall without a break,
for nowhere now
    shelter can I take.

> Daughter of a gentleman-in-waiting

No. 1637

This chamber built with barkèd wood
brought from the grove nearby,
and thatched with obana stems
shall stand a thousand years.

> EMPEROR GENSHO

No. 1638

We like this cottage built with trees
    cut and from Mt. Nara brought.
However oft we look,
    it tires us not.

> EMPEROR SHOMU

No. 1639

Incessantly the snow
    comes lightly down,
reminding me, who live afar,
    of Nara town.

> OHTOMONO TABITO

No. 1640

The plum trees on my hill
    are in full bloom, and oh,
I mistake the flowers
    for the fallen snow.

> OHTOMONO TABITO

No. 1641

Behold, our plums have bloomed
prompted by the recent snowfall.
I wish to offer you a spray,
but would it raise a rumor?

> TSUNUNO HIRONARI

No. 1642

Let the sky be overcast,
　　　and snow descend. Then I will get
joy therefrom instead
　　　of the plum flowers not opened yet.
　　　　　　　　　　ABENO OKIMICHI

No. 1643

Let the sky be overcast,
　　　and snow descend; then I will see
the copse all wrapped in white
　　　with the remainder of the scenery.
　　　　　　　　WAKASAKURABENO KIMITARI

No. 1644

If I pull and break a twig of scarlet plum
　　　the flowers will scattered fall and lie
upon the ground, but if I put them in my sleeve,
　　　it will be colored with their lovely dye.
　　　　　　　　　　MINUNO ISOMORI

No. 1645

The snow has fallen
　　　on our trees all bare;
and I enjoy the view,
　　　fancying plums are blooming fair.
　　　　　　　　　KOSENO SUKUNAMARO

No. 1646

To enjoy the fallen snow
　　　let us go out at once,
for if it vanish by the morrow,
　　　we shall lose the chance.
　　　　　　　　OWARIDANO AZUMAMARO

No. 1647

Like small plum petals
that flutter down
the snow is falling
wind-blown.

　　　　　　　　　IMBENO KUROMARO

No. 1648

O Plum tree, are you not aware
　　　that in December you'll have snow ?
Why not remain in bud awhile,
　　　why in this season blow?
　　　　　　　　　　KINO OSHIKA

No. 1649

Behold, the plum trees by my bower
have broken into flower,
vying with the snow
spread o'er the garden now.
　　　　　　　　OHTOMONO YAKAMOCHI

No. 1650

Let the snow fall on,
　　　and dress the garden pines in white
that on the morrow too
　　　I may enjoy the sight.

　　　　　　　　　　　　ANON.

No. 1651

The snow's been falling
　　　day after day.
I fear our plum flowers soon
　　　will pass away.
　　　　　　OHTOMONO SAKANOENO IRATSUME

No. 1652

Beautiful plum flowers have I seen,
　　　and sometimes plucked them off the trees,
lured by their grace,
　　　but by far the best are these.
　　　　　　Daughter of OSADANO HIROTSU

Note:　Perhaps written, admiring the plum
　　　　flowers at a banquet.

No. 1653

If nature loved flowers as you love me,
the newly-opened blossom would not fall
scattered by the wind,
but last for ever.
　　　　　　Daughter of AGATANO INUKAI

Note:　Motoori Norinaga says this verse was
　　　　perhaps written by a girl newly wed.

No. 1654

Lovely the snow laid on the sedge
　　　beneath the pine ! Is there no way
to keep the snow as it is now,
　　　and not to let it fade away?
　　　　　　OHTOMONO SAKANOENO IRATSUME

WINTER LOVE SONGS

No. 1655

Alas, I pine with love, and soon will perish
like the snow now on the sage leaves lying.
MIKUNINO HITOTARI

No. 1656

We'll put plum petals in our cups,
    and drink with saké, Comrades gay.
Then after that we shall not care
    if all the blossoms fall away.
OHTOMONO SAKANOENO IRATSUME

In response to the above
No. 1657

The law does not forbid us
    to hold a feast if small,
and we'll have more of them.
    So, Plums, let not your blossoms fall.
ANON.

To Emperor Shohmu
by Empress Kohmyo
No. 1658

My dearest Lord, if only I
    together with you now could see
the snow descending from the sky,
    in what joy I would be!

No. 1659

Though snow is falling ceaselessly,
come, my love, tonight to me.
Daughter of OSADANO HIROTSU

No. 1660

Oft have I heard about
    your beauty, and now I
see you to my delight
    before my eye.
OHTOMONO SURUGAMARO

No. 1661

The moon is clear tonight,
    and in full blossom my plum tree,
and oh! best of all here
    my darling do I see.
LADY KINO OSHIKA

To Sakanoeno Ohkiiratsume
by Ohtomono Tamurano Ohkiiratsume
No. 1662

Like snow I should have gone
long ago, but I live on.
Why, but to see you, my own.

No. 1663

On this cold night when snow falls ceaselessly,
without my love alone in bed I lie.
OHTOMONO YAKAMOCHI

THE MANYOSHU

BOOK IX

FOREWORD

This volume is divided into 3 parts: miscellaneous songs, love songs and elegies. Among the miscellaneous songs there are 12 longer lays, one Sedohka, and 89 verselets. Some of them were written on the occasion of royal progresses and other travels. The story of Urashima also seems to have been composed on the site. As to the love songs there are 5 longer lays and 24 verselets, and the elegies 5 longer lays and 12 verselets.

Taken as a whole, there are 22 longer lays, one Sedohka, and 125 verselets.

Broadly speaking, they are chronologically arranged, the oldest being the song by Emperor Yuryaku, which appears at the beginning of the book. One outstanding peculiarity of this volume is that it is rich in songs dealing with legend.

MISCELLANEOUS SONGS

No. 1664

When night falls,
    the cries of deer come from our mountain
      deep,
but no belling do I hear this eve.
    Are they then all gone to sleep?
              EMPEROR YURYAKU

No. 1665

O Billows of the offing, bring
    rare stones ashore
that I may gather them
    for her whom I adore.

                    ANON.

No. 1666

Does my husband go his way
clad in garments dripping
with morning mist
now along some mountain path?

                    ANON.

*13 songs written on the occasion when
Empress Jito went to Kii Province*

No. 1667

Same as No. 1665

No. 1668

O pretty Promontory,
    remain as you are, for again will we
come in a ship equipped
    with many oars your view to see.

No. 1669

Let no tide come into Minabe Bay,
    for I will go awhile
to see the men
    fishing on the offshore isle.

No. 1670

At dawn I will row out
    upon the ocean, there to see
the men at fishing
    off Yura Promontory.

No. 1671

The tide is ebbing
    at Yura Promontory,
and the boatmen rowing
    for the shore I see.

No. 1672

Pretty the girl that goes
    there at ebb tide,
sporting her scarlet skirt.
    She seems to be a bride.

No. 1673

Windless, the sea is calm today;
    only the waves come, breaking white
along the lovely shore, but none
    except myself enjoy the sight.
              NAGANO OKIMARO

No. 1674

Yearning for my love at home
who waits for word from me,
I pass this grove of Idetachi
with its lovely pines.

No. 1675

As I go over Fujishiro Slope
where Prince Arima met his end,
the tears run down my way-worn cheeks,
wetting my sleeves.

No. 1676

On Mt. Se golden maple leaves are falling now.
Are they falling too on Kamunabi's brow?

No. 1677

No one knows at home,
    that I fare sound,
living in a hut on Ohga Field
    with bamboo leaves spread on the ground.

No. 1678

This is the famed slope where
    in olden times a hunter is said
to have shot many deer with arrows—
    each with its turnip-shapèd head.

No. 1679

O God enshrined deep in the Woods of Spouse,
I will go to Kii
to see the namesake of your sacred place.
So let me meet my darling at her house.

No. 1680

My lord is journeying in Kii,
and 'tis today
for him to traverse Mt. Matsuchi.
May no rain come on now.

No. 1681

Yearning for my lover who
    is gone awhile, at home I stay forlorn;
while he perhaps is crossing now
    some cloud-capped mountain all alone.

No. 1682

Living in the mountain deep
where winter comes soon after summer,
a warm fur coat together
with a cooling fan I keep.

2 songs to Prince Toneri

No. 1683

The trees are blooming fair.
Now is the time for us to wear
these blossoms in our hair.

No. 1684

The cherry flowers on other hills
    have fallen away,
but the trees upon Mt. Miwa
    still burgeoning stay.

*2 songs written by the River Izumi
by Hashibitono Sukune*

No. 1685

Izumi's river
flows on for ever—
in pools now swirls,
now runs in rapids, tossing spray like pearls.

No. 1686

Perhaps the Cowherd shook his head,
    yearning for the Weaver maid,
and now the loosened gems that decked
    his locks are falling in cascade.

No. 1687

As night is spent, and still
so far the town, beneath this pine upon the hill,
waiting for daybreak,
shelter I will take.

No. 1688

I have no woman here
    for dripping clothes to care.
Shall I send them home
    to show how I fare?

No. 1689

Make your vessel sail along the bay
that I may longer see you go away.

No. 1690

The angry waves are roaring in the Ado River,
    but little do I care.
My thought is only of my home,
    and how you fare.

No. 1691

My sole companion is the moon
    now that I am a traveler lone;
but she goes down behind Mt. Takashima,
    leaving me alone.

No. 1692

Far away from home I rove,
    and again this eve
must lay my head at Tama Cove
    on my own lonely sleeve.

No. 1693

Calm is the night. How I would wish
    it would not dawn, were I at home this eve,
sleeping with my wife,
    but now alone I lie, my head upon my sleeve.

No. 1694

O white Azaleas on Mt. Sagisaka,
    let my garments catch your scent so sweet
to please my darling wife
    when again we meet.

No. 1695

Yonder on the river rocks
    the snow yet lingering
compells me to remember
    'tis winter still, not spring.

3 songs written by Nagi's stream

No. 1696

Does my wife at home
    know I am wet
with vernal rain
    by Nagi's rivulet?

No. 1697

Is it a messenger from my family—
this spring rain
which, turn how'er I may,
insists on being intimate with me?

No. 1698

I wish that I had some one who
    would dry my clothes for me.
Oh who is it that sends rain
    as messenger? Does she?

2 songs written by the River Uji

No. 1699

Listen, the inlet is resounding
    with the flapping of wild geese, and I
behold the honking flock
    winging their way on high.

No. 1700

I hear the flapping of geese in the sky,
and the rapids here
are roaring and resounding
in the cold autumn wind.

3 songs to Prince Yuge

No. 1701

The night is far advanced
    and from the sky
comes the honking of wild geese,
    where the moon is sailing placidly.

No. 1702

'Tis toward my home the wild geese go,
    crying in the sky
veiled in evening vapor.
    With envy I see them and sigh.

No. 1703

When wild geese cry
hidden in the foggy autumn air,
I crave to see the distant hills
all pranked with crimson leaves.

2 songs to Prince Toneri

No. 1704

The mist is thick that veils Mt. Tamu.
    And surely on that ground
the rapids in the River Hoso
    roar without cease, and resound.

No. 1705

I set a tiny tree,
    and lo, it is in flower.
Now I desire to see its fruit,
    and eagerly await that hour.

No. 1706

Behold, on this bright moonlit night
there hangs a mist,
half hiding yonder hill.
Oh what a lovely sight.

PRINCE TONERI

No. 1707

Oh how sacred is this hill
where, since the age of Gods,
in springtime trees have broken into leaf;
shed foliage, scattered by the autumn wind.

No. 1708

Alas, the wild goose goes
        over the hill indifferently,
bringing no word
        from home to me.

No. 1709

A votive offering!
On the Mountain of the Southern Pools
is fallen snow still clinging to the rocks?
                    KAKINOMOTONO HITOMARO

2 songs by Kakinomotono Hitomaro
No. 1710

This is the famous Kuranashi* beach,
which brings to mind my love I left behind
who plants rice, scarlet skirt tucked up,
but has no barn to put the harvest in.
        * Meaning "no storehouse."

No. 1711

Many an island did I pass,
        but none is worth my while
to go again to see
        except this Awa Isle.

Composed on Mt. Tsukuba, viewing the moon
No. 1712

The moon I love
is sailing now above
upon this cloudless night
serene and bright.

*2 songs written on the occasion of the Imperial
Visit to the Yoshino Palace*
No. 1713

From Mt. Mifune
        soaring above the waterfall
I hear a cuckoo sing.
        Oh whom, I wonder, does he call?

No. 1714

The current, falling, swirling, runs
        after gnawing rocks to rest
in an eddying pool,
        mirroring the moon upon its breast.
                    ANON.

No. 1715

The gale sweeps down the peak of Hira,
and passes o'er the waves
where I see angling fishermen
with fluttering sleeves.
                    YAMANOENO OKURA

No. 1716

How many years have passed
        since votive offerings first were tied
on the branches of this pine
        here at the beautiful seaside?
                    PRINCE KAWASHIMA

No. 1717

Everywhere along the stream,
        both in pools and rapids, I
cast my net, and am wet all through,
        but have no maid my clothes to dry.
                    KASUGANO OYU

No. 1718

Did that ship I saw
leading many others reach
the River Ado
to anchor for the night?
                    TAKECHINO KUROHITO

No. 1719

O Clouds, do not conceal the moon,
        for behind the isle
now I will moor my boat, but in the dark
        'twill be hard toil.
                    KASUGANO OYU

*3 songs by Genni
at the River Yoshino*
No. 1720

We all went to the river bank,
        riding abreast; and drawing rein,
took pleasure in the fine view of the stream.
        There will I not repair again?

No. 1721

The night is come,
        which deeply I regret,
for I have not enjoyed my fill
        of the landscape yet.

No. 1722

The wind is high, the crested waves
    are raving in the stream.
I must leave the falls unseen,
    and will about them only dream.

No. 1723

Matsuda's stream is lined with sallows green,
    where singing frogs so sweetly trill—
How fair the brook of which
    I only wish I could behold my fill.
                                        KINU

No. 1724

How sweet the murmur of Yoshino's stream!
To see its view has been my cherished dream.

No. 1725

I ne'er tire of Yoshino's view.
How our forbears loved it too!

No. 1726

O Maiden, gathering ocean herbs
    on this seaside,
tell me your name, and pray,
    become my bride.
                            TAJIHINO MAHITO

In reply
No. 1727

Regard me only as a maid
    who culls herbs of the brine,
and do not ask a stranger's name
    as now you query mine.

No. 1728

I'll be with you tonight,
    but from tomorrow on,
without you, oh
    how shall I live alone?
                                LORD ISHIKAWA

3 songs by Fujiwarano Umakai
No. 1729

This dawn again I dreamed
    of you, for as the wave
yearns for the shore,
    so do I my darling crave.

No. 1730

Where is my traveler?
    does he go
now along the mountain path
    overlooking Yamashina's oaks below?

No. 1731

If I offer gifts
    to the god enshrined
in the woods of Yamashina,
    can I see my darling kind?

No. 1732

The mist is hanging o'er Mt. Oba;
    and far advanced the night.
Oh where should we cast anchor
    without a landmark now in sight?

No. 1733

Fascinated,
    I left the promontory,
but so fair the landscape,
    I went the view again to see.

No. 1734

Has my traveler passed Ado Bay,
    and is he rowing on today
about other coves
    as beautiful as the bay?

No. 1735

Hark to the sweetest melody
    the stream frogs pour,
rejoicing in their home
    upon the shady pebbled shore.

No. 1736

How beautiful the landscape!
Hemmed in by lofty mountains,
Natsume runs in rapids
with foam like cotton flowers.

No. 1737

After passing the Great Fall,
I strolled along the stream so sweet.
And oh how beautiful the landscape
I saw beyond the rapids!

No. 1738

At Sue bordering on Awa Province
there lived Tamana, maiden fair.
Her breast was broad—the beauty's breast;
her waist was narrow as a belted bee's.
She was so pretty to behold
that when she smiling stood, she looked
like an open flower. The passers-by
entered her gate, as if spell-bound.
One of her neighbors, leaving his old spouse,
gave her all his keys without her asking.
Thus people catering to her fancies,
she kept on her coquettish ways.

Hanka

No. 1739

When anyone stood at her gate,
    even though it were midnight,
she forgot about herself,
    and always came out, smiling bright.

"The Young Man of Urashima"
A narrative poem, author unknown

No. 1740

When I stroll on a hazy day of spring
    about the shore of Suminoe Cove
the sight of fishing boats ne'er fails to bring
    to mind the ancient story that I love.

A lad of Urashima went to roam,
    proud of his skill, bonito, bream to take.
For seven days he sailed away from home—
    over the ocean quiet as a lake.
He came across a maiden sweet and fair.
    This young girl was a goddess of the sea.
He talked and talked with her and lost all care
    except to wed her. So with gladness he
married the maid; and in the Palace there—
    in its grand chamber in superlative
joy and delight they led a life so rare.
    And so it might have been his luck to live
most blessed and free from age and death;
    had not the folly of the worldly lad
led him to tell his bride with bated breath
        that he must leave her for some time, though
            sad,

to see his parents and with them to speak.
    But he would come back very soon, he said.
At this the bride asked with a manner meek,
    if he desired to come back to her bed—
and truly wished to live again as now—
    to take but not unclose her gift of love,
she earnestly implored; he gave his vow.

    Now when upon the old shore of the cove
our youth stood, not a house could there be seen,
    nor yet the near-by village once he knew.
In his surprise, before the puzzling scene,
    the boy considered it was but a few
summers he'd been away. What was amiss?
    If he but looked into the box, could he
not find his home again and feel its bliss?
    So thinking, he half opened it to see
the secret, when all suddenly he saw
    a thick white cloud appear, curl up, and flow
Horai-ward. Crying he rose in awe
        and waved his sleeves,—ran, stumbled, fell,
            and lo !
writhing the poor wretch fainted presently.
    His skin was now all wrinkled, and his hair
jet-black before, now white as white could be;
    and his faint breath expirèd then and there.
The end was come: there lay the body cold.

I see the village where he lived of old.

Hanka

No. 1741

Had the lad but had the wit to follow
    her command, together happily
they might have lived
    for eternity.

*Seeing a girl crossing the great bridge
of Kawachi*

No. 1742

O'er the vermilion-painted bridge
which spans the river Katashiwa
a lovely maiden goes
in clothes of blue and red.
I wonder if she has a husband,
if she sleeps alone at night.
O would I not ask it of her,
if but I knew her whereabouts?

Hanka

No. 1743

If near Ohashi Bridge
  I had a cottage of my own,
would I not let her come in
  and rest, who now is walking all alone?

No. 1744

Here in Sakitama,
in the marsh of Osaki,
the mallard, waking,
flaps his wings, and beats
from off his tail
the night-laid frost.

No. 1745

I like to view this spring
  ever gushing out. O what delight,
if I could have a love
  like the fountain beaming bright!

No. 1746

Alas, my wife is far away.
If she lived in Taka,
she would come to meet me here
upon this beautiful Tazuna Beach.

No. 1747

The cherry flowers above the falls
of Mt. Tatsuta have half fallen,
because the wind blows hard upon the lofty peak,
and there the rain falls ceaselessly;
but let the lower trees their flowers keep
until you who now start return.

No. 1748

I shall return within days seven,
so scatter not the flowers, oh Wind of heaven!

No. 1749

As I go over Mt. Tatsuta in the gloaming,
the cherry flowers above the falls are falling,
but elsewhere I see trees in bud which will soon
  blow.
Though all the trees may not be decked with
  bloom,
methinks it is time for the Emperor to come.

No. 1750

Had I time enough,
would I not wade across the river,
and climbing up the opposite hill,
take some flowering cherry branches home?

No. 1751

Yesterday I came along the mountain path,
and saw the cherry trees abloom.
Today, returning by the selfsame route,
I found the stream with petals strewn.
I fear the blossoms will not wait the royal call.

No. 1752

I wish I had my love with me beside this rill
to view the cherry trees in flower upon the hill.

No. 1753

Lord Ohtomo came to see
twin-peaked Tsukuba in Hitachi Province.
We climbed with him, perspiring,
clinging to the roots of trees;
and lo, the god of the one peak,
and goddess of the other blessed us,
for the sun shone upon the mountain
usually veiled in clouds.
We could view the landscape spread below,
standing on the brow so dense with summer grass.

No. 1754

The men of old went up Tsukuba, and enjoyed
  the view.
Today we climbed the sacred mountain too.

No. 1755

A cuckoo hatched within an uguisu nest
could not warble like his foster parents.
He came flying from the field
where the utsugi were abloom,
and perching on our orange tree,
sang throughout the day.
O Cuckoo, do not go away,
but in our garden stay.

No. 1756

Upon this rainy night do I
hear a cuckoo in the murky sky.

On climbing Mt. Tsukuba

No. 1757

I climbed up Mt. Tsukuba
to console me during my long travel,
heard wild geese coldly crying
above obana-falling Shizuku field,
saw white waves rolling
down in Toba Lake.
Truly I enjoyed the view;
it banished all my troubles in my bosom.

No. 1758

I'll break a spray of crimson leaves
upon the peak
to give it to a maid
who reaps the autumn fields below.

On a poetry party upon Mt. Tsukuba

No. 1759

Upon the eagle-dwelling Mt. Tsukuba
young girls and men assemble at a poetry party.
For the evening they are free.
Now men can lie with others' wives.
What the mountain godhead wills,
we must obey.

No. 1760

Even though clouds come,
and showers drench my sleeve,
this poetry party
will I not leave.

No. 1761

On Mt. Mikaki standing opposite Mt. Mimuro
in the early morning moonlight
stags cry for hinds to come and lie together
beneath the hagi flowers.

Hanka

No. 1762

If hinds come not tonight, they will tomorrow.
Why should the stags cry as in sorrow?
KAKINOMOTONO HITOMARO

No. 1763

Because the mountains are so high,
    the moon that rises late
at night is hindered, and for her
    to come out long have I to wait.
LADY SAMI

No. 1764

In the upper reach of the Celestial River
will I build a bridge,
and in the lower reach range boats
for my love to come to me
whether rain may fall
or wind may blow.

No. 1765

Is my lover coming now to me,
for spray upon the Heavenly Stream I see?

LOVE SONGS

No. 1766

Where my love a ring,
    I would wear her upon my hand,
and together we would travel
    in whatever land.
FURUTAMUKE SUKUNE

*3 songs by Nukikeno Ohito on marrying
Himonoko, maiden of Buzen Province*

No. 1767

This house I call my own,
    for here we dwell. And thou art mine,
my darling love. Together
    we live, and I am thine.

No. 1768

I show not in my face,
    but in my bosom I
love you, and ne'er a day
    without my yearning for you passes by.

No. 1769

Every day I live
    only yearning for thee.
My life I set at nought.
    Of thee am I unworthy?

2 songs at a feast held by the Hatsuse River

No. 1770

Flow on, Hatsuse,
girdle of the guardian god of Mt. Mimuro.
I love you, sacred river.
May our friendship like you last for ever.

No. 1771

You set out to trudge across the mountain
    veiled in the haze of spring,
and we left behind
    shall day and night be languishing.

To Lord Ohmiwa by Lord Abe

No. 1772

I envy you, my friend,
    who for Tsukushi start today,
and will enjoy the autumn hagi
    in Inami field upon the way.

To Prince Yuge

No. 1773

Even the lofty cedars of Kamunabi
from which the shingles come to shelter gods
tower less high than does my love for you.

No. 1774

Be filial to your mother's loving wish:
the time you have to wait is not so long.

No. 1775

Wading Hatsuse River
in the twilight,
now I approach
my truelove's bower.

2 songs to Lord Ishikawa
by a girl

No. 1776

When spring comes, and cherries on Mt. Tayuraki
  blow,
shall I not surely call you to mind, my Lord?

No. 1777

After you leave me, I will not
    care for my looks,
nor take out my comb
    to dress my locks.

To Lord Fujii by a girl

No. 1778

I shall yearn
from tomorrow for you
who will go over rocky paths
on Mt. Nahori.

In reply by Lord Fujii

No. 1779

If I survive this journey,
I will come to you again,
treading the rocky paths
on Mt. Nahori.

On seeing off Lord Ohtomo

No. 1780

When the scarlet-painted ship with jeweled oars
start from Kashima Point
at evening tide with sturdy sailors shouting loud,
we shall be standing on the seabeach,
treading on the sands.

Hanka

No. 1781

Start when the sea is quiet.
Why go now when 'tis raving?

To his wife by Kakinomotono Hitomaro

No. 1782

Why send me no word?
    Is your heart of snow
that fades away in vernal sun?
    Oh let me know.

In reply

No. 1783

I wait and wait for your return.
You come not, and I vainly yearn.

To the Envoy to China

No. 1784

I've prayed the Sea God
    for you, my friend;
so on your outward sail and in,
    may your vessel speed to journey's end!

No. 1785

How shall I live without you?
But by the royal order
you set out now, accompanied by many soldiers,
and left behind,
I shall be only yearning after you.

No. 1786

As you cross the mountain range all white
with snow, pray, think of me, my heart's delight.

No. 1787

Conscripted by the royal order,
here I lie on Furu field
in traveling clothes all dusty,
for which, were I at home,
my wife would care—
my wife I yearn for
all sleepless through this winter night.

Hanka
No. 1788

Mt. Furu overlooks the nearby city,
yet here I sleepless yearn for you.

No. 1789

Never will I loosen the sash
she bound for me, when I
left home. Should the girdle snap, it may;
but I never will untie it.

*By the mother of a man accompanying the Envoy
to China in the Tang Dynasty in 733*

No. 1790

'Tis said the doe bewitched by hagi flowers
will bear an only youngling.
Now my only son is on a weary journey.
I, piercing bamboo bits on a thread,
and decking saké jugs with cotton to appease the
  gods,
pray daily for his safe return.

Hanka
No. 1791

If frost should fall upon the field
    where, tired at night our travelers rest,
cover my darling with your wings,
    O Cranes that fly on high abreast.

No. 1792

I love a girl fair as a pearl,
but whom I seldom meet.
She dwells so deep in me
like the water flowing under fallen leaves.

No. 1793

Like a fence is others' gossip:
many months I have not seen her.

No. 1794

The days and months have passèd by,
but still is she before my eye.

ELEGIES

No. 1795

The prince is gone
who once beheld
the leafy pines
on yonder hill.

No. 1796

Yonder I see the old seashore
    where once we stood, my wife and I,
and am reminded of her
    in grief profound to sigh.

No. 1797

This is a wild, bleak shore,
    but I hold it dear,
for once my wife and I
    admiring it stood here.

No. 1798

Forlorn lies Kuroushi Bay
    I saw before
with my beloved wife
    whose death I deplore.

No. 1799

So dear Tamatsu Island's shore,
where once my darling and I came;
I would I could imbue my very clothes
from its memory-laden sands.

Seeing a dead man upon Ashigara Pass
by Tanabeno Fukumaro
No. 1800

I see a man in homespun hempen clothes
so wasted that his sash went thrice around him.
He had left the Court behind to see his family
    at home,
and came to Ashigara Pass, disheveled, shivering.
Though passers-by now ask him where his prov-
    ince is,
where his people live,
they can get no answer from the main,
for here he lies dead and cold.

On visiting the tomb of the maiden of Ashiya
by Tanabeno Fukumaro
No. 1801

I pass the tomb where sleeps
the well-known maiden of Ashiya,
for whose hand suing, two men desperately vied.
The tomb is made of rocks, and many travelers
    come
from the far ends of this land,
and weep, calling the tragic tale to mind;
and, standing by the grassy grave,
I too shed tears anew.

Hanka
No. 1802

This is Unai's grave
wooed by two warriors brave.

No. 1803

No wonder if those men vied, everything for-
    getting.
Even today the storied beauty of the maid en-
    chants us.

On his brother's death
by Tanabeno Fukumaro
No. 1804

My beloved brother is gone
like dew by the divine will.
If but he could come back again to us!
He must be wandering now in sepulchral gloom,
and disconsolate, I only cry and moan
day after day.

No. 1805

Though parted now, could I anticipate some meet-
    ing,
I could compose my grief-disheveled mind.

No. 1806

Leaving his remains upon the mountain wild and
    lone,
they have gone home, and now we guard the tomb
    alone.

"The Maid of Mama in Katsushika"
No. 1807

This legend has been told since olden times;
A maid of Mama, named Tekona, was attired
always in hemp with a blue kerchief at her neck,
and hempen also was her skirt.
She never dressed her hair, went barefoot,
but no sweet girl, though clad in rare brocade,
could vie with her in gracefulness;
and when the flawless beauty stood
fair as a flower, all men came wooing
as summer moths fly into flames,
or boats come crowding into ports.
Now two young men sued for her hand,
setting their lives at naught to win her.
She pitied them and thought:
if I only die, they'll cease their strife,
and threw herself into the sea.
Yonder bustling harbor is where she was drowned.
It came to pass in days of yore,
yet seems to have occurred but yesterday.

Hanka
No. 1808

When I behold the Mama spring
    in Katsushika County, I
picture to myself the maid,
    lovely Tekona, standing by.

On the maiden of Ashiya

No. 1809

From the time when Unai was but a child
up to the time when as a maid she had her tresses
   hanging,
parted in the middle,
her parents kept her even from the neighbors,
but rumors of her charms drew people to the
   place.
Two warriors bearing swords and quivers
came to woo her with spindle-wood bows in hand
willing to go through fire and water for her sake.
The maiden to her mother said,
"It is not meet for men to vie for me;
I will wait for my truelove in the other world,"
and later killed herself.
That night Unai haunted
the dreams of Chinu, one of the men.
Sorrowing for her death,

he took his life, and followed her.
At the news the other man too,
gnashing his teeth, fell on his sword.
People erected three tombs in a row,
setting that of the maiden in the middle,
and of the men on either side.
This sad event seems fresh
as if it happened only yesterday.

Hanka

No. 1810

Whene'er I pass the tomb where Unai and her
   suitors lie,
reminded of the tragic tale, I weep and sigh.

No. 1811

Why should the box tree planted by the Ashiya
   maiden's grave
lean but o'er the tomb of Chinu, her suitor brave?

THE MANYOSHU

BOOK X

FOREWORD

This volume is divided into 8 parts, just as Book 8, and the classifications are the same. The only difference is that while Book 8 contains poems whose authors are known, in this book anonymous writers alone appear. Considering that the miscellaneous songs are those written on a variety of things, and the love songs are songs in metaphor, this book may be called very similar to Book 7. In brief, this volume combines the peculiarities of both Books 7 and 8.

The number of the songs is 539. Quantitatively this is by far the largest of all the books of the Manyo Anthology, made up of 3 longer lays, 4 Sedohka and 532 verselets.

As the writers are unknown, the time when the poems were written also remains unknown. There is, however, one song which is annotated as having been written in the 9th year of Emperor Temmu. And it is conjectured from the contents and manner in which they are composed, that the majority of the songs were written at the beginning of the Tempyo Period.

MISCELLANEOUS SONGS OF SPRING

No. 1812

Lo, hanging over yonder hill
    I see the first mist of this year.
Winter is gone, and now the spring,
    the happy spring is here.

No. 1813

I came to you, my love,
    longing, yearning for you.
If I love you not,
    why am I now before you?

No. 1814

Behold, upon yon mountain
    with ancient cedar trees
a mist hangs.
    So 'tis spring with balmy breeze.

No. 1815

Mt. Makimuku clad with verdant foliage
is all hidden now in vernal mist.

No. 1816

Now in the twilight sky
    Mt. Yuzuki's seen
half concealed in mist,
    soaring serene.

No. 1817

Behold, Mt. Asazuma
    is veiled in haze;
and at the lovely view
    I, fascinated, gaze.

No. 1818

Over yon mountain cliffs
    spring vapors lie,
whereat I gaze
    and fondly sigh.

No. 1819

Spring, then, is come,
    for lo, upon our willow tree
is perched a warbler,
    singing so merrily.

No. 1820

As I sit in my hillside bower
surrounded by plums in flower,
many uguisu birds come near,
and their sweet songs I hear.

No. 1821

The vernal mist hangs over all;
    and now I hear an uguisu trill,
pecking at the willow twig
    with its tiny yellow bill.

No. 1822

Perhaps my lover now
is on Kose's brow.
So Cuckoo, fly away,
and call him back while it is day.

No. 1823

O Crow that come at dawning
to the weir, pray, do you also yearn
after your mate,
as I do for my love?

No. 1824

Spring at last has come
    and oh on field and hill
do I hear uguisu birds
    their sweetest music trill.

No. 1825

I roam the field of dayflowers
    yearning for you,
and hear the warblers.
    Are they yearning too?

No. 1826

When spring comes, uguisu
    calling for their mates, sing.
Behold, they flit from branch to branch,
    trilling as if chattering.

No. 1827

From yonder hill to Saho Town
    a cuckoo calling goes.
Whom the bird is calling
    no one knows.

No. 1828

However oft you may call, Cuckoo,
    none will reply.
Why do you townward fly now high now low,
    crying so loud across the sky?

No. 1829

Springtime it is, and since
    you live beside a hill
often you will hear
    sweet-throated uguisu trill.

No. 1830

When spring is here, the warblers come,
    touching with wings the bamboo spray,
and busily moving their small tails,
    sing among the trees and play.

No. 1831

I see a cuckoo
    fly on high,
all drenched in morning fog. And oh
    how clear his cry !

No. 1832

The spring is come,
    but still the wintry sky
is overcast with clouds,
    snow falling ceaselessly.

No. 1833

I took snow off my plum tree, and to show it you
    I tried to wrap it up with care,
but when I touched, 'twas gone,
    and naught whatever I saw there.

No. 1834

Our plums came into flower,
    and are leafy now, yet lo,
still to my garden ceaselessly
    descends untiring snow.

No. 1835

The tremulous heat waves are rising
from the ground as spring is here.
Can snow descend
still as in winter now?

No. 1836

Blown by the wind, the snow
is falling, but 'tis springtime
and often o'er yon mountain
vapor hangs low.

No. 1837

'Tis springtime, and afar among
the mountains warblers are in song,
but here in town
still tardy snow comes down.

No. 1838

Methinks these flakes come down
    not from the clouds on high, but from the
        snow
laid on the nearby mountains,
    carried by the spring gusts that now blow.

No. 1839

I went out to a marsh to gather
    herbs for you, and oh
I had my skirts all drenched
    with water from the melted snow.

No. 1840

The snow is falling everywhere
even on the wings of the uguisu
fitting from yon plum spray to spray
among the flowers twittering away.

No. 1841

From the high mountains snow comes down,
    though 'tis springtime, and I in imagination
        see
tiny plum blossoms falling,
    petal after petal, in front of me.

No. 1842

You prize plum flower so.
Why not the vernal snow?
Do you not abide
upon a mountainside?

No. 1843

The old year finished only yesterday,
    but already now
the vernal vapor veils
    Mt. Kasuga's brow.

No. 1844

Winter is over now, methinks
    and spring is come, for on
Kasuga hangs a mist
    dyed by the morning sun.

No. 1845

It is spring when
    sweet-throated warblers trill.
Now even in the evening
    haze is hanging o'er Kasuga Hill.

No. 1846

Lo, the frost-bitten willow tree
has put forth buds, and we
can plait the twigs so fair
into vernal wreaths to wear.

No. 1847

I see threads dyed in green
    hanging to dry in front of me,
but at a closer gaze I find
    that they are branches of a willow tree.

No. 1848

Snow is still falling in the mountains,
    but here already we behold
upon the willows by the river
    tiny buds unfold.

No. 1849

The mountains are still wrapped in snow,
but the willow trees which line
the raging torrent
have broken into tiny bud.

No. 1850

O Willows every morn I view,
    quickly grow into a leafy grove
where uguisu come and sing
    their sweet songs that I love.

No. 1851

Beautiful the weeping willow trees!
    O that here were a maiden fair
who could enjoy the sight with me: the breeze
    touching the branches with soft care.

No. 1852

I never tire of seeing
    these willow trees, with twigs of which
the courtiers weave
    vernal garlands fair and rich.

No. 1853

A traveler, I break a sprig
    from off a plum in flower,
and it reminds me of my home
    and budding willows by her bower.

No. 1854

As the time passes when sweet uguisu
    flit from a plum branch here
to another there, a different season
    wherein the cherry blows, draws near.

No. 1855

The cherry flowers are at their best,
    and yet they fall apace.
Do they think their short life makes
    us yearn more for their grace?

No. 1856

The spring wind comes into my garden,
    winnowing the willow trees.
Are your plum blossoms falling,
    my dear, now in the breeze?

No. 1857

The plum bloom comes year after year,
    but to me, oh
only joyless springs
    come and go.

No. 1858

Songbirds do not peck at plum flowers
    yet, apprehensively.
I stretch the votive rope
    around my tree.

No. 1859

What, I wonder, that can be
    veiling the hills in white?
Plum trees in flower
    that meet our sight?

No. 1860

Yellow roses blow,
but yield no fruit, I know;
and yet I wait and wait
for fruit despite their fate.

No. 1861

Even the Noto's bed is bright.
reflecting cherry flowers white
upon Mikasa Hill
standing serene and still.

No. 1862

When I behold the snow
'tis winter still I know;
but already vernal mist hangs there,
plums shedding petals fair.

No. 1863

The flowers she saw last year
    are open now again,
but alas, she is no more,
    and they will fall in vain.

No. 1864

I shall regret to see
    those cherry flowers
now brightening the mountain
    fall scattered in spring showers.

No. 1865

Spring is come,
    and the cherry trees
on yonder hill are breaking
    into flower by degrees.
      (Same as No. 1422)

No. 1866

On Takamado where
    pheasants cry, the cherry trees
though none view them, are shedding petals
    leaf by leaf in the breeze.

No. 1867

Are the cherry flowers on Mt. Aho
    being shed today,
with none to view the sight
    as they were yesterday?

No. 1868

Ashibi trees above Yoshino falls
    are now in flower, and river frogs
sing in the stream. I wish the bloom
    would ever thrive upon the crags.

No. 1869

The cherries by my bower
have broken into flower,
hearing the wheedling whispering
of gentle rain of spring.

No. 1870

O Spring rain, fall not hard.
I shall grieve to see
my cherries drop their flowers
ere I view them.

No. 1871

O Cherry flowers, you fall away
    as soon as you come out.
I wish your tree would longer stay
    in flower and bud and sprout.

No. 1872

I look out o'er Kasuga field
    all covered with a haze.
Oh are they cherry flowers I also
    view like gauze ablaze?

No. 1873

I eagerly wait the morning
    to see bush warblers come
and lightly fly from bough to bough,
    scattering the plum.

No. 1874

I will go out to Takamado field tonight,
and view the moon soft-shinning
through spring vapor light.

No. 1875

Even on the moonlit night
    beneath the leafy mountain high,
everything looks dim
    and obscure to the eye.

No. 1876

On the dark mist-covered
    eve of spring we wait
for the moon to rise among the trees
    making its appearance late.

No. 1877

I was caught in the springtime storm,
    alackaday,
and could not reach her bower,
    sheltering long on the way.

No. 1878

I wish to go and see
    Asuka swollen by the rain,
whose water must be raving now
    as it runs amain.

No. 1879

The wreaths of smoke there rise
    above Kasuga field.
Are the women boiling
    the springtime herbs they culled?

No. 1880

Never shall I forget the joy I had today
upon Kasuga field with good companions gay!

No. 1881

I like Kasuga field
in gauzy vapor veiled.
I will take joy in wandering
there spring after spring.

No. 1882

Eagerly do I wish
    the night would not come on,
for in Kasuga field
    I'm drinking with my good companion.

No. 1883

Behold, the courtiers there,
    in elegant leisure
pranking their hair
    with plum flowers for pleasure.

No. 1884

When winter passes
    into spring, the year
turns new, and yet
    man grows but old and sere.

No. 1885

All things are better
    when they are new;
but human beings are prized
    as they grow old and few.

No. 1886

In old Suminoe
    strolling an hour,
I met my own truelove
    as fair as a flower.

No. 1887

O that the moon would rise now from behind
  Mikasa
for me to view the cherry flowers on Saki Hill.

No. 1888

The snowy winter passes into happy spring,
and on the misty meadow uguisu sing.

No. 1889

I feel as happy as if I,
    standing beneath a peach tree blossoming,
were lighted
    by the moon of spring.

SPRINGTIME LOVE SONGS

No. 1890

We part now, as bush warblers part,
    one from the other, crying bitterly,
but keep me in your mind
    till you return again to me.

No. 1891

Culling a flower, I fondly stare,
calling to mind my love as fair.

No. 1892

Even an uguisu
    lost among the mountains high
veiled in the springtime mist
    would not yearn so for his mate as I.

No. 1893

Oh how fair she is!
    I will woo her,
and till at last I win her,
    never cease to sue her.

No. 1894

Now you are here at last
    though so late,
for whom, yearning,
    did I wait and wait.

No. 1895

My love, keep well and soon we'll meet,
I only wish you well, my sweet.

No. 1896

The spring has come when willow branches
    sway in the breeze, and how fare you?
I love you, darling, thinking of you
    all day long and all night through.

No. 1897

When springtime comes, some birds
conceal themselves in grass.
Your bower is invisible too, yet
I never cease to look your way.

No. 1898

I daily live
for you a yearning,
and the chance waiting
to see you, darling.

No. 1899

In need of spring repairs
leans every which way my love's hedge
with bushes of unkempt utsugi,
perhaps because so oft I leapt through it.

No. 1900

To the lovely bower
where plum trees are in flower
to see my darling will I go,
not waiting now for word from her so slow.

No. 1901

If I keep yearning like this
    in secret, never shall I move
her heart. So I'm determined
    now to confess my love.

No. 1902

The field is wrapped in haze
    where many flowers bloom,
but long have we not met,
    and I pass my days in gloom.

No. 1903

Oh how I love my husband
    who reminds me of the flower
of fair ashibi tree,
    sweetest at this hour.

No. 1904

If I to Shakyamuni pray,
    offering a sprig of flowering plum
together with a willow spray,
    will he let my lover come?

No. 1905

People spread ill rumors
    about me,
but my dear husband,
    never, never doubt me.

No. 1906

I will take every care
    to tend my flowering plum
and have my friend in Nara
    to see it come.

No. 1907

Why did I plant the yellow rose?
    'Twas but for him to take delight,
yet he never comes to me
    who yearn for him both day and night.

No. 1908

Like the frost that with the spring
disappears from the plants at the water's edge,
even thus will I, fading in love for you,
so disappear.

No. 1909

I saw her dimly as one sees
    a vernal mountain through a haze,
and yearn for her,
    wishing again on her to gaze.

No. 1910

Since I saw her on that day
when vernal vapor veiled the hill
not a single day has passed
without my yearning after her.

No. 1911

When I think of my lass
with rosy cheeks so fair,
even on a day of spring
I brood and yearn for her.

No. 1912

When you tell me to sit,
    I will obey your sweet command,
act gladly on your word,
    if you only bid me stand.

No. 1913

How beautiful Kasuga field
through vernal vapor viewed!
You are fair as the sight.
Oh how I yearn for you.

No. 1914

Sunk in thoughts of love I found it hard
    today to fritter time away.
How shall I pass tomorrow when
    spring brings a mist and longer day?

No. 1915

Yearning, unbidden
    my footsteps bore me to your bower,
my dear,
    despite this shower.

No. 1916

How can you say that you will go away?
    Do you not divine the kindly heart
of vernal rain that bids you stay
    with me alone and not depart?

No. 1917

Could your clothes be wet all through
    by this mere sprinkle? Should it rain
seven days, would you say I have
    to wait for seven nights in vain?

No. 1918

Where vernal rain is raining,
    and plum flowers fall
is my husband staying
    in a dilapidated cottage small?

No. 1919

Though the time is spring,
    I waste my youth,
only languishing
    for you in truth.

No. 1920

My love for you is verdant
as the springtime grass;
my love for you is ceaseless
as the waves along the shore!

No. 1921

I had a glimpse of you;
    and each long vernal day since then
I've wasted, yearning,
    yearning but in vain.

No. 1922

While the plum trees were in flower,
    I had a hope to see you here.
Now that the bloom is gone
    is it hopeless, oh my dear?

No. 1923

I part from you and go
    like a cloud above,
but my heart stays with you
    wherever I may rove.

No. 1924

Yearning for you all day long,
with my hands I wove this wreath—
longing for you all night through,
wove this with willow shoot and twig.

No. 1925

In the morning dark
    my husband leaves me
with a short farewell.
    Oh how it grieves me!

No. 1926

You are lovely as a flower
blooming upon a springtime hill.
I love you deeply; and whatever
you command I will obey at once.

No. 1927

I am old as the cedar
    standing before the Furu shrine,
but now a slave of love am I.
    Oh pray, let me be thine.

No. 1928

I shall be glad if only flowers
    be shown by the fruit tree;
and I shall be content when you
    will kindly smile on me.

In reply to the above by his love
No. 1929

The tree is laden with good fruit;
    and however rain may pour,
the time has passed by for the tree
    to come now into flower.

No. 1930

The flowers of the seaweed
    now bloom in the sea,
but still you will not have
    a tryst with me.

No. 1931

Pray, come to me.
    I keep open my door,
prepared to welcome you
    at any hour.
      (Same as No. 491)

No. 1932

Ceaselessly falls
    the springtime rain
my lover
    to detain.

No. 1933

I'm yearning after you
    until the spring rain seems to be
incessant tears
    all shed for me.

No. 1934

In unrequited love I suffer,
but she thinks not of me,
and yet I go on yearning still
throughout this long spring day.

No. 1935

You say that you love me,
    nor am I untrue.
I only wait,
    loving you too.

No. 1936

Almost the same as No. 1934

MISCELLANEOUS SONGS OF SUMMER

No. 1937

Upon Mt. Kamunabi where I go,
cuckoos sing loudly,
echoes resounding
among the mulberry trees
at dawn and dusk and even midnight,
delighting the villagers.
Are they calling for their mates?

Hanka
No. 1938

Is the cuckoo wandering
leaving his nest, and crying
for his mate upon Mt. Kamunabi
now at midnight?

No. 1939

Could I but keep your sweet, sweet voice,
    O Cuckoo, would I not
string it as an ornament of May
    with jewels exquisitely wrought?

No. 1940

I wait on tiptoe
cuckoo's songs to hear
when morning vapor covers
the summer's meadow.

No. 1941

O Cuckoo bird, you come
over hill and dale,
but here, alas,
you find no cottage.

No. 1942

O Maiden, gathering arrowroot
    upon the hillside where utsugi are ablow,
shedding their petals in the wind,
    did you see cuckoos singing go?

No. 1943

I tend my garden now and ask my friend
    to come and take delight
in cuckoo's lovely song
    this moonlit summer night.

No. 1944

Over Mt. Imaki crying
    cuckoos go,
crying at the fall of the wistaria flowers
    as in woe.

No. 1945

The cuckoo bird came flying
    over many a mountain high
where utsugi were in flower, singing
    in the mist that hid the sky.

No. 1946

I will not have a lofty tree
    beside my bower,
for it invites the cuckoo,
    and makes my lovesick heart ache more.

No. 1947

Here you are at last tonight
    for whom I have been yearning long.
And now I wish to have a cuckoo come
    that we two may enjoy his song.

No. 1948

In this evening twilight
among the foliage cuckoos cry.
Where are their bowers, I wonder,
that they sing about?

No. 1949

A cuckoo sang this dawn.
    Did you hear
it, or were you asleep,
    my dear?

No. 1950

I see a cuckoo perched
    upon the orange tree in flower
and to his music sweet
    leaf after leaf the petals shower.

No. 1951

O Cuckoo, what ails you?
    It is your time, you know.
Come and sing for me until
    your voice will husky grow.

No. 1952

Upon this pitch-dark night
    I hear a cuckoo-bird.
Hark, from afar the calling comes
    to be so faintly heard.

No. 1953

Upon this moonlit night of May
    with utsugi full abloom, on high
I hear a cuckoo. 'Tis so sweet
    I listen for another cry.

No. 1954

O Cuckoo, come
    and in my garden sing.
My orange trees are blooming.
    Scatter the petals with your wing.

No. 1955

I always like to hear a cuckoo,
but if I may choose,
let him come and sing his lay
when I wear an iris wreath of May.

No. 1956

You wing your way, O Cuckoo,
    Yamato-ward alone;
and you remind me of my love
    now dead and gone.

No. 1957

Seeking utsugi flowers,
    cuckoos to the meadow come,
and ever crying go again
    into the mountain range to roam.

No. 1958

I'll plant a grove of orange trees,
    O Cuckoo, for your sake; so come,
and live till fall, till winter—nay,
    forever, making it your home.

No. 1959

The rain has lifted; and there goes
    a cuckoo with a floating cloud
over Mt. Kasuga's brow,
    calling clear and loud.

No. 1960

I spent a sleepless night,
    and feel unwell this morn,
and adding to my gloom,
    a cuckoo, crying sadly, goes alone.

No. 1961

A cuckoo's perched upon my sleeve,
and will not leave,
telling me what to do—
to send this robe to you.

No. 1962

Cuckoo, my friend thou art.
I love thee from my heart,
and have been yearning after thee.
And oh! thou comest now to me.

No. 1963

In this summer rain
    is the cuckoo singing still
with his lovely throat
    on the utsugi-blowing hill?

No. 1964

Evening cicada, sing your fill
    when I feel jolly, pray,
but cry not now,
    for sad am I today.

No. 1965

O Hagi, though I know
you bloom in autumn,
now I want to dye her garment.
So pray, will you not blow?

No. 1966

In my sleeves I catch orange petals
    that through the air descend,
calling you to mind who once
    stood here where I now stand, my friend.

No. 1967

My love sends me a string
　　of orange blossoms every year,
but none I have received so far,
　　nor any word I hear.

No. 1968

Now cuckoos come and sing,
　　and our orange blossoms fall.
I wish you, my dear friend,
　　would come to make a call.

No. 1969

How glad I am to welcome you !
　　But I regret you've come today,
because our orange flowers already
　　have fallen all away.

No. 1970

I look out o'er the field
　　where pinks are full ablow.
How sweet ! O kindly Rain,
　　do not yet make them go.

No. 1971

I came out to the field to see
　　the flowering orange trees thereon,
sallying forth as rain had stopped;
　　but now, alas, the blooms are gone.

No. 1972

Behold, the pinks are now in flower
　　upon the field. The fall
I have been waiting
　　is approaching for us all.

No. 1973

The China tree outside my bower
　　is all abloom along the bough.
I wish the flowers would stay
　　long as they are now.

No. 1974

Alas, wistaria blooms are gone,
leaving the field forlorn,
and the hunting men can wear
no other flowers in their hair.

No. 1975

Though it is not the month of May,
I've made a nosegay
as my gift for you,
since I could wait no longer.

Question and Answer
(Nos. 1976 and 1977)

No. 1976

Did you see the cuckoo
　　winging his flight
over the hill utsugi deck
　　with their small flowers white?

No. 1977

The cuckoo of which you
　　ask is passing now this way,
heavily drenched with rain—
　　the drizzling rain of May.

No. 1978

If I frequent the town
　　where orange blossoms fall,
I fear the human cuckoos
　　will noisily call.

SUMMER LOVE SONGS

No. 1979

'Tis spring
　　and with no sight of her,
like the cuckoo of this season
　　I have grown slenderer.

No. 1980

I have met you, my dear,
　　though the cuckoo's calling now
hidden among the flowering oranges
　　upon the summer mountain brow.

No. 1981

If I sleep alone,
    even upon the shortest night of May
when cuckoos come and sing
    I only wait the break of day.

No. 1982

Evening cicadas cry
    only in summer's height,
but, lovelorn, I
    weep day and night.

No. 1983

Gossip is rampant
    as the summer grass,
but content am I, if only
    I can lie together with my lass.

No. 1984

What a thing is love!
'Tis like the summer grass.
I try to clear my heart of it,
but it comes again to harrow me.

No. 1985

If I pass my days like this,
    only languishing for thee,
how can I live on?—
    Dead soon I shall be.

No. 1986

I wish to know if thou
    so fair to see
lovest me too, or I
    alone yearn after thee.

No. 1987

After you yearning,
here I am twisting
thread beside my bower
to string leaves of the orange flower.

No. 1988

What has happened?
Why do you not come?
Every hour on tiptoe
I wait for you.

No. 1989

I am in unrequited love,
    for he does not confide
to me his own affection,
    and in this torment I abide.

No. 1990

Though you love me not,
    you love the orange flower.
Why not come to view
    the bloom beside my bower?

No. 1991

Cuckoos sing about our hill
    where wistarias are in flower.
Would you not care, my gentle friend,
    to make a visit to my bower?

No. 1992

You suffer, hiding love, my dear,
to lay it open have no fear.
Then daily will I come to you,
my flowering pink so fair to view.

No. 1993

I yearn for you
    all secretly,
and like a red, red flower in bud
    your love will be.

No. 1994

My sleeves are wet,
    and do not dry, alas,
though these are not the ones
    wherein I went through summer grass.

No. 1995

Even upon a day of June
    when earth cracks from the fiery sun
my sleeves are never dry, since I
    without you weep alone.

MISCELLANEOUS SONGS OF AUTUMN

No. 1996

Rowing the shining boat that brightened
    even the bottom of the river,
did the Cowherd meet
    after a year his lovely Weaver?

No. 1997

The Weaver maid waits for her lover
on the shore of the Heavenly River.

No. 1998

I, a poor weaver,
yearn for my Cowherd,
but no boat brings his message
across the Heavenly River.

No. 1999

If I saw the Weaver fair
oftentimes, aware
she has a husband, I fear
that I might love her dear.

No. 2000

Tell my love my boat is at the ferry
to carry me to her, come autumn.

No. 2001

Alas, I, who can fly on high, am fated,
when I meet my love, to row across the river.

No. 2002

Since days of old I've loved the Weaver maid,
which every one knows now, I am afraid.

No. 2003

Tonight the Weaver fair, my blushing bride
will lie with me upon yon riverside.

No. 2004

The Weaver loves her Cowherd so much that
    whenever
he comes, she gladly slumbers with her lover,
not waiting longer just beside the river.

No. 2005

Since heaven and earth were separated, aye
I have been waiting for one autumn day.

No. 2006

The Cowherd sends word to his Weaver
who yearns for him across the river.

No. 2007

Oh how I loathe
fate that parts both
of us for aye
by the Milky Way!

No. 2008

Prithee, send word to me, my Weaver,
though evening vapor veil the river.

No. 2009

The Weaver ne'er will cease to wave her sleeve of
    gauze
until her love is hidden in the cloud-like haze.

No. 2010

The Evening Star is out. O that the moon
would shine too on my Cowherd coming soon.

No. 2011

I live a lonely life, O Weaver,
separated by the river,
so pray, send word to me,
and in the fall I'll come to thee.

No. 2012

Without unloosening the sash adorned with jewels
    I
exist forlorn, and oh my sleeve is never dry.

No. 2013

'Tis autumn, and I see the grass
    upon the bottom land now quiver.
At last it is time when my Cowherd
    will come to me across the river.

No. 2014

Behold, the hagi is in flower,
and now I can go to her bower.

No. 2015

I hear out in the dark
    the oars' sound coming from the river
as I sit longing
    for my lover.

No. 2016

'Tis autumn, and I seem to hear
her calling in the wind.
Now is the time for me to go
and see my weaving maid.

No. 2017

How long have I awaited this one chance?
Let the night of our reunion come at once.

No. 2018

The river bed has changed this year.
I find it hard my course to steer.

No. 2019

Daily I waited for my lover,
passing the twelvemonth by the river.

No. 2020

Poling the boat, though dawning I may greet,
surely will I my darling Weaver meet.

No. 2021

O Cocks, pray, do not crow at dawning
when I still lie together with my darling.

No. 2022

'Tis dawning, and I must return
across the Heavenly River,
and through the long twelve months
I shall only yearn.

No. 2023

We've been together but awhile, alackaday,
and it is dawn, and now my love must go away.

No. 2024

A thousand years were brief, if I
    could be with you, my dear,
but, oh! alas, we only meet
    one night a year.

No. 2025

We meet but once a year.
    Is it not a pity, love,
to have the shining moon
    hide even awhile in clouds above?

No. 2026

Every day though veiled in mist the river,
I look across it, yearning for my Weaver.

No. 2027

Has my wife finished with the white cloth she
with love was weaving day and night for me?

No. 2028

Since you, my lover,
come not across the river,
with dust the cloth is soiled,
on which day after day I toiled.

No. 2029

I hear the oars' sound on the river:
will she meet tonight her lover?

No. 2030

When autumn comes, mist veils the river,
and through it comes to me my yearned-for lover.

No. 2031

Is there not a messenger to tell him that his wife
every day and every night in sighing spends her
    life?

No. 2032

Oh how the hours are fleeting
this evening of their meeting!

No. 2033

How fortunate the gods who meet at will,
and miserable we who meet one night of fall!

No. 2034

He'll wear the cloth I wove, come autumn—
my darling love, my sweetest Cowherd.

No. 2035

The Cowherd will lie on a misty eve
beside the river on the Weaver's sleeve.

No. 2036

At last the fall for which I waited long is here,
and I'll enjoy the love tryst with my Weaver dear.

No. 2037

Let us have our fill of this tryst, love of mine,
since from tomorrow we again shall only pine.

No. 2038

We are met, but from tomorrow on,
    my all-in-all,
we have to live apart
    until next fall.

No. 2039

After waiting long for our reunion,
why on this night of all nights does he tarry?

No. 2040

Let no waves rise upon the Heavenly River,
for 'tis tonight the Cowherd meets his Weaver.

No. 2041

I see on high a white cloud floating,
or else the scarf worn by the Weaver.

No. 2042

Cowherd, hasten now and pole your boat
    across the river.
This is the only night you have
    to meet your Weaver.

No. 2043

Tonight the autumn wind blows soft,
and he beholds the moon aloft.

No. 2044

From the Heavenly River veiled in vapor
comes the sound of oars rowed by the Cowherd.

No. 2045

Is Cowherd rowing to his Weaver?
For I see spray upon the river.

No. 2046

The autumn wind is raging,
    and the waves are running wild;
so moor your boat and wait awhile
    until the river calms, my child.

No. 2047

The splashing sound comes from the river.
Is the Cowherd rowing to his Weaver?

No. 2048

How oft did I stand at the ferry,
and now my Cowherd dear is coming.

No. 2049

Oh what delight to see my lover
I long awaited by the river!

No. 2050

Alas, you go, and from tomorrow,
again I'll sleep and wake in sorrow.

No. 2051

Lo, with a crescent bow in hand there hies
the old man in the moon for hunting in the skies.

No. 2052

Perhaps the Cowherd's paddle-spray
is falling as the rain tonight.

No. 2053

I see a fog like spray above the river,
Is the Cowherd rowing now to meet his Weaver?

No. 2054

The waves are high, the wind now blowing.
So let your boat be towed across the river.

No. 2055

Alas, I must await my love a year,
although the ferry is not far from here.

No. 2056

If a floating bridge were there
I would come every eve to her.

No. 2057

Only one night I meet my love
after a year of months has passed—
Oh could it but last the length of seven.

No. 2058

I'll go to see my Weaver
across the Heavenly River,
so Wind, pray, do not rave;
stay quiet now, O Wave!

No. 2059

Even though the waves roar in the river,
I'll hasten to row out to meet my Weaver.

No. 2060

Though I have not talked with you enough
yet already it is dawning now.

No. 2061

Though waves are raving in the river,
very soon I'll see my lover.

No. 2062

The foot-boards of my looms I'll set afloat
that he may cross the river with no boat.

No. 2063

I see a mist upon the river,
or perhaps the gauzy garments of the Weaver.

No. 2064

With the new garment I sewed for my lover
I wait for him to come across the river.

No. 2065

I wish to have the cloth all ready,
   when he comes across the river,
and jewels jingling on my wrists and ankles,
   I'm weaving it now for my lover.

No. 2066

Alas, we part now, after waiting one whole year.
Oh if but soon again I could meet you, my dear.

No. 2067

Even at the rapids
so deep the stream for him to wade
that he comes by boat, and now
I hear the splashing of his paddle.

No. 2068

Translated, almost the same as No. 4045

No. 2069

I will pray to the highest deity
that you may traverse safe to me.

No. 2070

I am waiting for him by the river,
and wish this happy night would last for ever.

No. 2071

Across the river I have waded to come here,
and already far advanced the night, my dear.

No. 2072

"O Ferrymaster, come and carry me across the
   river,"
I cry, but nowhere see a boat to take me to my
   Weaver.

No. 2073

Oh what delight to think tonight
   at last I'll dream
with her for whom I yearned a year
   across the stream!

No. 2074

I came across the river,
yearning for my Weaver,
and am so happy here
after a weary year.

No. 2075

We are happy with the Weaver
to see the boat rowed by her lover
nearing her side of the Celestial River.

No. 2076

Poor Cowherd, swiftly runs the Heavenly River,
and night is spent. When will you see your
  Weaver?

No. 2077

O Ferryman, bring me my Cowherd dear;
pity us who meet but once a year.

No. 2078

Everlasting is our love and sweet,
but only one night in a year we meet.

No. 2079

Almost the same as No. 2017

No. 2080

The happy Weaver meets her love tonight, but
  then
a year must pass before she can see him again.

No. 2081

Ranging boat by boat,
make a bridge afloat
to span the Heavenly River
for the lovely Weaver.

No. 2082

So many ferries are there on the river,
and where shall I await my coming lover?

No. 2083

Tell my Cowherd every night
'gainst the fall wind well bedight,
to welcome him, I wait and wait
beside the stream till late and late.

No. 2084

Alas, so changed the bottom of the river
that I know not from whence will come my lover.

No. 2085

Not waiting for the high waves to subside,
I came across the stream on foot, my bride.

No. 2086

I vow to you: yours is my heart.
Come what may, I shall not part.

No. 2087

Cast off now, Ferrymaster.
We shall await another twelvemonth's passing.

No. 2088

What use to call the ferryman, my love?
He can not find the rudder or the oars,
for I have hidden them.

No. 2089

Since the beginning of the world
the Cowherd and his love have lived
by the Celestial River set apart,
and only once in every autumn
been allowed to see each other.
Now across the stream his red boat goes,
pushing aside the silver waves
with flowering obana at the stem
in autumn air awavering.
Thus the Cowherd meets his Weaver
yearly on the seventh of July.

Hanka

No. 2090

This is the night whereon
the lovers in the heavens meet
with girdles of Korean rich brocade
loosened for each other.

No. 2091

I seem to see the very scene
  of the glad embrace
on his arrival at the ferry
  here before my face.

No. 2092

Month after month have I been standing,
counting the days that go
before I meet my Weaver
here by the Heavenly River
(which came into being
as Heaven and earth were set apart,)
until the autumn wind now puts my sleeves
　　aflutter;
and oh this is the very night
when I can sit with her.
O that it might last as the stream flows on for
　　ever.

Hanka
No. 2093

Many a month I spent beside the Heavenly River,
waiting for the night when I can see my Weaver.

No. 2094

I am sad to see
　　the hagi flowers fair and small
loved by the stag,
　　rain-beaten, fall.

No. 2095

The night airs on the tender leaves of hagi—
will they blast the young leaves ere the autumn?

No. 2096

On Ada field when'er
autumn winds come,
little hagi flowers
fall fluttering in the air.

No. 2097

I love the landscape of this field
where hagi are in flower,
where soon wild geese will come.
Oh let not rain descend and harm the bloom.

No. 2098

The hagi flowers are falling
　　in the field where deer
come from the mountains for the plants
　　before their leaves get sere.

No. 2099

I hate to see the hagi flowers
　　blasted by dew,
and think of plucking their sprays now
　　to show to you.

No. 2100

How beautiful the hagi
　　now in flower near
the shed built by the field
　　for me to guard the rice in ear!

No. 2101

My garment was not dyed intentionally.
　　I was enjoying Takamado's view
where hagi were in flower,
　　and now 'tis of a purple hue.

No. 2102

I hear this evening
the fall wind blowing.
The hagi that have been enduring
dew, tomorrow will come into flower.

No. 2103

Now the cool autumn breeze is here.
So let us go together,
riding abreast into the field
to view the hagi full abloom.

No. 2104

They say the bellflower blows
　　wet in the morning dew; but here
in the evening twilight
　　I see one blooming bright and clear.

No. 2105

In spring the hagi hide in haze,
　　but now in autumn there
I see them blooming.
　　So with their twigs let's deck our hair.

No. 2106

Behold, the hagi are in flower
in yonder Sanukata field.
Friends, let us break their twigs to wear
in our hair.

No. 2107

I will not have my clothes intentionally dyed.
Let me betake myself instead
out to Sakinu field where hagi are in flower,
and then they will be colored bright.

No. 2108

The autumn gale will come amain.
    So ere the hagi flowers yield
to it, I'll go and see
    them in the field.

No. 2109

The hagi by my bower
    have grown tall,
and they will be in flower
    blown by the wind of fall.

No. 2110

People choose the hagi first
    among the flowers of fall,
but I believe obana
    prettiest of all.

No. 2111

The hagi sprays
    your messenger brought
delight my eyes
    as does your thought.

No. 2112

If the hagi at my bower
always were in flower,
my lover would be glad to see
them when he comes to me.

No. 2113

I am repaid now for my pains:
    I set the hagi with good care,
and they have broken into flower
    outside my bower, and flourish there.

No. 2114

Who roped my hagi off?
    Can you call this fair?
I'd planted them outside my bower,
    and now am taken unaware.

No. 2115

I did not pluck the ominaeshi twig,
fearing the flowers might stain my robe,
and by the dew so thickly laid
now soon the bloom must fall.

No. 2116

Wakened by dew,
    the hagi now have blown.
O Rain, pray, come not with a wind
    lest the flowers be gone.

No. 2117

The time has come when summer meets
    with autumn, and it is the hour
also for folk to reap the field.
    Behold, the hagi are in flower.

No. 2118

I fear the hagi flowers
    will fall ere I can go
to see them in the field
    where morning mist hangs low.

No. 2119

Behold, the hagi are in flower
    which my husband set.
He told me, if I yearned for him,
    to see the pretty bloom dew-wet.

No. 2120

How can I keep from missing
    hagi flowers? Once they go,
I have to wait a year again
    to see the fair plant blow.

No. 2121

The autumn wind is blowing
    day after day,
and hagi flowers will fall
    if it continues in this way.

No. 2122

Where is my stalwart warrior heart?
I only love the autumn hagi.

No. 2123

The long-awaited fall at last is here,
but hagi have not blown yet anywhere.

No. 2124

How I longed
and yearned and waited !
Now beheld them—
autumn hagi
abloom all o'er the bough.

No. 2125

If in Kasuga field
    hagi flowers fall,
I would that morning breezes brought
    their leaves here, one and all.

No. 2126

Do hagi flowers hate to hear
    the wild goose cry?
They must fall when the bird is seen
    to wing the sky.

No. 2127

I set the hagi
    that my love might view
its flowers, but now they are all gone
    because of rime and dew.

No. 2128

Yonder wild geese
that wing their way Yamato-ward,
braving the autumn wind,
will vanish soon among the clouds.

No. 2129

O Wild geese flying in the morning fog,
    let me ask you
to go and tell my wife
    I love her, love her true.

No. 2130

The wild geese that oft cried beside my bower
    yonder among the clouds now fly.
Are they returning
    to their native sky?

No. 2131

These be the blissful trio of autumn:
the shining moon,
the stags that bell for hinds,
the wild geese honking in the clouds.

No. 2132

Since wild geese cried among the clouds,
    winging their weary flight,
frost has been falling;
    and oh how cold tonight !

No. 2133

I've reaped the harvest
alloted for my work,
and now hearing wild geese cry,
await the winter.

No. 2134

The autumn wind is soughing
over the leaves of rushes now,
and wild geese in the heavens
hear the dreary sound below.

No. 2135

There on the reedy shore
    have the wild geese gone to sleep
despite the chilly wind
    and the frost so deep?

No. 2136

Defying the autumn wind,
wild geese go over the mountains.
Soon their cries will fade
among the distant clouds.

No. 2137

The wild geese in the morning sky
    are sadly crying. Do they pine
for their native land
    as I yearn for mine?

No. 2138

I hear cranes crying,
and see wild geese
winging the sky
to vanish soon among the clouds.

No. 2139

Wild geese, how many nights
    do you go flying
across the sky,
    your own names crying?

> 'Kari' is the Japanese for wild goose, and
> also its honk.

No. 2140

We cry our names,
inviting friends to go
back to our native land.
Who asks such a simple question?

No. 2141

I take joy in the belling
with which stags call
their mates out of the morning mist.
It is like music.

No. 2142

Let the belling of the stag
    go sounding far away,
and let the hagi in the field
    with its echoes sway.

No. 2143

I hear the sad cries of a stag
when I sit yearning after you—
a stag that treads the autumn field
brushing dew from off the hagi flowers.

No. 2144

Wild geese have come,
    but hagi flowers are gone;
and now stags' cries
    sadder have grown.

No. 2145

I miss the hagi flowers gone
    for which stags too
keep on lamenting, and
    oh how I yearn for you!

No. 2146

Never live close by the hill,
    for there the stag comes by;
and even in your sleep
    you hear his mournful cry.

No. 2147

Many huntsmen ride
to the mountainside,
on hill and meadow I
hear stags who soon must die.

No. 2148

Had you come
across the mountain,
you would have heard stags call,
for their hinds yearning.

No. 2149

Upon the hillside
    keen is the hunter's eye,
where seeking hinds,
    the stags come nigh.

No. 2150

Hark, the stag is crying
over the fallen hagi flowers.
Sad and forlorn
he keeps on crying!

No. 2151

Living in the capital
far from the mountains,
no longer can I hear
stags belling near.

No. 2152

If the flowers of hagi fall,
    stags will cry
over the petals
    which scattered lie.

No. 2153

Here in the autumn field
I see the traces of deer's hoofs.
Did they seek their mates,
brushing dew from off the hagi bloom?

No. 2154

Hagi flowers are falling,
and stags are sadly crying.

No. 2155

I hear the sad cry of a stag
    out in the field where hagi are ablow.
He is crying now perhaps,
    seeing the flowers go.

No. 2156

O Keeper of the fields,
    do you not hear
from the mountainside
    the cries of deer?

No. 2157

Many cicadas, coming in the afternoon
    keep singing away.
I ne'er tire of their music,
    though I hear it day after day.

No. 2158

The autumn wind blows cold,
and near my bower I hear
crickets chirp in the grass,
quivering the stilly air.

No. 2159

I never tire of hearing
    evening crickets cry
about my cottage
    among the grasses high.

No. 2160

After the shower
    in my garden do I hear
the crickets chirp
    and know that fall is near.

No. 2161

From the rocks of yonder river
sweet singing of stream frogs I hear.
Is it because
they hold the limpid waters dear
that they are singing there?

No. 2162

By the mountain torrent
    sweet-throated frogs I hear.
Are the creatures telling us
    the golden fall is here?

No. 2163

After my family
    as I yearn alone,
sweet kajika's music makes
    me still more forlorn.

No. 2164

Where silvery sprays
    over the rapids fly
sweet-throated frogs
    morning and evening cry.

No. 2165

Hark, in this upper pool
    river frogs are singing sweet.
'Tis twilight cool. Do they desire
    their mates to meet?

No. 2166

The waterfowl are crying sad
    upon the waves of yonder pool:
it seems into cold winter now
    passes the autumn cool.

No. 2167

Does my dear wife
    who awaits me in her bower
hear the shrike now crying
    by our obana flower?

No. 2168

The dewdrops on the hagi
    jewels resemble.
Every morning on the flowers
    they assemble.

No. 2169

Whene'er a shower comes on,
I am reminded of the dew
laid on the obana flowers
upon Kasuga field.

No. 2170

Upon the hagi sprays lies rime,
and cold already is our clime.

No. 2171

Hagi flowers I love
    and also autumn dew.
I can't decide which I
    like better of the two.

No. 2172

Touch with your lovely hand
    the obana sprays that I may see
little pearls of dew fall scattered
    in front of me.

No. 2173

If you touch the dew
'twill disappear.
So Friends, let us enjoy
the hagi flowers bedewed
from here.

No. 2174

I built a shed
    the fields to reap.
As I lie therein
    I'm wet with dew, and can not sleep.

No. 2175

The autumn wind is blowing.
    How cold! Is frost of night
that withers hagi flowers
    lying white?

No. 2176

The mat-door of the hovel I live in
fluttered in the wind as if to say,
"Since you have reaped the fields, now there
    remain
no ears of rice for dew to fall upon."

No. 2177

The vernal hill is clad with trees in bud.
    Summer finds it in their foliage green.
In variegated colors red
    the autumn hill is seen.

No. 2178

Mt. Yanu's tinted now
    with dew and rime.
The trees will soon be bare,
    and cold the clime.

No. 2179

Let no rain fall upon the leaves
    by dew so beautified.
Would they might stay
    forever on the mountainside!

No. 2180

By the shower of September
    yonder Kasuga mountainside
with variegated autumn hues
    is beautified.

No. 2181

Lo, Mt. Kasuga's colored
red and golden
by frosts of dawning,
and now wild geese go crying.

No. 2182

In my garden
the frost of morning
falling on hagi leaves,
they are golden.

No. 2183

Wild geese have come.
O Maple,
it is your turn
now to color.

No. 2184

Talk not, friend, of the autumn hill,
for it invokes
the memories I cherish
of her still.

No. 2185

Crossing Osaka Pass,
I see the golden leaves
upon Mt. Futakami
falling in the autumn shower.

No. 2186

Autumn is come,
and the bush that sparsely grows
beside my cottage gate
is colored now by dews.

No. 2187

How fair the maple leaves on Mt. Makiki
colored by dews of morning!
I shall grieve to see them fall.

No. 2188

Fair all the golden leaves,
but if I must choose from among them
to wear upon my head, I'll pluck
a spray off a pear bough.

No. 2189

Behold, the pear leaves
are colored red and brown
dyed with the evening dews
by autumn's cold winds blown.

No. 2190

The bushes at my gate
have begun to redden.
Are autumn leaves now falling
on Nabari field?

No. 2191

I hear the wild geese,
and on Takamado field
I see the grasses
colored in autumn hues.

No. 2192

Behold, the mountain is all red.
Should my lord go there in garments white,
they will be dyed
with the autumn color bright.

No. 2193

The fall wind blows
day after day,
and the trees upon the hill
are colored gay.

No. 2194

I hear the wild geese, and bedight
is Tatsuta with red leaves and bright.

No. 2195

I hear the wild geese,
and now I will
see golden foliage shine
upon Kasuga Hill.

No. 2196

The rain has fallen ceaselessly.
Lo, even the evergreen black pine
could not resist its power to change
leaves into autumn colors fine.

No. 2197

Little rain fell, but Mt. Ohki's brow
is already colored yellow now.

No. 2198

When autumn winds come blowing,
withered tree leaves falling,
Aga's pine grove
will be sadly strewn.

No. 2199

I kept indoors for long,
and I see now
all colored golden
Kasuga's brow.

No. 2200

How fair the foliage
on the lofty mountains
all colored red and yellow
by cold dews of September!

No. 2201

Riding a saddled horse, I go
o'er Mt. Ikoma to her bower,
and see the golden leaves
fall like a shower.

No. 2202

The time has come for leaves
to color gold. Behold the moon,
the katsura tree therein
too seems adorned with golden leaves.

No. 2203

Does frost fall also on the town?
Here the foliage is bedight
upon the hill and field
with autumn colors bright.

No. 2204

Day after day
the fall wind blows,
and the frost-bitten hagi leaf
yellower grows.

No. 2205

Autumn is deep,
and cold the winds that blow.
Now the hagi leaves,
turned golden, glow.

No. 2206

Is dew falling
on Mt. Minabuchi,
and maples shedding
golden leaves?

No. 2207

The bushes in my garden
have colored yellow.
And in remote Nabari
maybe autumn showers are falling.

No. 2208

Wild geese came,
and coldly cried,
and leaves of arrowroot
with frost are dyed.

No. 2209

When hagi flowers go
and their foliage too,
how I shall miss their grace!

No. 2210

On the Asuka River
golden leaves are floating.
Do they come
from Mt. Katsuragi?

No. 2211

Yon Mt. Tatsuta is agleam
with variegated autumn colors.

No. 2212

Now is the season when wild geese in heavens call,
and on Mt. Mikasa golden tree leaves fall.

No. 2213

Our hagi from the morning dew
have taken on a reddish hue.

No. 2214

The maple trees on Mt. Tatsuta
over which at evening wild geese wing their
flight
now in the autumn shower
have turned so red and bright.

No. 2215

How fair the hagi shrub!
Let not the rain come in the night
lest it make the plants
shed their leaves so bright.

No. 2216

I have come from the capital
with a present for you now:
a spray of golden leaves
taken from off my maple bough.

No. 2217

Why did the maple trees shed leaves so soon?
    Is the reason
that they were beaten by the rainstorm
    of this season?

No. 2218

We shall not come again
    to see the autumn mountain till next year.
Why then to our hearts' content
    shall we not enjoy this outing here?

No. 2219

O Keeper of the mountain fields,
    though yet the rice plants have no ear,
do rope them in to show
    that on the watch now you are here.

No. 2220

Never shall I reap the field
    where a hart is heard to call his hind,
even though the hoar frost come
    upon the grain with chilly wind.

No. 2221

When I behold the rice plants
    outside my gate, I call to mind
the hagi- and obana-flowers
    swaying in Saho Village in the wind.

No. 2222

I like to hear
the music of the river clear
where sings kajika
in the waning twilit fog.

No. 2223

In the sea of heaven
I see the lone man row
the lunar boat so bright
with katsura oars tonight.

No. 2224

The night is far advanced,
    and there on high
where wild geese go
    the moon sails leisurely.

No. 2225

Upon the hagi flowers
worn by my friend there in his hair
night dew is laid, and oh,
thereon the moonlight sparkles.

No. 2226

As in a melancholy mood
    I sit this autumn night,
I'm made more lone and sleepless
    by the clear moonlight.

No. 2227

A shower came unexpectedly,
    but now the sky is clear
of rain-clouds, and the moon
    shines brightly there.

No. 2228

The moon is shining radiantly.
Is she telling us to see
the hagi in full flower
outside my bower?

No. 2229

In September do I love to view
    at dawn the moon still bright,
changing the dew
    into pearls glittering white.

No. 2230

Seeking the coolness of the fall,
    I built a shed upon my farming-land.
I sit therein,
    and by a balmy breeze now I am fanned.

No. 2231

Beautiful the field
    with hagi flowers, and there
sing cicadas too
    fanned in the autumn air.

No. 2232

Upon the autumn mountain
some tree leaves are still green,
but so cold this morning's air
that soon the frost will change them.

No. 2233

Many a mushroom
springs on the knoll
of Takamado
umbrella-fashion
with scent of fall.

No. 2234

The rain is falling
    on my love's bower
for whom I languish
    every hour.

No. 2235

Rain on my straw-built shed
    falls, and I
am wet and weary
    with no woman by.

No. 2236

I am a slave of love,
    and though a tempest rave,
dripping wet I'll come to you,
    all glad the storm to brave.

No. 2237

The rain and wind are scattering
    sodden leaves in flight;
and as I lie alone in bed,
    so drear and cold is night.

No. 2238

Behold, the flight of wild geese.
    How with their wings they veil the sky!
And yet the frost comes, as it were,
    leaking from on high.

AUTUMN LOVE SONGS

No. 2239

Amid the golden foliage
of autumn mountains
could I hear your voice,
then should I not rejoice?

No. 2240

Pray, never ask
anything about me,
for I await my truelove
wet with the night dew of September.

No. 2241

The night was veiled in vapor,
    making every vista blear,
but sleeping, in my dream
    I saw my darling love so clear.

No. 2242

The obana flowers of autumn
    lean but to one side,
as my heart is drawn
    only to you, my bride.

No. 2243

Tree leaves fall nipped by rime.
    Though I grow as sere
with the lapse of time
    I never shall forget you, dear.

No. 2244

To bed rice plants I tilled my field
    near Suminoe Cove.
Now comes the time to reap.
    So long have I not seen my love.

No. 2245

I wonder when
    I shall see my wife again,
toiling in the distant fields,
    languishing for her in vain.

No. 2246

Like morning dew
    upon the ear
of autumn rice, I too
    shall disappear.

No. 2247

As ears of autumn rice
        bend to one side, so I
yearn but for you,
        yet cold, you make me sigh.

No. 2248

Would I could see my husband
who labors now far off,
living in a straw-built shed
to reap the autumn rice.

No. 2249

I would my love could know
now living in a shed,
I hear the lonely cries of cranes.

No. 2250

I built a hut in spring
        when mist hung far and near.
Now I reap the autumn fields,
        yearning to see my dear.

No. 2251

The rice is past the time to reap.
Still he comes not with me to sleep.

No. 2252

Come to me, however late
        across the meadow bright
with hagi flowers now falling.
        Come, though wet with dew of night.

No. 2253

I lie without my wife tonight,
        hoping no cold dew
may fall and dye the leaves
        in autumn hue.

No. 2254

How can I go on loving thus?
        I'd rather pass away
like dew laid on
        my flowering hagi spray.

No. 2255

The dew on hagi flowers
        attracts the eye,
but I will love
        you secretly.

No. 2256

I can't love on like this.
        So let me pass away
like dew upon those golden-eared rice plants
        which in the wind now sway.

No. 2257

Late is the night, but I will come to you,
my darling, though my clothes be wet with dew.

No. 2258

I can not love like this.
        So let me pass away
like dewdrops on
        the flowering hagi spray.
            (Very much the same as No. 2254)

No. 2259

Whenever dew descends
        upon the hagi by my dwelling place,
I look on them with joy,
        reminded of you full of grace.

No. 2260

If my wife were clothes, then her
next to my skin would I not wear
now when the autumn wind
blows cold and drear?

No. 2261

The wind comes howling
        down the hill this eve;
and I lie alone,
        pillowing my head on my own sleeve.

No. 2262

Long falls the rain,
        scattering the hagi bloom,
and lovelorn sleepless
        all night I lie in gloom.

No. 2263

Gloomy I sit
   yearning for thee.
None else, my love,
   can solace me.

No. 2264

This autumn night I hear
   in chorus crickets cry,
but I have naught except my pillow
   to keep me company.

No. 2265

Alas, if but your voice I hear,
I will not ask for more, my dear.

No. 2266

If I set off upon a journey,
   my wife will grieve. So thinking, I
postponed the start from day to day;
   and thus the twelvemonth has gone by.

No. 2267

Does not the hart take care
to hide his grassy lair?
Prithee, keep your love for me
deep, deep in thee.

No. 2268

As beaten grass shows clearly
   where stags have slept,
so now out is our secret
   I sedulously kept.

No. 2269

As day is dawning,
   I hear the cranes on high;
and yearning for my love,
   I sadly sigh.

No. 2270

As this grass is ever found
   to grow obana near,
so I can't live
   without my husband dear.

No. 2271

Come to my bower
to see the hagi in full flower
among the grasses high
where many crickets cry.

No. 2272

I love him true. But he is unaware,
because to talk to him I do not dare.

No. 2273

Never believe the rumors, pray,
   for I love to see you
as I love newly-opened flowers
   of hagi bush to view.

No. 2274

Suffering and moaning, lovesick
   though I pass away,
our secret will I keep,
   and ne'er betray.

No. 2275

Like a budding bellflower
I conceal my love.

No. 2276

At the cries of wild geese newly come
   the hagi have burst into flower.
So my love, will you not come
   to see them to my bower?

No. 2277

As the obana flower
   your arm is sweet.
And oh! I'll lie thereon
   when soon we meet.

No. 2278

For a long, long time
   yearning for you I've been,
and now unbidden as the cockscomb flower
   in my face 'tis seen.

No. 2279

Within my town a flower has blown
   of such a lovely hue
that I can not but love,
   and that is you.

No. 2280

The hagi bush
   has broken into flower,
reminding me so long you have
   not been to my bower.

No. 2281

How like the dayflower
   bedewed and bright
am I, and fade so soon away
   with nearing night!

No. 2282

Liefer be the destined blossom
   scattered, gone
than thus be spending nights in longing,
   yearning on.

No. 2283

I spend my days in yearning
   after you within my dwelling place;
but never, never will
   I show it in my face.

No. 2284

How I wish to see my wife
   as lithe and fair
as hagi flowers
   beaming in the autumn air.

No. 2285

Like a lone plume grass
   in the field where hagi are in flower
all hidden lives my mistress,
   and I yearn for her bower.

No. 2286

For a long time I
   have not seen you, indeed.
My hagi flowered, withered,
   and now they are in seed.

No. 2287

My hagi bush is now abloom.
   Before the flowers fall
will you not come from Nara
   and pay a call?

No. 2288

My darling wife is fair:
a pretty flower and rare.

No. 2289

Within the deserted capital
hagi blew and fell,
   eagerly
awaiting thee.

No. 2290

Yearning for you, I break a hagi spray,
   and sadly stare,
for 'tis not you,
   although as fair.

No. 2291

Dayflowers blow in the morning,
   and at evening wither.
As brief will be my life,
   because you come not hither.

No. 2292

When you go on a journey,
   and in the field of fair Akitsu stay,
thatch your roof with hagi stalks
   together with the obana spray.

No. 2293

Even though in flower
   had you not shown the hagi spray,
I could go at peace.
   Now I must longer stay.

No. 2294

I think of you, dear, when I talk,
and yearn too for you when I walk.

No. 2295

The arrowroot leaves by my bower
   grow redder day by day,
telling that autumn is advancing;
   but you never come. Why, pray?

No. 2296

I have not seen you long,
   alas for me !
and golden leaves now prank
   many a mountain tree.

No. 2297

I love a girl demure
   now another's wife,
and all I can is but endure
   my lonely life.

No. 2298

As yearning after you
I sit forlorn,
the autumn wind soughs and
the moon goes down.

No. 2299

Like the moon of autumn night
hidden in the clouds,
alas, you come not
into my sight.

No. 2300

If but you come like this,
then I shall ever be in bliss.

No. 2301

Resignedly I live alone;
   but when the autumn wind I hear,
oh how can I but be reminded
   of you, my husband dear?

No. 2302

The townsfolk will think me unfeeling
   when this long September evening I
spend thus companionless.
   and alone within my bower lie.

No. 2303

The autumn night is long,
   and late dawns the day.
Still 'tis too short whereon to tell
   you all I have to say.

No. 2304

This robe is like
   a dragonfly's wing so light.
It shall be yours
   to wrap you at night.

No. 2305

I change clothes when I sleep
   even on a journey lone,
but oh how busy now, and I
   rest nightly with my day robe on.

No. 2306

Showers come off and on
as the moon sets in early dawn,
and I wish to remain with you in bed
who still keep the girdle not unloosened.

No. 2307

As dew upon the autumn leaves
   takes on their color red,
so though I strived to keep our secret,
   gossip is spread.

No. 2308

Rain makes the river rush and break
   against rocks in its course,
but I love you, and am not rain
   so cruel and without remorse.

No. 2309

Even the sacred tree roped off
   by the priest of the shrine
sometimes sheds golden leaves
   beyond its holy line.

No. 2310

As I lie sleepless, yearning after you, my dear,
near my autumnal bed a cricket's song I hear.

No. 2311

Because a glimpse of her I had,
love-struck I live a life so sad.

WINTER MISCELLANEOUS SONGS

No. 2312

From head to sleeve
    the hailstones leap,
I would bring them to my love
    for her to keep.

No. 2313

Lo, on the pines
    upon the hill
snow is falling
    thickly still.

No. 2314

Not a cloud above the hill I see,
and yet the snow descends on the pine tree.

No. 2315

The oak boughs on the mountain
    are bent with snow,
and I can not discern
    the path below.

No. 2316

The summit of Mt. Nara
is veiled with murky clouds.
No wonder there remains the snow
beneath my hedges even now.

No. 2317

Would I could have more snow
enough to melt and wet me through,
but it disappears up in the air.
and no more comes to me.

No. 2318

The night was cold; now in the morning
    opening the sliding-doors I go
out into a garden carpeted
    all o'er with the silvery snow.

No. 2319

How cold the wind this winter eve, and lo,
how fair the hill all white with snow!

No. 2320

I wish the snow
dancing on my clothes would go,
carrying my heart from here
to stay on the sleeve of my dear.

No. 2321

O Snow,
    do not descend today, for I
have no one here
    my clothes to dry.

No. 2322

I see descending but a little snow,
veiled though the skies with murky clouds and
    low.

No. 2323

Waiting for my lord,
I go abroad,
and see the snow descending light,
but of him no sight.

No. 2324

I see the mountains newly covered white.
Did the snow descend there too last night?

No. 2325

From whose garden come
these plum petals
riding the moonlit breeze?

No. 2326

I send a spray
    of my plum flowers to you
as a humble gift
    for you to view.

No. 2327

Who owns, would I could know,
these plums ablow?
They are so fair
that I stand and stare.

No. 2328

Though my plum flowers fall,
I do not care,
for none come to my bower
to look at them.

No. 2329

'Tis snowy and cold still
    for my plums to blow,
and well for them to stay in bud
    awhile unhurt by snow.

No. 2330

I try to break for you an upper spray
    of plum in flower now,
and am all wet with dew
    shaken off the lower bough.

No. 2331

Here the meadow grass is sere.
Is Mt. Arachi
over which my lord must go
cold now with wind and snow?

No. 2332

Oh when will the moon again appear
from behind the dark clouds and shine clear?

No. 2333

As sometimes falling snow melts in mid air amain,
so I may pass away ere I see you again.

No. 2334

Fall, Snow, fall copiously for me
who languish my dear love to see.

No. 2335

To languish ever for my wife—
is this to be my way of life?

No. 2336

'Tis late at night, Untoward
the wayside grass is frosted.
Go not abroad, my lord.

No. 2337

My love grows deeper
    when I hear her say
like frost on the bamboo
    lovesick, she will fade away.

No. 2338

Wind blows, and hail falls too.
    And on this night so drear,
here in Tatano Plain
    must I lie without my dear.

No. 2339

Henceforth openly, not secretly,
O my beloved, I'll love you.

No. 2340

I, loving at first sight,
languish now day and night.

No. 2341

From my thoughts of her I learn
how for her I yearn.

No. 2342

I saw you but awhile as in a dream,
and shall die like the snowflake on the stream.

No. 2343

He says he loves me true,
    so I will go now to his dwelling place;
but if it snows, my skirt will leave
    behind its telltale trace.

No. 2344

I want to send a messenger,
but fear they'll know that I love her.

No. 2345

I wish to die
like snow out of the murky sky,
but hoping to see you, my own,
I still live on.

No. 2346

If I love openly, her name will out,
and she will suffer then, no doubt.

No. 2347

For long my husband came not here,
but oh! his footsteps now I hear.

No. 2348

Tell her for me
    however rough the way,
I'll come
    with her to stay.

No. 2349

Pray, come to see my plums in flower
outside my bower.
I await you every night
with moonlight shining on them bright.

No. 2350

No mountain wind yet blows,
    but when you do not come,
I feel all cold,
    and pass my time in gloom.

THE MANYOSHU

BOOK XI

FOREWORD

This book is divided into two parts: songs taken from Kakinomotono Hitomaro anthology and from the ancient collection of songs, and other songs. They are all love songs. There are 17 Sedohka, and 473 verselets, and all are anonymous, but it is not hard to imagine that some songs taken from the Hitomaro anthology were written by Kakinomotono Hitomaro himself.

No. 2351

Come to cut obana stalks,
    friend, for my cottage new,
and I will let you choose
    a pretty maid and have her too.

No. 2352

The girls are dancing,
and the bells upon their wrists are ringing.
I will let one of them show you
into the cottage.

No. 2353

So bright this moonlit night
will not even my love whom I keep hidden be
    visible
for eyes of all to see?

No. 2354

Loved by a warrior brave do I live here,
and none shall see me though the moon shine
    clear.

No. 2355

Live I ne'er so long,
so people say, she'll never love me.
Heigh-ho, then what care I
though she go early to her grave.

No. 2356

Upon my floor he left his girdle of brocade.
I will return it when he comes tomorrow night.

No. 2357

In the grass you will get damp with dew,
and I together shall be wet with you.

No. 2358

What though I live, my sweet,
since we can never meet.

No. 2359

O that I were a breeze, my lady fair,
in secret to your bower to repair.

No. 2360

Forlorn I sit at home,
because you do not come.

No. 2361

"How can I cross the one-plank bridge?" asked I.
"Well shod," was my darling wife's reply.

No. 2362

A wretch from Kuse asking for my hand!
How dare that rascal such a thing demand?

No. 2363

Let not people tread this pathway,
since it is taken by my lover.

No. 2364

Prithee come in beneath the bamboo blind.
If Mama asks, I'll say it is the wind.

No. 2365

Upon my way to Court
such a charming housewife did I see
that since then, well-a-day,
my careless sleep has gone.

No. 2366

Once a pretty girl loved me,
and her again I wish to see.

No. 2367

I love another's wife, ah me!
and my mind is like a bark at sea.

*Songs expressing the heart without allusions
(original caption in the Manyoshu)*

No. 2368

Since I parted from my mother,
never have I felt so lonely.

No. 2369

Yearning for you, I can not sleep at night,
and only wish for sight of you.

No. 2370

Alas, now I shall die,
    die of love for her,
none bringing me her message
    though there goes many a passenger.

No. 2371

Only yearning for my love,
　　my time I waste away.
Only wishing to see her,
　　I pass my night and day.

No. 2372

That I must pine with love I then had been
　　aware,
I would not have approached, however fair.

No. 2373

For her I ever long,
but more, come evensong.

No. 2374

Alas, for me love is an endless strife—
maybe to the finish of my life.

No. 2375

Let future generations see
that they should never love like me.

No. 2376

To manliness I have no right,
pining with love from day to night.

No. 2377

Why have I lived so many years,
only weeping lovelorn tears?

No. 2378

I'm in despair,
　　for you come not to me.
Must I part from you
　　through all eternity?

No. 2379

Short is the way;
　　but making a detour, you come
only to shun the eyes of folk,
　　and eagerly I wait at home.

No. 2380

Oh, why does he not come? Did he forget the
　　way?
Or is aught interrupting him today?

No. 2381

Without you these two nights passed wearily,
and they seemed a thousand years to me.

No. 2382

To worship at the shrine
　　many go along the road,
but among them only one,
　　my dear, shall be my lord.

No. 2383

Hard is the way of life,
　　that I concede.
But why day in, day out must I
　　pine with love indeed?

No. 2384

Returning from a journey,
　　let some traveler tell
me that he met my husband
　　faring well.

No. 2385

After five years,
　　ah, sad to say,
I, a miserable slave,
　　love her still today.

No. 2386

Though I could traverse mountains rough,
I am a weakling now for love.

No. 2387

People will be upon the watch
　　after dark, so with me stay.
Oh, how I wish it were as long
　　as a thousand years today.

No. 2388

I do not know now whether
　　I stand or sit. So eagerly
I yearn, but she is cold
　　and no word comes to me.

No. 2389

Let morning never dawn,
　　for if it does, you'll go away,
and I've to wait again
　　throughout a weary day.

No. 2390

Were yearning death,
    I should have been dead then
a thousand times,
    over and over yet again.

No. 2391

Last evening but awhile
did I glimpse a lovely maiden,
and still this morning
I keep on yearning.

No. 2392

I parted from her at her door.
Now I've met her, I love her more.

No. 2393

Had I not strayed outside my neighborhood,
my heart would still be innocent of love.

No. 2394

Thin as a shadow cast by morning sun
have I grown since I glimpsed that lovely one.

No. 2395

However oft I come,
    of her I have no sight;
yet here am I again
    sadly wet with the dew of night.

No. 2396

I casually saw her,
    and love her now.
Can I see her again?
    Oh, how?

No. 2397

Daily I go my love to see.
How jealous people are of me!

No. 2398

How I long to be your wife,
but careless gossip renders hard my life.

No. 2399

I chastely sleep. Oh, never fear,
my love: I ever hold you dear.

No. 2400

Oh, where has gone my manliness?
Alas, a slave of love am I.

No. 2401

My love, do you want me to die,
passing my gate so callously?

No. 2402

Alas, you are not living near,
and I but pine for you, my dear.

No. 2403

I purify myself
in Kuse's stream today
and fervently pray
for you, my darling, and for me.

No. 2404

People may speak what they desire of me,
but thou shalt never find me cold to thee.

No. 2405

Alas, how people talk of us
who have done nothing scandalous!

No. 2406

Too soon I shall go to my tomb,
and now but wait for you to come.

No. 2407

However much my mother asks
    at whom I aim,
never, never will I say
    my lover's name.

No. 2408

When a maid's brows itch, or she sneezes,
    or her girdle loosens, people say
some one loves her,
    and pray, how do you fare today?

No. 2409

My girdle loosens as I yearn for thee,
and now I know thou truly lovest me.

No. 2410

A year has passed since then,
but how can I forget that eve
when I slept pillowing my head
upon your sleeve?

No. 2411

I only saw her in a garment bright,
and fell in love, and long now for her sight.

No. 2412

O for the sight of thee
even in a dream, but deep,
so deep my love for thee
that I can scarcely sleep.

No. 2413

My nether robe lace loosens
of itself—the lace
I fastened fast. Pray keep this secret
till I sit with you face to face.

No. 2414

I only cared for you,
and nothing caught my eye—
the hills and rivers on the way,
and now here am I.

*A note in the original text says that the
following verses were composed to
"express the feelings" of the
authors "with allusions"*

No. 2415

Long is the fence of Furu Shrine.
So long too for you did I pine.
(Same as No. 501)

No. 2416

I know that life is in the hands
of divinities,
but I wish to live long
for our ties.

No. 2417

Old as the sacred cedar tree,
I still continue to love thee.

No. 2418

If I give the gods
offerings through a priest,
can I see my love
in dreams at least?

No. 2419

O that I could keep our tryst
as sure as heaven and earth exist.

No. 2420

The moon is shining bright,
whereat my sweet love too
now looks perchance, but oh,
yon mountain separates us two.

No. 2421

There is no craggy slope
on the road he rides alone,
but still I pray his horse may not
stumble on a stone.

No. 2422

Though there lie no rugged mountain
on the way,
he has not come
for many a day.

No. 2423

Even awhile if I do not see you, my dear,
lorn am I as the island mountain here.

No. 2424

The ornamental tassel of a mirror
has no need of loosening, but I
at my lover's coming
my girdle untie.

No. 2425

I have a horse;
but not waiting for the groom to saddle it,
over the rugged path
came I to you on foot.

No. 2426

Wrapped in mist the mountains lie,
and pining for my love, I sigh.

No. 2427

The Uji River
runs for ever
as I keep
love in me deep.

No. 2428

As hard to cross the rapids of the Uji,
so hard, alas, for me to win that maid.

No. 2429

I know she will refuse to let me in today,
but I cross the stream, my garments wet with
    spray.

No. 2430

The river flows on, and
never returns,
nor shall you ever see
me retract my vow.

No. 2431

Down the lower reaches Kamo flows on leisurely,
and as slowly will I not persuade her to meet me?

No. 2432

I did love her,
    but naught whatever
said, and I felt myself
    like a raving river.

No. 2433

Like letters written on the stream
    my life will fade away,
but to let me live on for your sake
    the gods I pray.

No. 2434

Even though I die beside the roaring sea,
ever faithful to my darling shall I be.

No. 2435

I know not where she lives;
    but if she lets me come,
I'll traverse hill and dale,
    though seven days and nights I roam.

No. 2436

I wonder if there be a man
    who can rest peacefully
like that ship at anchor
    in the Katori Sea.

No. 2437

Wave after wave
    comes rolling from the blue,
and like the waves
    my thought will go to you.

No. 2438

Gossip I
never fly.
My love for thee
is as the sea.

No. 2439

I thought my love was secret
    as a lone island in the sea,
but now I find 'tis common knowledge,
    and people freely talk, ah me!

No. 2440

As a ship waiting for a wind
    I'll wait for what you have to say,
and with content and joy
    you will I obey.

No. 2441

Long I loved as secret
as the marsh beneath the grasses,
and then the name,
ever so near my lips, escaped.

No. 2442

Even if you could move our earth away,
you could not escape love's fateful sway.

No. 2443

My love for you,
    oh, my beloved one,
is like the water seeping down
    even underneath a stone.

No. 2444

Like rocks on Mt. Isobe can I be for aye?
Oh, no. Why then in love should I waste life
  away?

No. 2445

My love is like a jewel bright
that shines for me both day and night.

No. 2446

A maiden like a pearl I won,
and cherish her now as my own.

No. 2447

I won a maiden like a pearl,
and ne'er will I part from the girl.

No. 2448

Although like beads we be
  strung separate,
joined we shall be
  some day by fate.

No. 2449

I saw her dimly as in mist, not well,
but still in love I desperately fell.

No. 2450

I passed her as a cloud the moon,
and wish again to see her soon.

No. 2451

My truelove lives so far away,
but my conduct here shall none reprove.

No. 2452

I can not meet her, but live gloomily,
looking only at the clouds on high.

No. 2453

Almost the same as No. 2294

No. 2454

Across the cloud-capped mountains is my house;
but I will not return, because here is my spouse.

No. 2455

All because of me
  spread the rumors ill.
Now will she fade away
  like morning mist above the hill?

No. 2456

The grass on Kurokami Hill is blest by rain,
but ah, I yearn for you, my darling love, in vain.

No. 2457

As one caught in a shower
  takes shelter underneath a tree,
so every now and then, do think
  my bower a tree, and come to me.

No. 2458

I wait tonight again, yearning for you.
Soon I shall fade away like morning dew.

No. 2459

My husband, pray, be patient;
do not go away
as swift as the sea wind.

No. 2460

My love I left behind
  may now be viewing this moon bright,
and I hope the clouds may not
  conceal it from her sight.

No. 2461

Though I met my love, I parted soon
to yearn again as for the coming moon.

No. 2462

If you love me true, my dear,
pray, in my nightly dream appear.

No. 2463

I try to look upon the moon,
  deeming it you,
but oft it disappears behind the clouds;
  and then what can I do?

No. 2464

Clouds obstruct the moonlight,
    making it dim,
and things hindering my lover,
    seldom I see him.

No. 2465

The grass grows sere
even as I do,
pining for you.

No. 2466

What excuse, though it may prove
    futile as to rope a wasteland off,
can I invent
    here to invite my love?

No. 2467

You say
that we will meet some day,
but oh, how can you tell
tomorrow finds us faring well?

No. 2468

As can be known
the grass among
the seaside reed,
so all men read
my constant mind.

        (The original is based on a similar play of
    words between shiri kusa (a kind of grass)
    and shiri (know).

No. 2469

Love will never cease,
nor will my heart know peace.

No. 2470

I suffer, for I love thee,
and oh, how shall I move thee?

No. 2471

How kind thou art to me!
Grateful am I to thee.

No. 2472

Mine is unrequited love.
O that the lovely maiden were my lass.

No. 2473

With a kind heart
    my sash you tied,
and only you can loosen it
    for me, my bride.

No. 2474

In unrequited love
    have I been yearning after thee.
Now years have passed,
    and still with callousness thou treatest me.

No. 2475

Ferns have I, growing on my eaves,
but daylilies none—
that love-forgetting flower—
which I need the most.

No. 2476

Some millet stays
even in the well-threshed rice,
but thrown away by her
I sleep alone.

No. 2477

If you only promise a meeting,
no obstacle can come between us two.

No. 2478

Alas, alas, I languish all alone,
awaiting you to render me your own.

No. 2479

If even in a dream
    my lover I could see.
In such thoughts many a year
    has passed o'er me.

No. 2480

No one but is aware
I love you, Lady fair.

No. 2481

Her vow seemed aimless as to rope off a field;
so I went to ascertain her mind.

No. 2482

Hidden as plants under water,
I pass time, pining for my truelove.

No. 2483

How does she fare this eve,
not lying on my sleeve?

No. 2484

Thou settest a young tree
to treat my eye.
The tree and I
now *pine* for thee.

> The same pun is in the original, matsu (pin-
> ing) and matsu (pine tree).

No. 2485

Now my wife is hidden
    behind yon tall pine tree,
though still in earshot,
    vainly waving sleeves to me.

No. 2486

Now she is another's wife,
and I must live a lonely life.

No. 2487

Whatever obstacles may lie,
to win the maiden I will try.

No. 2488

She will not let me come,
and I love her in gloom.

No. 2489

She stood beneath an orange tree,
    and took a lower spray thereof;
then, smiling, gave it me
    as a token of her love.

No. 2490

Translated, almost the same as No. 2488

No. 2491

I spent a sleepless night,
    and now at dawn behold above
a mandarin duck on the wing.
    Is if flying to its love?

No. 2492

On fire for you,
though wet as any grebe,
not unobserved I came.

No. 2493

I did not wave my sleeve
    as you were departing.
There were too many folk
    to show my feelings at our parting.

No. 2494

Even now while the lofty ship
    they steer,
I yearn. Apart from you,
    how can I pass a year?

No. 2495

Like a silkworm in its tight cocoon
    her mother keeps her in her bower,
and no means whate'er have I
    to see my lovely flower.

No. 2496

I wish my heart were ribbons red
for you to deck your lovely head.

No. 2497

I have told you my name and house,
and now you can call me your spouse.

No. 2498

I'm thine, and what will I not dare
    for thee, my lord?
Glad will I die and die,
    treading the double-edgèd sword!

No. 2499

Of gossip I am not afraid.
I only wish to see the maid.

No. 2500

Though familiar as my comb you be,
yet you, my love, I ever wish to see.

No. 2501

So far from home now is my husband dear.
O that in dreams at least he could appear.

No. 2502

In the mirror that I take up in the morning
I see but you,
though 'tis myself.

No. 2503

When evening comes I set his pillow on my bed,
but he never comes thereon to lay his head.

No. 2504

No rendezvous whatever
can I have with my lover.

No. 2505

Why did I not refuse him then,
alas, to sorrow now in vain?

No. 2506

The fortuneteller at the crossroads
says I shall meet my long-awaited maiden now.

No. 2507

Very much the same as above.

No. 2508

Serving at court was I,
when you caught my eye.

No. 2509

Be not worried, love, but be at rest.
Our secret is well kept within my breast.

No. 2510

How soon the swift red horse
    will bear me on his cloud-zoned ride!
So pray, before we part, once yet again
    receive me lying by your side.

No. 2511

Slippery the stream with pebbles,
    and the paths rugged all the way.
It is my heart you carry;
    be careful of it, pray.

No. 2512

The moon rises above Mimuro,
that mount of sweetest wine;
and my lover whom I long to see,
ah, the sound of his horse I hear.

No. 2513

Let thunder roar, clouds lour,
and showers descend,
then you will stay
here in my bower.

No. 2514

Even though no thunder come,
    nor rain,
if you let me, I will
    remain.

2 songs by Kakinomotono Hitomaro

No. 2515

My pillow slides and will not
    let me rest.
If only I could lie
    against my darling's breast.

No. 2516

Your pillow waits long for your head,
and now with mold is coverèd.

*In the text mention is made that the following
verses were composed to "express the
feelings" of the authors "without
any allusion."*

No. 2517

If we heed our mothers much,
we two shall never come in touch.

No. 2518

When I left, my poor wife sighed,
and had her sleeves all wet with tears.

No. 2519

Open your door, your cedar door,
    and come out for me, pray.
Now is the chance. Unless 'tis seized,
    you will repent both night and day.

No. 2520

I lie upon a single mat,
　　　but could I only be
locked in your arms, no cold
　　　this winter night should trouble me.

No. 2521

With little chance
for our rendezvous
I only dream of you,
of your lovely countenance.

No. 2522

I thought you had a grudge against me,
and that is why I did not see you.

No. 2523

I do not show it in my face,
but in my heart is only love for you.

No. 2524

Were we meeting openly,
well might people talk,
but chastely corresponding—
why should gossip rise?

No. 2525

Such unrequited love is mine
I scarcely feel alive.

No. 2526

My love must be awaiting me.
I'll haste her smiling face to see.

No. 2527

Oh, who calls me
outside my bower?
Again at me
Mother will scowl.

No. 2528

Although a thousand nights he may not come,
yet I shall be awaiting him with constancy.

No. 2529

Along the thoroughfare many men I see,
but none from her bring messages to me.

No. 2530

If but I can glimpse her across the hedge,
the days of separation I'll not grudge.

No. 2531

I am determined not to tell your name,
and you shall never say I am to blame.

No. 2532

If I did not hold you dear,
for whose eyes, pray.
would I thus wear
my black hair long?

No. 2533

A girl can not forget the lover's face. Oh, never—
she thinking of him, longing for him ever.

No. 2534

Alas, thou never hast been kind to me
who have for years been yearning after thee.

No. 2535

We are deep in love,
and badly spoken of.

No. 2536

I love you with all my life,
and unawares
the years elapse.

No. 2537

Even my mother I'd betray
my lover's pleasure to obey.

No. 2538

Nightly alone upon my mattress stuffed with
　　rushes
will I wait your coming till it gets all threadbare.

No. 2539

Since first we met it seems
　　a thousand years have gone o'er me—
I, waiting, yearning and
　　languishing into eternity.

No. 2540

Her girlish hair
too short to plait
she braids with tender grass—
Ah, how I love her!

No. 2541

Leaving my love behind,
    I made a start,
and though my feet now tread my journey,
    far is my heart.

No. 2542

How many nights have passed, in vain,
since first I lay with you, my lovely lass?

No. 2543

Even your messenger
will not come;
and I have none to whom
I can tell how I fare.

No. 2544

We can not meet.
So let me dream of you, my sweet,
when alone I lie
that from fiery love I may not die.

No. 2545

I knew not what to say
    if asked, "Whose messenger is he?"
And so ere being queried
    in tears I sent him back to thee.

No. 2546

"Surprise, surprise" I'll say,
and already her delighted smile
I seem to see.

No. 2547

I did not know
I loved her so,
and now regret
that I was not more kind.

No. 2548

If but you knew my love for you is great,
and word from you I eagerly await.

No. 2549

Wet are my sleeve and pillow with the tears I
    weep,
for, yearning after you, I nightly go to sleep.

No. 2550

Whether I sit or stand, I dream
    of the maiden aye
who, trailing her red skirt,
    left me to go her way.

No. 2551

Yearning, languishing for thee,
I wandered out at least thy gate to see.
    (A folk song?)

No. 2552

In my heart
I think of you a thousand times,
but I have no means
to send you any message.

No. 2553

Even in an empty dream he gladdens me.
Should we really meet, oh, what joy would it be!

No. 2554

When I meet him, I am made shy,
but still to see him is a joy.

No. 2555

Keep the doors all shut tomorrow
    till late in the day,
for I shall have an honored guest tonight,
    and he will stay.
    (A folk song?)

No. 2556

Oh, come to me, my lover kind,
if but to lift my bamboo blind.
    (A folk song?)

No. 2557

Almost the same as No. 2517

No. 2558

She tied the sash for me
    as I was starting on my way.
Now of itself it came untied:
    is she yearning so today?

No. 2559

I saw my truelove yesternight,
but now again long for her sight.

No. 2560

Here I live in a village drear,
and soon shall die of love.

No. 2561

We've met, defying rumors scandalous,
and now more poisoned tongues will harry us.

No. 2562

How I love my truelove meek,
but oh, how the townspeople speak.

(A folk song?)

No. 2563

You departed early,
    and I accompanied you,
and had my skirt all wet—
    dripping wet with dew.

(A folk song?)

No. 2564

Does my love lie tonight alone in bed,
her lovely raven tresses careless spread?

No. 2565

Across the hedge she caught my eye,
and left me heaving many a sigh.

(A folk song?)

No. 2566

Can any one reprove
my lass, for hiding love?

(A folk song?)

No. 2567

All men know
that face to face
is love's consolation;
but as for me,
I yearn the worse thereafter.

No. 2568

Only love can make me bold enough
to pass through your forbidding portal.

No. 2569

I know you do not think of me.
How strange I nightly dream of you!

No. 2570

Since I have told my mother
now you can freely come here.

No. 2571

Men may console themselves in sundry fashions
    of their own,
but ah, alas, we women only suffer all alone.

No. 2572

Almost the same as No. 771

No. 2573

I am yours, heart and soul,
I swear, my all-in-all.

No. 2574

Although I clench my fist, and beat my breast,
the love within will not be dispossessed.

No. 2575

Now my left eyebrow itches,
so I shall see my lover.

        (It is said when one's eyebrows itch, one can
    see one's love.)

No. 2576

I only talked with her the hedges through,
and now townspeople tattle of us two.

No. 2577

We shall not see each other long.
　　It is our fate,
and months and years will pass
　　over us, separate.

No. 2578

Disheveled though it be this morn,
I shall not comb my hair;
for while we slept last night it lay
upon your stalwart arm so strong.

No. 2579

Impetuously I sought you out,
and now
what beatific calm of lassitude!

No. 2580

If I could cease to love you so,
then should I go on yearning?　No!

No. 2581

'Tis easy to say, 'I love you.'
'Tis easy to hear it said.
But oh, in my heart where truth lies,
there I love you.

No. 2582

'Tis ludicrous all else above
for me so old to fall in love.

No. 2583

As time is reckoned, but a little while
has passed since first we met,
and yet to us
already it seems years.

No. 2584

A manly man I thought myself to be,
but now a weakling she has rendered me.

No. 2585

I know man's life is not to be relied upon;
and only pray that you will come to see me soon.

No. 2586

People talk.　That's why I send no messenger,
but believe me, I love you the same, my dear.

No. 2587

I left my love in far Ohara Town.
Oh, how I wish I could but dream of her.

No. 2588

My dear, at dusk you used to come to me,
and at this hour now still I wait for you.

No. 2589

I prayed the gods I might see you at least in
　　dreams,
but all's in vain.　Not even there do you appear.

No. 2590

At night I'm loath
　　to cross the rugged hill,
but again and yet again
　　to see my love I will.

No. 2591

If we heed rumors much,
we shall lose each other.

No. 2592

After my death I shall have naught to say;
so come as often as you can, I pray.

No. 2593

Restless on my shifting pillow,
keeping vigil with my yearning,
—would that the night were past!

No. 2594

Tonight I can not go to her.
Does she keep unlatched her gate,
and wait and wait?

No. 2595

How I desire to see her in my dreams!
But I am too disturbed even for them.

No. 2596

I yearn to see my love again,
but days and months pass by in vain.

No. 2597

My love for you will grow and grow,
and now can I forget you?　No.

No. 2598

Far though you live, I love you dear;
no village girls shall take my heart.

No. 2599

Vain is my love for her
who sleeps upon another's arm.

No. 2600

We can not live a hundred years. Then why
must we our pleasant rendezvous deny?

No. 2601

Awake or adream, my dear,
I never thought of our encounter here.

No. 2602

I cease not loving you although my hair
grows white: my constancy I'll alter ne'er.

No. 2603

Translated, almost the same as No. 2573

No. 2604

My love, if you must weep, weep secretly;
and let not others see you heave a sigh.

No. 2605

At the young girl I had a glance,
and came to love her then at once.

No. 2606

Translated, much the same as No. 2517

No. 2607

Though we parted then that day,
yet you ever in me stay.

No. 2608

Away now from my own,
I nightly sleep alone.

No. 2609

Alas, alas, now almost threadbare is my sleeve,
since yearning for my love I wave it morn and
    eve.

No. 2610

Though I be deranged, I little care,—
though as disheveled as my hair.

No. 2611

My girdle loosens in my longing
when I lie not with you, my love.

No. 2612

My lover, ever since my sleeve touched yours,
I have been yearning for you days and hours.

No. 2613

The fortuneteller tells me you will come,
and oh, I vainly wait and wait.

No. 2614

I have been wondering if you could come, my
    dear,
my eyebrows itching. And how blessed, now you
    are here.

No. 2615

Alas, for many a year
I've slept away from her.

No. 2616

Her door I knocked at made a threatening sound,
and so I slept upon the frosty ground.

No. 2617

What stops my love for whom I wait,
keeping unlatched my cherry gate?

No. 2618

The moon was clear. I took the shortest cut
my truelove to be with,
and now, alas, far spent
already is the night.

*Mention is made in the text that the following
verses were composed to "expresse the
feelings of the authors with allusions,"
which, however, are not
always clear.*

No. 2619

So long I have not seen you
I waste away,
thin as a morning shadow.

No. 2620

I seem deranged in mind,
  yearning for you, and oh,
I have no friend who asks
  for whom I suffer so.

No. 2621

It is said when you dream
  of wearing colored clothes
people talk about you, and I dreamed
  such a dream, and surely rumor goes.

No. 2622

Though I see you often,
I long for you each moment.

No. 2623

Daily we grow closer,
and love each other more.

No. 2624

Very much the same as above.

No. 2625

Offerings I make the gods in hopes to see
my lover, but still he comes not to me.

No. 2626

As one who throws away old clothes repents
when autumn winds come wailing,
so you will sorrow soon,
your love forsaking.

No. 2627

My young bride flirts with me,
  laughing and whispering,
and yielding, unties
  her garment string.

No. 2628

You are the only one
I truly hold my own.

No. 2629

Although you stay away, I do not take it ill,
but send this pillow now my place to fill.

No. 2630

For long I have not seen my wife,
  because I roam,
and my wooden pillow
  must be molding now at home.

No. 2631

Is my love awaiting me, her head
upon her arm, and raven tresses spread?

No. 2632

Alas, unless I sit before her,
I never shall stop yearning for her.

No. 2633

As I look at my mirror every morning,
so daily I see you with joy, my darling.

No. 2634

Alas, you live afar,
  and how I yearn, my dear.
You never leave my mind,
  and nightly in my dream appear.

No. 2635

I am a man who wears a blade,
but love is not afraid of me.

No. 2636

Very much the same as No. 2498

No. 2637

I sneeze. Does she
now think of me?

No. 2638

In Suenohara field
with your catalpa bow
hunting birds with surest aim
your bow-string twangs unceasing.

No. 2639

Placing faith in me
as Sotsuhiko in his bow
(he of Katsuragi)
her name she has revealed.

No. 2640

Like drawing and letting go
your fine catalpa bow
draw near when you desire,
and, as you wish, retire.

No. 2641

I count the drum beats.
    It is the time appointed with my dear.
Oh, why then does
    he not appear?

No. 2642

Shining in the circle of the lamplight
her smiling face even now I seem to see.

No. 2643

Could we only meet
day after day, my sweet!

No. 2644

Even if the bridge decay, ne'er fear.
I will come, crawling on the girder.

No. 2645

Those who build a palace do not rest,
my love, nor does from languishing my breast.

No. 2646

Oh, why should I thus pining be?
Better to be buoyant, free.

No. 2647

Far off lives my sweet,
alas, nor can we meet.

No. 2648

As lines drawn by the skilful
carpenters of Hida,
my thoughts go straight to you.

No. 2649

The fire of love burns bright
within me day and night.

No. 2650

My parents do not let me see you,
though I hold you as my own.

No. 2651

Though my wife grow older,
dear all the same I hold her.

No. 2652

Now she will not see me.
Has she had enough of me?

No. 2653

When I heard the beat of hoofs,
expecting to see you,
I sallied forth and stood beside the tree,
but the rider was a stranger.

No. 2654

I've spent a sleepless night,
waiting for my lover,
and hear the clattering of hoofs.
Who goes riding now at dawn?

No. 2655

Shall I come, trailing the red skirt, my sweet,
or you to me across the narrow path?

No. 2656

Wishing to make you mine,
I worship at the Karu shrine.

No. 2657

Though I prayed to keep him as my love,
he is too fickle for the powers above.

No. 2658

I hear of him again and yet again,
but, oh, alas, the days pass by in vain.

No. 2659

My love, let people talk about us free.
I but wish peace will reign o'er you and me.

No. 2660

Day after day
I pray
that every evening I may meet
my sweet.

No. 2661

Bereft of love am I,
and I do naught but sigh.

No. 2662

Almost the same as No. 2660

No. 2663

Sacrifice I set at naught;
the shrine itself I would profane,
reckless of my proper fame.

No. 2664

I have wasted to a string,
for my sweet love languishing.

No. 2665

Ah me, I should have left your bower sooner
I took the dawning for the shining moon.

No. 2666

Now I wait on tiptoe for my love,
as one waits at twilight for the moon above.

No. 2667

While I was awaiting you,
    dusting the matting with my sleeves,
the moon went down, alas,
    dawn brightening my eaves.

No. 2668

How for her sleeve
I yearn at eve!

No. 2669

My husband may be thinking now of me,
    viewing this moon so bright.
Let no clouds come, therefore,
    and veil the sky tonight.

No. 2670

Though now the moon sinks in the west,
I, waiting for you, can not rest.

No. 2671

You are the only one
I await, my own.

No. 2672

Absent is my mind,
for I love you blindly.

No. 2673

I'm looking on the moon,
yearning for you.
When it goes down,
nothing will soothe me.

No. 2674

Even if me you betray,
will I not go my own way?

No. 2675

As clouds e'er veil Mikasa high,
so day and night with love I sigh.

No. 2676

O that a white cloud I could be
that daily I might come to thee.

No. 2677

I hear the tempest roar.
I will not leave your bower.

No. 2678

I kept the door unshut
    for a breeze and lay awake,
but like my lover
    it came not for my sake.

No. 2679

'Tis a stormy night, but moonbeams come
    into my room,
and I am thinking of you dearly,
    oh, my bridegroom.

No. 2680

When they hear of our love, they'll talk of us,
since they so much like rumors slanderous.

No. 2681

Bent on word from my husband, at my gate
hatless I am standing in the rain.

No. 2682

I made a gown for you
  in the Chinese way,
and waited for your coming
  all this rainy day.

No. 2683

'Twas raining when I led her
  into a hut that day,
and the floor itself was wet,
  as we together lay.

No. 2684

It was my lover dear who said
  he would not start, for he
with no umbrella could not go
  into the rain, and stayed with me.

No. 2685

Now I pass her gate, and wish that it would shower
to give me an excuse to shelter in her bower.

No. 2686

To consult the fortuneteller
I left my bower at eve,
and dew fell on my sleeve
only soon to disappear.

No. 2687

Though my mother may suspect, go not ere dawn,
my love, for now the dew of night lies cold.

No. 2688

Even though I be wet through with dew,
outside the gate I'll be awaiting you.

No. 2689

Howe'er old I may grow,
I'll wait for you as now.

No. 2690

Drenched with dew I stood
outside her gate
uselessly: she never let me in.

No. 2691

I think of no one else,
and though I be but dew,
my trust is all in you.

No. 2692

The grass is white with last night's rime;
do not leave telltale prints behind you.

No. 2693

Oh, how I languish for you, Maiden fair,
and wish I were the very ground you tread.

No. 2694

How strange I love the maiden still
I saw but once beyond the hill!

No. 2695

Only to see my love I'm yearning;
and like Mt. Fuji ever burning.

No. 2696

Glad I will bear the blame
for hiding my love's name.

No. 2697

Though I be ever burning like Mt. Fuji,
I'll try to stay away from you.

No. 2698

Nightly I can not sleep,
  for my sweet love
lives beyond the mountain deep
  beside Asaka Cove.

No. 2699

Alas, I can't have sight
of you though I yearn day and night.

No. 2700

Though I may die from love, ne'er shall you
  blame
me, dear, for I have not disclosed your name.

No. 2701

Tomorrow I will come again
   crossing the river.
I can not live without you, dear,
   for ever.

No. 2702

Daily more I languish,
and soon from love shall perish.

No. 2703

Long have I yearned for her, and oh, this eve
at last will I rest pillowing my head upon her
   sleeve.

No. 2704

As ever runs this river clear,
so I yearn after you, my dear.

No. 2705

You would not let me in,
though I forded the river to meet you.

No. 2706

So sweet the waters of Hatsuse.
As sweet were you who loved me once.

No. 2707

Alas, alas, we can not meet,
I pining ever for my sweet.

No. 2708

They speak of us loud as a mountain torrent,
and I, her parents fearing, can not see my truelove.

No. 2709

Overleaping all impediments,
   I love my lass for ever
as water courses down
   the weirs of the river.

No. 2710

People may ask my name of thee;
but, pray, speak not at all of me.

No. 2711

Only hearing of her,
I now deeply love her.

No. 2712

All people talk too much, my dear,
pray, cease for some time to come here.

No. 2713

How she must have awaited me today;
yet alas, I could not go, and stayed away.

No. 2714

However long for you I pine,
I never shall complain.

No. 2715

No longer shall I keep this secret,
but will see my lover openly.

No. 2716

Nights when alone I sleep
are spent in sorrow deep.

No. 2717

Though I seldom see my love,
gossip goes now like the sound of falls.

No. 2718

Though my love is violent
as the mountain torrent,
and though I die from it,
I shall not speak of you.

No. 2719

I told the secret, and I sigh.
Oh what a wretched fool am I!

No. 2720

Now I see you this evensong—
you for whom I pined so long.

No. 2721

Was I too rash, or did I yearn too clear?
For now our love is known, my dear.

No. 2722

Tell my love
that I have come
as far as the plain
of Wazami.

No. 2723

Thinking of my family name,
I love her secretly.

No. 2724

I do not know eventually
    what will become of me,
but now like driftwood to the shore
    my heart is drawn to thee.

No. 2725

I may look placid, oh, my love,
but that I pine my heart can prove.

No. 2726

Without trysts gossip is abroad
as if, all windless, billows rose.

No. 2727

Here intermittent breakers lave the shore,
but ceaselessly I languish for my love.

No. 2728

I keep her secret
like Biwa's unseen island mountain,
and people envy me.

No. 2729

Noisy as the waves that roar against Ohura
gossip goes, but unconcerned, I only love you.

No. 2730

We've never met; but people speak of us,
since they so much like rumors scandalous.

No. 2731

Though their slanderous tongues reprove,
they never can undo our love.

No. 2732

As the sea is lashed
    by waves that rave,
so people's tongues torment us.
    My sweet, we must be brave.

No. 2733

Being in a miserable plight,
love tormenting me both day and night,
I am like an island shore
where white-crested breakers roar.

No. 2734

I am unstable as a grain of sand
    when tides come the beach to lave.
Oh why will not this unrequited love
    send me down into the grave?

No. 2735

I wish that I could see
my sweet love oft and free.

No. 2736

I wonder if thou thinkst of me,
Beloved, as I think of thee.

No. 2737

Ceaselessly as the white wave laving Mitsu Beach
I yearn for her, but oh, she knows it not.

No. 2738

Ay me, how can I cease
to love, and sleep in peace?

No. 2739

I do not know, my friend,
how our love will end.

No. 2740

What people say I do not care.
For you all things I gladly dare.

No. 2741

Sometimes tranquil is the sea,
but I am ever deep in turmoil
for the sake of you.

No. 2742

With fervent love I pine,
wishing to be thine.

No. 2743

Had I been born into a fisherman's family,
I would be faring simply, and not in love with
  you.

No. 2744

You seem as far as fishing torches burning
out at sea, and I spend time in yearning.

No. 2745

Many obstacles came between us,
and oh, I have not been with you.

No. 2746

My love for you is ever burning in my breast
like rowing oars that ply without surcease.

No. 2747

Now thy name is known to me,
and I can surely come to thee.

No. 2748

My heart goes out to you
freely and ceaselessly.

No. 2749

My mind is ever filled with thought
of her, and other things are naught.

No. 2750

I have not seen my love for long, and now
the moss has grown upon our orange bough.

No. 2751

Fair the lone pine tree by Susa Cove.
So is my lass, and her alone I love.

No. 2752

I ever think of you, my dear.
I fear my looks are telltale.

No. 2753

Like that oak upon the isle
for long I have not seen my love.

No. 2754

Yearning for you, in bed I lay,
and in my dream you came to stay.

No. 2755

They speak of us, though innocent are we,
but never mind their talk, and come to me.

No. 2756

My love, we can not live for ever.
Why then speak only of the future?

No. 2757

Faultless do you remain, my sweet,
though ever and anon we meet.

No. 2758

I pine for you,
and my manliness is lost in love.

No. 2759

It matters not how long 'twill be,
if you consent to marry me.

No. 2760

I will go to the hillside herbs to gather.
So meet me there,
even though your mother scold you aftewards.

No. 2761

Deep are the roots of plants that grow by stones.
So is my fervent love for you.

No. 2762

Dissemble, for if you smile so,
that you love me all will know.

No. 2763

The while you hold
the reeds of Asaha
to reap them,
even that while, hold me in mind.

No. 2764

O sweet, feel pity now on me
whose sole wish is to live for thee.

No. 2765

I'd rather die, dear one,
than in this way live on.

No. 2766

You but pretend to love me so:
you do not truly; that I know.

No. 2767

The orange does not hide its color,
nor shall we hide our love.

No. 2768

I wish to win her hand,
but people seem to stand e'er in my way.

No. 2769

I cling to my husband, persistent as grasses that
  grow
again and yet again, however trodden they may
  be.

No. 2770

It matters not how long it takes, still I
shall be waiting for the girl's reply.

No. 2771

Hatless hurried I hither
to shelter 'neath your sleeves.

No. 2772

Unless you weave your hat
with sedge from Manu Pond
take care to cause no gossip.

No. 2773

My darling, when you come not, I am desolate;
when you come, afterward I feel more lonely.

No. 2774

His voice is sweet and clear
which through the crowd I hear.

No. 2775

O that I could see you
ever, continuous as the vine!

No. 2776

Pray, tell her that I have come here,
treading the winter grasses sere.

In reply
No. 2777

If he came oft to me, I know
the wayside grasses could not grow.

No. 2778

Moving as secretly as the plants
that grow beneath the water
will I go to her.

No. 2779

Reduced now to a bag of bones am I,
pining with love, and living wearily.

No. 2780

Translated, much the same as No. 2573

No. 2781

I yearn for thee, forgetting all;
so pity me, thy wretched thrall!

No. 2782

I little care for others with whom I can lie,
and only wait and wait, my lass, for your reply.

No. 2783

What boots it then, my loving thee
like this who dost not think of me?

No. 2784

I'll keep on loving you as secretly
as now, my dear, though yearning I may die!

No. 2785

Although the fairest flower has but its time,
my love for you is ever in its prime.

No. 2786

I dreamed about her dressed in red,
and still yearn after her in bed.

No. 2787

Yonder dwells my darling fair
with whom I wish to be for e'er.

No. 2788

Rather let our love be known
than live thus apart, alone.

No. 2789

Of love bereft, no more shall I have sight
of her, but wait for death's sepulchral night.

No. 2790

As two beads on the selfsame string will meet,
so we will be eventually joined, my sweet.

No. 2791

Oh must I waste away, a thrall
to love, till I am known to all?

No. 2792

Oh how can I be sane,
yearning for years in vain?

No. 2793

Alas for me;
afar lives she.

No. 2794

Like as the water oozes hard rock through,
as patiently now do I wait for you.

No. 2795

Years passing, aged I shall be,
still I'll be ever true to thee.

No. 2796

Many a year has passed now over me,
living in unrequited love for you.

No. 2797

No empty shell
beached on Suminoe Cove
is my love, but full and faithful.

No. 2798

Unrequited love is mine,
and who can blame me my complaints?

No. 2799

That none could spy us,
averting gossip,
amid the crying quail
we met in a deserted hut.

No. 2800

Cocks are crowing, as 'tis dawn,
but what care I who lie alone?

No. 2801

Every morning I desire to see
you, but, alas, you do not come to me.

No. 2802

How could I pass
this livelong night
without thought of my lass?

No. 2803

Freely any village cock
can lift its voice,
but my true love
in secret weeps.

No. 2804

I wait on tiptoe for my love,
fervently praying he may come.

No. 2805

Could I but pass some word with you,
I should not live this lonely life.

No. 2806

Oh, is it for my love of you
    that like a mallard on the breast
of yonder waves, no time have I
    for my poor heart to rest?

No. 2807

Already birds are singing
    telling that dawn is here
when I still wish to lie
    pillowed on your arm, my dear.

Dialogue
No. 2808

Did you await me, sneezing,
your eyebrows itching, and sash loosening?
To our delight now we are met.

No. 2809

I sneezed, my brows itched.
All good omens.
Now you have come.

No. 2810

Hearing of you, I love you. If I see
you, oh what will become of me?

No. 2811

So longing for some gentle word from you,
in mirror-bright moonlight I saw only dark.

No. 2812

They say, "If you lie wearing
    your night gown inside out, your love will see
you in his dream."
    I slept so doing yesternight, and did you dream
      of me?

No. 2813

You say you put your gown on inside out,
and surely did I have you in my dream.

No. 2814

You in my dream at least I wished to see,
but in vain the years have passed o'er me.

No. 2815

You say you do not see me in your dream, my
    love,
but every night without cease you in mine appear.

No. 2816

I am all thine: pray, trust in me.
I'll never turn my back on thee.

No. 2817

I love you secretly,
and you can trust in me.

No. 2818

I am betrothed, but waiting for the nuptial bed,
alas, year after year has passèd o'er my head.

No. 2819

My betrothed, I love you so
I shall wait, however old I grow.

No. 2820

Standing the livelong night outside your gate,
until the moon sank I awaited you.

No. 2821

Entranced with the moon's progression through
    the trees
I spent the night in wandering.

No. 2822

I only pine for you,
but you think naught of me.

No. 2823

Cold to me,
unkind, unkind
are you who will not come.

No. 2824

If I had only known that you would come to me,
I would have paved my gateway with smooth
stones.

No. 2825

For pretty stones about your gate I little care.
All I crave is to be with you, lady fair.

No. 2826

You start upon a journey, leaving me,
and pining, I shall wait and wait for you.

No. 2827

I part from you, and wish you were a flower
wherewith to dye the robe I wear for journeying.

No. 2828

None wears a scarlet undergown,
and goes unnoticed.

No. 2829

If from a bounteous wardrobe
I appeared in constant changes,
would you remember my unchanging face?

No. 2830

Can you not have a new band for your bow
to draw it with a spirit fresh and bold?

No. 2831

I'd rather be a stranded vessel
    waiting for the tide
than thus be yearning to see you
    who come not to my side.

No. 2832

For many a year did I frequent her bower,
though her parents were upon the watch so close.

No. 2833

If the water of the pond where mallards live flow
    out,
they fly away,
but never, never shall I leave you,
oh, my darling love.

No. 2834

As rich in promise as the peach trees
of Muro in Yamato
my vow shall be fulfilled.

No. 2835

To no man will I yield
my sweet grass of the field.

No. 2836

The sedge is still too young, and yet
    were I to wait till it can be
made into a hat, some one
    would reap ahead of me.

No. 2837

Reaping the riverside sedge,
why do you leave it ungathered?

No. 2838

O that a herb I were,
    floating downstream, and by
a maiden young and fair
    caught lovingly.

No. 2839

Like the frayed rope of the sacred tree
old and weak soon I shall be.

No. 2840

A little rain makes not the river roar,
but our few trysts have swollen the flood of gossip.

THE MANYOSHU

BOOK XII

FOREWORD

This book is, so to speak, Part 2 of the love songs appearing in Book XI, and has been classified by the commentators into 5 parts: "Songs expressing the feelings without allusions," "Songs expressed through allusions," "Songs in dialogue," "Songs on travel," and elegies.

Whereas Book XI has Sedohka and songs in metaphor, they do not appear in this volume.

Book XII contains songs on travel and elegies, not found in the preceding volume. We have only verselets in this book, which number 380.

Songs expressing the feelings without allusions

No. 2841

My lover took a hurried leave
    this morn and went away,
and left alone, I must
    yearn for him all day.

No. 2842

I long for you so fervently, my dear,
that every night you in my dream appear.

No. 2843

Yonder I see my sweet love now, but oh,
the thick crowd intervening, I must let her go.

No. 2844

These nights I have been sleepless,
    lying alone
without her arm to lay
    my head upon.

No. 2845

Only to cease to pine with love I talk with men,
but it avails me naught: all is in vain.

No. 2846

I can not sleep;
I can not be at peace,
nor can I change my clothes
until I see my love.

No. 2847

You told me then to wait, but many a year
has passed in vain since over me.

No. 2848

I wish at least to see my love
    while sleeping, but it seems
that rumor stops his coming
    even in my dreams.

No. 2849

Not a day passes over me without a tear;
and how I wish that I were in your dreams.

No. 2850

My days are spent in yearning after thee,
so in my dream at least, pray, come to me.

Songs expressed through allusions

No. 2851

I keep well tied my upper sash that people see;
but with the nether loosened, daily wait for you.

    (In ancient Japanese folklore a sash loosened
    is a charm to bring the wearer's love soon.)

No. 2852

When gossip is rampant,
my love like a garment
I would wear underneath.

No. 2853

Thinking of our future,
nightly now I sleep alone.

No. 2854

Before my sash frays I will pray
the gods may keep it strong until we meet.

    (It is an ill omen to have the sash break, for
    it means separation from the love.)

No. 2855

Glad am I to hear them tell
that my darling love fares well.

No. 2856

Though I prayed to see her,
my prayer is not yet answered.

No. 2857

Yearning for you, my sleeves are ever wet with
    brine,
and 'tis only you that have the power to dry them.

No. 2858

O Wind, no sleep comes to me yearning for my
    love.
If you have come from blowing o'er her bower,
    caress me now.

No. 2859

The Asuka stream has swollen, and a long way
  round
    did I come here,
and my reward is that till dawn
    I will not leave my dear.

No. 2860

Without cease flows the river,
so have I loved you ever.

No. 2861

Lest people talk about us,
I circumspectly love my dear.

No. 2862

I, without cease day and night,
yearn for you, my heart's delight.

No. 2863

Oh, for whom do I languish
but for you, my love, my darling?

Songs expressing the feelings without allusions
No. 2864

I eagerly await my lord;
    but vainly hours pass by,
and, alas, he coming not,
    sitting alone I only sigh.

No. 2865

Had I a love with whom I now could lie,
this night could be spent in an ecstasy.

No. 2866

Speak not such impudence.
Oh how audacious to think that I,
a married woman, would untie
the sash for such as you!

No. 2867

How I languish for my love!
I should have stayed the night.
Now my haste I but regret.

No. 2868

Only for trysts with her I pray,
and thus I live from day to day.

No. 2869

Not a moment am I free
from this sad unrequited love for thee.
Now fervently
I pray the gods to let me die.

No. 2870

Alas, the night is gone
he promised me to come upon.
Such is his word, and never he
will come again to me.

No. 2871

People spoke ill of me,
and since then even when we meet
casually on the street,
not a word of greeting utters she.

No. 2872

Without a chance to meet my love,
    sadly do I live
vexed with the gossip spread
    by people talkative.

No. 2873

If I pine with love and die,
the townsfolk with a nose
for news will spread it,
and you too will be talked about.

No. 2874

Having no messenger I can entrust,
I only sigh for you,
and wonder if
in your dream I now appear.

No. 2875

To heaven and earth not much inferior
    I thought myself to be,
but now where is my manliness,
    falling a prey of love for thee?

No. 2876

It is not good to live close by a town.
    fearing people's eye,
and not to dare to see your love
    as often as you wish, and only sigh.

No. 2877

Alas, a wretched slave of love am I,
wherefrom I can't escape, hard though I try.

No. 2878

Alone in bed to loneliness I yield.
When will my lovesick heart be healed?

No. 2879

Many years passed over me,
during which not a single tryst had we.

No. 2880

Alas, I live a lonely life,
only dreaming of my wife.

No. 2881

I know not what to do, my love,
passing months apart from you.

No. 2882

I ever love you,
though we can seldom meet.

No. 2883

How could I cease to love you,
my dear, unless I perish?

No. 2884

I pass today in sorrow.
How shall I be tomorrow?

No. 2885

At midnight I thought of you, my love,
and yearned upon my restless pillow.

No. 2886

No matter how they talk of us,
dare I not their tongues slanderous?

No. 2887

Although I stand on earth, do I
not feel my heart soar to the sky?

No. 2888

Serious is love with me;
I love you earnestly.

No. 2889

My dearest love will ever welcome me.
Why do I yearn then so impatiently?

No. 2890

The nights are long now; so my husband,
prithee often in my dream appear.

No. 2891

Alas, long have I yearned and pined for you.
How can I hope thus for long life?

No. 2892

Ay me, the months have passed
without a single tryst with you.

No. 2893

You leave my bower at dawn and come at even-
    song,
but in the daytime still for you I long.

No. 2894

A wretched slave of love,
I ever languish for my lass.

No. 2895

Only to shun folk's tongues so keen
for days my love I have not seen.

No. 2896

About our future thou art in anxiety;
but be assured, my dear, for I love none but thee.

No. 2897

When can I daily see
my darling love
with her trailing skirt
moving about me?

No. 2898

Alas, is it my lot to yearn for sight
of her? Oh, would I could but flee this plight!

No. 2899

Ay me, I, lovesick, ever moan.
Why did I not stay away from her?

No. 2900

Still now her smiling face and graceful brows
    remain
before me, and I can see them again and yet again.

No. 2901

After nightfall never can I rest
with love so fervid burning in my breast.

No. 2902

I ever pine for you,
and know not what to do.

No. 2903

The itching eyebrow that shall be a charm
to bring you, is in vain for me, it seems,
though I should rub my slender eyebrow off.

No. 2904

Had I no hope my love to see,
how could I live? I ask of you.

No. 2905

Our mortal span is sadly short,
but still I waste time, yearning for my love.

No. 2906

To a far country did I go to seek a bride.
I found one, but before I laid my sword aside
'twas morningtide.
    (A folk song?)

No. 2907

No stalwart soldier now am I:
a wretched slave of love will die.

No. 2908

Pining in lovesickness both night and day,
only for respite from my love I pray.

No. 2909

Oh why a man's wife would I woo,
my friend, unless I love her true?

No. 2910

I ever think of you, because I love you true;
but to flee people's eyes I do not come to you.

No. 2911

Never look upon me as untrue.
'Tis but to shun folk I do not see you.

No. 2912

So censorious is the world
    that I will come to thee
in thy dream tonight.
    Pray, keep thy door unlatched for me.

No. 2913

Oh, it is better far to die
than daily thus in love to sigh.

No. 2914

I dreamed of you so fair,
and woke in my despair.

No. 2915

Obscure, I can not call her 'love,' but oh,
what delight if I could call her so!

No. 2916

Who proposed this tryst? I ask of you.
You who now hide your lovely face from me.

No. 2917

Did she really come, or in a dream?
I can not tell. I'm so bemused by love.

No. 2918

With our parents' leave we are betrothed; and I
wait for the happy day, and long and sigh.

No. 2919

My love and I together tied my girdle then.
So I'll not loosen it till I see her again.

No. 2920

Oh, I shall die from love,
    but little do I care. I only grieve
that I can not see her
    before this world I leave.

No. 2921

Alas, I am a maiden who
ever yearns for you.

No. 2922

My dear, you come to me at evensong,
and from the morning for that hour I long.

No. 2923

Oh how I wished to see my love today,
but care for her name kept me from her bower.

No. 2924

Many and many a night had I
when with her I could not lie.

No. 2925

To seek a nurse
is but for tender babes,
and is it thus
you seek my breast?

No. 2926

Alas, I'm old, fit only for the hearse.
When young, I had obliged you as a nurse.

No. 2927

Time was when I loved her deep.
If I slept on her sleeve now,
could my love for her return again?

No. 2928

Pining with love, an early death I crave,
and soon I shall go down into my grave.

No. 2929

Night after night I stand beside the gate,
but you come not, although I wait and wait.

No. 2930

Of love I've yet to make acquaintance.
Can this be love that hurts me so?

No. 2931

I suffer, since I wait at home;
so at evening let me come.

No. 2932

With fervid love within I burn,
yet shunning people, I but yearn.

No. 2933

Thou dost not think of me,
but how I yearn for thee!

No. 2934

I see you oft, but have not sat,
conversing with you tête-à-tête.

No. 2935

Alas, I loved for years,
and ever lived in tears.

No. 2936

Ay me, I soon shall pass away,
pining for you both night and day.

No. 2937

They say, "Sleep with your garment inside out,
    and you
will see your darling in your dream," which has
    proved true.

No. 2938

They talk, and though my lover come,
I can not see him now at home.

No. 2939

Short and easy is the word of love,
but to me 'tis life and death above.

No. 2940

Better to die than live on in this plight,
unable to distinguish day from night.

No. 2941

I ever live in rue,
not blessed with sight of you.

No. 2942

Yearning for you, my husband,
nightly I cry like a baby.

No. 2943

You ne'er come, though you promise. Will not I
live to blame you for the lie?

No. 2944

People's poisonous tongues I fear.
They make me languish for my dear.

No. 2945

Many a night now do I spend,
calling to mind those nights of yore
when messengers from you would find me waiting.

No. 2946

How I wish to have as my own
the maiden I met on the street today !

No. 2947

Not knowing what to do, I told your name.
For that rash act I surely am to blame.

No. 2948

I'll pass her gate tomorrow. She perchance
may pity me my haggard countenance.

No. 2949

My darling, how depressed you look today !
Be cheerful when we are together.

No. 2950

He's gone away. With empty breast
I tread the earth, and have no rest.

No. 2951

My partner in the dance tied me my sash;
I will untie it for another with regret.

No. 2952

As older and as weaker we
grow, dearer you will be.

No. 2953

Pining for my dear love,
I dampen my sleeves with tears.

No. 2954

Alas, tears ceaselessly stand in my eyes. I fear
it is an omen that you no more love me dear.

No. 2955

After months now hearing word from you,
it seems to me a joyous dream scarce true.

No. 2956

I've dreamed of you, my dear,
for years and months.

No. 2957

We part and no more shall we meet.
I only wish to dream of you.

No. 2958

Come in my dream at least, my dear,
where people's tongues we need not fear.

No. 2959

As we can't meet, my dear,
pray, in my dream appear.

No. 2960

I do not feel alive,
since I have not seen her for years.

No. 2961

Unctuous are these words you utter
sounding true by repetition.

No. 2962

I sleep tonight without my love,
and care not at all how soon it dawns.

No. 2963

Languishing with love, alas,
I can not have a peaceful sleep.

Songs expressed through allusions
No. 2964

If you were a gown—
you who are like this—
I once thought I would wear you
as an undergarment.

No. 2965

You are so dear to me, and I
ask you to come, and vainly sigh.

No. 2966

At first so deeply did I not love you.
Now from the bottom of my heart I do.

No. 2967

"Traveling, though years pass over you,
ever look at this, and think of me, dear," said my
  love,
giving me a garment of her sewing.
But now 'tis worn to rags.

No. 2968

So kind to me is she,
whom I love fervently.

No. 2969

No friends concern themselves, although
'tis plain with love I suffer so.

No. 2970

Believe me, I meet you
with a heart all true.

No. 2971

Oftentimes my love I see,
but she never wearies me.

No. 2972

Daily I yearn for you.
Oh why not come to me?

No. 2973

My girdle shall not be untied, my sweet,
until the happy evening when we meet.

No. 2974

My purple sash kept fastened,
I only want my wife.

No. 2975

I pray to the divinities, and lie alone,
    my girdle of Korean brocade tied tight,
but the prayer unanswered, never
    does my lover come by day or night.

No. 2976

Hiding love deep in my breast,
pining for you, I know no rest.

No. 2977

Translated, very much the same as No. 2966

No. 2978

Cherish this mirror for my sake
    when you are on the road,
and look whenever you
    wish to see me, my lord.

No. 2979

I'll be content, can I come face to face with you,
but else consumed by love I shall soon die.

No. 2980

Without my love I do not feel alive.
Oh how can I these dreary months survive?

No. 2981

I am reminded of my love
by every woman I see on the street.

No. 2982

My sash will fray,
as if to say,
"You have none to mend me."

No. 2983

Korean sword!
for my own reasons
I can not meet you
whom I want so much.

No. 2984

Since so much for her I care,
obloquy I gladly bear.

No. 2985

I know not how my love for you will end,
but be sure I ever love you true.

No. 2986

As one draws and lets go
the catalpa bow,
so on impulse and reflection
my heart stays yours.

No. 2987

Alas, I am a weakling now to serve
a girl, though once a warrior of steel nerve.

No. 2938

I met you today,
and life's no longer gray.

No. 2989

My mind is now at rest,
since I rely on you.

No. 2990

Happy am I in passionate love for you,
and love is now the only thing with me.

No. 2991

My love, I keep indoors alone
like a silk worm in the cocoon.

No. 2992

Ever I yearn for you, my dear.
Ever I wish to have you here.

No. 2993

Today so beautiful a girl saw I;
and she'll remain long in my memory.

No. 2994

I ever languish for my love,
but have no chance for rendezvous.

No. 2995

Till we've a happy time to meet,
come in my nightly dream, my sweet.

No. 2996

Your words are good enough to hear,
if only they prove true.

No. 2997

Alas, already night is far advanced, and I
may not see my darling waiting now.

No. 2998

Alas, I cannot see her now,
but shall be with her soon enough.

No. 2999

Like millet cast away from fields am I,
weeded out from among her happy suitors.

No. 3000

If we love, together we can lie,
    but my mother keeps a watch o'er me
as against a savage boar
    that harm the harvest free.

No. 3001

Like the glow of sunset
over Kasuga slope
I glimpsed you in the distance,
and still my heart is sore.

No. 3002

Pretending that I wait to view the moon
rise from behind the mountain,
here I stand to see
my lover come.

No. 3003

Dimly as in the earliest dawning
with the moon already set
I saw her.
That vision haunts me still.

No. 3004

While the sun shines above,
I shall not change, my love.

No. 3005

Refulgent as the fifteen-day-old moon
you shine upon me,
and all my life is silvered.

No. 3006

So full of promise seemed the moon
inviting me outside my gate;
"Yes," "No," "Yes," "No,"—I walked a fortune-
  walk.
In vain! I can not see her.

> (The person who wants to know his fortune
> sets a mark on the ground, and repeating "good
> or bad" he goes toward it. If at the moment
> when his foot is on the mark, the word is good,
> then he will be fortunate, and vice versa.)

No. 3007

I had wished the moon were bright
  the other evening when we met;
but cloudy, I could not behold
  your beauty well to my regret.

No. 3008

Lofty trees stand on the mountain,
retarding the moonrise and my darling.

No. 3009

My first love was the best:
I care not for the rest.

No. 3010

Calmly flows the Saho River.
Would that we lived thus for ever.

No. 3011

Yoshiki's Stream, tell me
the means my love to see.

No. 3012

I yearn for my darling ever
as water courses in the river.

No. 3013

Never cease to love me, never,
but love me on forever
as runs our Sodefuru River.

No. 3014

I live a happy, happy life
with you as my beloved wife.

No. 3015

Would I could see my lover's face
here now within my dwelling place!

No. 3016

Alas, my secret love for you is out,
and rumors now are being spread no doubt.

No. 3017

My love has flown from me.
Now some man's wife is she.

No. 3018

As the Noto's tributaries meet,
so we too shall be one at last.

No. 3019

My darling, come what will, 'tis clear
I'll never cease to hold you dear.

No. 3020

Whatever people speak of you, my dear,
I'll go on loving you. So have no fear.

No. 3021

I languish for you ceaselessly,
but none shall see me heave a sigh.

No. 3022

Secret my love for you I keep,
My dear, like water hidden deep.

No. 3023

Ay me, my face betraying me,
now people know my love for you.

No. 3024

Like white waves to and fro on Horie shore
my heart is ever yearning after you.

No. 3025

If only we could meet,
love truly would be sweet.

No. 3026

Alas, you do not come to me,
and how can I, a maid, go out to you?

No. 3027

O Waves upon Lake Biwa,
none know but you I am in love.

No. 3028

She plights herself to me,
and ever true will be.

No. 3029

I yearn for her incessantly,
and yet she is indifferent to me.

No. 3030

All things remind me of her,
since so deep I love her.

No. 3031

If you do not love me true,
ask me not to wait for you.

No. 3032

Toward her bower I look,
and take delight.
Oh Mt. Ikoma, never, never
let rain clouds veil your brow.

No. 3033

A stranger then was he,
but now so dear to me.

No. 3034

From out my smoldering breast
when I slide open the doors at morn
the vapors of love do I exhale.

No. 3035

I always leave your bower at dawn.
How strange our secrecy is known!

No. 3036

Day and night do I pine
after that love of mine.

No. 3037

Oh what delight if even awhile
I could see my darling smile.

No. 3038

I am lovelorn,
and grieve and moan.
I envy dew that falls at night
to vanish in the morning light.

No. 3039

Can I survive
this love, or shall I be
like dew that falls at night
only to vanish in the morning?

No. 3040

I am a slave to love. Oh pity me
who live but for the hope my lass to see.

No. 3041

"Let's die together when we die, dear," said my
     lass,
"vanishing like the morning's dew upon the
     grass."

No. 3042

Lovelorn, I wish to pass away
like dew before the morning's ray.

No. 3043

Weak and lovesick though I be,
I strive to live till you agree.

No. 3044

I'm in the garden waiting now for you,
and on my hair is laid the evening dew.

No. 3045

I ever languish for my love until
I wonder why I am so weak of will.

No. 3046

My passion for the girl has no surcease,
and oh! this wretched bosom knows no ease.

No. 3047

Thankful am I for you, whose judgement is as
  sound
as the pine deep-rooted in the rocky ground.

No. 3048

My love, I hold you dear,
but you remain so cold.

No. 3049

Younger than I the woman is.
Married are we to live in bliss.

No. 3050

Oh how I wish her to love me,
as I love her ceaselessly!

No. 3051

My dear, how I love you—
you so fair and true!

No. 3052

You come not to my bower.
You mean you've had enough of me?

No. 3053

Almost the same as No. 3051

No. 3054

Why must I pine for you
when you're so cold to me?

No. 3055

My breast is void, ah me;
my heart, it is with thee.

No. 3056

I passed her gate before I started on my way,
  and tied together grass.
So Wind, pray, blow it not apart
  until I come back to my lass.

No. 3057

Lovesick, I roamed about the field
near the bower where lives my love.

No. 3058

Though many handsome men at court we have,
you are the only man whose love I crave.

No. 3059

No matter what they speak of me,
my heart shall ever be with you.

No. 3060

I tied day lilies in my sash,
unable to forget her pretty face.

> (A day lily is a flower which is said to make
> one forget love.)

No. 3061

I send this gift to you, my love; so for my sake
look at it when every morning you awake.

No. 3062

I set day lilies by my bower
that they might make me forget love.
They grew and grew,
but alas, I suffer still in love.

No. 3063

Even your empty words to hear
would be welcome to my hungry ear.

No. 3064

Days and months and years may pass,
but still let us not lose our hopes to meet.

No. 3065

I, languishing with love,
sleepless spend the nights.

No. 3066

Believe me, I shall go on loving,
my beloved, you alone.

No. 3067

If you love me, I shall not mind, my dear,
even though you come not for a year.

No. 3068

Oh why is it that she
so seldom comes to me?

No. 3069

Though I like to hear from you,
pray, sometimes come to me.

No. 3070

Soon, if not now, pray, meet me
where you desire, my love.

No. 3071

I have no mind whatever
to part from him. Oh never.

No. 3072

For long have I been waiting eagerly
for her to render me her fair reply.

No. 3073

Like tendrils that entwine
I would that we could be.

No. 3074

For you, false-hearted, many years
have I spent in woful tears.

No. 3075

Alas, a man can perish in this wise.
If only on my love I could set eyes!

No. 3076

How strange the maiden will not let me come,
although she told her name and home.

No. 3077

Even if my parents learn of us and blame
me, never, never will I let them know your name.

No. 3078

Unrequited love is mine,
and day and night for you I pine.

No. 3079

I await you eagerly;
prithee, come and lie with me.
(Maybe a folk song.)

No. 3080

Even though I die lovelorn,
my sweet, your name shall not be known.

No. 3081

Ah! from my lover now I have to part,
although I love him still with all my heart.

No. 3082

What care I whether I live or die,
if my lot be but for you to sigh?

No. 3083

For you I yearn and sigh,
alas, and soon shall die.

No. 3084

You ever shall be in my mind—
you who are lovely and so kind.

No. 3085

Thin as a shadow
cast by morning sun am I
now for the glimpse I took
of a maiden passing by.
(Same as No. 2394)

No. 3086

I would liefer be a silkworm
than a man thus lovesick, suffering.

No. 3087

I'm yearning after you as ceaselessly
as o'er the River Soga plovers cry.

No. 3088

As birds are ever singing on Mt. Nara,
so I ever yearn for you, my darling.

No. 3089

Whether I stand or sit,
I ever languish for my lass.

No. 3090

Only hearing of him,
now I deeply love him.

No. 3091

On finding food a mallard
always calls his mate, 'tis said;
and I, a lonely traveler, so thinking,
long and sigh for mine.

No. 3092

Oh why
must I sleepless lie
tonight? Because
I languish for my lass.

No. 3093

After the married girl still ceaselessly
I yearn. She is so beautiful to see!

No. 3094

After a weary night I spend awake,
even the cock crows sadly at daybreak.

No. 3095

O Chanticleer, cry not at morning
and make my lover leave me early.

No. 3096

My parents now reprove
me, since I have a love.

No. 3097

Pray, stop at the river
and let your horse drink
for me to see you longer
before you go away.

No. 3098

My parents scold me if you come, but then of
  course
a woman could not come to you upon a horse.

No. 3099

The doe desires to lie upon the tender grass.
  So does the buck, my own.
Therefore, even when they live on different hills,
  their choice is one.

No. 3100

If you say you love me when you don't,
with you the forest deity will be severe.

Letters and Conversations between Lovers

No. 3101

I love the maiden still that at the dance I met.
Oh why to ask her name did I neglect?

No. 3102

How can she tell her name to one,
a stranger, and his name to her unknown?

No. 3103

My dear, if you can not come here,
at least send me a messenger.

No. 3104

A thousand times I truly wish to come to you,
but many people passing your gate hinder me.

No. 3105

Alas, if I should die of love due to your pride,
your name shall be made known—the name you
  wish to hide.

No. 3106

Pining with love, it will be I
who shall die before you die.

No. 3107

Avoiding gossip do I live alone
without a tryst with you, my own;
and feel now as if I were dead,
long years passing o'er my head.

No. 3108

If you come not, since gossip people spread,
will I not dream about you in my bed?

No. 3109

But for gossip, I would come to you,
my dear, because I love you true.

No. 3110

Pray, do we part, if people speak,
my love? Is your resolve so weak?

No. 3111

I wonder if you dreamt of me
dying from unrequited love for you?

No. 3112

I dreamt of you, and dressed for a holiday
was setting out just when your letter came.

No. 3113

My dear, you promised me to come,
and vainly do I wait and wait.

No. 3114

Every day I wish to meet you,
but gossip hinders me, my darling.

No. 3115

I yearned for her, not knowing
she'd been already married.

No. 3116

Sorrow not, I pray,
for we shall meet some day.

No. 3117

I tightly closed my sliding doors and slept,
nevertheless, I saw you in my dream.

No. 3118

You say you tightly closed your doors and slept.
Perhaps then in through some hole thieves had
    made I crept.

No. 3119

I shall be vainly yearning for you from tomorrow,
so pray, come here, my love, now and untie your
    girdle.

No. 3120

The night is still too young for us to lie, my dear,
so after you leave, nightly in my dream appear.

No. 3121

Bent on word from my husband, at my gate
hatless I was standing in the rain.

> (Same as No. 2681, appearing here again as
> a love letter.)

No. 3122

Oh what relentless rain ! Today did I
intend to visit you safe from the jealous eye.

No. 3123

Tonight I tried to sleep alone in vain,
and came here, fending off the rain with my long
    sleeves.

No. 3124

The rainy night is far advanced. So pray,
untie your girdle now with me to stay.

No. 3125

I wonder who stands at my gate
upon this rainy day so late.

No. 3126

The mountain's veiled in clouds, my dear,
rain falling hard, but I came here.

Songs of Travel
No. 3127

So far since my departure have I come,
longing for my wife I left at home.

No. 3128

That I might see my truelove in my dream
to the gods I prayed whene'er I crossed a stream.

No. 3129

Like the cherry flowers falling as soon as they
   blow,
behold, these countless people come and go.

No. 3130

Even now as I go my way,
love holds me in its sway.

No. 3131

You say that next month you return,
but ere you go, now I already yearn.

No. 3132

I thought that she might come to take me home
   again;
so, as I went my way, I looked back now and then.

No. 3133

Now on my journey I
yearn for my wife and sigh.

No. 3134

I am not yet come
so far from home,
yet for my wife I yearn
already wishing to return.

No. 3135

Unable I shall be to hear
of my love, once I depart.

No. 3136

Roaming so far from you, I yearn
for you and wish soon to return.

No. 3137

I am away from home, and for some while
save in my mind, I can not see you smile.

No. 3138

I dream of my dear
wasting away in love,
longing to see me back within this year.

No. 3139

Ever since I left her behind,
I have kept her within my mind.

No. 3140

Alas, I'm doomed to live so wearily:
you traveling, I languishing for you.

No. 3141

Fair was the girl I met,
and that makes my journey lonelier yet.

No. 3142

Traveling far away from home,
   after my wife I yearn,
and nightly wish to dream
   of her till I return.

No. 3143

If I had known that I should languish so,
before we parted, I'd have talked my fill.

No. 3144

Traveling, now many a night
have I spent in a loney bed,
sleeping as in the day
without unloosening my scarlet sash.

No. 3145

My girdle came unloosened in my sleep.
Is my darling's love for me so deep?
      (When some one yearns for you, your sash
      comes untied.)

No. 3146

My girdle is unloosened; oh,
is she yearning for me so?

No. 3147

Almost the same as the above two.

N. 3148

Leaving my bridal bed, alas,
I must set out to cross the mountain pass.

No. 3149

I did not know what was in store for me,
but came across the mountain pass with you.

> (Written perhaps by a girl eloping with a
> man.)

No. 3150

Upon a misty spring day yearning for my lass,
I go my endless way across the mountain pass.

No. 3151

My dear, without time to take leave
tomorrow I go over Mt. Tamuke.

No. 3152

Ah! must I sleep this livelong night
wet with the dew on Shima hill?

No. 3153

Crossing the snowy Mt. Ohyama,
when can I see my native village?

No. 3154

Hasten, hasten, Pony fleet,
to reach her bower
before I die of longing, longing
for my love so sweet.

No. 3155

Would I could remove the trees on Mt. Ashiki
that I might see my yearned-for village where
  she lives!

No. 3156

Why must I wade Suzuka's stream at night?
Have I a darling love, my heart's delight?

No. 3157

Upon my weary journey I,
yearning for home, sleep but fitfully.

No. 3158

I yearn for you, my darling,
as restlessly as billows
surging now shoreward,
now seaward.

No. 3159

I think of her I left at home
as over hill and dale I roam.

No. 3160

Same as No. 2732

No. 3161

How beautiful the view
    of Arichi cove
which now I pass
    hurrying to my love.

No. 3162

My wife yearns after me, meseems;
for oft do I see her in dreams.

No. 3163

Crossing the shore my clothes were wet with
  brine,
my darling, not with blissful tears of thine.

No. 3164

Walking along the island shore,
my clothes are wet by waves.

No. 3165

O for the opportunity
oftentimes my love to see!

No. 3166

My darling love is not an island in the offing.
Why then absent-minded, should I thus be viewing the ocean?

No. 3167

Why are these rumors spread?
We've never lain in bed.

No. 3168

Alas, without cease do
I long and yearn for you.

No. 3169

Lighted by fishing fires I'll go to see my love
rather than wait for the moon to rise above.

No. 3170

O for a sight
of her this night!

No. 3171

I sailed out from Naniwa Bay, leaving my wife,
and for her now I vainly long and yearn.

No. 3172

I daily view boats coming to this lovely cove,
nor a day passes but I languish for my love.

No. 3173

No matter where I roam,
I long and yearn for home.

No. 3174

O my darling love,
how my heart you move!

No. 3175

I gathered shells reputed to make one forget,
  dripping wet in Waka Cove,
but all in vain. In spite of them
  still I yearn for my love.

No. 3176

Not a day passes but I sigh for home,
now far from my beloved wife I roam.

No. 3177

Although I know her name now, she
is yet too shy to welcome me.

No. 3178

Grieve not, my love, because from you I go.
I'll write as frequently as white clouds flow.

No. 3179

Not a minute passes by,
my darling, but for you I sigh.

Songs of Parting
No. 3180

Alas, you set out and left me alone,
and daily I yearn for you who are gone.

No. 3181

Prithee, let me tie your girdle, O my sweet,
hoping to undo it when again we meet.

No. 3182

My hands were on thy sleeves at parting, but,
  ah me!
to wipe away my tears I loosed my hold on thee.

No. 3183

My sash comes loose oft when he is away.
Oh, is my husband longing night and day?

No. 3184

At parting I waved not my sleeve,
heeding the folk, and now I grieve.

No. 3185

You are upon the journey, and I strive,
my husband, all alone to keep alive.

No. 3186
Along the rugged mountain paths you go your
        way.
All I can do is to await you night and day.

No. 3187
Over many a mountain wild you go,
and how to send you word I do not know.

No. 3188
Over the misty hills you roam,
and I but yearn for you at home.

No. 3189
Though I may go o'er many a hill,
you ever shall be in me still.

No. 3190
My husband, though some day I'll surely be with
        you,
We'll long be set apart by seas and mountains.

No. 3191
I strive hard not to yearn for you, my darling, but
        in vain;
your image comes across my mind again and yet
        again.

No. 3192
Is my husband trudging o'er the mountain brow
overlooking the Araki promontory now?

No. 3193
Do you go now across Mt. Shimakuma
all alone in the weary gloaming?

No. 3194
My dearest husband, are you now
traversing some mountain in the East?

No. 3195
When you return, return across Mt. Iwaki;
I will be waiting at Konuma Bay.

No. 3196
You left Kasuga field behind,
but you shall never leave my mind.

No. 3197
Never a day has passed since last we met,
but I hear this voice in me: I love you true.

No. 3198
Tomorrow you start on your journey,
and till you come back I'll be pining.

No. 3199
Although it takes a longer time,
        sail nearer the seashore,
for fearsome is the boundless sea
        where raving billows roar.

No. 3200
Like waves that lave
beautiful Kehi Cove,
my love I left behind
ever comes to mind.

No. 3201
'Tis only for your sake
        that I go to Fuke beach,
and purify myself
        the heavenly blessing to beseech.

No. 3202
From Nigitatsu you have taken ship for home.
Every day I wait and wait, but oh you do not
        come.

No. 3203
Once the ship, waiting for the tide upon the strand
        where ospreys live, puts out to sea,
I shall be yearning for my husband
        till again he comes to me.

No. 3204
Speed thy journey, and return to me
who only wait and wait for thee.

No. 3205

I wish I were a woman diver
on the beach of Tago where you are,
for left behind, alone
I languish night and day.

No. 3206

Are you playing truant,
    gathering seaweed at Tsukushi Bay?
Why do you not return
    to me who wait you night and day?

No. 3207

Tomorrow on his journey must my husband start—
my husband whom I love with all my heart.

No. 3208

When I think of my husband traveling all alone,
the radiant moonlit night itself grows dark to me.

No. 3209

I see the sailing clouds above Mikasa,
and am reminded of my traveling husband.

No. 3210

My husband, how shall I live on
once you leave me alone?

Sad Letters and Conversations between Lovers
No. 3211

How shall I live, ah me,
once you put out to sea?

No. 3212

When my ship is hidden by an isle at sea,
my wife will wave her sleeve in vain for me.

No. 3213

Are you wet in October rain, my darling,
or in some country cottage sheltering?

No. 3214

When without cease falls October rain,
in what village shall I shelter then?

No. 3215

For my darling who has come so far with me,
I'll not take ship as yet, but lodge at Aratsu by
    the sea.

No. 3216

I could not part from you, my dear,
and together we are here.

No. 3217

With gifts I will appease the sea divinity,
so soon return, my husband, safe to me.

No. 3218

Daily will I look toward Tsukushi,
and sigh, yearning for my darling.

No. 3219

All day I have been tramping over Kiku Beach,
and now at twilight long and yearn for you.

No. 3220

My dear, on tiptoe do I wait,
but ah already night is late.

THE MANYOSHU

BOOK XIII

FOREWORD

This book is divided into 5 parts: miscellaneous songs, love songs, songs in dialogue, a song in metaphor, and elegies. The songs number 127, including 66 longer lays and 1 Sedohka.

MISCELLANEOUS SONGS

No. 3221

When winter passes into spring,
dew falls at morn,
mist hangs at eve;
and songbirds warble
among the trees
stirred by the breeze.

No. 3222

How sacred Mt. Mimuro!
At its foot ashibi bloom;
and on its brow camellias.
Noble is this mountain
where priests keep constant vigil.

No. 3223

At the time when September rain
falls from the leaden sky,
even if wild geese have not yet arrived,
the autumn foliage of the sacred trees
upon the shore of Kamunabi Pond
is already beautiful to view.
I am a little maid who take delight
in tinkling tiny bells upon my wrists,
and for your sake, now breaking maple sprays
from off their boughs, have brought them all.

Hanka
No. 3224

Too fair the maple leaves alone to view,
I have brought a golden spray to you.

No. 3225

Though clouds reflect themselves upon the clear
  Hatsuse,
it has nor pool for boats to come in
nor shoal for fishermen to catch fish nigh.
Even though no pool be found,
nor any shoal,
like billows following fast
I would that fishing boats might come into the
  river.

Hanka
No. 3226

Alas, the river clear with silver foam afloat
has no pool where a fisherman can moor a boat.

No. 3227

Mt. Mimuro, storied since the age wherein
millions of gods lived, is in springtime veiled
with mist; in autumn clad in golden leaves.
The Asuka River lovely as a sash
the mountain god would deign to wear
courses so fast moss finds it hard
to grow on boulders in the stream.
O Guardian Spirit of the mountain, come
into my dream and bless me
that I may nightly see my love until
fresh green moss shall thrive around the river
  rocks.

Hanka
No. 3228

Shall I forget my love, though time may pass o'er
  me,
and moss on moss grows round the sacred cedar
  tree?

No. 3229

Noble are the shinto priests
who deck with flowers and leaves their hair,
presenting the god with papered bamboo sticks
and votive wine.

No. 3230

When I see our sovereign starting
from Nara, passing through Hozumi,
and Sakate, lodging at Kamunabi,
and finally arriving at the Yoshino Palace,
I am reminded of the other rulers
who traveled by the selfsame route in days of old.

Hanka
No. 3231

All things change as time and tide pass by;
only the Palace stands here lastingly.

No. 3232

We, making rafts with cypress trees
cut down upon Mt. Nifu, and
equipped with oars on either side
sailed down the river, saw the isles,
and the awe-inspiring falls
of Mt. Yoshino and their sparkling waves.

Hanka
No. 3233

O that my darling love could view with me
this sparkling water falling thunderously!

No. 3234

Fertile the land, lofty the peaks,
and crystalline the streams of Ise
which provide with foodstuffs
the Sovereign reigning o'er Japan.
Its sea is vast, and isles therein all famed.
These must be the reasons why at Ishi field
was built a palace bright as morning sun,
fair as evening glory, prosperous as the spring hill,
and radiant as the autumn mountain.
Here the courtiers shall enjoy long life and bliss.

Hanka
No. 3235

The flowers upon the hills are bright and red
as if some brilliant brocade were spread.

No. 3236

I stop and pray with offerings to the god
of the forest of Ishida that I ever
can go across Mt. Nara,
Tsuzuki field, over the Uji River,
and on, traversing Osaka Hill to see my love.

No. 3237

Almost the same as the above.

Hanka
No. 3238

I cross Osaka Hill, and now ahead I see
Lake Biwa where a myriad waves dance joyously.

No. 3239

Many are the inlets in Lake Biwa.
On its shores orange trees stand bearing flowers.
Now I lime the upper sprigs thereof,
upon the middle boughs set as decoys
grosbeaks and on the lower finches.
Hark, the poor creatures twitter unaware
their fathers and their mothers will be caught.

No. 3240

Banished by His Majesty, I cross Mt. Nara,
row over fleet Izumi's stream
where lumber pools are dotted,
and enter Uji's foaming waters.
I worship at Osaka Hill,
and come to Karasaki on the shore of Biwa,
hoping, if fortunate, again to see these places.
Many towns and hills I saw in front
I leave behind with sighs.
Oh! I know not what will become of me.

No. 3241

To heaven and earth in flowing tears I pray
that I again may see this Karasaki Bay.

No. 3242

I hear a lovely girl lives to the west
of the Kukuri Palace, and desire to see her,
but two peaks obstruct the way,
soaring forbiddingly on high.

No. 3243

Yearningly into Nagato Cove
comes morning tide,
and evening tide.
Like the tides now I hasten,
longing for my love,
and see upon the shore
a group of maiden divers culling herbs.
They notice me, and wave their sleeves
and scarfs bright in the sun,
bracelets clinking on their arms.

No. 3244

Continuous as the waves on Ago's shore
I'm yearning for my darling I adore.

No. 3245

Would that the bridge of heaven* were longer,
and that the mountain higher still for me to go
up to the sky to get the water from the moon,
and bring my lord his youth again.

* stairs leading to heaven.

Hanka
No. 3246

You are the sun and moon to me,
but, unlike them,
I see you aging with each passing day.

No. 3247

A priceless jewel lies, 'tis said,
down in the bed of Nuna's stream.
You, alas, have aged—
you who are precious as the gem.

LOVE SONGS

No. 3248

Many people live here in this land,
but you are the only one I love;
and all night long
like vines that yearn to cling around a tree
I only long for you

Hanka
No. 3249

Were there another just like you here in this land,
my dear, then should I thus pine ceaselessly?

No. 3250

Blessed is our country by the gods,
but it seems they love me not,
because I have not seen my love
for many a day and many a month,
and live in sorrow inconsolable.
O merciful Gods,
let me come face to face with him,
or I shall die.

No. 3251

Trustworthy as a lofty ship are you,
and oh I love you true.

No. 3252

Leaving the capital,
you go on a long journey,
and I shall wait and wait
for your return.

No. 3253

This is a country where since olden times
people have loved to be taciturn,
but now I pray aloud again and yet again
as wave comes rolling after wave,
that by its incantation you may safe return.

Hanka
No. 3254

Since subject is our country of Yamato
to the sorcery of words,
I pray and pray that you may safe return.

No. 3255

It has been said since olden times
that when one falls in love one suffers.
I frankly speak my mind to her,
but know not hers,
and drooping as the reapèd reeds
I only yearn.

Hanka

No. 3256

Although to me she is not kind,
yet she is ever in my mind.

No. 3257

I longed to see you,
and taking the rough Kose road,
came across the stream,
walking o'er the stepping stones.

No. 3258

Years have come and gone,
but no messenger comes from you;
and on a long spring day I keep indoors
like a silkworm pent in the cocoon,
only yearning after you.
I have none I can speak my mind to,
pining in tears both day and night.

Hanka

No. 3259

You are indifferent to me.
Oh why did I not keep away from you?

No. 3260

As people like to draw clear water
from Ayuchi's well,
and drink it day and night,
so do I ever pine for you.

Hanka

No. 3261

Alas, I'm doomed to weary tears
without a tryst with you these years.

No. 3262

So long have I yearned after you, and oh
daily my sash seems longer yet to grow.

No. 3263

Only had I a woman I could love
as I love a jewel or a mirror,
I would fain go back home,
but, alas, for whom could I return?

Hanka

No. 3264

Though others can wait long
for their traveling husbands,
how can I live without mine?

> (This does not seem to be the hanka to the
> above.)

No. 3265

Weary of life,
I renounced the world,
nor have I any mind
to seek it out again.

No. 3266

In springtime flowers come,
and autumn brings the bright red leaves.
For long I wooed a lovely maid,
and what delight, now she is mine.

Hanka

No. 3267

A slave of love am I;
for her I fain would die.

No. 3268

The clouds that topped Mt. Kamunabi
swirl overhead with wind and rain.
I pray my husband may get home
soon across Magami field.

Hanka

No. 3269

I love my husband deep,
and when alone can't sleep.

No. 3270

Within her hovel (would that I could burn it),
upon the tattered mat fit for the rake,
and on her greasy arm (would I could break it),
I know he lies now—he for whom I yearn
and wait indoors though bright the sun may
    shine,
for whom the livelong night forlorn I pine,
and till the flooring creaks, in bed I turn.

Hanka
No. 3271

I am doomed with love to burn,
and in this wise for him to yearn.

No. 3272

The woman I yearn for has married,
and I am thrown into deep grief.
Now living with my parents,
I feel as if I were a traveler lone.
Inconsolable am I, but she,
alas, is unaware of this my sorrow.

Hanka
No. 3273

Alas, I've pined away in love for her,
and now my girdle goes three times round me.

No. 3274

With grief I leave my bower at dawn,
not knowing what to do,
and sorrow finds me coming back at dusk.
I can not sleep at ease as others do,
spreading their tresses long;
but with a mind perturbed
like a ship rolling on the sea
I spend the livelong night.

Hanka
No. 3275

Although I try to count the number
of nights I have slept all alone,
My mind is too perturbed,
too heavy is my heart.

No. 3276

Parting from my love, I go my way
astride the stumbling horse,
deep in the thought of her.
People upon the road look wonderingly.
Should they inquire now what ails me,
I fear that I might say one word in me: her name.
I would endeavor to reply, however,
that I am waiting for the moon to rise.

Hanka
No. 3277

Oh why does not my lover come this eve?
Is he now pillowing on some other woman's
sleeve?

> Note: this does not seem the hanka to the
> above.

No. 3278

Yearning for my lover,
like a hunter
waiting for a stag upon the hill,
I am hiding in the bush.
O Dogs, be quiet, do not bark!

(Perhaps a folk song)

Hanka
No. 3279

O Dogs, bark not so noisily,
now through the bush comes he to me.

No. 3280

Vainly waiting for my lover,
I go out to look at the sky.
The night is far spent, and the wind
freezes the snow upon my sleeves.
Now so late he'll never come, think I,
I will go to sleep, hoping to dream of him.

Another version
No. 3281

Though I wait, my husband does not come.
The wild geese coldly cry;
the night is far advanced.
The wind blows hard
to turn the snow upon my sleeves to ice,
and freeze the frost upon the ground.
He'll never come; so wishing for a dream
wherein he comes, I go to bed.

2 Hanka
No. 3282

Upon this windy night so cold
you do not come,
and oh, I must sleep all alone.

No. 3283

Since you come not, my dear,
pray, in my dream appear.

No. 3284

Setting the wine jar in the ground,
and hanging stringèd bamboo rings,
I pray the gods my husband
may not make some slip of the tongue.

No. 3285

Even from my mother I conceal
my love for you, obeying but your will.

No. 3286

Same as No. 3284

No. 3287

Shall I be kept from seeing you? Oh, nay;
since to the gods in heaven and earth I pray.

No. 3288

Now tucking up sleeves with a ceremonial sash,
and setting saké jars firm in the ground,
I pray for him I hold so dear
to the gods in heaven and earth.

No. 3289

My mother tells me
not to see and talk with my love,
but never, never can I rest
till I see him whom I love
as deep as Kiyosumi pond.

Hanka
No. 3290

Meseems that in our former life
we were devoted man and wife.

No. 3291

Ordered by the Emperor,
my husband goes now to a distant place.
After his departure of this morning
I shall only yearn for him;
and he too will for me.
Alas, we part in grief.

No. 3292

I shall be waiting,
praying the gods for your safety.

No. 3293

'Tis said on Mt. Ohmine
rain falls incessantly,
snow descends without cease.
And like the rain and snow
ceaselessly do I yearn for you.

Hanka
No. 3294

What can I do? I love
a maid I caught a mere glimpse of.

No. 3295

"Treading through the knee-deep summer grass,
what lady will you go to see, my son?"
"I will tell you about her, Mother.
Raven is her hair
wherein she wears a boxwood comb.
Oh, she is lovely to behold."

No. 3296

Now across the summer field I go,
to see the girl my parents wot not of.

No. 3297

I can not see my love,
and all day long
I yearn for her:
the livelong night
sleepless I lie,
only pining after her.

Hanka
No. 3298

I wish to die,
for bereft of love,
I have no heart to live on.

No. 3299

Across the river waits my love,
and on this side I only sigh.
Would that I had a scarlet boat
along with jeweled oars.
Then I would cross the stream
and nightly talk and talk with her.

No. 3300

Long have I kept
our love in secrecy,
but people are inquisitive.
Alas, they know it now,
and wag their tongues about it.

No. 3301

Deep, deep in the Sea of Ise
grow herbs called miru,
and I love you as deep.
As floating miru comes ashore
at morning calm,
and at evening calm,
I shall come back to you
when my journey's done, my darling,
with you for e'er to stay.

No. 3302

As I was leaving Muro Cove,
before the crowd who saw me off
my wife wept like a child.
Now I recall that parting scene,
and long and yearn anew for her.

No. 3303

A village woman tells this tale:
her husband met my man so haggard
who rode a jet-black horse
upon Mt. Kamunabi
where autumn leaves were falling,
and disappeared across the seven streams.

No. 3304

I did not ask the girl about my husband.
Why does she worry me with such a story?

No. 3305

I wish to wander like a cloud,
and when I see a hill
blooming with cherries and azaleas,
I view their sheen with constant joy.
You are as lovely as these flowers.
People say we are in love.
Oh how I wish that it were true!

> Note: This appears to be the first half of
> No. 3309.

Hanka
No. 3306

Love is a fiery passion that will ever stay,
and now in vain for its surcease the gods I pray.

No. 3307

For this reason during these eight years
though I've outgrown my friends with parted hair,
and now am taller than our orange tree,
I've loved you quietly as a deep, deep stream,
only awaiting your poposal.

> Note: This appears to be the second half of
> No. 3309.

No. 3308
Translated, the same as No. 3306

No. 3309

"I wish to wander like a cloud,
and when I see a hill
blooming with cherries and azaleas,
I view their sheen with constant joy.
You are as lovely as these flowers.
People say we are in love."
"I have outgrown my friends with parted hair
during the lapse of these eight years,
and now am taller than our orange tree.
Quietly as a deep pool have I loved you,
and only wait and wait for your proposal."

(Nos. 3305 and 3307 put together.)

No. 3310

I have come to the district of Hatsuse
to see my love and lie with her.
Suddenly the sky is overcast,
and snow begins to fall;
Suddenly the sky is overcast,
and rain starts to descend.
Pheasants cry; cocks crow
to tell the dawn of day.
Before me is the house.
"Do let me in, pray, for a rest."

(A folk song?)

Hanka
No. 3311

In the Hatsuse district lives my love so sweet,
and treading stony river-beach, here now I go.

No. 3312

His Highness came to sit with me
here to the district of Hatsuse.
My mother slept within the inner room;
my father in the outer room.
"If I go out, they'll know,"
I hesitated with the thought for long
when suddenly day broke.
Oh, 'tis hard to meet a secret love.

Hanka
No. 3313

Pray, across the rapids,
astride the jet-black steed,
nightly come to me.

No. 3314

Along the road to Yamashiro
on horseback other husbands go,
but oh, how sad! You go on foot.
Take these silks, this mirror
left me by my mother
therewith to buy a horse, my dear!

Hanka
No. 3315

Izumi's river is so deep, I fear
that drenched will be my husband.

No. 3316

Buy a horse, pray, with this mirror,
keepsake of my darling mother,
for I can not endure to see
among the riding travelers you only walking.

No. 3317

Better to walk with you, my own,
than ride the finest horse alone.

No. 3318

My husband went o'er many a hill
far to the shores of Kii Province
to gather pearly shells.
Eager to know when he comes home,
I consult a fortuneteller.
"In seven days, if late;
if early, in two days.
Do not worry, Lady,"
is what he says.

Hanka
No. 3319

Although to meet my dear I wish to go,
by which way he returns I do not know.

No. 3320

Yearning for you, I've come to meet you here,
crossing the stony river cold and clear.

No. 3321

"Dawn bids me go," he said,
and vanished through the gate;
and day and night I wait his coming back.

No. 3322

If you, my dear, so yearn,
posthaste will I return.

No. 3323

The little sedge
out in Ochi field
is reaped, but kept unwoven,
Poor little sedge!

ELEGIES

No. 3324

Many a prince lives in the capital,
but he was the only one I wished to serve.
Still his gates serenely stand,
majestic to behold.
In springtime our prince used to go
up pine-clad Uetsuki Hill
to contemplate the land below,
in autumn he enjoyed the hagi flowers
wet with September dew, and in the winter
went hunting to the field,
catalpa bow in hand.
But now, oh what is this I see before me?
The residence is veiled in white;
the men are dressed in hempen robes
his bier to carry
along Kinoe highway past Iware.
Ah! I know not what to think,
and only embrace the pine tree
the prince's sleeve once touched.

No. 3325

White clouds hang over Mt. Iware.
Did they rise from the funeral pyre?

No. 3326

The prince's tomb is made:
he rests therein.
Though the men, numerous as a flock of birds,
who served his Highness
wait eagerly for his word,
yet it comes from him no more.
They only sigh and moan in tears.

No. 3327

In the western stable
horses of the prince are kept,
and in the eastern stable other horses.
They are fed
with fodder good and water sweet,
but they keep sadly crying now.

Hanka
No. 3328

The grays keep crying sadly with hard breath,
perhaps lamenting o'er their master's death.

No. 3329

In this vast world
am I the only one who loved you deep?
Even now my love for you
increases day by day.
Oh woe worth that September day.
I remain beside your stone-built tomb
to tend it morn and eve
crying, and sleepless lie throughout the night.

No. 3330

Moaning her death I spend my days.
When clothes are rent, they can be mended;
when strings of pearls are raveled, they can be
   restrung.
But oh! how can I meet my love again?

No. 3331

Osaka Hill
lies by Mt. Hatsuse,
and is so beautiful to view.
There my beloved wife now sleeps
within her grassy tomb.

No. 3332

Changeless the mountain soars;
immutable the ocean lies,
but alas, ephemeral man's life.

No. 3333

Ordered by the Emperor,
my husband went aboard at Mitsu Beach.
Large was the crew who sailed the ship.
Since then no word has come from him.
The fortuneteller I consult
tells me to my dismay he passed away
like autumn leaves upon Tsukushi's mountains.

No. 3334

Word of his death now comes to me,
and I moan, wondering if true it be.

No. 3335

Here lies a traveler dead.
Has he tramped over hill and field,
and traversed stormy straits
upon his way home to his folk—
he who lies stranded now cold on this shore?

No. 3336

A dead man lies upon the beach
where only birds are seen
with the mountain high behind him
and tufts of seaweed are here spread
around his senseless head.
Oh where lives his wife?
How frail and sad man's life!

No. 3337

I see a dead man lying here.
Where are his wife and children?

No. 3338

Now I will go along the mountain path,
avoiding the perils of the wind-blown shore.

No. 3339

Same as No. 3336

No. 3340

Same as No. 3337

No. 3341

Translated, the same as No. 3337

No. 3342

Same as No. 3337

No. 3343

A man lies dead away from home
here on the shore where wild waves come.

No. 3344

Long have I waited for my husband
to return this month, but now
word comes to me that he is dead.
O that I could go with the floating cloud
to where he lies, or tired, I too might perish.
Alas, is it my lot to mourn his death alone?

No. 3345

When I see wild geese fly o'er the reedy shore,
I am reminded of my husband's arrow's feather.

No. 3346

Alas, my wife is dead and buried
at yonder Toba where the pine trees stand.
She died when I was far from home.
I only wish that I had been at home
to tend her day and night.

Hanka

No. 3347

My darling wife I left behind is dead,
and wearily my homeward way I tread.

THE MANYOSHU

BOOK XIV

FOREWORD

This book is unique in the anthology, because here are collected so-called "Eastland poems."

They are divided into 2 parts: 90 songs of which the authors' provinces are known, and 140 songs whose authors are unknown. All of them are verselets.

EASTLAND POEMS

No. 3348

I sleep tonight in Unakami Bay,
and on the morrow we will anchor weigh.

No. 3349

Out in Mama harbor sailors cry.
It seems that now the seas are high.

No. 3350

For my new silks I do not care.
I only wish your clothes to wear.

No. 3351

Is snow descending on Tsukuba,
or is it white cloth maids are spreading?

No. 3352

I hoped to go home in the spring, but cuckoos
crying in Suga field tell it is summer now.

No. 3353

I shall not come tonight. So go to sleep,
and be not waiting by the stockade woods.

No. 3354

I'll get beneath your counterpane,
and lying there, with you remain.

No. 3355

If I arrive too late,
all closed will be her gate.

No. 3356

The way was long and rough but here
along Mt. Fuji's foot I came.

No. 3357

If Mt. Fuji be all hidden in a mist when I
come to its foot then which way will my darling
  face to sigh?

No. 3358

Few are the nights we pass in bed,
but loud the gossip that is spread.

No. 3359

My kind mother I defy,
and on your promise I rely.

No. 3360

Now I can see my love as ceaselessly
as white waves rolling on the Izu Sea.

No. 3361

My darling, when the noises we hear nigh
are over, loosening our girdles, we shall lie.

No. 3362

Having come so far, I long less for my wife.
  Why make me hear,
O fellow Traveler, about your love,
  and call to mind my dear?

No. 3363

When my darling husband comes home from the
  capital to me
among the cedars on Mt. Ashigara waiting will I
  be.

No. 3364

Though we are betrothed, how strange,
I see in her no change.

No. 3365

Never sorry shall you be
for this nuptial vow with me.

No. 3366

I go along the inlet with my love to lie,
but oh, the tide is up and seas are high.

No. 3367

I deeply love the man, but he
goes here and there, an does not come to me.

No. 3368

Why do I doubt my love?
She's chaste—that I can prove.

No. 3369

Why use a pillow stuffed with sedge in bed,
my love? My brawny arm is for your head.

No. 3370

Now you are mine. Why not untie
your girdle when with me you lie?

No. 3371

Amid the fearsome pass of Ashigara
I called on my love's name.

No. 3372

I love my lass so fair and bright
as is Yorogi beach.

No. 3373

Fair as cloth bleached in limpid Tama
is she,
and I love her with all my heart.

No. 3374

Divinéd through the votive burning,
the stag-bone from Musashi field,
your name—the name I never spoke—appeared.

No. 3375

Since we parted, daily
as a pheasant for her mate I cry.

No. 3376

Though you yearn and long for me,
never show it in your face, my love.

No. 3377

With all my heart I trusted you,
but you, alas, have proved untrue.

No. 3378

Like the tendrils that entwine
in the field of Ohya
along Irima Road
if I draw you,
come to me.

No. 3379

My lover dear, I languish for you,
but oh I can not tell you to your face.

No. 3380

Shall we separate? oh never,
though the mooring rope may sever.

No. 3381

I love you secretly,
and night and morning sigh.

No. 3382

My sleeves were wet with tears when I left you,
as bamboo grasses were with morning dew.

No. 3383

How shall I pass my days
when I go farther off,
for already I feel sad to see your bower
hidden behind the hill?

No. 3384

Tekona, Tekona of Mama,
of Mama in Katsushika,
is it true, is it true that she loves me,
Tekona of Katsushika?

(Probably a folk song.)

No. 3385

Like the waves that lave the shore of Mama
men of yore came from afar to woo Tekona.

No. 3386

I will not make you wait
outside my gate
even at such a time as I
am offering new rice ears to the deity.

No. 3387

O for a charger which without a sound could run
that I might come to see you frequently.

No. 3388

Let your lover in and with him lie
who stands now at the gate with many a sigh.

No. 3389

I wave my sleeve now ere
the mountain hides her bower.

No. 3390

Like the eagle crying on Tsukuba
I am crying ever yearning for you.

No. 3391

Like Ashiho's peak that soars above
noble and peerless is my darling love.

No. 3392

Ulike the cataract down Mt. Tsukuba
    calm is my mind,
though deep in love with you
    myself I find.

No. 3393

My mother must know 'tis too late
now for us to separate.

No. 3394

I go back, looking on Tsukuba's peak above,
longing and pining after you, my love.

No. 3395

Since that clear night we together lay
over me has gone many a lonely day.

No. 3396

We lay together once,
but since then no more chance.

No. 3397

Though the seaweed may be severed
from the rock of Nasaka Inlet,
none shall ever see us separated.

No. 3398

For word from others do I little care,
eagerly waiting yours, my maiden fair.

No. 3399

The road is newly laid and rough;
therefore be well shod, my love.

No. 3400

If you tread on pebbles
    upon the shore of the Chikuma River,
I will go gather them
and treasure them for ever.

No. 3401

Stay with me, for when the ship departs,
no more shall we be able then to meet.

No. 3402

When my husband goes across the hill at eve,
he too, as I for him, will wave his sleeve.

No. 3403

My love will never cease,
but only will increase.

No. 3404

Happy are we, my darling love and I,
since now locked in each other's arms we lie.

No. 3405

Hoping to meet my mistress fair,
to the river bank will I repair.

No. 3406

Though you come not back this year,
I will be awaiting you,
gathering Sanu's herbs
together with village maids.

No. 3407

I sit with you now face to face,
and you seem bright as the morning sun.

No. 3408

As Mt. Niita stands alone,
so the maid belongs to none.

No. 3409

Yonder mountain mingles with the clouds.
Likewise, my love, shall we not lie together?

No. 3410

Worry not about tomorrows, sweet.
Care only for today that we enjoy.

No. 3411

Though I pulled, yon mountain would not move;
and you are like the peak to me, my love.

No. 3412

My wife lives far off left behind,
and I fondly call her now to mind.

No. 3413

How lucky you and I !
We've caught no people's eye.

No. 3414

If only we
contented be,
what matters though our secret may leak out
for folk to speak about?

No. 3415

I saw a pretty flower in Ikaho's marsh.
O that I could transplant it to my pond.

No. 3416

This is my fervent prayer
to be with my darling fair.

No. 3417

You are pretty at a distance,
but attract me more seen closer.

No. 3418

I am so grateful for your words to me,
but I, betrothed already, am not free.

No. 3419

Man of Ikaho, you say that you love me,
but I know that you have a secret love.

No. 3420

To sever us my parents now beseech,
but trust me: there is no fear of a breach.

No. 3421

O Thunder, you can't make me fear,
but do not roar, and scare my dear.

No. 3422

Sometimes the Ikaho wind will cease,
but my yearning only will increase.

No. 3423

I linger at your gate as if to prove
'tis hard to pass the bower where lives one's love.

No. 3424

Married is that country lass
fair as a mountain sapling !

No. 3425

My eager foot scarce touching
the pebbles in the river bed
of Aso in Shimotsuke,
I came here as on air !
Now, what is in your heart?

No. 3426

Tie my sash when I leave you behind
that I may from afar call you to mind.

No. 3427

For the sake of a lovely maiden in Tsukushi
the girdle that my wife tied I unloosened.

No. 3428

Changeless like the vigil of the shishi*
lying on Adatara's peak am I:
await me; do not leave your bower.

   * wild boar.

No. 3429

Deep-set the watermark I see.
I wish it were your love for me.

No. 3430

Every ship comes to its port from sea;
and why does not my husband come to me?

No. 3431

If you come at all to me,
come not like this, but willingly.

No. 3432

If you love me, pray, elope with me,
though obstacle on obstacle there be.

No. 3433

If thou art true to me,
so shall I be to thee.

No. 3434

We have long been in love;
no severance you need to fear.

No. 3435

The cloth I wear is new,
dyed with a purple hue.

No. 3436

O Trees that guard Mt. Onihita
where men dig whetstones for their sickles
be fresh and green forever.

No. 3437

One can not easily string a bow
that has been long unstrung.

No. 3438

Bells ringing in the field I hear,
and know the prince is hunting near.

No. 3439

The horses' bells I hear:
our stage is drawing near.
Pray, in your hands cup water
for me to drink, fair daughter.

No. 3440

Woman, washing pot-herbs in the river,
you and I have stalwart children—
will you give my son your daughter?

No. 3441

Hasten now, oh, Charger fleet,
to yonder bower where lives my sweet!

No. 3442

I shall not reach the slope ere sunset,
but spend tonight amid the mountains.

No. 3443

A budding willow did I pass,
and was reminded of my lass.

No. 3444

Diligently though I seek for herbs,
my basket is not full.
O Lady, learn from me: go not alone
but with your gentle lord.

No. 3445

Gather sedge at the estuary,
and I'll weave it together for your mat.

No. 3446

Reeds and rushes are alike, my sweet;
so are we, and for each other meet.

No. 3447

Towards Asuna's shady grasses
a road was laid,
but none sought out Asuna's grasses,
and so the road is overgrown.

No. 3448

My lord, may you enjoy longevity
until these hills are leveled to the sea!

No. 3449

Where Makuraga lies, white-sleeved in foam,
the sailors bending to their oars strain forward.
Rise not, O Waves.

No. 3450

Okusa lad, Ogusa lad—boats floating on the wave,
the 'G' boy leads the 'K' boy: it is he that I
would have.

No. 3451

Though, sowing millet in the fields, I see
my lover coming up to me,
by the bridle walking his old bay,
never will I drive it away.

No. 3452

Do not burn the winter field, for though
you leave it as it lies, young grass will grow.

No. 3453

My love gave me this garment when we parted.
So long I'm gone, and now 'tis old and threadbare.

No. 3454

Counterpane, counterpane, woven of hemp
grown in my own little yard,
Counterpane, counterpane, bring him to me—
my husband, my lover, my lord.

No. 3455

My husband, come,
if you long for me.
I am waiting at the gate
with all the willows trimmed.

No. 3456

My sweet, the gossip is not true;
but ever I believe in you.

No. 3457

O my husband serving in the distant Nara Palace,
think of me even when you lie with other women
of Yamato.

No. 3458

My darling is out of sight with the turning road,
and left behind I can do naught but weep.

No. 3459

The rice needs pounding;
ah, but then this evening
taking in his own my roughened hands,
will he not grieve, my lover?

No. 3460

Who is knocking at the door
when I keep the dwelling pure
after seeing off my husband
to the Harvest Festival?

No. 3461

Does he love me? He never comes
early in the evening,
but always late at night
or at dawning.

No. 3462

Many people live here in this village,
and, since my lass is fair, they talk about her.

No. 3463

Here in this noisy populous town we meet.
O that it were in a country field.

No. 3464

My darling love, why should we care for envious
rumors,
if we can lay our heads upon the selfsame pillow?

No. 3465

I lay with her, my girdle of Korean brocade
    untied,
and yet my fiery passion was not wholly satisfied.

No. 3466

If with my lass I lie, I'm spoken of.
If I do not, I am consumed with love.

No. 3467

My lover, knock loud at the cedar gate,
and I will let you in, however late.

No. 3468

These rumors slanderous
are but to trouble us.

No. 3469

The fortuneteller told me I could see my lover,
but what is wrong with him?   He comes not.

No. 3470

It seems a thousand years have now passed o'er
    my head,
because night after night I've spent alone in bed.

No. 3471

Would I could have unbroken slumber
even for a while,
but you come into my dream;
you will not let me sleep.

No. 3472

You say so oft she is another's wife.
Do you not sometimes borrow garments from a
    neighbor?

No. 3473

His ax rings on Mt. Sano—
from the distance comes its song to me
to tell me soon, oh soon we'll be together.

No. 3474

How will my darling wife yearn left behind
after I'm speeded by my kindly neighbors?

No. 3475

With patience though I try to wait my lover's
    safe return,
yet even as he disappears beyond the hill, I want
    him.

No. 3476

Word from her tells she yearns for me; and well
    she may,
for many a day and month have passed by since
    I took my way.

No. 3477

As you go over Yobi pass in Tago,
even though therefrom you will return,
still I needs must sigh.

No. 3478

Whether or not I sit with you, my dear,
my heart is ever with you.   Do not fear.

No. 3479

She clears the ground for us on Mt. Akami,
and yet she will deny she has a lover.

No. 3480

Conscripted, I depart at midnight,
leaving behind my wife so dear.

No. 3481

Same as No. 503

No. 3482

Of late I have not come to you,
but doubt me not, since I am true.

No. 3483

'Tis strange my girdle cannot be unfastened in
    the daytime,
but when at night I see my love it loosens of
    itself.

No. 3484

Weaving, always busy with the household are you,
but leave it for tomorrow, and come near.

No. 3485

Now far away from home
where my dear wife is ever kind to me,
I feel as lonely as a homesick child.

No. 3486

Any soldier can I beat in archery,
and yet a weakling to my love am I.

No. 3487

My mind adream with future days,
the close-by maid escaped my gaze.

No. 3488

If I consult the fortuneteller,
he'll know my secret love.

No. 3489

I'll make my darling stand the forest nigh
till I can find a place where we can lie.

No. 3490

Since many guests are now with me,
pray, wait till I come presently.

No. 3491

When the willow bough is cut
a shoot comes out afresh,
but man is different.
Will you let me yearn and die in vain?

No. 3492

Though wedlock may not favor us,
let what there is between us two remain.

No. 3493

Sooner or later you will come to me,
so, dear, I shall await you patiently.

No. 3494

O that I could be lying thus with you in bed
until the fresh young maple leaves turn red.

No. 3495

For long I have awaited you, my own.
Why do you not come, making me forlorn?

No. 3496

In Koba with its orange trees
there lives a maid who loves me so.
She loves me, and I yearn for her,
and thither I shall go.

No. 3497

I lay with her in bed,
and gossip now is spread.

No. 3498

Numerous are women as the reeds along the seashore,
that you may forget me, but I never shall forget
you.

No. 3499

It seemed that I could woo her easily,
but she is tougher than she looks, ah me!

No. 3500

As pretty and persistent as the purple grass
is she: I wish that I could sleep with that fair
lass!

No. 3501

As with the hand one gently draws
the tendrils of the vines on Awa hill,
so smoothly may she come to me.

No. 3502

I shall keep loving you year after year—
you lovely as a flower, my sweet, my dear.

No. 3503

Know you not, sweet, mere liking doesn't unfold
the secret you now in my face behold?

No. 3504

Ever yearning, longing after you,
my sleep is always light,
and as wistaria flowers caressed by vernal air,
would I could rest at night.

No. 3505

I could not come to her last night
    and alone in bed will she
lie this evening too,
    lonely, yearning after me?

No. 3506

To my regret I couldn't find you
among the guests who came to view
the residence built anew.

No. 3507

Persistent as the vine
I ever shall be thine.

No. 3508

Had I never seen the maiden,
prithee, how could I be lovesick?

No. 3509

With only the white-sheeted wind
    from the mountain for my counterpane,
sleepless, I languish
    for my love's warm gift in vain.

No. 3510

I wish I were a cloud, away
up, floating in the sky
to go and see my love today,
to meet, and by and by
return tomorrow.

No. 3511

Like a cloud that flees the wind across the sky,
my heart is ever troubled restlessly.

No. 3512

Alas, so like a floating cloud
is my fickle, faithless lass.

No. 3513

She vowed that severed we would never be,
but ah, against it has forsaken me.

No. 3514

Clouds will rest on a lofty mountain.
Am I not a cloud, and you a mountain?

No. 3515

Whenever my face you forget
the clouds above our peak
will teach you to remember me.

No. 3516

Unclouded are these lower slopes
    of the mountains where I roam,
but my mind dwells in upper clouds
    and thinks of you at home.

No. 3517

Gone like a cloud my love,
    and why should I,
yearning still,
    in this manner sigh?

No. 3518

Behold, yon clouds embrace the mountain blue,
my darling, let us lie together too.

No. 3519

Rejected by your mother, now I go away,
so come out of the bower if but a minute, pray.

No. 3520

So long ago I left my love behind
that she is wellnigh out of mind,
and oftentimes I try
to recall her, looking at the sky.

No. 3521

"Caw, caw," the cries of lying crows I hear,
as if to tell me you had come.

No. 3522

It was but yesternight we lay so cosily,
but now it seems already long ago to me.

No. 3523

Over the slope, upon the fields of Abe
the crane stands...oh, my love,
will you not come again tomorrow?

No. 3524

Though closely ringed the jointed reeds,
they do not meet.
Forlorn as the wild duck upon the pond I sigh.

No. 3525

On the field of Mikugu the wild ducks are
    waddling.
As to my little dear, the promise is yet vague,
nor have I slept with her.

No. 3526

Though fowls may fly between two marshes,
I swear that I am true to my one nest
wherein you, my darling, rest.

No. 3527

I had to leave my love behind me,
a little wild duck on a lonely pond.

No. 3528

Hurriedly I bade adieu
to her and now my trip I rue!

No. 3529

With a light heart I went to see my sweetheart
only to be scolded by her mother.

No. 3530

Even though my love I do not meet,
if I pass her gate I feel so sweet.

No. 3531

I went to glimpse my darling standing at her
    door,
but they drove me away as if I were a savage
    boar.

No. 3532

Like the pony
eagerly grazing
in fields of spring,
so, without ceasing,
of me she is thinking,
that darling love.

No. 3533

When I am bent on getting to my love,
what to me is the bird upon the beach,
the horse that stumbles?

No. 3534

When I must needs leave home,
and mounted my red horse to ride away,
how sad my wife to see me go that day!

No. 3535

You have come riding up to me, my dear,
and to behold your smiling face I'm here.

No. 3536

You try to worm yourself into my favor
to come to see me in my bower—in vain.

No. 3537

I only glimpsed the maiden,
and ever since keep yearning.

No. 3538

My horse can't cross the bridge so narrow;
I only send my heart to you, my darling.

No. 3539

'Tis dangerous I know to love his wife,
and yet I dare it at the peril of my life.

No. 3540

'Twas she, 'twas she, the maid of Sawatari,
and oh, you prankish horse
that galloped on, and would not let us talk!

No. 3541

Dangerous as a horse upon a beetling cliff,
I keep on loving her, already wed.

No. 3542

Like a horse fatigued from galloping on pebbles
am I before my yearned-for maiden's bower.

No. 3543

"Married are we," says she,
but keeps herself from me.

No. 3544

I gave you all, all unaware
that such a faithless man you were.

No. 3545

Had I known one would so soon interfere,
many more nights had I spent with my dear.

No. 3546

At the ferry by the budding willow
I wait for you;
I should be drawing water, but forgetting,
I only stay.

No. 3547

I have not seen my love this while,
and find the time hard to beguile.

No. 3548

Like hapless driftwood in the roaring rapids,
so are we caught in wagging tongues, my lover.

No. 3549

The tide has risen. How will he
come o'er the flooded sands to me?

No. 3550

Last night awaiting you,
I paid no mind to housewifery.
So now tonight though you are here,
I must be diligent, and husk the rice.

No. 3551

Fair as the wave at Ajikama is my lover,
and for him only I untie my girdle.

No. 3552

Like the incessant waves of Matsuo Cove
is gossip: can your mind,
any more than mine, untroubled be?

No. 3553

Though like the flooding tide in Ajikama Cove
are people's noisy tongues, yet I
ceaselessly long to lie with you.

No. 3554

Water can find its way
even beneath a living rock. Had I
such power, then I would come
secretly into your bed to lie.

No. 3555

Like lapping, overlapping sound of oars
that throng at Koga ferry
comes rumor, hearsay, gossip all around me,
and why? Still chaste that maid and I.

No. 3556

How lorn to be alone like floating ships,
but if we sleep together,
oh what a tide of gossip must we cope with!

No. 3557

You are another's wife, alas,
but even now my heart harass.

No. 3558

I must embark now for the main,
and wish I could see her again.

No. 3559

I can trust my betrothed,
for he will keep his vow.

No. 3560

Although I cherish love within,
like the Nifu clay
hiding iron in it,
I never show it in my face.

No. 3561

As the dry harrowed fields yearn after rain,
so do I wait for you to come to me.

No. 3562

With hair outspread like waving seaweed
must she be sleeping now without me!

No. 3563

With mind like strands of seaweed
that intertwine in Hita Cove
is she awaiting me night after night, my love?

No. 3564

All day long and all night through I pine,
and wish I could forget dear love of mine.

No. 3565

Too late, too late!
The moon is sinking behind Urano:
no night of love is mine tonight.

No. 3566

It will be rumored, if I perish from this love,
that I am rightly punished by the gods above.

No. 3567

How I regret to leave my darling.
If only she were my catalpa bow!

A frontier-guard

In reply

No. 3568

Sad it will be to part,
    and yearning for you, I stay here.
I wish that I could be the bow
    you carry to the field, my dear.

No. 3569

When I was leaving home, conscripted as a frontier guard
she weeping bitterly, could not let go my hand.

No. 3570

Upon a wintry evening when a mist hangs over rushes,
and wild ducks plaintively cry, I shall remember you.

No. 3571

Leaving the town where lives my dear,
sadly came I along the weary road.

No. 3572

The soft breeze urges sage-buds to unfold.
Can I not woo you though you are not yet of age?

No. 3573

Can I leave and let wither
the vine in the gorge?

No. 3574

The flower of all the village,
would I could bend it to me,
break it for myself,
but no, too young it is, too tender.

No. 3575

O Bellflower in bud, pray,
burgeoning stay.

No. 3576

With the purple flowers of Konagi
I dyed my gown
to make the lovely color that you see.

No. 3577

Alas, my love is dead, and left behind
I regret that I was not more kind.

THE MANYOSHU

BOOK XV

FOREWORD

This book is composed of two different collections: the first contains songs by envoys to Korea, and the second a series of impassioned love songs exchanged between Nakatomino Yakamori and his love Sanuno Chikami.

According to the record, the envoys were sent in June, 736. The songs were composed before their departure and on the way in the Inland Sea, and at other places, but we do not find a single song after their arrival in Korea. There are, however, 5 songs on the return trip at Iejima in Harima Province.

The number of the songs is 5 longer lays, 3 Sedohka, and 137 verselets —145 in all.

The love songs in dialogue were written before and after the departure for exile of Yakamori. All of them are verselets—40 by Yakamori, 23 by his sweetheart.

The following 11 songs are written by a man starting for Korea and his wife.

No. 3578

Once my husband starts from Muko Cove,
soon I shall perish, languishing with love.

No. 3579

If only my beloved wife could come,
together hand in hand we would leave home.

No. 3580

If a mist rises when you stay
beside some bay,
think that it is caused
by my sighs.

No. 3581

My dear, in autumn shall I not return?
Why then with such sighs do you yearn?

No. 3582

My lord, you sail across the sea;
unhindered may you soon return to me.

No. 3583

If only my beloved pray for me,
no roaring waves will do me harm at sea.

No. 3584

How sad you will be once you go; so, pray,
wear this gown of mine upon the way.

No. 3585

Never shall I part with this gown, my sweet,—
this gift of yours until again we meet.

No. 3586

Same as No. 3581

No. 3587

Daily will I pray to the Deity
that safe you may return across the sea.

No. 3588

You go far across the sea,
my lord, but ever stay in me.

No. 3589

Crossing Mt. Ikoma where at eve cicadas cry,
yearning after you, my darling, here came I.

HATANO HASHIMARO

No. 3590

Treading the rocks of Mt. Ikoma,
here I go to see my darling.

No. 3591

I left my wife behind,
and now how cold the wind!

No. 3592

Sea Wind, forbear to blow, for here I sleep
without my love upon the ocean deep.

No. 3593

I take ship, parting from my heart's delight,
and on what island shall I sleep tonight?

No. 3594

My ship must wait the flood tide in the cove,
oh, why then did I haste to leave my love?

No. 3595

At dawn my ship left Muko Cove
where I heard cranes crying
behind the ebbing tide.

No. 3596

To see Inamitsuma I wish to go nigh,
but the sea is rough, and billows high.

No. 3597

The maiden divers hasten shoreward,
for suddenly the seas are rising.

No. 3598

I hear the cranes from Tama Bay.
Then already is it day?

No. 3599

Late though it be, it is a moonlit night, and so
seaward, passing Kami Island, let us row.

No. 3600

For scores of years
so perilously clinging to the cliff
that island juniper has stood!

No. 3601

Weary to me is life
without my wife,
but that island juniper
long has been standing there.

No. 3602

I shall not tire of seeing clouds o'erhanging
Nara Town where reds and greens commingle.

No. 3603

I, a humble maiden, pass my days,
yearning after you, a mighty lord.

No. 3604

Many a day has passed since I left you behind,
but you, my dear, are ever dwelling in my mind.

No. 3605

Oh, shall I ever cease to love you?
Such a day may come to me
when our Shikama flows no more
into the unbounded sea.

No. 3606

Passing the cove where maidens gather seaweed,
I build a hut upon Nujima Point.

No. 3607

The fishermen at white Fujie Cove
might they not think me one of them,
passing traveler though I be?

No. 3608

Aboard a vessel as I come,
yearning to see my darling love,
yonder I view Yamato's land
from this Akashi's lovely cove.

(Same as No. 255.)

No. 3609

The Sea of Muko is so calm today:
the fishing boats are out now in the bay.

(Same as No. 256.)

No. 3610

Do the court ladies take delight
in boating now on Ago Bay,
on the rising tide with scarlet skirts
sparkling amid the azure spray?

(Same as No. 40.)

No. 3611

Rowing the bright Moon's boat its man goes there
over Heaven's sea so calm, so fair.

KAKINOMOTONO HITOMARO

No. 3612

O that I had a man aboard this ship that he,
returning home, might tell my family of me.

No. 3613

Since my departure many an island have I passed,
but ne'er can I forget old Nara and my love.

No. 3614

On my way home I'll gather pretty stones for you,
my love, upon some island out at sea.

No. 3615

Is my dear wife sighing now for me?
For I view a mist out on the sea.

(Note: assimilation of breath to mist is
common in the anthology.)

No. 3616

Blow, Wind, and bring here from the sea
the mist, my darling's breath to me.

No. 3617

With the sound of the falls cicadas' cries I hear,
and am reminded of my cherished native town.

OISHI MINOMARO

No. 3618

How beautiful this limpid mountain stream,
but even here of Nara still I dream.

No. 3619

How beautiful the view! I will delight
in it again in fall when leaves are colored bright.

No. 3620

On the isle yearning for my dear,
cicadas' orchestra I hear.

No. 3621

How many years have passed, I wonder,
over these pine trees on Nagato Isle?

No. 3622

The moon is clear tonight, and on the sea
the men are rowing, singing merrily.

No. 3623

As the moon descends behind the mountain,
the fishermen's lights glimmer on the water.

No. 3624

We are not alone tonight upon the sea,
for from afar there comes a sound of rowing.

No. 3625

Even a drake that cries among reeds on the shore
    at eve,
and spends the day afloat upon the wave
can sleep together with his mate that thus
each may keep frost from falling on the other;
but ah, I lie alone beside this garment of my wife
now gone for ever like the flowing river
or the blowing wind without return.

Hanka

No. 3626

Alas, I am sad as a crane left all alone
by his mate that to some reedy shore is flown.

No. 3627

For Korea we took ship at Mitsu,
piloted out of the cove.
The waves rose, and the evening clouds concealed
    Awaji Island.
Off Akashi Bay we stopped to pass the night.
I saw some fisherwomen in small boats.
Soon cranes among the reeds ashore told by their
    cries
that day was breaking and the tide was rising.
The sailors plying oars, left Iyejima far behind.
I went ashore at Tama Cove then, and beheld the
    lovely view,
but yearning after home, I still felt lonely.
There I found a stone that had come off the sea
    god's bracelet,
but with none to take it to my wife for me,
I returned the gift back to the sea.

2 Hanka

No. 3628

Though I picked up a lovely pebble of the main,
my wife not being there,
into the sea I threw it back again.

No. 3629

O Waves, bring pretty shells out of the main,
and keep for me who come in autumn here again.

No. 3630

If but my vessel stopped beside yon isle,
thereon this weary night I might beguile.

No. 3631

'Twas my long-cherished dream to see the isle
of Awa, but I can not go there on this voyage.

No. 3632

O that our ship would anchor here tonight
for me to take delight,
viewing Marifu Cove
that I so love.

No. 3633

"Returning home, again my darling I shall see,"
I murmur, still I can't sleep peacefully.

No. 3634

She never leaves my mind—
my love I left behind.

No. 3635

O that my darling wife were here
to see Marifu's view with me.

No. 3636

Oh how my people must be praying
the gods now for my safe return!

No. 3637

This pretty island 'Isle of Prayer' they call.
'Tis an auspicious name for travelers all.

No. 3638

Behold, they are the diving maids who came
to gather seaweed near Naruto's whirlpools.

No. 3639

I dreamed happy dream at sea,
wherein my wife appeared to me.

No. 3640

I wish there were a vessel in this cove
to take a message to my yearned-for love.

No. 3641

Now at dawn I long and yearn for home,
and hear the sound of sculls
plied perhaps by maidens young.

No. 3642

Is the tide coming in? I hear
cranes searching for food, crying near.

No. 3643

Yonder I see a ship Yamato-bound upon the foam,
and wish I could ask some to take my message
    home.

No. 3644

We are bound for Korea, ordered by His Majesty,
but overtaken by a tempest in this port we lie.

No. 3645

My wife is eagerly awaiting me
who vainly chafe at days spent on the sea.

No. 3646

We sailed within sight of the land,
but driven by the wind,
anchor now beside an island out at sea.

No. 3647

Nightly in the dream I see
my wife who's yearning after me.

No. 3648

Let yon fishing torches burn more bright,
and bring my home, Yamato, into sight.

No. 3649

Like the wild duck sleeping on the wave
so slept I, and the night bedewed my hair.

No. 3650

I view the yearned-for moon above,
but still I can not see my love.

No. 3651

Eagerly I await the moonlight shining bright
that o'er the sea I may look homeward by its
    light.

No. 3652

Day after day the fishermen at Shika burn
salt; day after day for home I yearn.

No. 3653

Now their families must be waiting
for those fishermen home to return,
but they are fishing still by torchlight.

No. 3654

Behold, the cranes go crying in the sky.
Perhaps at Shika Cove the waves are high.

No. 3655

Autumn cicadas in the pines are singing.
Oh! is it already fall?

3 songs at a feast on the legend
of the Milky Way.

No. 3656

What though my garments dyed with hagi flowers
    be wet,
if I can keep you from departing in your boat?

No. 3657

Even the Cowherd longing for his Weaver maid
    above
yearns less than I so yearning for my love.

No. 3658

I wish I were the Cowherd of this evening,
rowing to see his wife across the river.

9 song written by the sea, viewing the moon

No. 3659

The autumn wind is blowing drearily,
and how my love must be awaiting me.

No. 3660

As ceaseless as the billows off Aratsu Point
for my darling wife at home I yearn.

No. 3661

Wave after wave advances in the breeze,
wetting the skirts of fishing girls caught unawares.

No. 3662

I look up at the sky,
    and find the night well gone;
but oh what matters though day break,
    because I am alone.

No. 3663

Is my wife expecting me to come back home
this month? Alas, 'tis wellnight gone, and still
    I roam.

No. 3664

I hear the sound of oars: 'tis day
and fishermen return from Shika Bay.

No. 3665

Yearning for my love, a sleepless night spent I,
and now hear wild geese in the misty morning
    sky.

No. 3666

'Tis nightfall, and the autumn wind blows drearily,
now shall I don the robe my wife made warm for
    me.

No. 3667

Long is my journey and forlorn;
and even the clothes, fresh given by my dear
now soiled and worn.

No. 3668

Of import is my duty here, I know,
but still I yearn for Nara town.

No. 3669

Though far away these quarters are well lighted,
while in the dark at home my dear wife must be
    yearning.

No. 3670

There may be days when waves rise not in Noko
    Cove,
but none whatever when I yearn not for my love.

No. 3671

Were I the moon that sails above,
I would go now to see my love.

No. 3672

The moon is shining bright above;
the fishing torches light the cove.

No. 3673

The wind was roaring, and the billows raging,
and we spent these three nights in Noko Harbor.

No. 3674

As I am yearning for my dear,
stags crying on the hill I hear.

No. 3675

Does my family know, I wonder,
we were o'ertaken by a tempest?

No. 3676

O that I had a wild goose as a messenger
to wing on high to Nara Town with word to her.

No. 3677

Though hagi flowers begem the field,
I am too far from home to take delight.

No. 3678

Translated, same as No. 3674

No. 3679

Waiting for the tempests to die down,
I passed a month here in this seaside town.

No. 3680

No slumber comes tonight to me,
and now stags crying for their mates I hear.

No. 3681

The hagi and obana I hoped to behold
have fallen, leaving desolate my garden.

No. 3682

I pray to all the gods of heaven and earth that I
soon may see your home-coming from Korea.

No. 3683

In yearning after you I spend the time
every month and every day.

No. 3684

Oh why can I not sleep this autumn night?
Is it because I lie without my heart's delight?

No. 3685

The month already goes, alack,
wherein I said I would come back.

No. 3686

Although my wife is far away,
she lives within my mind.

No. 3687

O Wild Geese, winging Nara-ward above,
come back and let me know how fares my love.

*Lamenting the death of Yukino Yakamaro
on Iki Island*

No. 3688

The autumn is come, but my friend
has not returned yet from Korea.
His family is praying to the gods,
taking good care of his mat*.
The time he told his mother that he would return
  has passed,
and they thought, "Will he come home today;
will he come home tomorrow?"
But even word of his arrival
in the foreign land comes not.
Now he sleeps upon a far-off island
within sound of the breakers dashing on the shore.

* The ancients took good care of the mat belonging to
a person during his absence.

2 Hanka

No. 3689

What shall I answer if his folk ask me about him
now dead and buried on the hillside of Iwada?

No. 3690

Alas, alas, my dearest friend has passed away,
leaving me behind to trudge life's weary way.

No. 3691

They prayed you might live long;
but your ship storm-tossed
during the voyage to Korea,
you spent days and months upon the sea till
  autumn came
when wild geese visited our land.
Your mother and wife often waited at the gate,
drenched in the morning dew and evening mist.
But now, alas,
You are dead and buried on a distant hill
where hagi fall, and obana nod.

2 Hanka

No. 3692

Alas, now dead and buried on the island
are you, awaited by your wife and children.

No. 3693

Alas for them who wait for you that met your end,
and sleep upon a hill with autumn leaves.

No. 3694

He came at last to Iki after many stormy days;
and praying that no accident might come,
consulted there a fortuneteller
who burned stag's shoulder-bones for divination,
but ah, ere leaving the island
death came to him.

2 Hanka

No. 3695

Hard it is to cross the sea and reach
Korea. Now he sleeps on Iki beach.

No. 3696

Whether to go on to Korea or return
am I wholly at a loss on Iki Isle
since he is dead.

No. 3697

The maple leaves on Mt. Asaji
are turned red in the autumn showers.

No. 3698

Even here in this distant isle
the harvest moon shines clear,
but oh! I must view it alone
without my dear.

No. 3699

Are Nara's mountains colored too
like this by autumn frost and dew?

No. 3700

Coloring the autumn mountains bright
the maple leaves are at their height.

No. 3701

These golden maple leaves at Takashiki Cove
tell me next fall I shall return home to my love.

No. 3702

O Maple leaves at Takashiki Cove,
fall not till I come home from Korea.

No. 3703

Behold, Mt. Uyekata is alight
with variegated autumn colors bright.

No. 3704

Amid the beauty of the falling maple leaves
I stand and watch your gorgeous ship go by.

No. 3705

Your ship goes, setting seaweed waving in the bay.
My lord, when will you come again here to this
isle?

No. 3706

The tide is coming in, and I must go aboard the
ship,
but I will see this view again upon my homeward
trip.

No. 3707

I was delighting in sight-seeing,
wearing red leaves in my hair
when the tide came in before I had my fill
of the lovely landscape there.

No. 3708

Many a month has passed since I left home,
and, yearning for my life, alone I go.

No. 3709

Gathering seashells for remembrance,
I am caught unawares by crawling waves.

No. 3710

Now I hear the sea roar, and must go away,
but at low tide I'll come again into this bay.

No. 3711

Though wet, I'll get a shell that makes
   me forget home at this cove,
braving the waves, because I suffer
   from pining for my love.

No. 3712

My raven-tressed wife—would she were here
to deftly spread and dry my clothes,
but clumsy I—what shall I do?

No. 3713

The maple leaves are falling fast like rain;
the time I told her I would come back goes in vain.

No. 3714

I hoped to dream long of you,
because I deeply love you;
but the autumn night was gone,
and I was left forlorn.

No. 3715

If I untie my sash away from you,
who will refasten it for me?

No. 3716

Many a weary day have I spent on my journey.
Now crimson leaves have faded on September
   mountains.

No. 3717

How soiled the sash my darling tied for me
at my departure, praying for my safe return!

No. 3718

Is this 'Home' Isle*? But here
I can not find my dear.

   • Iyejima (Iye means home.)

No. 3719

"I shall soon return, my love," said I
to my wife, but now a year's gone by.

No. 3720

Soon I shall see my darling, for from here
I can behold Awaji Island clear.

No. 3721

Sailors, row the ship without cease night and day:
the pines must be awaiting me at Mitsu Bay.

No. 3722

When can I cross Tatsuta Hill to reach
home, disembarking at fair Mitsu Beach?

4 songs to Nakatomino Yakamori
by Sanuno Chikami
No. 3723

Alas, my banished love goes, leaving me behind,
and peace and happiness go also from my mind.

No. 3724

Had I the Heaven's fire consuming all,
I would roll up and cast your long, long way
into the flames to let you stay.

No. 3725

When you go, my husband, wave your sleeve for
   me,
that I may keep the picture in my memory.

No. 3726

I scarce can bear my grief with you near by,
but then when once you go, oh how can I?

4 songs by Nakatomino Yakamori on the way
No. 3727

Worthless though I be,
yet my wife weeps for me.

No. 3728

Good though to walk along the streets of Nara,
yet hard indeed to go across the mountains.

No. 3729

My darling wife comes oftentimes to mind,
as I now trudge on, leaving her behind.

No. 3730

Since I was ordered banishment
all speechless have I been,
but now your name comes to my lips,
standing upon this mountain pass.

No. 3731

If to yearn passionately were to meet,
I ever could be with my darling.

No. 3732

Alas, throughout the ruddy day
for you I pine away,
throughout the dark night too
weeping I sigh for you.

No. 3733

To be kept in my memory
at parting my kindly wife
gave me this robe wherewith I now
beguile my weary life.

No. 3734

Crossing barriers and mountains, came I here,
and now no hope have I again to see my dear.

No. 3735

Nightly in my dream comes she,
she who is ever yearning after me.

No. 3736

How far from me you are away,
and I yearn for you night and day!

No. 3737

Even against you oft I have a spite,
because you make me languish day and night.

No. 3738

Yearning for you, I go to sleep, my dear,
and nightly in my dream see you appear.

No. 3739

Alas, I suffer so from love.
Oh why did I see you, my dear?

No. 3740

Were there no gods in heaven and earth to pity
me,
then I should die before I see my love again.

No. 3741

If alive, I then
shall see my love again.

No. 3742

When again shall I behold my wife—
I who live a weary banished life?

No. 3743

One may think a journey quite an easy thing,
but an ordeal to me now with love languishing.

No. 3744

Languishing for my dear,
I think naught of my life.

No. 3745

My darling, worry not about me, pray,
for if we live on, we shall meet some day.

No. 3746

You went away, my husband dear,
and no serving man is here;
so what to do I'm at a loss
with none for our fields to care.

No. 3747

I will be waiting,
      dear lord of mine,
at the gate
      as constant as our pine.

No. 3748

It must be hard in other provinces to rove;
so pray, return before I die of love.

No. 3749

When can I have you sitting face to face
with me, returning from the far-off place?

No. 3750

Believe me, you have none in life
who love you deeper than your wife.

No. 3751

My husband, keep my garment for me
until again you sit before me.

No. 3752

On a spring day I feel forlorn.
Without you how can I live on?

No. 3753

With care this cloth I wove
for you to wear, my love.

13 songs by Nakatomino Yakamori
No. 3754

O that I were a cuckoo flying high above
that I might come to you without a permit, love.

No. 3755

With hills and streams between us
we live a life so lonely.

No. 3756

When I was at home I saw you daily,
but now a month has passed without you.

No. 3757

My heart is in the capital with my dear
beyond so many barriers, many mountains.

No. 3758

Are the courtiers, free from care,
gaily teasing her so fair?

No. 3759

Nightly I lie alone in bed,
and oh! my tears are vainly shed.

No. 3760

Many the nights I lie alone,
and few that I spend with my own.

No. 3761

Thus it is, and worldly laws,
where each effect must follow cause,
have brought me to this pass.

No. 3762

I've crossed the 'Meeting' Hill* alone,
and weep, unable to behold my own.

* Osaka (O means to meet.)

No. 3763

'Journey' is an easy word to say.
Why is it hard to me thus all the way?

No. 3764

Parted are we by hill and river,
but not our hearts, my love; oh never.

No. 3765

I give this mirror clear
　　to you who love me.
Show it to none, my dear.
　　Keep it to be reminded of me.

No. 3766

Call me to mind whene'er you pine,
looking in this gift of mine!

8 songs by Sanuno Chikami
No. 3767

Morning and night I pray the gods to still my soul,
but have no peace now, yearning for my all-in-all.

No. 3768

I daily spend time in sad tears,
yearning after you, my love.

No. 3769

Night after night I spent then with my dear,
but he is gone: no longer with me now.

No. 3770

How long have I to wait ere he
comes home from banishment to me?

No. 3771

Anxious and eager, your friends are waiting,
and oh why do you not return?

No. 3772

Hearing that some have returned,
my heart welled up in joy,
but still as yet I see no sign
of him for whom I pined so long.

No. 3773

Here in the capital I live in grief;
my husband, why did I not go with you?

No. 3774

Till you return
I will exist somehow,
so forget me not,
but come back safe to me.

2 songs by Nakatomino Yakamori
No. 3775

Though I have not seen my wife these years,
yet ever faithful shall I be to her.

No. 3776

Were I in Nara Town, I should be waiting
now for our tryst beside the western stable.

2 songs by Chikami
No. 3777

With no means whatsoever to see you,
I only weep, not knowing what to do.

No. 3778

My dear, hold up the garment I gave you and pray
each day until the time of your return.

7 songs by Nakatomino Yakamori
No. 3779

Is the orange flower
falling by your bower
wherein you live alone
now I am gone?

No. 3780

Do cuckoos sing
that I may die,
for now when languishing for you I sit
they come near and cry?

No. 3781

I'm lonely, yearning after home,
so Cuckoo, cease
to cry so loud and let
me be at peace !

No. 3782

Melancholy enough it is to stay inside
throughout this day-long rain;
must you too, Cuckoo, add your note
to make me sadder still?

No. 3783

In this far province am I yearning after home,
and yearn the more, hearing the cuckoo's song.

No. 3784

O Cuckoo bird, I ask of thee
how so heartless canst thou be
as to add thy plaintive moan
when I grieve my lot alone?

No. 3785

O Cuckoo, from your plaintive cry
some respite give !
Sad enough already, at your song
my sorrow deepens.

THE MANYOSHU

BOOK XVI

FOREWORD

This book consists of two parts: songs based on legend and miscellaneous verses.

The number of the songs contained in this volume is 104, including 8 longer lays, and 92 verselets.

The distinguished poets appearing are Nagano Okimaro, and Ohtomono Yakamochi.

Once upon a time there was a maiden named Sakura (Cherry). Two men made love to her, and each vowed to win her though he might risk his life. The girl said, "Since olden times it was never heard that one woman married two men. These young men will never be reconciled. Therefore I will kill myself so that both of them may cease to fight."

She went into the woods, and hanged herself there. The men, lamenting her death, composed these songs:

No. 3786

THE FIRST MAN'S SONG

Alas, alas,
gone is my Cherry Flower
I so longed to wear
in springtime in my hair.

No. 3787

THE SECOND MAN'S SONG

O Cherry Flower,
namesake of the maiden I adored,
I shall love you year after year,
when in springtime you appear.

There were three men, it is told, who competed with one another for the hand of a girl, Ivy by name. She sighed and said, "Man's life is ephemeral as dew, and the will of the three is hard as adamant."

She roamed around the pond and finally drowned herself. The sorrow-stricken men composed these songs:

No. 3788

THE FIRST MAN'S SONG

Why were you not dry,
oh, Pond, when she came nigh?

No. 3789

THE SECOND MAN'S SONG

Alas, the maiden died unknown,
when I was journeying alone.

No. 3790

THE THIRD MAN'S SONG

I roam along the margin of the pond,
thinking of Ivy wandering beyond.

One upon a time there was an old man. He climbed a hill on a day of spring, and came across nine beautiful shinsen* who stood around a boiling cauldron of broth. They looked at the man, and said, "Come here and blow at the fire." The man complied, and sat before the cauldron. After a while one of them said, "Why did you come here where we work?" The old man replied, "I have unexpectedly met you, girls. Far be it from me to trespass," and composed the following song and hanka.

* an archaic term for a kind of fairy or witch.

No. 3791

When I was a babe, my mother carried me within
    her bosom.
I was crawling then in swaddling clothes.
As a lad, I wore robes with spotted sleeves.
When I was at your age, I took delight in combing
    my black hair,
now braiding, and now loosening.
I had red-colored silks,
girdles of bright brocade,
hagi-dyed gowns with Korean sashes, and such
    things.
One day a lovely maiden came to see me,
accompanied by a burly old man in black boots,
who waited in the yard outside.
I heard the girl say to the man, "Don't leave, but
    wait for me."
However, seeing I was there, she drew to me,
the silken girdle glittering round her waist
slender as a belted bee's
adorning the eaves of the Dragon Palace.
Thus people were glad to see me when I was
    young.
When spring came, and I roamed the fields,
pheasants came on the wing to me.
In autumn as I roved amid the mountains, clouds
    came overhead.
As I walked along the streets of Nara,
court ladies and their valets looked admiringly
    on me.
But now alas, you, pretty girls despise me.
Oh, look not down upon old men.
Know you not of that nefarious man
who, trundling his aged sire upon a cart,
would fain abandon him? It was the sage,
the venerable Genkoku who rescued him
to teach succeeding generations
the rule of filial devotion.

2 Hanka

No. 3792

Had I died young, you would not see me, Ladies
  fair.
Now that I am alive, blame not my snowy hair.

No. 3793

If your heads grow as white as snow like mine,
the young will scorn you too, my ladies nine.

9 girls in reply

No. 3794

THE FIRST GIRL

Now we nine foolish girls all prize
your lovely story, old man wise.

No. 3795

THE SECOND GIRL

Taught by the ancient man today,
with a good grace we all obey.

No. 3796

THE THIRD GIRL

The other girls seem to obey,
and I too follow them with joy.

No. 3797

THE FOURTH GIRL

I will obey him in the selfsame breath
with t'others I am bound in life and death.

No. 3798

THE FIFTH GIRL

Oh, what else can I do? I too
will act as t'other sisters do.

No. 3799

THE SIXTH GIRL

Proudly I also can
obey the aged man.

No. 3800

THE SEVENTH GIRL

The thoughts I hid within me are all clear
to him. I will obey too with no fear.

No. 3801

THE EIGHTH GIRL

Like cloth so hard to dye
with hagi flowers am I,
but I'll obey like t'others willingly.

No. 3802

THE NINTH GIRL

Like vernal grasses young which softly sway
in the wind, him I too will obey.

*There were a man and a beautiful girl. They
were in love, and she wanted to let her parents
know about it. Composing a song, she sent it to
her lover:*

No. 3803

Better for the moon to rise and shine above
than be hanging low behind the hill, my love.

(The reply from the lover is missing.)

*There was a young man newly wed. Soon after
the marriage he was sent to a far province as an
express messenger. The bride became sick, and
took to her bed. Years passed. He came back,
and reported his mission. He then hastened home
to see his wife. The emaciated woman was dying.
The man moaned and composed a song in tears:*

No. 3804

My wife who has awaited me for long is dying.
Alas, no more can we live happily together.

*The wife, hearing the song, raised her head and
sang:*

No. 3805

His black hair powdered with white snow
at last has come my lord who loves me so.

(It seems, when the husband returned, it was
winter, and snow was falling.)

The following verse is concerning a girl who loved a man without permission of her parents. Fearing their reprimand, the man hesitated. Therefore, the girl wrote the following song to send it to her lover.

No. 3806

Even if my parents know our secret love, be brave,
my lover. We can die, and rest together in the grave.

The following song is about Prince Katsuragi who was sent to the Northern area of this country. On the way he showed displeasure at his treatment by the chief of a province. Though the latter subsequently asked to hold a banquet in his honor, he refused. An ex-court-maiden came up to him with a cup in her left hand and wine in the other and sang the song. Immediately the prince's anger was gone, and he gladly sat and drank all day.

No. 3807

For my lord's pardon now we pray,
and glad your pleasure we obey.

Once some men and women went on a picnic. Among them was a couple. The wife was so lovely that the husband's heart went out to her. He composed this song and praised her beauty.

No. 3808

Among the throng I see my wife so dear,
as bright and pretty as a mirror clear.

A girl was loved by a nobleman, but soon fell into disfavor. He returned the gown she had given him as she was leaving his residence. The girl, feeling bitter, composed this song.

No. 3809

Is there a law allowing buyers
to return an article bought?
My lord, why do you give me back
the gown I brought?

There was a woman who was living for years separate from her husband. He sent her a gift as he married another woman. She made this song in return.

No. 3810

Alas, I brewed good wine for you to drink, but all
is now in vain, since at my bower you will not call.

Once there was a woman, whose husband did not come to see her for a long time. The girl pined with love, and finally took to her bed. Every day she became thinner, and soon was on the point of death. Thereupon they sent for the husband. He came. But she was delirious and sang these songs in tears, and died.

No. 3811

No messenger from my lover comes to me,
and I lie on a bed of illness.
This comes not from the curse of gods.
No use asking fortunetellers,
since I am languishing with love.
I know death is approaching me,
and neither prayers nor fortunetellers now avail.

Hanka
No. 3812

No fortuneteller is of use, nor any doctor.
Alas, I have no means whate'er to see my lover.

No. 3813

To see you I've no opportunity,
my darling, and so I would rather die.

There once lived a girl who was forsaken by her husband. She married another man. A young man, without knowing that she had been remarried, asked her parents for her hand with the following song. The parents replied to him with the other verse.

No. 3814

The priceless pearl now has come off the string, they say,
and I wish it for mine to cherish night and day.

The reply

No. 3815

The pearl was off the string, 'tis true,
but now 'tis on another new.

At a feast Prince Hozumi composed this song:

No. 3816

Though I lock Love in the chest I bought,
yet he comes out to grip me by the throat.

The following songs were sung by Prince Kawamura, accompanied by the koto:

No. 3817

The mortar is now resting in the barn,
and my husband smiling at the gate.

No. 3818

Morning mist in the valley
and the little kajika singing,
and I in the shade of yearning
for a maid, and none to tell her.

The following songs used to be sung at the beginning of a banquet by Prince Kodai, accompanied with the koto:

No. 3819

My friends, no shower that comes but brings to
   mind the view
of Kasuga field, and its obana wet with dew.

No. 3820

People come to the new pavilion by the stream
to see the sunset and the evening sky agleam.

There was a girl who refused all proposals from handsome noblemen, and married a vulgar wretch. Thereupon Princess Konobe wrote the following song in derision:

No. 3821

All like the beautiful,
   so think I at least,
but strange, this woman chose a man
   as ugly as a hornèd beast.

No. 3822

The lass I took into an empty house to sleep together
is grown up, and now wears her glossy hair like
   other women.

No. 3823

Same as the above

8 songs by Nagano Okimaro

(Note: several of these songs are examples of
a kind of game, in which the writer is challenged to
combine certain words.)

Friends were drinking at a banquet. The night was far spent when they heard the cries of foxes. Thereupon Okimaro sang No. 3824 song.

No. 3824

Boil water, Children, in the pot
   to pour upon the foxes sly
that, crossing yonder cypress bridge
   athwart the stream, come furtively.

A song composed, using 'Hunting trousers,' 'herbs,' 'feasting mat,' and 'crossbeam.'

No. 3825

Bring a feasting mat and dish
of boiled herbs to this rider
who rests now hanging
his hunting trousers on the crossbeam.

No. 3826

Is this a lotus leaf indeed?
   Well then, that I was wrong I grant,
and those which are found in my yard
   are but the leaves of taro plant.

On the backgammon die

No. 3827

Not only one and two, but five, six, three
and four has our backgammon die as you can
   see.

Song composed, using 'perfume,' 'tower,' 'nook,' 'dirty,' 'carp' and 'hag.'

No. 3828

O Hag, you are defiled, because you took
and ate a dirty carp half-dead found at the river
    nook.
Therefore ne'er come here
the perfumed tower near.

Song written, using 'vinegar,' 'sauce,' 'leek,' 'sea bream' and 'waterplant.'

No. 3829

Do not bring a waterplant which smells like leeks
    with vinegared sauce to me who wish
to have sliced raw sea bream
    with garnishings, my favorite dish.

Written, using 'broomcorn,' 'reaping hook,' 'juniper tree' and 'jujube tree.'

No. 3830

Reap the broomcorn with a hook for me
to clean the earth beneath this juniper- and
    jujube-tree.

Written, using 'egret,' 'branch in the beak' and 'fly.'

No. 3831

Are the egrets mimicking a sumo* dance on high,
flying with branches in their beaks so merrily?

* Japanese wrestler.

Written, using 'bramble,' 'storehouse,' 'defile,' 'comb' and 'woman.'

No. 3832

I'll clear the earth of brambles to erect a store-
    house high.
Therefore, Combmaking woman, ne'er defile the
    ground near by.

Written, using 'tiger,' 'crevasse,' 'dragon' and 'blade.'

No. 3833

A sharp blade and well-tempered I desire
to go astride a tiger high and higher
to the crevasse and there to catch a dragon dire.

Looking at the food before him at a feast

No. 3834

I see a pear, a jujube, millet dark and brown,
and creeping arrowroot
laid on the table with geranium flowers adorning
    them.

A nobleman said he saw lovely lotus flowers in Katsumata Pond. Whereat a lady, making this verse, ridiculed him:

No. 3835

No lotus flower is found
in Katsumata Pond.
Of that I am as well aware
as that you have no beard whate'er.

Scorning double-faced wretches

No. 3836

Mean, double-facèd wretches
are they. How I despise them!

No. 3837

Oh, how I wish a shower would come to dot
the lotus leaves with little jewels bright!

2 nonsense songs:

Prince Toneri at a banquet asked for meaning-less songs, offering the writer cash and silk. Thereupon Lord Abe composed the following songs, and got two thousand mon together with the cloth.

No. 3838

There's a backgammon board
on the forehead of my wife,
and a boil upon the ox's back.

No. 3839

A boulder for my lord to wear for trousers,
and a whitebait hanging on the mountain.

Exchanges of banter:
To Lord Ohmiwa

No. 3840

The female devil of the temple said,
"Wed me to lean Ohmiwa
that I may bear him a skinny bratling."

LORD IKEDA

In reply

No. 3841

Vermilion if you lack to make a Buddha's image,
dig for it the big red nose of Lord Ikeda.

LORD OHMIWA

To Lord Hozumi

No. 3842

O Children, trouble not to go to reap the meadow,
since you have plenty here to mow in Lord
Hozumi's armpits.

LORD HEGURI

In reply

No. 3843

Where do you get vermilion?—
Dig for it the nose of Lord Heguri.

LORD HOZUMI

No. 3844

Whene'er I see the darker Hida,
I am reminded of the less black Kose.

In reply

No. 3845

Hibimaro the dollmaker is so pale, alack,
that fervently he must wish to be black.

In derision of a priest

No. 3846

Such a beard our priest has!
    Horses we could tie there.
Ah, but if they pulled away,
    how our priest would cry there!

The reply

No. 3847

Hold your tongue, parishioner—
    talk of 'pull' and 'crying'!
When our headman pulls your tax,
    you cry as if you're dying.

A song composed in a dream

No. 3848

Long have I pined with love,
and yearned for you, my dove.

*2 songs written, weary of life
(inscribed on the koto kept in the
Kawaraji Temple)*

No. 3849

Of the sea of life and death I'm weary,
and long to go to yonder restful mountain.

No. 3850

Living long in the temporal hovel,
vainly do I yearn now for Nirvana.

*Song on the philosophy of Laotse
and Chungtze*

No. 3851

If only your mind stayed in nothingness, your eyes
would see the mountain where abide the hermits
    wise.

No. 3852

Never will the sea go dry,
nor the mountain naked lie.
Oh, yes, they do;
the tide recedes,
the old trees die.

ANON.

*2 songs written in derision of a thin courtier,
by Ohtomono Yakamochi*

No. 3853

My friend, thy weal is
    My concern. 'Tis for thy sake:
the summer eel is
    the food for thin men to take.
    Go catch one hiding by a stake.

No. 3854

Though lean, 'tis better
    to be alive, and so do not
be drowned to get a
    slippery eel. Know it would be a blot
    on thy escutcheon all for naught.

2 songs by Prince Takamiya

No. 3855

Could I but serve eternally
at court, what joy 'twould be!

No. 3856

Behold, the impious crow that robbed the sacred
  paddy
is perched with swollen eyelids on the temple
  pillar.

*The following song is said to have been written
by a maidservant in the service of Prince Sai.
She had no chance, living at the prince's residence,
to meet her lover, and yearned for him so much
that in a dream she saw him.*

*As she awoke, however, she felt for him in bed
in vain. Thereupon she wept and sang this song
aloud. The prince heard it, and sympathizing
with her, he let her go home.*

This song is a very short 'longer' lay.

No. 3857

Alas, though I eat rice,
I can not relish it,
and though I take a walk,
I do not feel at ease,
for I am here
without my dear.

2 songs

No. 3858

If recorded, then my pains in love
would be worth the fifth court rank.

No. 3859

If no prize is given for my pains in love,
I will go to the court of justice for a suit.

10 songs

*In the era of Jinki the local government of
Kyushu ordered Munekatabeno Tsumaro, a man
of Chikuzen Province, as captain to go with a
cargo of provisions to the Island of Tsushima.*

*Tsumaro asked his friend named Arao to take
his place, because he was now too old.*

*Arao complied, and set sail from Matsura of
Hizen Province for Tsushima Island.*

*But during the voyage overtaken by a storm,
the ship sank.*

*These songs are said to have been written by
either Arao's family or Yamanoeno Okura, the
governor of Chikuzen Province, which is more
probable.*

No. 3860

Arao who sailed for his friend is waving
his sleeve aboard the vessel in the offing.

No. 3861

Boiling rice, the wives await
their husbands daily at their gate.

No. 3862

Don't fell trees on Mt. Shiga
where sleep Arao and other sailors.

No. 3863

Arao and his crew are gone,
leaving their paddy fields all lone.

No. 3864

Very much the same as No. 3860

No. 3865

Why Arao and others think not of their wives,
spending years and years away from them?

No. 3866

If you see a ship returning with the sailors,
prithee, tell us at once, O Yara's Keeper of the
  sea.

No. 3867

Alas, there's none to tell the ship
is nearing Yara's headland tip.

No. 3868

I wish the crimson-colored ship
  that will be under sail
would take my parcel for my love,
  but, should a thief come—what avail?

No. 3869

They turn the ships; they gravely search around.
They find him not. Deep lies Arao drowned.

No. 3870

If the cormorant pick up a pearl from the ocean
  bed,
let me have it as my own to wear upon my head.

No. 3871

The young weed growing in the sea
is rough, but soft and sweet to me.

> Note: Wakame, seaweed, and wakame, young
> girl, are homonymous. This is a song
> in metaphor.

No. 3872

Many the birds that come to eat
  the berries of my ripening tree
that stands within the gate. Why then,
  my friend, do you not come to me?

ANON.

No. 3873

Waken, my sweetheart, waken ere it is too late.
Many a bird I hear now singing by the gate.

No. 3874

Where is the woman gone I slept with
when I was a stripling?

No. 3875

Would that I could meet my sweetheart in this
  place
and for her hat exchange my gilded lace.

> (Perhaps a folk song.)

No. 3876

Alas, did my wife wet her garments for my sake,
trying waternuts to gather in the lake?

No. 3877

Rain never fades my clothes dyed red,
my love: they will improve instead.

> (The meaning: my love for you shall never
> change in adversity, but shine brighter.)

*The following song was written in mock con-
solation for a man who dropped an ax into the
sea, and was foolish enough not to know that iron
does not float on water.*

No. 3878

You dropped the ax into the sea, but do not weep,
for soon 'twill to the surface rise out of the deep.

No. 3879

O poor wretch, come out of the brewery.
Naught brews but scolding, it is plain to see.

No. 3880

Gathering shellfish on the isle,
did you break them with a stone,
wash them cleanly in the stream,
rub them well with salt,
put them on a tray,
and give them to your mother dear,
and to your father dear?

> (A folk song.)

No. 3881

Narrow is the leafy path, my lord,
but if you visit here, we'll make it broad.

No. 3882

Hatched now are young eagles on the rugged
  mountain
feathers for long-handled fans to give your Highness.

No. 3883

This sacred Iyahiko Hill is drear,
even when fine, the drizzle falling here.

No. 3884

Is the antlered stag
  still asleep
dressed in a silken hide
  at the bottom of the mountain deep?

> Note: Shakamuni is said to have left his
> footprints before he entered Nirvana,
> and they were later carved in stones.
> In Yakushiji Temple of Nara there
> are 21 verses written in praise of
> Buddha's footmarked stones in 575777
> syllabled six Japanese lines. Hence
> this verse form is called 'Buddha's
> footmarked stone' style.

2 songs by a beggar

No. 3885

In April and May people hunt deer to acquire
their horns for medical use.
Now there stand two yew trees close together
on Heguri Hill.
One day I take my place beneath them,
bow and arrow in my hands
when I see a stag appear.
He talks to me: "Soon I shall perish,
shot by folk who serve the Emperor.
My horns will deck his hat,
my ears contain his China ink,
my eyes will be his mirror clear,
my nails adorn his bow;
and for his writing brush my hair,
my skin for his box cover, will be used.
My venison will become his food,
and even numbles be preserved
in salt to lend variety to his table.
Is this not a joy supreme
to an old deer like me?"

No. 3886

"The Emperor sent for me."
said the crab living on the seashore of Naniwa
 Bay.
"But why? I know I can be of no use.
Does he desire to hear me sing,
play on the flute or koto?

"At any rate I hastened to Asuka town
past Okina, Tsuku field,
and through the eastern gate
entering the palace ground, reported.
But oh, woe worth the day.
Horses and cows are tied with ropes,
but far worse fate awaited me.
Into a mortar I was thrown, and pounded well.
They had prepared fine powder—
dried and ground elm bark.
With it and thick salt water
brought from Naniwa Inlet I was mixed
to be served for the Emperor's board."

3 songs on frightening things
Author unknown

No. 3887

Reaping the field you see
quails start from underneath you suddenly.

No. 3888

A vessel boarded by a governor great
heavily rolling in a stormy strait.

No. 3889

When on a dreary rainy night
will-o'-the-wisps' appalling sight
appears to me, in fright
do I await the morning light.

THE MANYOSHU

BOOK XVII

FOREWORD

In this book the songs are arranged in chronological order, as are the following three books.

At the beginning of the book there appear songs written in November, 730 by men of the retinue accompanying Ohtomono Tabito, governor of the local government at Tsukushi, on his way to the Capital.

There are also songs written by Ohtomono Yakamochi, Tabito's son, after his appointment to the local government at Etchu. It is quite evident that this book was compiled by Yakamochi himself.

The number of the songs is 14 longer lays, 1 Sedohka, and 127 verselets—142 in all.

No. 3890

From the pine grove toward the ocean now I
    stare,
and see young women divers gathering seaweed
    there.

MINUNO ISOMORI

No. 3891

The tide now rises, now ebbs in the sea,
but I without cease yearn for thee.

No. 3892

The fishing boats are moored all in the bay,
but oh, I have no place where I can stay.

No. 3893

Our ship left Kyushu yesterday, and now
Hijiki's Sea I view afore the bow.

No. 3894

With every sound of oars upon the blue,
my darling wife, my heart yearns after you.

No. 3895

As the night falls upon the brine,
I muse on home and love of mine.

No. 3896

Even at home life's filled with dangers,
and far more here upon the ocean.

No. 3897

As I was starting for Tsukushi o'er the foam,
my love for whom I yearn asked, "When will you
    come home?"

No. 3898

My friend, sing merry songs. We have
naught else but sky upon the wave.

No. 3899

Dimly from aboard I view
Tsunu's pines across the blue.

No. 3900

Is the Weaver being taken
    across the Heavenly River to her love,
for on this moonlit night
    white clouds like spray appear above?

OHTOMONO YAKAMOCHI

No. 3901

Winter has passed, and now is spring
    with plums in flower,
but Friend, none come to view them
    from my bower.

No. 3902

Plum flower on flower you have here in your
    garden,
and hour on hour you ne'er tire of their guerdon.

No. 3903

Are you in bud mid vernal shower,
Willows, to vie with plums in flower?

No. 3904

My friend, though you should break the flowering
    plum,
spare it at least the moment of full bloom.

No. 3905

Decking our hair with fair plum flowers
    and willows, we take pleasure
here in the garden,
    and enjoy our leisure.

No. 3906

Behold, the petals of the plum flowers
    in the garden, scattered by the breeze,
fly up into the air, descending lightly
    as snowflakes on the trees.

In praise of the new Capital
No. 3907

The capital, Kuni, is adorned with flowers in
    spring,
and in the fall with golden leaves.
Here we have a bridge above the upper rapids,
and o'er the lower pool another floating one
to come and go and serve at court.

Hanka

No. 3908

As the Izumi River
goes on for ever,
so a courtier let me stay
to serve the Sovereign night and day.

No. 3909

O that the orange trees were e'er in flower that I
might have the cuckoo come and sing incessantly !

No. 3910

If I set a china tree outside my bower,
would mountain cuckoos come invited by its
    flower?

No. 3911

I live upon a mountainside and every day
cuckoos come flying to these woods to sing their
    lay.

No. 3912

Why but in May when we string orange bloom,
oh, Cuckoos, calling loudly do you come?

No. 3913

If cuckoos perch upon your china tree,
will its blossoms fall like jewelry?

No. 3914

Should cuckoo's cry be dowered on our banquet,
we'll make his song immortal with our verses.

No. 3915

Now's spring, and coming over hill and dale,
    among
the trees bush warblers must be singing their
    sweet song.

                              YAMABENO AKAHITO

6 songs by Ohtomono Yakamochi

No. 3916

Perhaps the fragrance of the orange flowers is
    gone
with the night's rain, and cuckoos cry forlorn.

No. 3917

Nightly do I take joy in the çuckoo's music.
    If a net were spread around
my garden, could I still hear it
    after the orange flowers are fallen to the
        ground?

No. 3918

To our garden cuckoos come and sing
    where the orange trees are now in flower.
O that I could e'er keep the birds
    near my bower.

No. 3919

Deserted, Nara is so drear,
but cuckoos still come, and sing here.

No. 3920

The house is old, and from the grass quails greet,
but still the flowering orange trees smell sweet.

No. 3921

Now is April
when we dye our clothes in iris color,
when we go to cull medicinal herbs.

No. 3922

Blest shall I be,
if I can serve His Majesty
till these smooth hands all wrinkled grow,
and this black hair as white as snow.

                              TACHIBANANO SUKUNE

No. 3923

Charming is the sight of snow
    that has already wrapped the ground,
still falling thick and fast,
    dancing away without a sound.

                              KINO KIYOHITO

No. 3924

The gorge between the mountains has become a
    pure white lane,
wrapped with the snow of yesterday and of today
    again.

                              KINO OKAJI

No. 3925

Happy on New Year's Day we have a snowfall!
We shall be blessèd with a heavy harvest.

FUJIINO MOROAI

No. 3926

The earth around the palace is bedight
with snow, and no one grows tired of the sight.

OHTOMONO YAKAMOCHI

*2 songs to Ohtomono Yakamochi
from his aunt, Sakanoeno Iratsume*

No. 3927

Now to speed the parting guest I offer wine
to the gods whom in my alcove I enshrine.

No. 3928

Oh, if I miss you, dear, in days to come,
how shall I console my heart in gloom?

2 more songs sent to Etchu

No. 3929

Night after night I dream of thee!
How far away thou art from me!

No. 3930

Gods of Etchu Province, bless my nephew
who is now living under your protection!

*12 songs sent to Ohtomono Yakamochi
by Lady Heguri*

No. 3931

They spread our rumors, but now you are far
away,
and know not how I yearning live day after day.

No. 3932

Alas for me
who after you must pine.

No. 3933

Yesterday's gone, and today still I live on.
Why? Only to see my love, my own.

No. 3934

I would as lief rest buried
as live like this without you.

No. 3935

I hide love in my bosom,
but now my face betrays me.

No. 3936

It is for you to roam, leaving me who
stay wearily at home, yearning for you.

No. 3937

Afar still does my traveler roam.
Oh, when will he come home?

No. 3938

My girdle has not been untied since he,
my darling, left to go away from me.

No. 3939

When you lived in the near-by village you could
come
whenever you desired to see me to my home.

No. 3940

The parting playful pinch, although I winced,
has left my arm with sign of love convinced.

No. 3941

Even after I am burned upon the pyre,
still my bones will yearn on for my heart's desire.

No. 3942

You treat me lightly as a poor pine flower,
but I yearn after you at every hour.

*13 songs written at a feast in the residence
of Ohtomono Yakamochi*

No. 3943

I know you culled these flowers for me
when the eared rice you went to see.

OHTOMONO YAKAMOCHI

3 songs by Ohtomono Ikenushi

No. 3944

I roamed the autumn field where I found these
abloom, and brought them here my friend to
please.

No. 3945

Away from home so cold the autumn dawn.
O that I could now have my wife's warm gown.

No. 3946

Down the mountainside where cuckoos sang in
  summer
I hear the dreary autumn wind now wailing.

2 songs by Ohtomono Yakamochi
No. 3947

How cold the autumn wind this morning; and
  now I
know the time for geese to come is drawing nigh.

No. 3948

Though a month has gone by in the country,
the sash she tied for me is not unloosened.

No. 3949

Is my wife at home now sleeping
with her sash for me unloosened?
                    OHTOMONO IKENUSHI

No. 3950

I love my distant wife so deep,
and here, my sash fast tied, I sleep.
                    OHTOMONO YAKAMOCHI

No. 3951

My friends, when you feel lonely, hearing the
  cicadas sing,
look upon autumn flowers about the meadow
  wandering.
                    HADANO YACHISHIMA

No. 3952

Whenever spring comes I enjoy wistarias
so graceful, brightening Ikuri forest.

No. 3953

The fall wind blowing cold and drear,
wild geese will soon come flying here.

No. 3954

Let us go, riding to see waves come rolling,
rolling, lovely Shibu laving, laving.

Toward the end of the banquet
No. 3955

It seems now far advanced the night, for lo,
above yon mountain hangs the moon so low.
                    Clerk HAJI MICHIYOSHI

No. 3956

The fishermen will put yon ships to sea,
sailing out beating gunwales merrily.

Mourning the dead brother
by Ohtomono Yakamochi
No. 3957

When I left the capital
for the appointed post in Etchu Province,
my brother saw me off past Narayama
until I came to the Izumi.
There we parted,
stopping our horses in the river bottom,
and wished each other well.
Since then with many peaks and streams between
  us,
I have kept yearning after him;
but now a messenger comes from home,
bringing me word he died,
not waiting for the fall
to see his favorite flowers: hagi and obana.

No. 3958

I thought that sound
was my brother dear,
but now I hear smoke of his funeral pyre
hangs above the hill.

No. 3959

If I had known that he must die so soon without
  awaiting me
back home, I would have taken him to view the
  Koshi Sea.

2 songs by Ohtomono Yakamochi
on welcoming Ohtomono Ikenushi

No. 3960

Though deep upon the garden lie the snow,
deeper my thought of you is you must know.

No. 3961

As ceaselessly
as the white waves roll,
and rudder's plied,
I think of you.

"Lying ill abed"
by Ohtomono Yakamochi

No. 3962

Sent by the Emperor I came to Etchu Province,
but ere I settled down I yielded to an illness,
growing worse day after day.
Oh, how my family must be awaiting me:
my mother anxious about my welfare,
my dear wife standing at the gate at morn,
and lying with her raven tresses spread at night,
my little children bothering others with their
　　noises.
Many are things I have to tell my folk at home,
but there is no quick means to send them word,
I only lie like this regretting my sad lot.

Hanka

No. 3963

How brief man's life! As soon I go
as cherry blossoms now ablow.

No. 3964

Many a hill and stream divides us two,
and my dear wife, I can't have sight of you.

2 songs to Ohtomono Ikenushi
by Ohtomono Yakamochi

No. 3965

Alas, though cherry trees are blowing everywhere,
no strength have I to pluck a sprig to deck my
　　hair.

No. 3966

The uguisu must be scattering cherry flowers
　　now,
and when together with you can I wear them o'er
　　my brow?

In reply
2 songs by Ohtomono Ikenushi

No. 3967

If only I could show
the cherry blossoms in the gorge to thee,
then well contented I should be.

No. 3968

Songbirds come and scatter petals
　　of the yellow rose, but oh,
'tis sad you can not come and touch
　　the plant ablow.

Again to his friend, Ohtomono Ikenushi,
by Ohtomono Yakamochi

No. 3969

I came, appointed by the Emperor, to govern here,
but now lie ill in bed;
and separated by high hill on hill,
I only yearn for home.
How I wish to go out
with friends to view the cherry flowers,
or hear bush warblers trill in vernal woods,
flitting from bough to bough,
or see fair maidens cull herbs on the mead,
their red skirts dripping with spring rain.
My friend, in thankful tears I read your words.
With gratitude I could not sleep last night.
With the same feeling do I think of you today.

In answer to No. 3967

No. 3970

Could I behold the cherry flowers with you,
no need to think of you so yearningly.

In answer to No. 3968

No. 3971

I envy you who can hear songbirds trill
among the yellow roses on the hill.

No. 3972

As I lie yearning after thee,
I feel as weak as weak can be.

3 songs by Ohtomono Ikenushi

No. 3973

You who, ordered by the Emperor,
govern the northern provinces,
lie ill, and yearn for home;
but you know messengers post night and day
along the highways to serve you.
Are not the cherry trees bedecking now the
  mountainside,
warblers singing on the bough,
and maidens culling violets in the field,
their snow-white sleeves and red skirts billowing
  in the breeze?
My friend, how all these wait for you to come out
  and greet them!

No. 3974

Daily my flowering yellow rose I view,
and daily too I long and yearn for you.

No. 3975

Longing for you I stood
outside your hedge.

2 songs by Ohtomono Yakamochi

No. 3976

My friend, you sent a spray of yellow rose to me,
making me sad, because the bush I can not see.

No. 3977

Because you stood with love for me
outside the hedge, I dreamed of you.

5 songs to his wife
by Ohtomono Yakamochi

No. 3978

How I yearn for my wife,
even when we live together!
To me she's ever the first flower in the spring;
but by the order of the Emperor
I came here over hill and field,
and have not seen her long.
I dream of her night after night,
but have no means to see her face to face.
Yet in May when cuckoos come,

and the utsugi flower adorns the hill,
I will go to Ohmi. From across the lake
at last, all wayworn, I'll return to her.

No. 3979

Winter is gone, and spring is come, but my dear
  wife
I can not see, and yearning, lead a lonely life.

No. 3980

O that it were but in reality:
My darling wife, I only dream of thee.

No. 3981

I have come over many a hill and stream,
and yearning, of her every night I dream.

No. 3982

I have not seen my wife long and the cherry
  flowers are gone.
Eagerly she must be waiting, counting days alone.

2 songs by Ohtomono Yakamochi

No. 3983

'Tis April, and the mountains stand near by.
Oh, why does not the cuckoo come and cry?

No. 3984

But a few orange trees are flowering in our village.
Is that the reason why the cuckoo does not come
  here?

> (Cuckoos come to sing on the first day of
> summer, but here in the province of Etchu
> orange trees, their favorite plants, are rare.
> Ohtomo Yakamochi composes the above verses
> on March 29.)

3 songs by Ohtomono Yakamochi

No. 3985

ON MT. FUTAGAMI

Mt. Futagami, the Izumi River flowing at its foot,
is fair, seen even from afar when in the spring
ablaze with cherry flowers
or radiant with red foliage in the fall.
The guardian god keeps watch
over this noble mountain,
from ancient times, a peak revered by all.

No. 3986

As ceaselessly waves lap the shore,
so do I miss the days of yore.

No. 3987

The time is near
when the cuckoo's song I hear
upon Mt. Futagami here.

(All written on March 30.)

No. 3988

Somewhere in the moonlight do I hear
a cuckoo; I regret it is not near.

OHTOMONO YAKAMOCHI

*2 songs at a farewell banquet
for Ohtomono Yakamochi in the
residence of Hatano Yachishima*

No. 3989

As ceaselessly the white waves run,
so shall I yearn when you are gone.

The host

No. 3990

Would my friend were a jewel fair
for me upon my wrist to wear!

OHTOMONO YAKAMOCHI

2 songs by Ohtomono Yakamochi

No. 3991

We rode abreast along the shore,
and came to the Unabi River,
passing Shibutani Point
where angry waves were dashing on the rocks.
Fishermen were catching fish with cormorants in
  the stream.
We had our fill of the fine view.
Then launching boats upon the sea,
we saw a flight of crying fowl above the beach,
and the isles bright with fair flowering trees.
I promised me to come here every year with
  cronies as today.

No. 3992

How fair the waves there in the offing to my sight!
I wish to come here every year to take delight.

2 songs by Ohtomono Ikenushi

No. 3993

"Wistaria flowers are gone, but now utsugi in full
  bloom,"
the cuckoos tell us. So unable
to subdue my lust for outing,
I started, taking horse, together with my bosom
  friends.
We passed the sand bank at the estuary
where birds were hunting for their food,
saw seaweed drifting on the waves.
Launching boats upon the lake,
we enjoyed the scenery around.
The point of Ofu was white with the flowers,
mallards were crying on the shore.
In autumn golden leaves, in springtime cherry
  flowers
enhance the beauty of this place.

No. 3994

As long as I live, oftentimes shall I
come to this beach to view the scenery.

*4 songs at a farewell banquet for
Ohtomono Yakamochi in the residence
of Ohtomono Ikenushi*

No. 3995

I start upon a journey long and weary,
and many, many days I shall not meet you.

OHTOMONO YAKAMOCHI

No. 3996

The cries of cuckoos will sound lone
in merry May when you are gone.

UCHINOKURA NAWAMARO

No. 3997

Oh, do not grieve since I'm away
  in May when cuckoos sing,
but take delight in putting
  orange flowers upon a string.

OHTOMONO YAKAMOCHI

*Composed by Ishikawano Mimichi,
and recited by Ohtomono Ikenushi*

No. 3998

When orange flowers are gone, I will soothe me,
stringing the fruit, although yet green and wee.

At a banquet in his residence
by Ohtomono Yakamochi

No. 3999

The day of my departure's near at hand, and I
will fully feast my eyes upon my company.

On Mt. Tachi (now pronounced Tate)
by Ohtomono Yakamochi

No. 4000

Many are famous mountains in this province,
but by far the noblest peak is Tachi
where snow is ceaselessly descending.
Many are noted rivers here,
but by far the clearest is the Katakai
over which mist hangs morning after morning.
How I love the sight: the mountain girded with
  the stream!
Oh, let me tell about the beauty grand, serene
  to all posterity.

Hanka

No. 4001

How fair the summer snow
upon Mt. Tachi's brow!

No. 4002

Deeply the limpid river do I love,
and e'er will go to see the view thereof.

On the same theme
by Ohtomono Ikenushi

No. 4003

The lofty peak stands, rending cloud on cloud
with snow descending all the year around.
There mossy rugged crags for ages lie so grand
  to view.
Mist in the morning veils the stream which foaming runs beneath,
and in the evening clouds hang o'er the mountain
  top.
How proud I am to tell about the beauty of this
  peak!

No. 4004

The snow remains
even in summer,
because Mt. Tachi
is so sacred.

No. 4005

As the Katagai courses day and night,
so people will repair here for its sight.

Written nearing the Capital
by Ohtomono Yakamochi to Ikenushi

No. 4006

Like hemlocks green upon Mt. Futagami
our Ohtomo clan has thrived for ages.
Ere my departure for the capital
we used to stroll along Imizu's stream
where in the evening wind
we saw white waves, heard sea birds cry,
and sound of oars from boats for reaping reeds.
Over lofty mountains wrapped in mist
have I come, spending many a weary day and
  night.
Oh, my dear friend, I only wish you were a
  bracelet
that I could carry round my arm.

No. 4007

O that you were a jewel fair
which I upon my wrist could wear!

3 songs in reply by Ohtomono Ikenushi

No. 4008

My dear friend, I was with you in this place
far away from Nara,
leading a happy life until you left.
Now I think nothing but of you.
In vain do I endeavor to suppress myself,
for life is void without you.
I'm praying to the god of Mt. Tonami
that I may welcome you with pinks in bloom.

No. 4009

O Gods of travel, earnestly at your shrine
I pray with offerings. So protect this friend of
  mine.

No. 4010

O that you were a pink's flower in my garden
which could delight me morning after morning!

5 songs on lost falcons
by Ohtomono Yakamochi

No. 4011

This is a distant province of the Emperor
with mountains high and rivers large.
The fields are wide with forage rich.
On summer evenings men catch sweetfish
with cormorants in the stream;
in autumn I go hunting with my favorite hawks.
One day the aged falconer took the birds without
  my leave,
and came back, losing them all.
I was beside myself with anger at the news,
and to retrieve them I tried every means.
I gave a precious mirror to the shrine,
praying for the help divine.
In my dream that night a maid appeared and said,
"Your falcons went across the cove of Himi,
and flew far, far away o'er many an isle,
but will return within a week.
Therefore rest assured, O Man, and do not sorrow."

No. 4012

Alas, I lost my favorite falcons,
and out to Mishimanu I can not go hawking.

No. 4013

In vain I spread nets everywhere upon Mt.
  Futagami
for the falcons, but now in my dream I have a
  revelation.

No. 4014

I doubt the proverb: wait with patience, and you
  need not grieve;
since the old falconer the lost birds can't retrieve.

No. 4015

Alas, have I to live thus night and day,
sorrowing for the hawks that flew away?

No. 4016

Ay me! There is no shelter on the field
where wind and snow now whip the withering
  obana.

TAKECHINO KUROHITO

4 songs by Ohtomono Yakamochi

No. 4017

The east wind sent the Nago fishermen away,
and not a single boat is seen out in the bay.

No. 4018

Coldly from the sea
  the wind is blowing. All
aloud above the estuary
  for their mates cranes flying call.

No. 4019

Living in a distant province,
I yearn unceasingly for Nara.

No. 4020

Throughout the long spring day of Koshinomi
  I roam the shore,
with inward eye fixed on the capital
  that I behold no more.

9 songs by Ohtomono Yakamochi

No. 4021

Behold, red skirts are mirrored in the water,
for maids are gathering moss there in the river.

No. 4022

Crossing the rapids in the river, I
am all wet with the spray my charger sent up
  high.

No. 4023

With torches every rapids is aglow,
and men are catching fish with cormorants.

No. 4024

It seems the snow upon Mt. Tachi thaws,
for swollen is the stream, and wet my stirrups.

No. 4025

I came across the pass; I view the balmy sea
    below.
I wish that I could find a boat with oars for me
    to row.

No. 4026

How deep the forest on the isle of Noto
where men cut trees with axes!

No. 4027

No moment do I have
but that I spend it yearning
for Nara.

No. 4028

Long have I not seen my wife who lives far, far
    away;
now at Nigishi river for her welfare do I pray.

No. 4029

I sailed out from the harbor in the Suzu Sea at
    sunrise,
and now behold the moon upon the beach of
    Nagahama.

2 songs by Ohtomono Yakamochi
No. 4030

A month has passed in vain,
though spring has bathed in mist the hill,
and long have I been waiting
for uguisu birds to trill.

No. 4031

With the Nakatomi prayer now at the shrine,
purifying me with water, offering wine,
for whom else would I be praying?

THE MANYOSHU

BOOK XVIII

FOREWORD

This book is one of those compiled by Ohtomono Yakamochi, and the songs, without being divided into kinds, are all arranged, as in the preceding volume, in chronological order from March, 748 to February, 750, extending for two years.

The songs number 107, including 10 longer lays and 97 verselets.

*4 songs by Tanabeno Fukumaro
at a banquet in the residence of
Ohtomono Yakamochi*

No. 4032

O for a ship
   to go to view
the roaring billows
   out on the blue.

No. 4033

For years I have been yearning for you dear,
and face to face now I sit with you here.

No. 4034

The cranes are crying, waiting
   for the tide to go out soon
that they may catch fish
   on the bare lagoon.

No. 4035

O Cuckoo, come and cry
whene'er you wish, but come, if I
may choose, when in my hair
iris flowers I wear.

No. 4036

You tell me of the lovely scenery
of the cove I so desire to see.

TANABENO FUKUMARO

No. 4037

Oh how I love
this Ofu Cove,
and the scenes thereof!

5 songs by Tanabeno Fukumaro

No. 4038

How I wish the morning would come soon
to let me gather shells on yon lagoon!

No. 4039

Ere I see Fuse Cove never shall I
return home though a twelvemonth may pass by.

No. 4040

If I go and see the cove at Fuse,
on my return
the nobles of the splendid court
will hear my tale.

No. 4041

The plum flowers in the garden I will see,
waiting for your messenger to me.

No. 4042

As I see wistarias blow
flower after flower, I know
that now the spring
is gone, and cuckoos soon will come and sing.

No. 4043

I wish I could hear cuckoos singing when I go
   tomorrow
to behold wistaria flowers upon the beach of Fuse.

OHTOMONO YAKAMOCHI

*2 songs composed, riding along the Fuse Sea,
by Ohtomono Yakamochi*

No. 4044

I go riding by the sea, a whip in hand,
and wish to have a boat row me out from the
   strand.

No. 4045

Is yon boat coming now
to take me out to sea?

No. 4046

For many hours the boatmen rowed about the
   sea,
but I never grew tired of the scenery.

TANABENO FUKUMARO

No. 4047

Rowing about, enjoy the seascape, friends,
and note the view to hand down to posterity.

No. 4048

We row about the sea and view the scenery of
   Taruhime,
and every rowing sound is mingled with the
   yearning after Nara.

OHTOMONO YAKAMOCHI

No. 4049

I never thought this beach so fair.
Its beauty is beyond compare.

TANABENO FUKUMARO

No. 4050

The cuckoo! Friend, you soon will hear its lay:
I told the bird to come for you today.

KUMENO HIRONAWA

No. 4051

O Cuckoo, come and let me hear among
Tako's leafy trees your summer song.

OHTOMONO YAKAMOCHI

4 songs at a feast
No. 4052

O Cuckoo, if you do not sing today
    to give us pleasure here,
your song would not avail tomorrow
    when we trudge the mountain drear.

TANABENO FUKUMARO

No. 4053

The wood is leafy now and dark, O Cuckoo.
Why come not to let us hear your song of summer?

KUMENO HIRONAWA

No. 4054

O Cuckoos, come this moonless night,
and sing on in our candlelight!

OHTOMONO YAKAMOCHI

No. 4055

When you leave
    let me hope
that you will wave your sleeve
    on Itsuhata slope.

DITTO

7 songs at the Court of Naniwa
No. 4056

If I had known the visit of your Majesty,
I would have had the shore all strewn with stones
    for thee.

TACHIBANANO MOROE

No. 4057

Worry not; we'll come again,
and see the path with pebbles strewn.

EMPRESS GENSHO

No. 4058

Never shall we
forget your orange tree*
laden with thousands of
fair fruit we love.

* Tachibana (orange tree) is also the family name of
the nobleman.

EMPRESS GENSHO

No. 4059

Her Majesty beholds the garden
where orange trees with fruit are glowing,
now at a banquet
this day of summer.

PRINCESS KOHCHI

No. 4060

I will leave soon
with the rise of the moon,
adorning my hair
with a tiny golden orange.

LADY AWATA

No. 4061

O Men who the Imperial vessel steer,
take every care of danger to keep clear!
    (Written probably by TACHIBANANO MOROE)

No. 4062

Steer the vessel up the river, climbing rapids after
    rapids,
for night is murky now in May; the highway full
    of danger.

No. 4063

Aglow with fruit the orange trees,
eager her Majesty to please.

OHTOMONO YAKAMOCHI

No. 4064

Very much the same as No. 4063

No. 4065

Ceaselessly as the rowing sound I hear
now from the inlet, I long for my dear.

4 songs at a feast in the residence
of Kumeno Hironawa
No. 4066

April is come, so Cuckoo, come thou also, for I would
enjoy thy song, although utsugi are still in the bud.

OHTOMONO YAKAMOCHI

No. 4067

O Cuckoos, hiding in Mt. Futagami,
come out and sing now for my master.

A singing girl

No. 4068

Let us drink out the night to take the pleasure
of cuckoo's song on the first summer morning.

OHTOMONO YAKAMOCHI

No. 4069

Tomorrow I shall hear first cuckoos sing,
and long to me seems this last night of spring.

NOTONO OTOMI

3 songs to Priest Seiken
by Ohtomono Yakamochi
No. 4070

But for you, whom do you think
I plant here by my bower this flowering pink?

No. 4071

Oh, how I wish to take joy every spring in wearing
willows in my hair with people of this province!

No. 4072

My wife must be awaiting me,
    viewing this moon so bright,
counting the days till my return
    in Nara town tonight.

3 songs sent to Ohtomono Yakamochi
from Ohtomono Ikenushi in Echizen Province
where he was transferred.
No. 4073

Though the same moon now shines on you
and me, the mountains part us two.

No. 4074

The cherry flowers are at their best, they say,
but where is joy now, since you are away?

No. 4075

Why should it be
that I yearn so
for you, who never think of me,
that strangers see it written in my face?

4 songs in reply by Ohtomono Yakamochi
No. 4076

The mountains separate us, but we see
the same moon shining bright for you and me.

No. 4077

The cherries by your now-deserted house
    are burgeoning.
My dear friend, will you not return
    to see the flowers of spring?

No. 4078

Even such a reverend word as love
can not suffice
to name the depth of feeling
in me for you.

March 16
No. 4079

The mist hangs o'er the field, but yesterday
it snowed, and oh, it snows again today.

2 songs from his mother-in-law in Nara
to Ohtomono Yakamochi
No. 4080

My beloved son, I love you true,
and day and night pray to the gods for you.

No. 4081

If I put love for you upon a horse today
to send to you, will robbers steal it on the way?

3 songs in reply from Omtomono Yakamochi
in Etchu
No. 4082

Glad do I live this country life, though drear,
since a distant angel loves me dear!

No. 4083

This horse-borne love from Nara
if added on to what I carry daily
will overwhelm me quite.

No. 4084

As I love the cuckoo's lay to hear,
so do I to recite your songs, my dear.

To the priest Hiei of the Todaiji Temple
by Ohtomono Yakamochi

No. 4085

At trusty Swordwave Barrier
starting from tomorrow
I'll set a double squad of guardsmen
to influence you to stay with me.

3 songs at a feast

No. 4086

How beautiful your lily garland
now glowing in the radiant lamplight!

OHTOMONO YAKAMOCHI

No. 4087

Oh, how I wish for pleasure
again like this at leisure.

NAWAMARO

No. 4088

How sumptuous has this banquet been!
I hope it may occur again.

4 songs by Ohtomono Yakamochi
On hearing the cuckoo

No. 4089

Here in this province ruled o'er by the Emperor
mountains soar, and birds of various kinds
in springtime fill the air with their sweet music,
but the best of them perhaps are cuckoos.
They come in April when small-flowered utsugi
  blow,
singing on till May when irises break into flower.
We hear their song, and are enraptured by the
  echoes.

No. 4090

O Cuckoo-bird, you cry and disappear,
making me wish more your song to hear.

No. 4091

Utsugi flowers
are cuckoos' bowers,
wherefrom mid echoes high
they fly across the sky.

No. 4092

'Tis sad to see the orange flowers fall.
So Cuckoo, bring not yet your plaintive call.

No. 4093

The east wind brings wave after wave,
which lovely Awo seabeach lave.

In the reign of the Emperor Shohmu while
the famous Buddha's image was being made in
Nara, and they were in sore need of gold, the
precious metal was found in Mutsu, a north-
eastern province of Japan.

Ohtomono Yakamochi wrote in the follow-
ing congratulatory song and 3 hanka:

No. 4094

Since the advent of the grandson of the great sun-
  goddess
the Imperial line has ruled this fertile land
of mountains high and rivers large,
producing innumerable presents for the Court.
Our Emperor, in answer to the Buddha's mercy
planned the construction of a temple grand,
for which he sorely needed lustrous gold.
How great indeed then his delight to hear
a gold mine was discovered in the East.
This all comes from the blessing of the gods and
  Buddha.
He thinks too of his loyal subjects,
especially of the Ohtomo family
with a motto since their first brave ancestor:
Fear not a watery death at sea,
nor grassy death upon the field.
Die in whatever way
if but you die beside the sovereign.
O Clansmen, keep these words in mind.
Protect the Liege with bow and sword.
Never fail to do or perish in his service.

Hanka
No. 4095

When we hear
the Sovereign speak
his words impress
us all with thankfulness.

No. 4096

Set a large monument upon the grave
of our ancestors so noble and so brave!

No. 4097

Oh, in this grand, auspicious reign,
 behold, as if your eyes to feast,
the radiant flower of gold has bloomed
 upon the mountain of the East.

*3 songs by Ohtomono Yakamochi
Composed beforehand for the Royal Visit
to the Yoshino Detached Palace*
No. 4098

Our Sovereign comes now to the Palace
built by his forbears
to take joy in the landscape of Yoshino
with a retinue of nobles
whose service is as ceaseless as the river,
as all-engirding as Yoshino's mountains.

No. 4099

Our Liege, remembering his forebears,
comes oft to this Yoshino Palace.

No. 4100

As Yoshino's river
flows for ever,
so the courtiers bend
themselves the Liege to tend.

*5 songs with the pearls to send home
by Ohtomono Yakamochi*
No. 4101

The women divers go to the isle at sea,
and search for pearls.
How I wished to have some for my wife,
waiting at home, leading a lonely life,
and counting the days she has to pass

before again she meets me.
Now I have got good pearls
which with the orange flower and iris
will prank her shining raven hair
in the merry month of May
when cuckoos come to sing.

No. 4102

Here I send a parcel of pearls to your bower
for you to string together with the flag and orange
  flower.

No. 4103

My love, now I will go to yonder island out at sea
to get a pearl out of an oyster shell for you.

No. 4104

O for a pearl they get by yonder isle
to send my darling to beguile her while.

No. 4105

How I admire the divers who
bring pearls from out the ocean blue!

*4 songs, admonishing his clerk, Owarino Okui,
in a facetious mood
by Ohtomono Yakamochi*
No. 4106

Since ancient times men have esteemed
their parents, loved their wives and children.
Before you rose in your position, and became a
  clerk,
on a fine summer day when flowers beamed in
  Kasuga field
you vowed you would remain true to your love;
but after you came here to serve,
you were enamoured of a woman light,
and waste your time away,
associating with her day and night.
Oh, what would your wife think
if she knew this deed of yours?

3 Hanka
No. 4107

Your wife in Nara left must yearn
on tiptoe after your return.

No. 4108

How will the townsfolk look upon you
enamoured of the wanton Saburuko?

No. 4109

Bright color fades away too fast
but brown is known for long to last.

No. 4110

Lo, riding posthaste, comes the wife from Nara
now to where lives Okui with his mistress.

2 songs on the Orange Tree
by Ohtomono Yakamochi
May 23 of the leap year.

No. 4111

In the remote reign of the Emperor Suinin
a man named Tajimamori brought back
some orange branches from abroad.
They were replanted in this land and thrived.
In spring they put forth shoots,
and in May when cuckoos come
all people take joy in their flowers;
when the autumn rain falls, and tree leaves change
    color,
the orange fruit becomes more ripe and bright.
Even in snowy winter they retain green leaves.
No wonder people call them seasonless fruit trees.

No. 4112

I have a fondness for the orange tree,
and ever wish its flowers and fruit to see.

3 songs by Ohtomono Yakamochi

No. 4113

I have spent five long years,
sent by the Emperor here in this snowy province.
So to console myself I set pinks in my garden,
and from the summer field transplanted lilies.
These pretty flowers remind me of my love at
    home,
and somehow let me live on in this dreary place.

No. 4114

Whene'er I see the pinks around my dwelling
    place,
I am reminded of smiles on a maiden's face.

No. 4115

My dreary days would all be passed in vain
but for a hope of meeting you again.

3 songs at a feast
by Ohtomono Yakamochi

No. 4116

Months passed since my dear friend had left for
    the capital,
taking the records of this year's occurrences.
Over hill and down dale did he go;
and though I held a banquet with a wreath of
    iris flowers,
I never could console myself.
But now he has returned, and I am happy,
beaming like a summer lily.

No. 4117

Last autumn when the hills were clad
    with foliage red and bright
you went a rustic. Now you have
    returned an urbanite.

No. 4118

You know not in what joy I am to see you:
such months have passed by since we parted.

Song on hearing a cuckoo in May
by Ohtomono Yakamochi

No. 4119

People of old too loved the cuckoo's lay,
and what delight it is to hear it now in May.

2 songs prepared beforehand for a feast in Nara
by Ohtomono Yakamochi

No. 4120

What joy to see you, Lady fair
with summer flowers in your hair!

No. 4121

I've lived long in this far-off place,
and wish so much to see your face.

*2 songs on a raincloud during drought
by Ohtomono Yakamochi*

No. 4122

In this land ruled by the Emperor
rice is presented to the throne
as the foremost staple food.
Now, this summer little rain has fallen,
daily the rice plants withering,
and we yearn after rain,
as babes yearn after mothers' breasts;
but now I see
a dark cloud over yonder peak.
May it bring pouring rain upon parched hill and
field !

No. 4123

I see the heavens overcast
    with clouds spread from a tiny stain.
I pray out of the murky sky
    may come the needed bounteous rain.

No. 4124

Behold, the pouring rain so long for which
we prayed. Assured are we now of a harvest rich.
                    OHTOMONO YAKAMOCHI

*3 songs on the seventh night of July
by Ohtomono Yakamochi*

No. 4125

Since the first royal ancestor reigned o'er this
    land,
the Cowherd and his sweet love have been stand-
    ing
with the Heavenly Stream between them,
yearning each for the other.
The ferrymaster lets them cross the river
only once a year.
Were there a bridge for them to get across,
the lover could embrace his love,
caress and soothe her oftentimes,
but alas, he has to wait with patience
for one autumn eve: the seventh of the seventh
    month.

No. 4126

Were there a bridge across the Heavenly River,
the fervent lovers could meet in all seasons.

No. 4127

After waiting for a dismal year,
the night the lovers can meet on is here.

*4 playful songs to Ohtomono Yakamochi
from Ohtomono Ikenushi*

No. 4128

Needles you gave to me who now upon my journey
    go,
and gladder will I be if you give also cloth to sew.

No. 4129

Alas, a thing of patches sad
is my wretched needle pad.

No. 4130

Though I show every townsman
the needle pad, none likes it.

No. 4131

I search for fortune's feast to the east, but sad
and lone with nothing but the needle pad.

2 more songs by Ohtomono Ikenushi

No. 4132

I'm nothing but a servant poor,
daily working at your door.

No. 4133

I thank you deeply for the needles. Do
let me for other things again thank you.

*On snow, moon, and plum flowers
by Ohtomono Yakamochi*

No. 4134

The moon is shining on the snow.
    O that I had a lady friend
here in this country town to whom
    a spray of plum flowers I could send !

*At a feast to the host
by Ohtomono Yakamochi*

No. 4135

When I hear you play upon the koto, I
am moved with pathos and with admiration high.

No. 4136

I found some mistletoe upon the hill, and praying
for long life, wore a stem in my black hair.

OHTOMONO YAKAMOCHI

No. 4137

On this New Year's Day we enjoy a feast with
   you,
my friends, and why not ever in the future too?

DITTO

No. 4138

How I miss my wife,
sheltering here at Yabunami village,
wet in the vernal rain!

THE MANYOSHU

BOOK XIX

FOREWORD

This book is edited in the same fashion as the preceding volume. That is to say, it is arranged in chronological order, and no classifications are made according to varieties of songs. The book contains songs written during three years by Yakamochi, i.e. beginning in March, 750 when he was staying as governor of the local government at Etchu; in August, however, of the following year he returned to the capital permanently.

The longer lays contained in this book are 23, and verselets 131; and out of 154 songs 103 come from the pen of Yakamochi.

2 songs by Ohtomono Yakamochi

No. 4139

In the spring garden where peach trees
are blossoming red, a maid is standing
upon the path beneath the bloom—
in its lovely glowing shadows.

No. 4140

Here in my garden damson flowers are falling,
or are they snowflakes I behold descending?

No. 4141

Lonely I feel in spring,
   and all the more now as I hear
a snipe cry, flapping wings
   out in the dewy meadow near.
                    OHTOMONO YAKAMOCHI

No. 4142

I hold a budding willow sprig in hand,
picturing the vernal streets of Nara grand.

No. 4143

Lo, here is gathered many a flower-like daughter
drawing water at the temple fountain.

2 songs on wild geese returning home

No. 4144

"Now is the time for swallows," thinking in this
   wise,
the wild geese go honk-honking through the
   cloudy skies.

No. 4145

Do not forget to come again
   though now you go away,
O Wild geese, when the autumn wind
   blows o'er the maples colored gay.

2 songs on plovers

No. 4146

Waking now in the midnight drear,
above the stream sad plovers' cries I hear.

No. 4147

At lonely midnight comes the plover's cry,
and men of old shed tears as well as I.

2 songs on the pheasant

No. 4148

My little pheasant in Sugino field,
quiet, quiet your crying!
Else our secret you will yield.

No. 4149

When in the mountains wrapped in morning mist
   we hear
a pheasant's lonely plaintive cry it seems so drear.

No. 4150

From afar I hear the boatmen's cry.
as now awake in bed I lie.

*3 songs at a feast in the residence
of Ohtomono Yakamochi*

No. 4151

Behold, refulgent are the cherries
I roped off for this entertainment!

No. 4152

O Friends, enjoy the banquet at my bower
here beneath the cherries in full flower.

No. 4153

In China too they float toy boats
   down their garden stream today*,
taking delight, decking their hair
   with vernal flowers gay.
   * the third day of March.

*On the white-speckled hawk
by Ohtomono Yakamochi*

No. 4154

I have lived long here in this country town,
and tried to think that capital and village are one
   to live in,
but now I have few friends with whom
I can talk and console myself.
So in the autumn I go hawking to Iwase Field
bedecked with little hagi flowers,
to have sight of my falcon
soaring on high, his white bells tinkling,
and then I bring him home to put him on the
   perch.
Oh, how brave my silver-speckled hawk!

Hanka

No. 4155

I take delight in keeping and caressing
my silver-speckled falcon.

On cormorant-fishing

No. 4156

When old year changes into new, and springtime
  comes,
the flowers adorn the hill and field,
and waterfalls thundering into the Sakita River,
sweetfish in the foaming rapids leap.
Then I take a cormorant fisherman at night,
and with lighted torches go into the waters,
though wet the garments given by my love.

Hanka

No. 4157

I see myself dressed in red clothes agleam
clearly reflected in the crystal stream.

No. 4158

So many flashing ayu here—
Sakita teeming every year!
Into the rapids, Cormorants, dive
and bring the silver fish alive.

No. 4159

Deeply rooted there I see
a noble ancient camphor tree.

On the uncertainty of life
by Ohtomono Yakamochi

No. 4160

Since the beginning of the world
life has been vain.
Even the moon now waxes and now wanes.
Plants break into flower in spring,
but come the fall, their leaves turn dun and sere.
It is the same with man:
black hair grows all white;
morning blushes into evening wrinkles.
Like the blowing wind, the flowing stream,
everything will go without return.
These vicissitudes we see,
and can not but weep tears.

Hanka

No. 4161

Even the speechless tree breaks into flower in
  spring,
but in the fall winds come, the old leaves scattering.

No. 4162

Man is mortal, and however great,
he must resign himself to fate.

No. 4163

O Mist, now rise and veil the Heavenly River,
because this is the very night I meet my Weaver.

On reading Yamanoeno Okura (see No. 978)
by Ohtomono Yakamochi

No. 4164

Every man is brought up with parental love.
The warrior ought to lead a manly life,
practising with bow and arrow.
and girded with a trusty sword must go where'er
  his duty calls him,
and leave a name that goes down to posterity.

Hanka

No. 4165

The man-at-arms should leave a reputation high
behind him that shall go down to posterity.

On cuckoos and flowers
by Ohtomono Yakamochi

No. 4166

As seasons come and go, change also flowers and
  birds.
They make us sad or joyful, then the leafy April
  comes,
and we hear the songs of cuckoos
which, the ancients tell, are hatched in uguisu's
  nests.
In May when maidens play with leaves of iris
  bloom and orange flowers
they sing on, flying o'er the mountains,
and making echoes in the moonlit night.

Hanka

No. 4167

One can enjoy flowers in all seasons
amid the mountains wild or brought home.

No. 4168

The cuckoo I was wont to hear
at this time. Then why not this year?

Writing on behalf of his wife,
who is now with him, to her mother
by Ohtomono Yakamochi

No. 4169

Now in May we hear the cuckoo's song
among the flowering orange trees,
but no word we hear from you, O Mother,
and in this dreary place we live forlorn,
looking only on the mountain cloud.
Like the divers yearning for a pearl
day and night we yearn for sight of you.

Hanka

No. 4170

Our life is dreary here
without you, Mother dear.

2 songs on the cuckoo
by Ohtomono Yakamochi

No. 4171

O Cuckoo, every one will rise to hear you.
So sing your first song on this April morning.

No. 4172

I failed to plant the orange for the cuckoo;
alas, it is too late now to regret it.

No. 4173

Day after day I have no peace
without you in this country place!

No. 4174

The height of joy in springtime is to wear
a flowering plum twig in your hair.

2 songs on the cuckoo

No. 4175

The cuckoo's come to call today,
and we shall hear his song till May
when we wear iris garlands gay.

No. 4176

O Cuckoo that now fly across the sky,
how I love to hear your echoes clear!

Songs on cuckoos sent to his friend,
Ohtomono Ikenushi,
by Ohtomono Yakamochi

No. 4177

Behold, upon the mountains vapor hangs,
and in the fields camellias blow.
The spring has passed now into summer, and the
   cuckoos sing,
but I find no joy in hearing them alone.
I long for you with Mt. Tonami separating us.
Presently the cuckoos will go flying o'er the peak,
and perched on pine tree tops at morning,
passing the moon at night,
will let you hear their throats, my friend.

Hanka

No. 4178

Cuckoo, your sweet song is too precious by myself to hear.
Therefore, fly to Nifu Hill where lives my comrade
   dear.

No. 4179

Cuckoo, go flying for my sake,
and nightly keep my friend awake!

On cuckoos again
by Ohtomono Yakamochi

No. 4180

After spring as summer comes,
I hear the long-awaited cries of cuckoos every
   night,
echoing among the hills;
and never do I tire of them.
They sing on till the month of May
when we make garlands, stringing orange flowers
   with iris bloom.

Hanka

No. 4181

I love to hear the cuckoo singing on
as night gives way to dawn.

No. 4182

The cuckoo's song I love so deep,
and wish I could catch one to keep.

No. 4183

I wish that I could keep a cuckoo
to hear his earliest cry next summer.

*From her sister in Nara to the wife
of Ohtomono Yakamochi*

No. 4184

The yellow rose of Nara in my hand
evokes you, sister, from your distant land.

On the same theme by the same lady

No. 4185

I long for you, especially in spring,
and with a wish to be consoled by yellow roses,
beside my bower I transplanted them I'd found
   down in the dale,
but whenever I behold them wet with morning
   dew,
I am reminded of you, and yearn all the more.

Hanka

No. 4186

To soothe my heart I set a yellow rose outside
   my bower,
but I am made to yearn more by the flower.

*On the Sea of Fuse
by Ohtomono Yakamochi*

No. 4187

I go out on the sea with friends
to enjoy the view, and row about.
The bay is veiled in mist;
wistarias blow on Taruhime Point.
Like the white waves that lave the shore
my heart yearns for this scenery.
I wish to come here every year
to see flowers in the spring,
and golden foliage in the fall.

No. 4188

Every year
I will come here,
and take delight
in fuji flowers' sight.

*On sending waterfowl to his friend,
Ohtomono Ikenushi,
by Ohtomono Yakamochi*

No. 4189

We lead a lonely life, both spending years
afar off from the capital,
and try to soothe ourselves by listening to cuckoo
   songs,
or making wreaths with orange flowers.
Sometimes, accompanied by servants we go to the
   river
to catch fish, casting nets, or using cormorants.
Let me greet you, my friend, now with these
   waterfowls.

Hanka

No. 4190

I give these cormorants to you, my crony,
take them and catch fish in the river.

No. 4191

Send me the ayu's fins* I wish
to have, pray, when you catch the fish.

   * they are considered a delicacy.

On cuckoo and wistaria flower

No. 4192

The cuckoos that go flying over shadowy valleys
   of Mt. Futagami,
or summer meadows both at dawn and in the
   moonlit night,
scatter wistaria flowers, winging their way too
   near the clusters.
I love the purple blooms. They are so beautiful
that now I put them in my sleeves.

Hanka

No. 4193

Petal after petal the wistaria flowers,
scattered by the cuckoo's wings, now come descending.

3 songs on the tardy cuckoo

No. 4194

They tell me that the cuckoo was in song, but I heard it not, though fuji's season has gone by.

No. 4195

O Cuckoo, how I love your lay,
but o'er the hills you fly away.

No. 4196

April is here, and I await you,
and why do you not come, O Cuckoo?

2 songs by Ohtomono Yakamochi

No. 4197

I roped off the yellow roses bright as gems
to be reminded of your beauty, but
stolen, alas, now are some stems.

No. 4198

I did not leave thee heartlessly,
but truly do I yearn for thee.

4 songs on wistaria flowers of Tako Bay
by Ohtomono Yakamochi

No. 4199

Wistarias blow reflecting purple shadows in the
    waters where
every pebble in the crystal bay looks like a jewel
    fair.

No. 4200

I'll go, bedecking my black hair
now with wistaria
which renders fair
Tako Bay
upon this summer day.

No. 4201

I'm still here for the beautiful wistarias' sight:
their fascination holding me o'ernight.

No. 4202

I shall be taken for a fisherman as I stop here,
building a hovel to behold wistaria flowers near.

No. 4203

No souvenir for my family.
O Cuckoo, come and sing for me.

KUMENO TSUGIMARO

2 songs on the big oak leaf
by Ohtomono Yakamochi

No. 4204

Behold the big oak leaf my friend has.
Does it not look a green umbrella?

No. 4205

When our ancestors met to dine,
they used this oak leaf to drink wine.

No. 4206

I'm riding now for Shibutani
    on this moonlit night,
but stop my horse awhile: so beautiful
    the sight.

OHTOMONO YAKAMOCHI

On the cuckoo
to Kumeno Hironawa
from Ohtomono Yakamochi

No. 4207

The cuckoo birds that come into your garden
to perch upon the alder boughs,
or in the twilight near the clusters of wistaria
    flowers,
call not at my bower,
because our orange trees are not in blossom yet.
I do not scold the tardy birds,
but could you not have sent me word of them?

Hanka

No. 4208

In vain I wait for cuckoos eagerly.
You hear their sweet throats, but say naught to
    me.

In reply to the above
by Kumeno Hironawa

No. 4209

Although I live beside a vale,
and leafy is my town,
cuckoos do not come.
To hear them cry I wait outside at dawn,
and in the twilight search the dale,
but ah, no song comes to my ear.

Hanka

No. 4210

Now wistaria flowers are past their time,
and why do I not hear the cuckoo's rhyme?

On the virgin of Ashiya
by Ohtomono Yakamochi

No. 4211

We hear with tears the story
how two warriors, Chinu and Unai vied
desperately for the Virgin of Ashiya,
and how, moved with the men's sincerity,
the budding maiden, lovely as the vernal flower,
fair as the autumn leaf,
left home, stood on the beach, and threw herself
into the sea.
Forlorn, the warriors fell upon their swords, and
followed her.
Now people chose the site to raise a tomb
in memory of the three.
Behold, a boxwood comb left here
has grown into a tree.

Hanka

No. 4212

Some maiden visited the tomb, and left her comb
behind.
It grew into a tree whose leaves now quiver in the
wind.

No. 4213

Without cease rolling white waves reach
Nago Beach,
and as incessantly
I yearn for thee.

Consoling his nephew Fujiwarano Jiro in grief
for the loss of his mother,
by Ohtomono Yakamochi

No. 4214

From ancient times the chiefs of clans,
by the Imperial order, used to govern provinces
however distant.
Today too we go over hill and river to our posts,
communicating with our families through messengers.
Now suddenly from home comes to your ear
the sad news of your mother's death,
and sunk in sorrow deep you live;
but you know this world is of vicissitudes:
Flowers, however fair, soon fade away.
No one could stem the flow of rivers,
man too must pass away in time.
What can we do? We but shed tears.

Hanka

No. 4215

Alas, your mother is no more,
and her sudden death do I deplore.

No. 4216

Alas, life here below is only vain.
but upright courtiers shall we remain.

2 songs by Ohtomono Yakamochi

No. 4217

The rain has brought much driftwood here, and I
could wish some pretty girls would now come
drifting by.

No. 4218

Do I betray by chance
secret love in my countenance?

No. 4219

The hagi by my bower has blown already
before the autumn wind comes cold and dreary.

2 songs by Ohtomono Sakanoeno Iratsume
to her daughter,
wife of Ohtomono Yakamochi

No. 4220

My daughter I hold dearer than the jewel
the ocean god is said to cherish,
went to a distant province, staying with her husband.
Ever since her lovely crescent brows
haunt me night and day.
Thus yearning for her, I grow old.
Alas, I may not live till she returns.

No. 4221

Alas, you went away from me, my dear,
and every day I wish that you were here.

2 songs at a feast

No. 4222

Would I could show my wife these maple trees.
O Showers, were it only you that came between
us !

KUMENO HIRONAWA

No. 4223

The autumn rain falls heavily
upon the maple tree
that you roped off
so fondly for your love.

OHTOMONO YAKAMOCHI

No. 4224

How I would our hagi flowers could allure the
wild geese
longer to stay there in the field veiled in the
morning vapor.

Said to have been written
by EMPRESS KOHMYO

At a farewell feast

No. 4225

Along the mountain path will you go, treading
the fallen leaves wet in the rain of autumn?

OHTOMONO YAKAMOCHI

No. 4226

Oh, let us go now to the slopes
where snow reposes still so white,
but shining 'mongst their deep green boughs
hang golden oranges round and bright.

Written in December
by OHTOMONO YAKAMOCHI

2 songs on snow by Mikatano Sami

No. 4227

Tread not the snow I see around the palace,
for it descends here seldom in the capital,
though thick in mountains wild,
Let no sandal-prints be seen.

No. 4228

Keep the ground unsullied, let our lord
behold it spread all white with snow.

At a feast

No. 4229

The snow is spread on earth
upon this New Year's Day:
a carpet white to welcome guests
here to our banquet gay.

OHTOMONO YAKAMOCHI

At another feast

No. 4230

I joined the New Year's banquet now,
trudging through the knee-deep snow.

OHTOMONO YAKAMOCHI

On the snow-made crag bedecked with
Artificial Pinks, by Kumeno Hironawa

No. 4231

It is in autumn that pinks blow,
but yours bloom on a crag of snow.

No. 4232

I wish the pink ablow
upon the crag of snow
would bedeck for e'er
your head of raven hair.

A singing girl

No. 4233

Even though morn's cock flap wing and crow,
stay yet: no path lies through this snow.

The host

No. 4234

What shall I do?
I hear the chanticleer,
but the snow lies deep,
so deep, my dear.

OHTOMONO YAKAMOCHI

To the Emperor
by Lady Inukai

No. 4235

In an ecstasy I stood
before you, Sovereign good!

On the wife's death
recited by a singing girl

No. 4236

Alas, my wife is gone
with whom I yearned to live for ever.
She fell ill, and I prayed the gods,
cotton sash slung across my shoulder,
and votive offering in hand,
but all in vain.
Ay me! Now I behold
only the last pyre's smoke
hovering through the lonely air.

Hanka

No. 4237

Gone is she, but love still yearns;
awake, adream, desire still burns.

At a farewell feast

No. 4238

My friend, if you are gone long on your journey,
with whom shall I make plum and willow garlands?

OHTOMONO YAKAMOCHI

On the cuckoo

No. 4239

The cuckoos which lived in the woods last year
have not yet come their songs to let me hear.

OHTOMONO YAKAMOCHI

To Fujiwarano Kiyokawa
by the Empress Dowager Fujiwara

No. 4240

Aboard a vessel rowed with many oars you go
across the sea
to China. Oh, may the protection of the gods be
now on you!

No. 4241

O Flowering plum trees on Kasuga's sacred lane,
luxuriant as now wait till I return again.

FUJIWARANO KIYOKAWA,
Envoy to China

No. 4242

Though well assured you come back safely
from Cathay,
my lord, still I feel sad to see
you go away.

FUJIWARANO NAKAMARO

No. 4243

Says the priest at the Suminoe Shrine,
"Your vessel shall sail fast across the brine."

TAJINO HANISHI

No. 4244

Alas, the days are drawing near
when I shall miss my wife so dear.

FUJIWARANO KIYOKAWA

To her husband, an envoy, bound
for China

No. 4245

Traveling from Nara to Naniwa,
then taking ship at Suminoe,
my husband goes across the ocean
to the land where sets the sun.
The god enshrined there at the stern
will stand upon the stem to guard the ship
which calls at many a port.
Left at home, I daily pray his safe return.

No. 4246

Let not the billows rise and gulf the vessel as
they steer,
and may the deities protect my husband dear!

No. 4247

Alas, the day is nearing on which I must say goodby
to my mother whose love is as boundless as the sky.

ABENO OKINA

2 songs to Kumeno Hironawa on the occasion
when Ohtomono Yakamochi was called back
to Nara after spending 5 years as
governor in Etchu Province

No. 4248

So many years to me you have been kind;
with gratitude must I leave you behind.

No. 4249

I start forthwith: no hawking with you now,
riding across the field where hagi blow.

At a farewell feast
by Ohtomono Yakamochi

No. 4250

After many years now I am leaving you behind,
but this night shall e'er remain with me, my comrades kind.

No. 4251

Blest by your farewell today,
my friend, I take my homeward way.

No. 4252

At your departure we shall wear
flowers of your hagi in our hair.

KUMENO HIRONAWA

No. 4253

With friendly greeting
upon our meeting
hagi let's wear
in our black hair.

OHTOMONO YAKAMOCHI

Song composed on the way to Nara in
preparation for a coming feast
by Ohtomono Yakamochi

No. 4254

Since the gods surveyed this Akitsu Island
aboard the lofty ship
with many oars from stem to stern,
sailing o'er the heaven's clouds
and came down, conquering the outlaws,
the Imperial family has ruled the land;
and our liege, herself a god, loves true
her subjects as well as the officials
serving at court.
Therefore, everywhere appear auspicious signs
to bless her reign which shall remain
like heaven and earth, for ever.
Now the good sovereign who knows her courtiers well
as she knows each autumn flower well
holds a feast with all of them.

Hanka

No. 4255

Courtiers differ much like flowers beneath the autumn sun,
but Her Majesty knows each particular one.

To Lord Tachibanano Moroe

No. 4256

Although a lone retainer may have spanned
three Emperors' reigns in days of old,
the glorious history of the Tachibana
stretches back for seven generations.

OHTOMONO YAKAMOCHI

3 songs at a feast in the residence of
Kino Iimaro

No. 4257

With bow in hand, on morning hunting
our lord is setting out to Tanakura.

No. 4258

The capital has moved without me—still
I linger, loving here each stream and hill.

No. 4259

The October rain will strip the pear tree
of all its maple-reddened foliage.

2 songs after the War of the Jinshin Year

No. 4260

Like a god's, the Emperor's word
has changed the empty meadow
with red horses grazing
to gorgeous Kiyomihara.

No. 4261

Out of a marshland fluttering with wings
our Emperor's god-like word has raised his capital.

No. 4262

To China's court you go.
    I drink your health in wine,
and when the mission's done,
    safe home, dear friend of mine!
                        TAHIHINO TAKANUSHI

No. 4263

I care not for my hair unkempt, my littered
    chamber,
I only wait upon your safe return.

*On sending wine to Fujiwarano Kiyokawa,
the Envoy to China by the Empress Kohken*

No. 4264

In this blessed country of Yamato
people can go safely over land and water.
The four ships bound for China shall sail stem
    to stern,
and swift come home again.
This saké we give you
that you may drink with us
upon your safe return.

Hanka

No. 4265

For the safe return we earnestly pray
of the four vessels for the envoy.

*Written beforehand for the New-Year's-Day
feast in the Palace
by Ohtomono Yakamochi*

No. 4266

The Liege who rules this land,
enthroned in Nara, thrives
as ever as the spruce and pine
standing on the peak.
Now on this happy day,
behold, the courtiers in their hair
fragrant orange blossoms wear,
and leisurely stroll about the garden,
all laughing merrily for joy.

Hanka

No. 4267

The Imperial Reign shall last for e'er, and here
may New-Year's-Day feast be repeated year by
    year.

No. 4268

Daily the frost descends now in this village.
Turned yellow is the green grass of last summer.

*4 songs at a feast in the residence of
Tachibanano Moroe*

No. 4269

This first-time welcome to ourself we cherish;
our loyal subject we shall yearly visit.
                        EMPEROR SHOMU

No. 4270

Had I known of your call before,
I would have strewn my gateway
with pebbles from the ocean floor.
                        TACHIBANANO MOROE

No. 4271

If I strew this shore
    where stands my villa new
with pretty stones, will you
    return to take the view?
                        FUJIWARANO YATSUKA

No. 4272

Our Sovereign now comes here,
and joy's spread far and near.
                        OHTOMONO YAKAMOCHI

*6 songs at a harvest-festival feast
November 25*

No. 4273

Like heaven and earth the Imperial Reign shall
  last for aye,
and proud am I thus as a courtier e'er to stay.
                KOSENO NATEMARO

No. 4274

To bless the reign auspicious,
hundreds of ropes are fastened
to the ridge beam of the palace.
                ISHIKAWANO TOSHITARI

No. 4275

The Emperor's palate serve I day and night;
now the dark saké brew him, now the white.
                FUMUYANO MAHITO

No. 4276

Behold, the courtiers in the palace garden wear
fragrant orange flowers in their hair.
                FUJIWARANO YATSUKA

No. 4277

Come to my bower to see the plums now flowering,
my friend, and hear among them uguisu sing.
                FUJIWARANO NAGATE

No. 4278

So content am I
    with the green vine in my bower.
I can not bear to leave
    even for trees in flower.
                OHTOMONO YAKAMOCHI

*3 songs at a farewell feast held in honor of
Tachibanano Naramaro*

No. 4279

We'll meet again, but now I send
you off with sorrow deep, my friend.

No. 4280

You leave us for your station at Tajima,
and we who stay in Nara town shall miss you.
                OHTOMONO KUROMARO

No. 4281

I pray for you, my friend, who go
now over mountains veiled in snow.
                OHTOMONO YAKAMOCHI

3 songs at a feast

No. 4282

How glad you're here! I feared lest, ere you
  come,
the hostile snow might strip the flowering plum.
     The host: ISONOKAMINO YAKATSUGU

No. 4283

As yet unopened plum flowers—do they yearn
for snow, or for another guest's return?
                LORD UMARADA

No. 4284

How happy I am now
    at the beginning of New Year
to sit together with my friends
    whom I respect and hold so dear!
                LORD FUNADO

3 songs on spring snow

No. 4285

Everywhere we see the fallen snow
in and outside the palace garden.

No. 4286

Songbirds among the bamboos trill,
and yet spring snow comes falling still.

No. 4287

I fear the plum flowers in the garden
will be scattered by this snowfall.

No. 4288

Plovers are crying in the palace garden.
It snowed too on the sandbank in the river?

No. 4289

Accept this garland woven from the willow,
and with it, prayers for your prosperity.

2 songs written impromptu
by Ohtomono Yakamochi

No. 4290

So lonely do I feel now in the twilight still,
although the field is veiled in mist and songbirds
trill.

No. 4291

In the twilight do I hear the breeze
rustling softly our small bamboo trees.

No. 4292

Pathetic on a vernal day am I,
hearing soaring skylarks sing on high.

OHTOMONO YAKAMOCHI

THE MANYOSHU

BOOK XX

FOREWORD

The last four volumes of the anthology can be regarded as Yakamochi's memoranda, for the greater part of the contents come from Ohtomono Yakamochi and his group, and no classification is made as to varieties of songs, the order being merely chronological.

The number of songs in this book is 224 including 6 longer lays, and 218 verselets.

The characteristic of this book is that we find here songs by frontier guards from various provinces of the East.

No. 4293

This is a song a hermit wrote
for us among the hills remote.

EMPEROR GENSHO

No. 4294

Our Sovereign is as noble as an eremite,
and he who wrote the song presents it with delight.

PRINCE TONERI

3 songs written under Mt. Takamado

No. 4295

I will enjoy the breeze of autumn coming
through the obana flowers of Mt. Takamado.

OHTOMONO IKENUSHI

No. 4296

Hidden in the clouds wild geese are crying,
and Takamado's hagi leaves will soon be crimson.

NAKATOMINO KIYOMARO

No. 4297

This is the pretty field of Takamado
where stags go belling through the autumn flowers.

OHTOMONO YAKAMOCHI

*3 songs at a New-Year's-Day feast in the
residence of Ohtomono Yakamochi*

No. 4298

So glad am I to come, my comrade dear,
to your banquet now, and every year.

OHTOMONO CHIMURO

No. 4299

To see you at each New Year's start
brings special blessing to my heart.

OHTOMONO MURAKAMI

No. 4300

Amid my friends in happiness,
auspicious dawns the year.

OHTOMONO IKENUSHI

No. 4301

In autumn only, sire, the leaves are golden,
but golden are my thoughts of you all seasons.

LORD ASUKABE

*2 songs written under the zelcova tree
at Ohtomono Yakamochi's villa*

No. 4302

The yellow roses I will foster fondly
that they may deck your hair as is your wont.

OKISOMENO HATSUSE

*In answer to Hatsuse who came out
with yellow rose flowers and a jug of wine,
by Ohtomono Yakamochi*

No. 4303

I will come here
year after year,
friend, to this bower
to see the rose in flower.

No. 4304

I pray for our longevity
every year the yellow rose to see

OHTOMONO YAKAMOCHI

No. 4305

I hear a cuckoo crying
over the forest flying.

DITTO

8 songs on Tanabata
by Ohtomono Yakamochi

No. 4306

Now that the long-awaited autumn wind I hear,
I can untie my girdle for my Weaver dear.

No. 4307

In autumn I yearn all the more to see her at the
bower,
thinking of the night I meet her lovely as a flower.

No. 4308

Alas, each ever to pine for the other,
both doomed to live divided by the river.

No. 4309

The autumn wind is swaying grasses by the river,
and what delight, now I can go to my sweet
Weaver.

No. 4310

Were boulders laid across the Heavenly Stream
mist-hidden in autumn,
could the sad-fated young man come and go
throughout all seasons?

No. 4311

With loosened sash in early autumn breeze
I await my lover's longed-for yearly visit,
and ah, alas, already has the moon
turned her face toward moon-set.

No. 4312

Only one autumn night I meet my yearned-for
lover,
and have to wait another year across the river.

No. 4313

I fear the day may break before
my boat can reach the other shore.

No. 4314

Planting sundry flower plants in my garden,
I will take delight throughout the twelvemonth.
                    OHTOMONO YAKAMOCHI

6 songs on the autumn field
by Ohtomono Yakamochi
No. 4315

As bright the courtiers at the Takamado Palace,
as are the hagi flowers before them in the garden.

No. 4316

Upon the hill the palace stands, and lo,
down in the meadows autumn flowers blow.

No. 4317

We'll go out to the field where courtiers
and their ladies
appear all dressed as gaily
as the autumn flowers.

No. 4318

If we do not enjoy
the hagi flowers coy
now in the dewy autumn meadow lone,
we shall regret it when they're gone.

No. 4319

Are stags that bell for their mates wandering
about the foggy field of Takamado?

No. 4320

Listen, yon hunters play their flutes to lure the
deer,
and, brushing hagi flowers aside, the animals
appear.

No. 4321

Conscripted as a frontier guard,
night after night I'll sleep upon the grass.
                    MONOBENO AKIMOCHI

No. 4322

I know my wife thinks daily of me, yearning,
and in the water cupped within my hands I see
her smiling now at me.
                    WAKAYAMABENO MUMARO

No. 4323

I can see flowers when their season's here,
but all the year round not my mother dear.
                    HATSUKABENO MAMARO

No. 4324

Wandering far away from home by Nié Cove,
how I yearn for Shiruba Beach where is my love!
                    HASETSUKABENO KAWAI

No. 4325

Were my parents flowers, would I not take them
carefully with me upon my journey?
                    HASETSUKABENO KUROMASA

No. 4326

I will pray for the safety of my parents fervently
till I have spent my years across the sea.
                    IKUTAMABENO TARIKUNI

No. 4327

Would I could pause to draw a picture of my love,
and have it ever with me on the rove!
                    MONOBENO FURUMARO

No. 4328

Sent by the Sovereign, I must leave
my aged parents presently,
and go, my vessel grazing sunken rocks at sea.

HASETSUKABENO HITOMARO

No. 4329

I wish my people could see us
    now gathered at Naniwa Bay
with lofty decorated ships on which
    we are to sail away.

TAJIHIBENO KUNIHITO

No. 4330

The decorated ship now starts to sail along
without my darling mother in the waving throng.

MAROKONO OHMARO

"The Coastguardsman"
by Ohtomono Yakamochi
No. 4331

The counties of Tsukushi where the local govern-
    ment is
are the bulwark to protect this land
against its enemies.
We have brave men everywhere
here in the country,
but no warriors can compare
with those of Kanto.
Therefore I, a native thereof, start now,
leaving my mother and my wife;
and, after months of traveling to reach Naniwa,
I will set sail from Mitsu Harbor there
aboard a lofty ship with many oars
to do my duty in the distant province, well aware
that my wife is praying every day for me,
setting a jug of saké in the alcove,
and at night, lying all alone
with her black tresses spread.

No. 4332

The man leaves with a quiver
    on his back, and sorrowing
for his departure
    weeps the loving little thing.

No. 4333

At their parting, well they may shed tears,
for once he leaves, they shall not meet for years

3 songs on the coastguardsman
by Ohtomono Yakamochi
No. 4334

Guardsman, thou goest far across the stormy sea,
but ne'er unbind the sash thy wife now ties for
thee.

No. 4335

Now to relieve the old set forth the new coast-
    guardsmen.
O Billows, do not rise, but let them safely reach
Tsukushi!

No. 4336

The ship with frontier guards aboard
    now sets sail with the wind;
and how they must be yearning
    for their wives left behind.

No. 4337

Bitterly I regret with no words kind
to have left my parents both behind!

UTOBENO USHIMARO

No. 4338

How sad to travel
to Tsukushi,
leaving behind
my mother kind!

IKUBENO MICHIMARO

No. 4339

To go to far Tsukushi now I leave you,
but, my love, praying to the gods, await me.

OSAKABENO MUSHIMARO

No. 4340

My parents, praying for my safety, wait for me.
I will return with pearls of the Tsukushi Sea.

KAWARANO MUSHIMARO

No. 4341

Leaving my father in the village lone,
I go my way toward the West alone.

HASETSUKABENO TARIMARO

No. 4342

The palace ever stands majestic there;
and may my mother be as strong and fair.

SAKATABENO MARO

No. 4343

Hard is a solitary traveler's life,
but feeding children, harder lives my wife.

TAMATSUKURIBENO HIROME

No. 4344

Farther and farther I roam, leaving hill and field
    behind,
still not a day goes but I call my parents dear to
    mind.

AKIOSANO MARO

No. 4345

O for another sight of Fuji in the sky
in which so oftentimes delighted she and I !

KASUGABENO MARO

No. 4346

My parents patted me upon the head,
and said,
"Safe home !" Their simple love I treasure
past measure.

HASETSUKABENO INAMARO

No. 4347

Rather than thus vainly yearning, filled with care,
how I wish I were the trusty sword you wear !
Father of KUSAKABENO MINAKA

No. 4348

So far away from you, my mother dear,
how can I peacefully sleep here?

KUSAKABENO MINAKA

No. 4349

Road after road I left behind since my departure.
Now, putting out to sea, I'll pass as many islands.

OSAKABENO ATAIMINU

No. 4350

New brushwood now adorns my garden shrine.
There I pray for your safety, Son of mine.

Father of WAKAOMIBENO MOROTO

No. 4351

My love, with many gowns in bed I lie;
still the cold pinches, since you are not nigh.

TAMATSUKURIBENO KUNIOSHI

No. 4352

How can I start, O Love of mine,
if you cling thus like a vine?

HASETSUKABENO TORI

No. 4353

Though east winds daily come,
they bring no word from home.

MAROKONO OHTOSHI

No. 4354

As if I could forget my wife !   How she,
busied among my guests, found words for me.

HASETSUKABENO YOROMARO

No. 4355

Daily I look east and pine
for those darling folk of mine.

HASETSUKABENO YAMASHIRO

No. 4356

Oh, how can I forget my darling mother
who took my sleeve and wept at my departure?

MONONOBENO TETORA

No. 4357

Never shall I forget that love of mine
who stood behind the fence, her sleeves all moist
    with brine !

OSAKABENO CHIKUNI

No. 4358

Clinging to me close,
bitterly wept my wife.

MONONOBENO TATSU

No. 4359

When will my vessel reach Tsukushi o'er the foam,
and, my duties done, return me home?

WAKAOMIBENO HITSUJI

*On the Detached Palace of Naniwa
by Ohtomono Yakamochi*

No. 4360

Once the seat of government stood here in Naniwa;
and still stands an Imperial villa here.
Therefrom one can see flowering trees in spring,
and all the year round mountains high and rivers clear.
Through its harbor precious gifts from all parts of the country come
up the canals to be presented to the throne.
The silver waves are rolling in the bay,
and men are fishing for the Imperial board.
Well the capital was here in days of yore!

No. 4361

Where still these cherries blow,
once the Emperor reigned.

No. 4362

I would that I could live year after year,
viewing the calm sea of Naniwa here!

2 songs by Wakatoneribeno Hirotari

No. 4363

Who will tell my wife that I
sailed from Naniwa for far Tsukushi?

No. 4364

Me gone, who will support my wife? To earn
her daily rice must she some trade now learn?

2 songs by Monobeno Michitari

No. 4365

Very much the same as No. 4363

No. 4366

O that there were a wild goose flying homeward
to take this message to my wife I yearn for.

No. 4367

Lest e'er I fade out of your memory,
look toward Tsukuba's peak and think of me.

URABENO OTATSU

No. 4368

Placid Kuji, flowing, flowing,
soon I return, and no more going.

MAROKOBENO SUKEWO

2 songs by Ohtoneribeno Chifumi

No. 4369

Fair by day and fair by night
is my sweet love, my lily white!

No. 4370

After obeisance at Kashima's shrine,
as frontier guard, I set sail o'er the brine.

No. 4371

How I yearn to see Tsukuba's mountain
soaring high, far in my native province!

URABENO HIROKATA

No. 4372

I came across the slope of Ashigara,
not even looking back,
and passed the barrier of Fuwa fast
where the lusty often stop for breath.
Duly I reported in Tsukushi,
and now, living at the cape,
I'm praying for my family
who pray for me.

SHIDORIBENO KARAMARO

No. 4373

How proud I am to start
with joy within my heart
for the distant field
as the Sovereign's shield!

IMAMATSURIBENO YOSOFU

No. 4374

To the gods of Heaven and earth I pray,
and, bow and quiver on back, I take my way.

OHTABENO ARAMIMI

No. 4375

The sentinel pines that watch my journey
watch like my people at our parting.

MONONOBENO MASHIMA

No. 4376

Ay me, conscripted suddenly,
I left my parents with but brief goodby.

KAWAKAMINO OMIOYU

No. 4377

O how I wish my mother were
as close as the gem that pins my hair!

TSUMORINO OKURUSU

No. 4378

Alas, the days and months pass drear,
but never I forget my parents dear.

NAKATOMIBENO TARIKUNI

No. 4379

O white Waves lapping at my shore,
if I must part from you,
how sadly, eightfold
will I wave my sleeve!

OHTONERIBENO NEMARO

No. 4380

I set sail from Naniwa Harbor,
and see white clouds above Ikoma's range.

OHTABENO MINARI

No. 4381

How sad to see the wayworn fellow soldiers
from many provinces set sail at Naniwa!

KAMUOMIBENO SHIMAMARO

No. 4382

"Alas for me," the guardsman said,
"conscripted when I'm ill abed."

OHTOMOBENO HIRONARI

No. 4383

Would I could see my mother once again
before we leave Naniwa for the main!

HASETSUKABENO TARIHITO

No. 4384

Where now has got the guardsmen's vessel
which at break of day departed?

OSADANO TOKOTARI

No. 4385

Let not the waves rise on my voyage;
my wife and family wait behind me.

KISAKIBENO ISOSHIMA

No. 4386

Busied about her work with me in mind
yearns my mother dear I left behind.

YAHAGIBENO MANAGA

No. 4387

My wife was but a budding dear,
who now waits for me year on year.

OHTOBENO TARIHITO

No. 4388

Long have I been upon this journey:
sadly soiled with dirt now are my garments.

URABENO MUSHIMARO

No. 4389

Little did I dream, ah me,
of this long sail across the sea!

HASETSUKABENO OHTOSHI

No. 4390

With so much virtue is she graced,
no question if my wife be chaste.

OSAKABENO SHIKAMARO

No. 4391

Whene'er I pass a Shinto shrine,
I pray for you, dear wife of mine.

OSHINOBENO IHOMARO

No. 4392

May some divinity of earth or heaven
accept my prayer, maintain me strong and healthy
until once more I greet my loving mother!

OHTOMOBENO MAYOSA

No. 4393

Praying for my parents' safety,
I set off as a frontier guardsman.
                    SASAKIBENO HIROSHIMA

No. 4394

I am enlisted; in the future
my bow shall be my bed companion.
                    OHTOMOBENO KOHITSUJI

No. 4395

I was blest to pass Tatsuta's Hill
    where cherries were ablow.
I hope they may be fair again when, duty done,
    I homeward go.

No. 4396

Every morning driftwood lies along Naniwa's
    shore:
no pretty shells for souvenir when I go home once
    more.

No. 4397

Whose lass is she who stands upon the river's
    shore,
basking in the sun, so radiant as a flower?

*3 songs on the thought of a newly-enlisted
frontier guardsman
by Ohtomono Yakamochi*

No. 4398

Ordered by the Emperor, I parted from my folk.
So sad was I, but taking heart was leaving home.
My mother came out to embrace me,
and my wife, clinging to my garments, would not
    let me go.
They vowed they would pray for my safe return.
'Twas hard for me to part,
and with difficulty could I leave.
My home receded far and farther.
I crossed the mountain range, and duly reached
    Naniwa.
There now I wait for wind and tide
to set sail for Tsukushi.
A spring mist hides the island
of Awaji in the offing.
Somewhere cranes sadly crying.
I call to mind my distant home,
and weep until my quiver rattled loud.

Hanka

No. 4399

The sad cries I
hear of cranes from the misty sky
above the vernal brine
bring thoughts of home and mine.

No. 4400

Somewhere from the shore I hear
the cries of cranes so drear,
as thinking of home, sleepless now I lie.
All is wrapped in mist—sea, beach, and reeds
    grown high.

No. 4401

My motherless children clung to me in tears,
as I set out on my journey of long years.
                    OSADANO TONERI OHSHIMA

No. 4402

At Kami Slope I rendered offerings
    as I passed the shrine,
cleansing myself and praying
    for those parents dear of mine.
                    KAMUTOBENO KOOSHIO

No. 4403

Since enlisted as a frontier soldier
I have traversed many a cloud-capped mountain.
                    OHATSUSEBENO KASAMARO

No. 4404

Alas, the girdle is now frayed
my love tied for me at my start.
                    KAMITSUKENUNO USHIKAI

No. 4405

I never shall untie my girdle fastened
by my love, although it may grow threadbare.
                    ASAKURANO MASUHITO

No. 4406

Will not some traveler come
to take my message home?
                    OHTOMOBENO FUSHIMARO

No. 4407

Behind me looms Usui Pass,
and how I miss my wife beyond it!
OSADABENO KOIWASAKI

5 songs on the parting sorrow of a
coastal guardsman
by Ohtomono Yakamochi

No. 4408

Conscripted as a coastal guard,
as I was leaving home,
my mother said, caressing me
together with my father
whose tears streamed down his snow-white beard,
"We are sad to see our only son depart;
we thought to have you by us somewhat longer."
My wife and children stood beside me, piteously
    weeping.
They clung to me, and would not let me go;
but taking heart I started,
looking back at each turn of the road
to see my people standing still.
I went my way to take ship at Naniwa.
There praying at the Suminoe Shrine,
with a votive offering
for the god's protection to let me survive
many outward and homeward sails
from isle to isle,
I embarked for the perilous sea at dawn.

No. 4409

My ship is sailing safe across the sea.
Are my people praying now for me?

No. 4410

"Even a cloud will serve as messenger,"
    so I have heard,
but ah, I know not how to make
    it carry home my word.

No. 4411

Against the shore the boiling waves were dashing
    high,
but for a souvenir to take home seashells gathered
    I.

No. 4412

Although we lie at anchor by an island,
I have no means now to send home my message.

No. 4413

When will return my lord,
wearing his trusty sword?
OHTOMONO MATARIME,
wife of a frontier guard

No. 4414

Enlisted as a frontier guard, far from my love
through the Inland Sea Tsukushi-ward I rove.
OHTOMOBENO OTOSHI

No. 4415

I wish now I beheld my wife so closely
as this fair pearl that in my palm is shining!
MONONOBENO TOSHITOKO

No. 4416

Now my husband does not change his clothing,
and I, his wife, must not untie my girdle.
Wife of MONONOBENO TOSHITOKO

No. 4417

Loosed to summer pasture his one red horse ran
    away,
and now my husband has to go afoot upon his
    way.
Wife of KURAHASHIBENO ARAMISHI

No. 4418

Oh, my camellia flower so fair,
fall not but by my hand, no, ne'er.
MONONOBENO HIROTARI

No. 4419

Here in Tsukushi I yearn for my cottage bare
where on the blackened hearth the rushes
    smoldered e'er.
MONONOBENO MANE

No. 4420

Take this needle on your journey, pray,
to sew the girdle when it starts to fray.
Wife of MONONOBENO MANE

No. 4421

Whene'er you sigh for me, my darling, feeling lonely,
look at the vapor on Mt. Ashigara which I traversed.

HATORIBENO UEDA

No. 4422

I miss my husband in Tsukushi,
and sleep, the girdle tied securely.

Wife of a frontier guard

No. 4423

Should I wave my sleeve on Ashigara's mountain,
I wonder if my wife so darling could behold me?

FUJIWARABENO TOMOMARO

In reply to the above
No. 4424

Had I only dyed his garment deeper,
I could see him wave it on the mountain.

No. 4425

I envy her who easily can ask
"whose husband is he?"
among the crowd that see off
frontier guardsmen.

No. 4426

If thou lovest me, upon thy journey
at each shrine
pray with offerings for the welfare
of this wife of thine.

No. 4427

The sash I tightly tied is loosened.
So must my wife at home be yearning.

No. 4428

Very much the same as No. 4422

No. 4429

A horse, when loosened, sallies forth out of the stable.
So fast my love ran after me at my departure.

No. 4430

Strapping on the quiver,
I left my people weeping.

No. 4431

Upon this frosty night with rushes coldly rustling,
far better is my wife's warmth than gowns sevenfolded.

No. 4432

Conscripted to serve in a distant place,
I leave home and my darling wife's embrace.

No. 4433

Oh, how I wish I were a morning skylark
to come and go upon the wing to Nara!

LORD ABENO SAMIMARO

2 songs by Ohtomono Yakamochi
No. 4434

The spring is come at last,
and larks are singing in the sky.
The city lies beneath a mist
that veils the scenery.

No. 4435

I left the capital when cherry trees were budding.
When I return, their flowers will have already fallen.

No. 4436

She asked me when I could return—
my poor dear wife for whom I yearn.

A frontier guard

No. 4437

O Cuckoo, do not cry so sadly, for
your sad song calls to mind the days of yore.

EMPRESS GENSHO

No. 4438

O Cuckoo, come and sing now, pray:
Her Majesty awaits your lay.

KECHINO MYOKAN

No. 4439

Keeping indoors, you can not see the snow
bending the branches of these pine trees low.

2 songs to Lord Oharano Imaki
by the wives of local Governors

No. 4440

Once you are gone across Mt. Ashigara,
whom shall we respect and hold so dear?

No. 4441

Ever in our memory your face
shall be with its nobility and grace.

No. 4442

Despite long days of summer rain
your pinks their lustrous hue retain.

OHARANO IMAKI

No. 4443

The pinks are colorful in this rain of May;
you look as graceful, my dear friend, as they.

OHTOMONO YAKAMOCHI

No. 4444

Think of me upon an autumn night,
my dear friend, when your hagi will blow white.

OHARANO IMAKI

No. 4445

The uguisu have now ceased to trill,
but oh, my ear yearns for their music still.

OHTOMONO YAKAMOCHI

3 songs at a feast held in honor of
Tachibanano Moroe

No. 4446

O sweet Pinks blowing in my garden, pray,
be ever, ever radiant in this way.

The host: TAJIHINO MAHITO

No. 4447

The flowering pink attracts my visit, but
even more your presence, flowering pinks or not.

TACHIBANANO MOROE

No. 4448

Like the eightfold ajisai full in bloom
may you be flourishing for years to come.

DITTO

3 songs at a feast held in Tachibanano Naramaro's
residence in honor of
Lord Tachibanano Moroe

No. 4449

It's good to place a pink upon your palm,
my friend, and closely see its beauty calm.

LORD FUNE

No. 4450

I wish your pinks so fair
would here remain for e'er.

OHTOMONO YAKAMOCHI

No. 4451

I never tire, beholding pinks in flower,
nor weary with thee hour on happy hour.

OHTOMONO YAKAMOCHI

2 songs at a feast

No. 4452

Maidens go trailing their red skirts
about the garden
where the wind goes scattering
the hagi flowers.

LORD ASUKABE

No. 4453

Beautiful the garden on this moonlit night
where the autumn hagi are now blowing bright!

OHTOMONO YAKAMOCHI

At a feast

No. 4454

Deep on the mountain, lo,
lies the virginal snow!

TACHIBANANO MOROE

No. 4455

Too busied in the fields by day, at night
I culled this water cress for your delight.

LORD KATSURAGI

No. 4456

Lo, a warrior brave in kindliness
has culled for me the curly water cress.

Wife of KECHINO MYOKAN

3 songs at a feast in the residence of
Umano Kunihito

No. 4457

Yon field of grasses so serene and fair—
would no one needed to set sickle there!
OHTOMONO YAKAMOCHI

No. 4458

Even though the stream should cease to flow,
how can I ever talk with you enough?
The host

No. 4459

They use small boats to reap the rushes at Naniwa,
and music for the courtiers is the slap-slap of the
oars.

3 songs by the creek at Naniwa
by Ohtomono Yakamochi

No. 4460

Somewhere from the small boats rowing near
the music of the oars comes to my ear.

No. 4461

Not a day passes here
but I yearn for Nara dear.

No. 4462

Boat after boat there comes and goes along the
river
where I hear plovers sadly crying on the wing.

2 songs by Ohtomono Yakamochi

No. 4463

This morn I heard a cuckoo sing its lay.
I wish it would stay on, not fly away.
March 20

No. 4464

Soon from the pines will come the cuckoo's song,
dropping upon us as we stroll along.

3 songs of admonition to the Ohtomo Clan
by Ohtomono Yakamochi

No. 4465

Since the advent of the god upon Mt. Takachiho
our ancestors have served the Imperial family
with bow and arrow,
and led the warriors throughout the land,
vanquishing all who did not obey the Emperor.
The conquest finished, at Unebi
a palace was erected in Yamato,
and the Sovereign sat upon the throne.
Ever since, the Ohtomo have been in favor with
the court.
Remember all this, my beloved clansmen,
and ne'er disgrace the good name of our forbears.

No. 4466

I exhort you, Chiefs, to be
loyal to His Majesty.

No. 4467

Too bright no blade can be
to live up to our history.

2 songs on the mutability of life
by Ohtomono Yakamochi

No. 4468

Man's life is brief. So turn your eyes to nature,
taking care to follow Buddha's teachings.

No. 4469

Let us not pass our time in vain, but practise
now's austerities for next's existence!

No. 4470

Albeit life is light as foam,
long may I lease this transient home.
OHTOMONO YAKAMOCHI

No. 4471

To the hill I go
striped with snow
in late pursuit
of golden fruit.
Nov. 5

OHTOMONO YAKAMOCHI

2 songs at a feast
No. 4472
Fair is Izumo's Oho Cove, but I,
bound by decree for Nara, hurry by.

ASUKABENO NADOMARO

No. 4473
The shining courtiers,
    Traveler, tell:
though far from Nara
    I fare well.

LORD YAMASHIRO

No. 4474
It makes me glad to hear about you
in this dreary life without you.

OHTOMONO YAKAMOCHI

2 songs at a feast by Oharano Imaki
No. 4475
Falling, falling, Snow so fair,
blur the edges of sharp care!

No. 4476
Like the shikimi
flowering in the deep mountain
I long for you.

No. 4477
None pass the road of Saho
to visit Princess Chinu.
The plover's mournful voices
proclaim she is no more.

LADY MAROKATA

No. 4478
Ever in my breast,
my friend, you stay a guest!

OHARANO MAHITO

No. 4479
Alas, alas, now you are gone,
and day and night I cry and moan.

No. 4480
Alas, my awesome Emperor is no more,
and day and night I his demise deplore.

At a feast given by Oharano Imaki
No. 4481
I never tire of seeing yon camellia flowers,
nor do I of thus being in your company.

OHTOMONO YAKAMOCHI

No. 4482
You came a long, long way to speed me,
my friends, and ne'er shall I forget it!

FUJIWARANO TORIYUMI

At a feast
No. 4483
These downward changing times as I behold,
I yearn and long for sterling men of old.

OHTOMONO YAKAMOCHI

No. 4484
The flower withers soon,
but weeds go prospering on.

DITTO

No. 4485
The varied flowers are bright in autumn weather,
would you and I were seeing them together.

DITTO

2 songs at a feast held at Court
No. 4486
Like sun and moon for ever shining
the Imperial Reign shall prosper.

CROWN PRINCE

No. 4487
O friends, rejoicing in this sacred land,
let us obey the Emperor's command.

FUJIWARANO NAKAMARO

3 songs at a feast held on December 18
No. 4488
Happy am I today to know
that winter closes and its snow,
and that tomorrow sets in spring
and soon the warbling birds will sing.

LORD MIKATA

No. 4489

The vernal mist that veils the moon
proclaims that spring is coming soon.

            IKAGONO MAHITO

No. 4490

O Uguisu, come the spring,
first at my bower sing.

            OHTOMONO YAKAMOCHI

No. 4491

With thoughts as deep as ocean,
trailing my skirts behind me,
used I to go to see my lover
in Sugawara village.

            LADY ISHIKAWA

At a feast

No. 4492

My friends, it is December still,
but veiled in spring mist is yon hill.

            OHTOMONO YAKAMOCHI

*Written when Ohtomono Yakamochi was
given a broom by the Emperor*

No. 4493

With the Emperor-given broom
I meetly sweep my room,
its small bell tinkling clear
on the third day of the year.

No. 4494

The waterfowl! The wild duck's wing!
Who sees a snow-white horse today
lives long, lives long.

            OHTOMONO YAKAMOCHI

No. 4495

O Uguisu, sing
there among the foliage
to prove at last here is the spring.

            DITTO

*10 songs at a feast held by
Nakatomino Kiyomaro*

No. 4496

I wish I had come to your bower
when the fair plums were in flower.

            OHARANO IMAKI

No. 4497

Did I not wait my friend to see
when lovely flowers were on the tree?

            The host

No. 4498

May our host enjoy longevity
as much as yonder thriving old pine tree!

            OHTOMONO YAKAMOCHI

No. 4499

A thousand thanks, my dear friend! I shall pray
the gods of earth and heaven to meet your lay.

            The host

No. 4500

I came a long way to your bower,
yearning for you and plums in flower.

            LORD ICHIWARA

No. 4501

Frail flowers soon fade, O friend of mine,
but be you lasting as the pine.

            OHTOMONO YAKAMOCHI

No. 4502

How fair your garden where
descend plum petals fluttering!
I never tire of seeing them
upon this day of spring.

            IKANO MAHITO

No. 4503

Ever refreshing yonder rippling pond;
ever delightful, friend, your company.

            OHTOMONO YAKAMOCHI

No. 4504

How glad I am my friend to see!
Your visit is a joy to me.

            NAKATOMINO KIYOMARO

No. 4505

Mandarin ducks yearn for your waters;
and my dear friend, I for your dwelling.

OHARANO IMAKI

5 songs on the Takamado Palace
No. 4506

Alas, the Emperor is gone,
and Takamado's Palace is forlorn.

OHTOMONO YAKAMOCHI

No. 4507

Although the Palace now stands desolate,
I never shall forget my Sovereign great.

OHARANO IMAKI

No. 4508

Year after year may come and go o'er me,
but never shall he quit my memory.

NAKATOMINO KIYOMARO

No. 4509

Faithful as the twining vine
    for my dead lord I yearn,
and would rope off the votive field
    where he will not return.

OHTOMONO YAKAMOCHI

No. 4510

Takamado's field so lone
reminds me of the Sovereign gone.

IKANO MAHITO

3 songs on the garden
No. 4511

Oshidori will come back and swim
    upon your pond;
already we see white ashibi shrub
    in bloom beyond.

LORD MIKATA

No. 4512

O for a spray of flowering ashibi
reflected in the stilly waters.

OHTOMONO YAKAMOCHI

No. 4513

Oh, do not fall, Ashibi flowers
reflected radiant in the waters!

IKANO MAHITO

At a farewell feast
No. 4514

No wind shall blow, calm be the sea.
I pray no harm will come to thee.

OHTOMONO YAKAMOCHI

At a farewell feast
No. 4515

Alas, now you must part from us before
the time of wearing hagi in our hair.

DITTO

No. 4516

The yearspring comes
with falling snow—
thrice happy omen.

DITTO

INDEX OF WRITERS

The references are to the number of the poems